PENGUIN HANDBOOKS

WOODSTOCK CRAFTSMAN'S MANUAL

Born in Nebraska, Jean Young grew up in
Hollywood, California, where she studied
fashion design at Hollywood High School.
After her marriage to Jim Young she moved
to the San Francisco area, taking courses in
art history and English literature at the
University of California at Berkeley and
studying with Alan Watts at the American
Academy of Asian Studies. Moving east,
she studied painting with Hans Hoffmann
and Karl Knaths, and her paintings were
subsequently exhibited at galleries in
New York City and San Francisco. In
1969 at Woodstock, New York, she and
her husband founded The Juggler, a shop
offering used, out-of-print, and new books;
art supplies; and old prints and paintings.
It was there that she saw the need for a
book with a new approach to crafts—a
realization that led to her *Woodstock
Craftsman's Manual*. Other books to
her credit include *Woodstock Kid's Crafts*,
People's Guide to Country Real Estate,
and *Succeeding in the Big World of Music*.

WOODSTOCK CRAFTSMAN'S MANUAL

Compiled by
Jean Young

PENGUIN BOOKS

Penguin Books Ltd, Harmondsworth,
Middlesex, England
Penguin Books, 625 Madison Avenue,
New York, New York 10022, U.S.A.
Penguin Books Australia Ltd, Ringwood,
Victoria, Australia
Penguin Books Canada Limited, 2801 John Street,
Markham, Ontario, Canada L3R 1B4
Penguin Books (N.Z.) Ltd, 182–190 Wairau Road,
Auckland 10, New Zealand

Woodstock Craftsman's Manual first published in
the United States of America by
Praeger Publishers, Inc., 1972
Woodstock Craftsman's Manual 2 first published in
the United States of America by
Praeger Publishers, Inc., 1973
Published together in one volume, with revisions,
in Penguin Books 1978

ISBN 0 14 046.340 2

Printed in the United States of America by
Command Web Offset, Inc., Jersey City, New Jersey

The quotation on page 345 is taken from
Black Elk Speaks by John G. Neilhardt.
Reprinted by courtesy of the author and
Simon & Schuster, Inc., the publisher.

Book design by Jean Young
Photographs, except when otherwise acknowledged,
by Jean Young

Contents

CANDLES
·11·

CROCHET
·39·

ORGANIC LEATHER
·65·

EMBROIDERY
·79·

POTTERY
·111·

WEAVING
·136·

TIE DYE·BATIK
·167·

SILKSCREEN
·187·

MACRAME
·203·

2
·219·

PATCHWORK·APPLIQUÉ·QUILTING
·225·

SANDALMAKING
·265·

WOODBLOCK AND
CARDBOARD-CUT PRINTS
·285·

BRONZEWORKING
·315·

TIPI-MAKING
·345·

VIDEO-MAKING MEDIA
·378·

NEEDLEPOINT
·403·

STAINED GLASS
·433·

PREPARING COPY AND ARTWORK
FOR OFFSET PRINTING-
GETTING IT IN PRINT
·455·

Woodstock Roots

This book grew out of experiences I had while working in the Juggler book-store in Woodstock. The typical craft book wasn't with it--the people who came into our shop knew this, and we would rap about crafts and craft books. The idea of a craftsman's manual evolved.

The idea was to put together a manual written by craftsmen that would give more information for less bread, be fun to read, and identify with our New World. Besides trying to give clear instructions, we wanted the book to be a liberation trip, free from patterns and designs to copy. It's <u>you</u>, your imagination, your interest, and your time that are the essentials.

I want to thank all the authors--with special thanks to Carol Abrams for her great positive vitality--and David Bell at Praeger, who listened and acted.

Many of the authors illustrated their own chapters. Carol illustrated <u>Weaving</u>. Albert illustrated <u>Leather</u>, Rick and Gloria illustrated <u>Silkscreen</u>, and Peggy Farber illustrated <u>Macrame</u>. I also want to thank Lenny Busciglio, who took some of the photographs, and Arnie Abrams, who took most of them; my family, Jim and Michael; Fran Danowski, Diane, Jean Shaw, Bea Binger, Estelle, Bell Abrams, Jim Matteson, Dennis and Barbara, Dennis the drummer, Alfie and Susan, Cris, Emily, Betsy Bocci, and Ellyn, the editor.

Jean Young

WOODSTOCK CRAFTSMAN'S MANUAL

Candles
Duncan Syme

Chapter One of John Muir's
beautiful book on fixing VWs is
really direct. He says, "Now
that you've spent your bread for
this book--read it! Read it all
the way through like a novel,
skipping the detailed steps in the
procedures, but scan all the com-
ments and notes. This will give
you a feel for the operational
viewpoint I took when I wrote it.
The intent is to give you some
sort of answer for every situation you'll run into. . . ." This
states his case and mine very
succinctly and much better than I
could have. For you people who
will be bored by elliptical com-
ments I have included cookbook-
type recipes for making some
candles. These recipes are self-
contained and tell you all you
need to know about making that
particular type candle, but they
tell you nothing about the art to
which I hope to introduce you.
Good reading and good luck.

WICKS

The main thing to get behind you first is the hassle about wicks. I could list long, boring tables and things to remember, but the best thing is to figure it out for yourself because there are many different kinds on the market and they all behave differently with the various waxes. Very quickly, the general idea is the bigger the wick the larger diameter of melted wax it will make. The main problem is that if you get too much melt it is possible the wick will drown. They make metal-cored wicks to keep them upright, which helps. The metal is very soft lead-type stuff which burns away nicely. If you're doing huge stuff cast in bowls, Chinese woks, etc., then one metal-cored number might be braided with a couple of cloth ones. No, you cannot use ordinary string just the way it comes. At least not with any real effectiveness. The wicking is so cheap that it's not worth the risk of having an unburnable candle. You might just as well buy the stuff which is made for candles.

One formula for making wicking says to take "strong string and soak overnight in 1 tablespoon salt and 2 tablespoons borax dissolved in 1 cup water. Hang the string up to dry and stiffen by dipping in melted paraffin." I assume that they mean some kind of thick cotton string, but that wasn't mentioned. The salt-and-borax treatment is to stop smoking when the candle is extinguished. This may work fine, and I would be curious to know, so no doubt someday I'll give it a try.

The metal-cored wicks start about as big as a skinny pencil lead and go up in about four sizes to a fat pencil lead. Same with the cloth ones, but they get even bigger. Some sennits are round and some are flat, but they all do the job. Usually the hobby shops will have them packaged in little plastic bags with about six feet of wicking per bag. Actually you can make quite a slew of candles with six feet of wick. Local stores have it on spools and will cut off whatever you want. Get two sizes of metal-cored and two or three sizes of cloth. What you don't need you'll soon discover, and the education is cheap.

One last thing about wicking. On a big candle sometimes a weird thing will happen. Let's say you made a really nice candle in a milk carton, and so you send it off to your sister who lives in an overdone house in Elizabeth, New Jersey. She is so overwhelmed at such a touching show of conventional emotion that it is given the place of honor in the center of grandma's damask tablecloth at Thanksgiving, and she lights it up. It goes great for a while, making a melt pool about two-and-a-half inches in diameter, but not quite in the middle. After dinner, and while waiting for dessert, they're all out throwing the main course dishes into the Kitchen Aid. When they come back into the dining room you need never worry about having to go and visit them again. The melt pool got so close to the edge that the thin dam of solid wax was softened and the hot stuff in the pool ran down onto the table, draining the pool completely. The wick, being big, then melted some more wax, which also immediately ran out, cutting the channel a little deeper. This keeps going and you wind up with a hollow shell with a tiny slit down one side where the hot wax ran out and the wick has burned a hole through the table-cloth, the finish, and into that precious cherry wood. Of course, wax all over the place too. Once the dam breaks the whole thing happens quite quickly and inside of five minutes, you have no candle or place to crash in Elizabeth, New Jersey.

Of course, you can't predict which way the wick will bend as it burns, and this will in effect move the point of heat closer to the wall. Sometimes when the melt pool becomes quite deep, the wick will want to bend from the bottom of the pool, so it can move quite far. This can happen with all kinds of wax. A guy who was into candles on a really big scale tells me that wicks are usually braided out of three strands, and one is pulled tighter than the other two to make the wick bend on purpose. If you have excess trouble with bendy wicks maybe a home-braided number would be the answer.

WAX

The next thing is waxes. There are two kinds of things you can do here. One is to set out with the idea that you will turn out those charming little Black Forest numbers with all the Slavic peasant folk art decorations. This requires apprenticing yourself to a little old candlemaker from . . . etc., and spending the rest of your life analyzing eutectic gradients and other MIT sounding stuff. Or, secondly, you can figure out what the WAX wants to do, and let it do it. This saves enthusiasm, and you have a ball discovering what it's all about. In this light, I recommend that you start out with what-ever the local hobby shop has to offer. If you live in a rural area ask the telephone operator for the number of a hobby store. She will give yellow-page information, especially if you are rural. Once you have the name of a big city place, write and they should be helpful. You can expect to pay from 24 to 40 cents a pound for their "special" blend. Nonsense of course, but don't fight it. Let them play their money-trip game, and you put your heart into the wax. If you plan to make more than a couple of candles, get a slab of wax (from eight to twelve pounds) and a candy thermometer, or maybe it's called a deep fry thermometer. The best kind are about seven inches long, are enclosed in a test tube about an inch in diameter with a sort of pointed end. They have a metal spring clip with a wooden ball, and all this slides up and down on the test tube so that you can keep just the tip in the hot wax. They start at 100°F. and go up to 400°.

Since the rough draft was completed, I've looked around in the stores and they don't seem to make that kind anymore. It's probably a case of Owre's Law (a friend of mine has discovered that whenever a product ap-pears on the market that is too good, then it is immediately replaced by one of inferior quality and serviceability). My commercial friend told me

that he had good luck with a pasteurizing thermometer.   These are the
things that the milk destroyers use, and they are cheap.   They have been
around a buck-and-a-half or so.   You get them from Agway feed-and-farm-
supply stores.   You city types will just have to be content with meat or
candy thermometers.   Don't get the type that has a wand and a dial of the
kind that is tucked into the meat, for the first time they fall into the wax,
they're done.   What you need is a range from roughly 120°F. to 250° and
something that is easily cleaned so that the scale can be read even if it
becomes coated with wax.

A gas stove has better karma, but of course you use what's at hand.
Start out by using a double boiler (with this rig you don't need a thermometer).   It takes much longer, but until you and the wax know each other, play
it safe.   Remember this stuff burns and is dangerous.   The flash point (the
temperature at which it will burst into flame without directly applying fire)
of melted wax is as low as 290°F.   Should a pot of wax catch fire the easiest
way to put it out is to cover it with a lid.   If you have a thermometer stuck
into the pot you will have to take it out first, but that can easily be done with
a long knife or something along those lines.   Just don't panic and tip the
thing over for then you will be in real trouble.   A large pot for the water
champer on the bottom will work best.   A Chinese wok with a ring is really
good, for it is easy to add more water as it boils away.   You don't want too
much water, for then the wax pot will float and it gets harder to work with.
You should only use just enough heat to keep the water simmering, for a
violent boil will only splash water into the wax, and then the candle won't
burn too well.   Also, when you pour, remember to set the pot down briefly
with a wiping motion on an old towel or rags so that the water on the bottom
of the pot won't run off into the mold and ruin the candle.   When you get the
hang of the thing you'll put the wax pot directly over the flame and eliminate
the double boiler.   But don't expect to go and try to sue us should something
go wrong, for you have been warned.   Even though I've been doing this for a
time I still don't heat directly over an electric stove.   There's just too much
localized heat, and even if you turn it off there is a lot of residual heat that
takes a long time to disappear, and by that time the house may have gone

with it. Be cautious. Also don't plan to get too involved if you are being interrupted. I once forgot about what I was doing and discovered that the temperature had gone up to over 300°F. and was smoking like crazy. I was lucky.

But I didn't mean to get started on that, so let me say some more about the wax. The stuff is some kind of by-product of gasoline, I think. Maybe they make it directly from crude oil on purpose; I'm not sure. The main thing is that it exists. There also seems to be something that can be done to it to achieve different characteristics, for there is great variety among name brands. These are subtle differences, though, and you don't have to worry about anything unless you get into production.

The basic stuff has a melting temperature of around 133°F., and you will quite often find that this information is either part of, or its entire name (for example, Chevron XB-212133). Usually, at the hobby-shop level they will call it just 133 and pretend it's their special blend. There is a possibility they might have recast it with some additive, but this only adds to the price and doesn't do much. Paraffin (or canning wax) will make candles fine, but it is expensive and has a lower melting temperature. This means that it burns more quickly, and will make a melt pool that is larger. Nothing wrong with this, but just keep it in mind. I sometimes use it to lower the melting point when I'm stuck with the high-temperature stuff. It is also handy for making the color clearer. By this I mean that the flame will light up more of the candle under it. The general rule is, the lower the melting temperature of the wax, the brighter the candle will glow. The light from the flame of a candle also shines downward. If the wax is translucent, like low-melting-temperature wax is, then the candle itself will seem to glow with an inner light. This is sometimes a very nice effect and will even work with colors if they are kept relatively thin. High-temperature waxes are quite opaque. So much for paraffin.

The high-temperature stuff (also in your local hobby shop) has a melting point around 156°F. The thing about this stuff is that it will last longer. But it's tricky, and I like the 133. The big harangue I gave you about your sister in Jersey is a classic example of what this 156 will do to you. In smaller diameter candles, where the melt pool is big or bigger than the candle, it will drip and run all over the place. Of course they don't last too long, but fine for special effects. If you're going to give these away, just tell them first what to expect. Oh yeah, one thing this reminds me of is this. Burn your own. I got into the whole thing by accident (luck?) and before I knew what was happening, I was giving them away, and selling them so fast I never really had a chance to find out how they behaved. Some I was lucky on, and with others I wiped out. I kind of like to have one or more going anyway while I'm messing around. I guess what I mean is that making them is only part of the trip.

OK, so back to 156. Colors will be darker with the 156, and of course more opaque. The outside of the candle may be smoother, but not necessarily. There may be fewer bubbles, but not necessarily. It may take more scent to do the same job, but not necessarily, etc., etc. Try it, and find out what you want. You probably won't care too much about this type of thing, which is better anyway, for it means that what the candle wants to be is more apt to reach you.

BEESWAX

Man, does this stuff have soul! Getting it and getting the bread for it is the hassle. If you know any apiaries, go there. Ask the guys in the health food store where they get their organic honey and go there. Big orchards either keep bees or know who does. Sometimes it's available in New York, Boston, L. A., but following the beekeeper out to a half-falling-down barn on a beautiful spring day with the apple trees pouring out their blossoms and nectar and bees flying all around can really turn you on. After moving his hand-cultivator and a pile of burlap bags--THERE IT IS. Fantastic! He's got a whole damn barn just filled with the stuff. A beautiful, kneadable yellow that looks kind of like Little Black Sambo gold. And it is, too. From 45 to 70 cents a pound (in stores, $1 to $2). What the hell, man, blow it and get ten pounds. Get twenty, so you don't get tight with it. To become tight with a material is for the art to die. Great for technology, but you're an MIT dropout--remember? What does it do? Smell it. Take a small piece in your hand and warm it--push it with your thumb--bite it. Oh, by the way, it burns. Don't waste it on your sister in Jersey. Let the people there burn Chevron XB-212133, they've already choked on the air they ruined by making the stuff in the first place. Have you ever seen a bee in Elizabeth?

Working with it . . . Melting temperature? I don't really know--it doesn't behave at all like Chevron's stuff (by the way, I'm not knocking them. Theirs is the best on the market)--I'd guess around 140°F. or so, but it's funny. It takes a lot of heat to melt it and as it cools down it won't skim like petroleum wax, it kind of congeals in a gooey mass. I don't know what its flash point is because I've never had it over 165°. I would imagine that it would ruin it to get it too hot, but I don't really know. Try some and

16

COOKBOOK #1

    Go to the grocery store and get a one-pound box of paraffin or canning wax. It is sold by both Esso and Gulf under their names, and they mention candlemaking on the box so you will know that you have the right stuff. Go to the local hobby or craft shop and get the smallest diameter candle wicking they have. If you can't do this, get some Cotton string, like kite or butcher string, and test it by setting it on fire. It should burn about like a cardboard match and if you hold it down, it will burn quite quickly and evenly. White is a must. Go home. Get out a biggish pan (two-quart) and put an inch of water in the bottom. Put a smaller pan in the water and put the burner on a medium heat so as to just boil the water. Open the box of paraffin, which will have five slabs inside, and put one in the top (dry) pot. When it has melted take out the other slabs and lay them flat on the counter. Take the pot with the melted wax out and dry the water off the bottom. Put the string or wicking into the wax, then take it out and spread it on the counter in a straight line

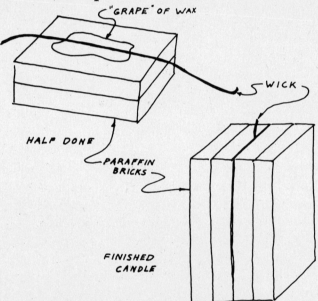

    and allow to harden. Next, pour about as much wax on one lying-down slab as would be contained in a grape-sized volume and immediately put another slab on top. Be careful to align the ends reasonably. Lay the prewaxed wick on the center of the second slab the long way and pour on another grape, or grape-and-a-half. Put on another slab and align the ends. One more grape, and the last slab, and align the ends. When cool (in about five minutes) take a pair of scissors and trim the string or wick flush with one end and leave about one little finger thickness (a half-inch) sticking up from the opposite end. Stand up with this end up, strike match on appropriate surface, apply to string (hereinafter referred to, if at all, as wick). Blow out match and turn off burner under the water.

see what it will do, I'll bet some really great things. Wicks are a whole different number with this beeswax, so make sure that you burn before you give. I've found that fat wicks seem to work better, although a friend has had very good luck with regular sizes. The metal jobs help, but they have to be fat. If you have the thin metal ones, braid up some cloth wicks around them. They are hard to light because it takes a lot of heat to melt the wax in the wick, but once they're burning they will last a long time--a candle made in half a beercan will last for maybe forty hours. It will do that same weird number, so gauge the melt pool to give a fairly heavy wall thickness in a fat candle. After burning a long time the melt pool will get fairly large and anything less than a half-inch wall thickness will sag and leak. Even though the wax smells nice, the flame burns clean and there is no really noticeable aroma in the air, except while extinguishing, so don't be too disappointed in that respect.

COLOR

Now we're making some headway. This is the most beautiful and elusive aspect of the whole thing. Before I forget the bees completely, I might as well say I've never added color to beeswax. The stuff is so wonderful just the way it is, I could never bear to frig with it. But then, the Greeks painted that fantastically beautiful Hellenic marble with what we now think of as gaudy colors, so what the hell.

Color is available at the hobby shops usually in little bricks sometimes in things like Thayer's Slippery Elm Throat Lozenges, sometimes cast into tricky plastic vacuum-molded packages like marzipan. The buttons can pretty much just be dumped in the molten wax but the bigger ones have to be sort of shaved down. Since the color is so intense, little quantities make a tremendous difference so it is practically impossible to get two batches to have the same color. This is what makes it so much fun--because you never really know what it is going to look like until it has cooled. I assume that the hobby shop junk is a super-intense dye that has been added to paraffin to cut it and make it manageable. The dye itself can be had directly, but at the beginning don't bother. Too much mess and expense. I'll give the poop on that later under turning pro.

There is an awful lot of stuff that you can use that really wasn't designed with candles in mind. One is crayons. They work pretty well, give all kinds of different colors and are cheap and readily available. They are sometimes hard to melt and don't give quite as clear a color as the real stuff. They also seem to leave some sediment in the bottom of the pan, so don't plan to dump all of the wax into a mold. Leave the crud behind in the bottom of the pot. A guy told me that he used paint. I tried Sherwin-Williams show-card enamels and they didn't work at all. I guess there is too much other junk in the pigment. Maybe right-from-the-tube artist colors

COOKBOOK #2

Take a mayonnaise or salad-dressing jar (sixteen-ounce is best) and wash out and dry leaving the label on and intact. Go to the hobby store and get at least a pound-and-a-half of their ordinary candle wax and a length of wicking. If this isn't possible, obtain materials as per Cookbook #1. Melt all of the wax in a double boiler. Tie a nut (steel, please, as in "nut-and-bolt") or small pebble or something with some weight to it to the wick and then prewax it (see Cookbook #1). Dangle the wick in the center of the jar. Shut an overhead cabinet door on the wick, or fasten it with a spring clothespin to something like a knife balanced across the top of the jar or any way you can as long as it is carefully centered (see illustration). Pour in the wax. (Another way is to drop the wick in right after pouring. Also, you can pour in one inch of wax and let it harden in cold water--put the jar in the sink--to secure the bolt at the bottom.)

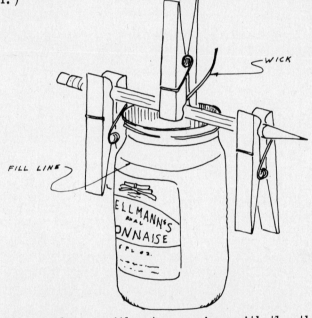

Wait about one hour without messing with the thing at all unless you have to recenter the wick immediately after pouring. You will notice that the top of the wax is no longer level, but has started to dip down making a depression. Add enough extra melted wax to fill the depression. In another hour you will see that another depression, or well, has started to form. Refill again. You might have to do this three times, but two should usually take care of it. A slight well will not cause any problem. Remove the wick-suspension apparatus and trim the wick to about as long as a lima bean is wide. Congratulations, you are now the proud owner of a Mayonnaise Candle. Tee-hee-hee. If you want to get the candle out, wrap a towel around the jar and break it, or put the jar under hot water and then immediately in the freezer so it will crack.

would be OK, but I never tried it. Lipstick should work, but I don't know. Try things and if you find something that is good, spread the word. A trick from the kitchen might help here. Try blending some of the color with just a small amount of wax. You can get the lumps and unevenness out here. Then when you want to color the main bulk of the wax just add some of the colored mixture. Children's poster color in powder form might do. If there is a printer that you could get friendly with I'll bet his inks would be great. Probably fairly opaque, but think of the great colors they have. If you are even slightly versed in candlese, any guys you know who are making a bag of candles will usually be really helpful. I ran into one exception in Colorado, but usually they like to swap new ideas. The world isn't so small that it won't support one extra candlemaker. If the guy's on a money trip, forget him. If he won't share what he knows, then he probably won't learn from you either and the art will soon outdistance him. What is hot in stores this year you probably won't be able to give away in five years.

One problem that is apt to occur with impure waxes or coloring agents is the clogging of the wick. Since the wick lifts the molten wax above the surface by capillary action, if solid matter is allowed to fill up the spaces between the fibers then the candle will not burn. If you are having trouble with this you can try to eliminate the impurities or, if this is not possible, then a coarser wicking might solve the problem. The braided stuff that you will get from the stores is apt to be fairly tightly woven. If you can find some fairly fine stuff and braid it yourself it will help. When I suspect a candle is giving me trouble for this reason I make a test by taking two pure pieces of wax and sandwiching a piece of the wick between. Once it has established a fair size melt pool I will hold a little bit of the coloring agent over the flame and melt some into the pool. If the flame starts to diminish immediately, then I know that the color and the wick are incompatible. I try again using a different wick or color and when I'm through with the tests I just blow the candle out and dump the still molten wax with its impurities out and toss the sample into the pot for remelting. This technique is also good for establishing the diameter of melt pools with different waxes and wicks. It takes a long time for the melt pool to reach its maximum size, though, so don't give up on them too quickly. At least an hour (if not two) is required.

SCENTS

These are all phony baloney except for the beeswax, which smells like honey, but everyone digs it so it doesn't hurt to know something about it and try it. More about this later. I've bought scents in little bottles in a liquid form and in translucent crystals. I'm sure that it probably comes in other forms too (try your local hobby shop or candle shop to start with). I kind of like the liquid because you just dump it in and that's it. Once I gave a really beautiful candle as a wedding present and even though I put in about five tiny bottles of the stuff, it just didn't seem to be as smelly as I wanted, so I just

COOKBOOK #3

Go to the hobby store and get some of their ordinary wax, some wicking, and some color. If they want to know any details to help in the selection of the materials tell them that you are going to make your candle in a half-gallon milk container. If there is any choice ask them for low-melting-temperature wax and a metal-cored wick. Color is color is color. Bring the stuff home. Melt enough wax and prewax the wick (see Cookbook #1). Wash out a half-gallon milk container, cut to about six inches high (two-thirds of the way up from the bottom) and dry thoroughly. Add the coloring agent to the melted wax until the tip of the bowl of a teaspoon held vertically in the molten wax is no longer visible. Just the bowl is put into the wax so, in other words, you can only see about an inch-and-a-half down into the melted wax. With yellow, two-inch visibility is good. On how to install the wick see Cookbook #2. Then fill the container with wax to one-half inch from the top. Keep topping off at hour intervals as per Cookbook #2, only this time it will take at least three refills and about six hours before the candle is really hard. When it is finally cool to the touch, and I mean <u>Cool</u>, all trace of warmth gone, you can strip off the paper container by tearing, or with a razor blade or scissors, and you have your candle. Trim the wick down to a half-inch high before lighting.

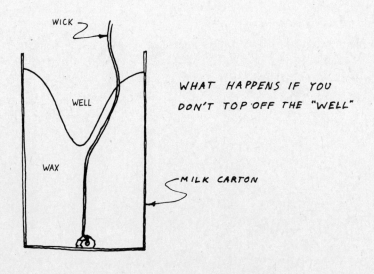

WICK

WELL

WAX

WHAT HAPPENS IF YOU
DON'T TOP OFF THE "WELL"

MILK CARTON

took a little more and rubbed it around on top with my finger. That really did it and it also made the top of the candle (which was about ten inches across) have a really nice sheen on it. Unfortunately, it kind of attracted the lint and dust so that after a couple of days, it began to look like fuzz city. Oh well. It's a good trick to remember if you want to peddle the things, though, as it will really snow the hell out of Old Mrs. Willowby, Prop., The Owl's Eye, Gifts. Here again try experimenting. Somehow the idea of putting all these hydrocarbon imitation scents in kind of turned me off and I always figured it would be nice to put in some real ones. Those little bottles of oil that they sell in the health food and head shops; are they real? I sort of figure that they are, but I'm not sure. How do you get oil out of cedar wood? Anyway they should work fine, but you'll have to do something about the price. I once tried using Dr. Bronner's Pure Castile Soap because it has such a strong mint smell, but it must be water based and there was no mixing at all. It just kind of sat there and sputtered. With all experiments, it's a good idea to try to use stuff that appears to have an oil or paraffin base, but that still won't guarantee success.

When I lived in Colorado I was making a sort of volcanic-looking number that was really great. For a while I used hydrocarbon pine scent which is the best of the batch. (The strawberry doesn't even come close and really turns your stomach.) After a while even that didn't do much for me and I picked a batch of sage brush which has a potent smell. I figured on doing a rugged-type candle with mostly natural components. Ground it in a blender and it was sort of OK, but just too many floaters. Never did get back to that, but I always thought a juicer might bring just the straight oil or I considered solvents like in Marijuana Consumer's Handbook's formulas for extracting concentrated resins from plants. I imagine that there is real room for an organically scented product if you'd like to get into that. Again, if you find out, spread the word; you don't have to work at the Max Planck Institute to add to the ocean of knowledge.

ADDITIVES

There are a bunch of these, but you don't really need them, so I won't go into it except for the main item, which is stearic acid. It comes in crystal form and goes under a variety of names such as Stearic Acid, Louisa's Magic Glow Flakes, Tuff 'n Tall, etc. Triple-pressed stearic acid is the whitest type. The idea is that it raises the melting point and slows burning. Of course, it then does all the things that I talked about under the higher-temperature waxes. It's not too bad an idea if you start off small and don't want to get involved with a lot of wax just to buy one slab of 133 and some stearic acid so you know what the higher stuff is like. It isn't quite the same, but it comes pretty close. I suppose there is some other boring information I should tell you about stearic, like keep it out of reach of children in a cool dark place, or something, but I can't think of anything. Actually, all it is is vegetable or animal fat, or both, and not dangerous.

HOW TO

This I can't tell you. The Rosicrucians can't tell you about that "split second of cosmic truth," but they can tell you what they did to get there. This article is about what I've done and some of what others have done and some that I've wanted to do, but got all hung up in other things instead. The very first thing I tried was with some pretty nice wax that I got in Frisco. It was down under the highway as you come over from Berkeley, but I can't remember the name or the street. It doesn't matter, for I'm sure that there are places just like it all over that can get you started. Since the wax was nice, if you live there you could let your fingers do the walking and come up with the place. I bought from them a recast slab of about fifteen pounds. What they had done to it I don't know, but it wasn't just the straight refinery stuff. Anyway, after dragging the materials halfway across the country, I finally wound up living in a sort of house, but with a real stove and I got the hots to try it. I'd always kind of liked the sandcast numbers that I'd seen, with the three little legs on the bottom like a colonial cast-iron fire pot, and so I thought I'd start there. Unfortunately, two feet of snow on the ground and no sand. So I tried snow. Fantastic. Not at all like you imagined, but fantastic. The hot wax melted the snow and cut all kinds of channels through the snow which I then let melt away from wax. You wouldn't believe the incredible lacy structure that was left. Not much use as a candle in quite that form, but I could have abandoned wax candles and gone into wax and bronze-from-wax sculpture right there. If you live where there's snow, try this. Try it with loose snow, try it with packed, try it with hot wax, try it with cold; here are four different possibilities right off the bat. Mix sand with it, freeze it, shape it while soft, let it harden and reshape it with a Bernzamatic torch. Glue extra pieces on, break some off. Step on the whole thing and re-fuse it with a little heat. In getting into something, do everything that can be done, has been done, ever will be done, and can't be done. There is no reason why this idea isn't as good for music and drawing as for wax.

Getting the big sheets into smaller pieces so that you can get them into the melting pans is a sweat. I've tried all techniques and first used a knife and sort of ice-picked it to death. An ax worked pretty well, but a lot goes shooting all over the place. Putting a knife or dowel or piece of wood down on the floor and bridging the wax over it works about the best. Then you can just stand on it and it will crack nicely. Smaller pieces can be made by just hitting the piece on the floor at about a thirty-degree angle. Sharp smacks will usually break off about tennis-ball-sized chunks.

If you ever get past this to the wick stage, here are a few possibilities. I first tried putting the wick in first. A hole in the bottom of the mold (snow, paper, glass, metal) and something to hold it straight up. It'll probably leak when you pour the wax in. This can be good or bad depending on

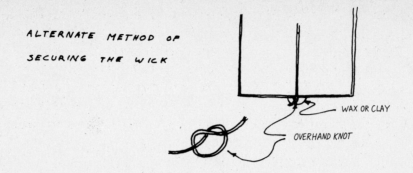

ALTERNATE METHOD OF SECURING THE WICK

WAX OR CLAY

OVERHAND KNOT

your outlook. One way to solve the leaking problem is to put a little model-ing clay around the wick where it comes through the hole. Since this stuff has an oil base it will not contaminate the wick.

Next I tried a coat hanger carefully propped up and pulled out later be-fore the wax got completely hard--then I shoved the wick down the hole (a little hot wax kept the thing from wiggling). Fair, but the hole was pretty small. Next, used screwdrivers. OK, but the end gets stuck if you let it get completely hard. A smooth rod as big as a pencil and slightly tapered would be the best; I had one of these but it still stuck and had to be pulled out at just the right moment. Don't ask when that is, you'll find out. The one idea that I did get out of that Colorado guy, after he'd laid his ego all over the place about two feet deep, was to use a quarter-inch electric drill and make the hole afterwards. One thing I can add to his idea is a bell hanger's drill. These are drill bits that are made especially for electri-cians going through thick walls and as I remember, the quarter-inch size is around eight or nine inches long. They are not the easiest thing to find, so I would recommend this really for the pros. Also there is the hassle of the electric drill motor, and of course electricity, if you're camped out on a deserted island in Maine or B. C.

They make little tin numbers to hold the wick in the bottom of the mold and these are not too bad, but they don't have any real weight. If you decide to try these, poke the wick through the hole and tie a knot in the wick to pre-vent it from pulling out. Place the wick in the mold so that the tin jobbie is in the center and pour in about a half inch of wax. After this has cooled you can easily pull on the wick and straighten it out as it cannot pull out of the wax. Actually just the knot alone will do the same thing, which is the route that I usually went. The real metal molds sometimes come with an alligator clip to hold the wick upright. These are fine, but I never really got into the commercial mold thing, so on that score you'll have to experiment.

One thing I haven't mentioned yet about the wax, related to wicks is the incredible amount of shrinkage of cooling wax (coefficient of expansion for you MIT freaks). If you pour a candle into a beercan, without top of course, and fill it right to the top, you're in for a surprise. When it cools it will shrink and form a well. You'll wind up with a sort of funnel-like hole that is about a fifth of the volume of the candle. Now if you've got a wick in there the wax will solidify around the wick and the outside of the beercan first. As the wax cools, it will pull the wick to the side of the well, so that even though you started off with the wick in the middle, now the damn thing is halfway to one side. This is why I like the rod or drill method. If you have to put the wick in first, it's better to keep adding wax as it cools so that no well forms.

Realize that you just don't make a candle in a couple of minutes. You can do your part in about that time, but they take a while to cool. A candle cast in a half-gallon milk container will take about six hours to cool completely. Of course you will get impatient like I did and ruin the first few by trying to take them out too soon, but you'll get over that. The easiest way out is to work in the evening and then the next morning they're ready. A big candle like the half-gallon jobbie will form an enormous well so that will have to be topped off from time to time, so don't expect to just sit back and wait, otherwise you will get that pulling-over-the-wick thing.

One trick to use is to add heavily scented wax to the hole around the wick when topping off. This saves on scent and does the same thing as a heavily scented candle. There's no federal law saying how the finished item must relate to gravity so make the bottom of the mold the top of the candle if you want, or the other way around if you want. So much for wicks into candles, except for the fact that prewaxed wicks seem to work better. Use hot wax for this for better penetration into fibers--easier to light the first time and much easier to insert if you're doing wick-laters. When I say hot here, I mean around 200°F.

I've noticed that sometimes a carbon crud builds up on the wick and tends to change the size of the flame slightly, but it's no big deal. It probably means that the wax was contaminated in some way, but I don't seem to lose much sleep over it.

My next experiment was with uncolored 133 in beercans with designs poked through the aluminum with a pocket knife after the wax had cooled. The light from the flame made the entire thing glow and all the holes became illuminated. Beautiful. Keep a tiny wick on this or you'll get a leak. Then I tried different colors added on top of each other. I'd fill the can up, say, halfway with red and tip it until the level of the wax was at a crazy angle, let it cool and then top it off with yellow. Wick later on this one of course. Four or five colors are nice with this. The wax shrinks away from the mold wall when it is entirely cool, which makes it easy to get out. Also it means that if you wait too long between pours, the new color will find that space and run down and cover the first color. Also, when you add wax in stages if you

COOKBOOK #4

Now you're starting to get into it. You really had better read the whole article now, and don't say I didn't warn you if you try this and wind up with a miserable mess. At least you should read the previous recipes. You've obtained the materials as per Cookbook #3 only this time you've bought several different coloring compounds. We melt the wax just the same way and prepare and hang the wick as in previous candles, only this time we don't heat all of the wax with only one color in it. Melt enough uncolored wax in one pot to do the whole candle and set up a second double boiler outfit. When everything is ready to go, pour off about a tennis-ball volume of wax from the main pot into a secondary pot. This second one is the one that you will add the color to. You really should have a wide glass container as a mold for this one. A four-cup pyrex measuring cup would be great. With the wick all set up in the mold (the measuring cup) dump in your tennis ball of colored

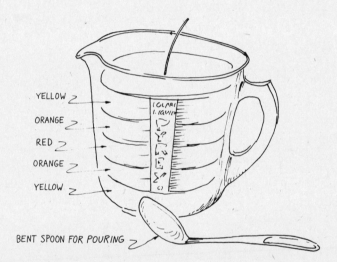

YELLOW

ORANGE

RED

ORANGE

YELLOW

BENT SPOON FOR POURING

wax. Let's say that it was yellow. Pour off a second tennis ball from the main supply and color it orange. When the yellow has formed a cloudy scum on the surface, wait five more minutes. Take a tablespoon and bend the bowl to about a forty-five degree angle to the handle. Hold the spoon just above the yellow and pour the orange into the bowl. Keep repeating this process with red, purple, then red again, orange, and yellow or until the mold is full. With the last color make about two tennis balls of colored wax, but pour only one in. The rest will be used to top off the well (see Cookbooks 2 and 3).

Great, you're coming along fine; oh yes, trim the excess wick to about as high as a hot dog split in half is above the surface of the frying pan.

let it get too cold then the layers won't stick properly which is apt to make Mrs. Willowby distraught. I found that if you've blown it and waited too long then you can actually save it by heating the next layer very hot, which will sort of remelt some of the underlayer and allow a good fuse. Of course, then you don't have a sharp separation of color, but who says that's bad. How hot you actually make it depends on the volume you add and how much volume the first layer had. Obviously if you add a quart of wax at 250°F. to a quarter-pint of cold stuff, it will completely melt the cold and mix the colors. I never did this, because at the time I wanted the layers to show. I'll bet though, that with care you might get the two to only partially mix with interesting convection swirls especially if the color agents are different types. So what if you want a red and yellow candle and wind up with an orange one, it's still going to be nice.

I like to use a thermometer all the time, as it kind of gives me a base of reference and then I know when to pour, add, etc. If you're heating a previously colored wax and can't see the bottom of the pot, you can tell when the wax is all melted by watching the thermometer. The 133 will go fairly quickly to around 140°F. or so and stay there until all the wax is melted. Then you will see an increase in temperature. Since solid wax sinks to the bottom it will be hard to tell how you're doing otherwise. This is especially true when reclaiming wax and sand chunks that you had left over from sandcasting. If the thermometer goes too deep into the wax, then it will cloud the test tube and you can't read what it says. Very hot water, from the tap, if you have it, will clean the wax off the tools and molds. Don't use abrasives, as the tiny little scratches give the wax something to grab onto and it becomes increasingly harder to clean your things. Somehow the test tube broke on my thermometer and I was able to chip the rest of the glass away until I wound up with just the core. Now I use it held in place with the spring clothespins and it works even better, so don't throw it out, should it break.

SANDCASTING

It doesn't need to be sand as I've already mentioned, but let's group all non-mold molding operations under this head. The snow I've mentioned. When I finally got some sand (from the highway department) it had clinkers mixed with it which was the way I got those volcanic looking numbers The sand was moist with melted snow when I tried it, which turned out to be good. Of course dry sand won't hold its shape. Also if you are using coarse stuff the wax will leak all through it. The wetness seems to help cool the wax and prevent this. Maybe it just allows the sand to pack closer so as to stop the leaks; anyway, a little water helps. Once I cast a candle in a cardboard box which contained the sand and I had so many leaks that the entire box wound up being the candle.

Next--temperature. Pour at 140°F. (I'm always talking about 133° unless otherwise mentioned) and the sand won't stick at all. You'll wind up

COOKBOOK #5

Materials as per Cookbooks 3 and 4, plus some scenting agents. This time we're going to make a candle with more than one wick and so we need a fairly fat mold. A dog dish, stainless mixing bowl, or something about eight inches in diameter and smaller at the bottom than the top would be suitable. Revere Ware pots are OK, but because of the straight sides they make it more difficult to get the finished candle out. What we do this time is to heat the wax according to Cookbook #4 and create small amounts of differently colored wax as before. Only this time we need golf balls rather than tennis balls. Don't worry about the placement of the wicks yet, but do prewax them as in #1 and set them aside to harden. We will need three separate wicks. Tie the weight on the bottom prior to prewaxing and make sections about eight inches long each. Pour a golf ball of yellow melted wax into the dog dish and quickly pick up the mold and tip it first one way and then the other. Cool wax is best, and a cold mold will work easier. The object here is not to completely coat the inside of the mold but rather to have an open effect with lacelike swirls and blotches. After the yellow is completely cold, repeat the process with red. Then blue, green, or whatever colors you decide on. The idea is to wind up with the inside of the mold completely covered with about four different colors so that when you take the candle out it will have a four-color marbleized surface. The actual swishing around of these first layers will take a little practice, so don't get discouraged if the first one doesn't look quite right. With the swirled layers all in and <u>cold</u>, then you can proceed as in Cookbook #2 with the filling. If the scent is liquid in a small bottle, just dump it into the rest of the wax now. If it is a wax-type lump, throw it in now and allow it to melt. Just add uncolored wax for the core, as the outside is already colored and you don't need to waste the coloring agent on the center. Also the flame will light the uncolored core and cause it to glow. If the outer, colored layers are thin enough the light will glow through them creating a stained-glass effect. The core must be poured rather cool, though, otherwise the great quantity of hot wax in the middle will remelt your outer coating and you then have nothing. To get the right temperature for the core-pour, take the pot out of its water pan and let it cool until there is a skin on the top that is thick enough to keep a lead pencil when held point down from poking through. Arrange the wicks, poke a hole in the skin and make the pour using only the liquid wax. Top off the well as in Cookbook #2, trim the wicks to a pea-and-a-half high and you're finished. Oh yeah; the wick arrangement. They should form a triangle, with the wicks about two inches from each other and the triangle centered in the dog dish. Of course they must hang straight down.

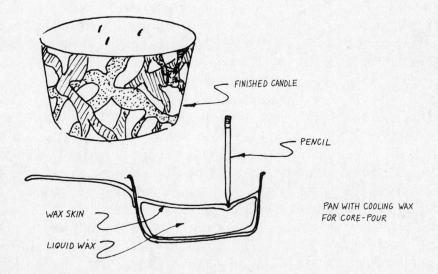

FINISHED CANDLE

PENCIL

PAN WITH COOLING WAX
FOR CORE-POUR

WAX SKIN

LIQUID WAX

with the shape of the sand and zillions of tiny air bubbles and no sand. Pour at 260° and it'll leak all over the place. I found with a damp mold 200° seems about right. Probably sand from Provincetown is quite a bit different from sand supplied by the Colorado Department of Highways, so play around. At 200° I got good adhesion and varied penetration from a half-inch to one-and-a-half inches into the sand. At first I used to clean them by brushing and brushing till most of the loose stuff was off, but they still shed. Then I discovered that by dipping the whole candle into a batch of scrap wax quickly at around 180° the outer grains were held securely and also given a gloss with the outer coating.

This is my favorite area so you'll have to bear with me as I devote most of my time to it. I thought I was doing some nice stuff with this until I saw some other guys' things. But first I have to digress a bit about the making of nothing: in other words, the hole into which you pour the wax. Anything goes. I shaped by hand at first. This should be good if you're using Prov-incetown- or Big-Sur-type stuff. Mine was too coarse and I needed some packing to keep the leaking down, so I got into putting a plate into the box, then a liquor bottle on top of the plate and packing the moist sand all around. Pull out the bottle and you've got it. The plate gave a smooth bottom and kept the candle from scratching beautiful tables in Elizabeth. I still like the hand forming though. Trouble is that the bottom is apt to be uneven and there isn't really much to rest it on. Easiest way to get around that is to poke your fingers down into the bottom of the mold three or four times. This gives it feet to sit on. If they're uneven, careful paring down with a knife later will fix it up.

Anyway, this other guy had done that. His candle was oval, about four by eight inches, and very shallow, maybe only two inches deep. It was a two wick job, wouldn't last too long because it was shallow, but so what. Off to one side there was a very smooth beach pebble only half imbedded in the wax and looking kind of like a Japanese sand garden. Really beautiful. Along one side, which evidently had just been laid along the inside edge of the mold be-fore casting, was the jawbone of a deer. Sounds kind of weird, but it was just right. The bone was pure white with a slight grainy texture from weathering, and the rock was flawless. A light lemon-colored wax kind of set it all off. One night in the spring we all got stoned and burned it. Amazing.

What about sandcasting combined with other techniques? Ever seen the ones where they form separate bodies for the various wicks and then with tunnels or channels in the sand connect them all together? They don't have to be all at the same level either. There could be waterfall-type numbers. I always wanted to get some heavy, crude wrought-iron rings and bury part of them into the sand so that the iron and wax would be combined. Then leather straps maybe, but that's old-hat now. I've always dug mixed bags. In the true spirit of phony imitation in America, I faked the sandcast number in order to try to reduce the waste through leakage by putting the sand direct-ly into some wax and then applying it around the outside of a mayonnaise jar that I had already filled and wicked. It was fine and had the advantage of being refillable. Did you ever make drip castles on the beach with wet sand? Why not try this with candles? I imagine great pagoda types soaring up and up. It's funny when you think about how important the wick is to Mrs. Willowby. How about those Santa Claus candles that people used to give your mother and she never burned? They bought them because they were candles, not because they were little statues. You can see a really nice construction a couple of feet tall made of wax, sand, shells, iron, etc. "Oh! That's lovely, what is it? Not a candle? Well thanks anyway, we're just looking." Stick a couple of bits of string here and there, call them wicks and you couldn't keep up with the volume at $50 per. And chances are, no one would ever try to burn it anyway.

So much for sand, but don't forget such things as powdered coal, Styrofoam beebees, or a box lined with leaves, and grass. (Feathers?)

RIGID MOLDS

Glass, tin, paper, plastic. All these work and others I haven't even thought of. Probably--at least with plastic and paper molds--but not necessarily, you are going to want to get the thing out. (How about my mayonnaise jar?) If the candle is to be left in the mold like the perforated beercan, no sweat, just fill it up and you're home. Luckily, because of the shrinkage of the wax you will be able to get it out of most smooth hard molds: glass and metal. Aluminum beercans, you just peel away. Paper, ditto. Milk cartons are widely used and are fine, although the sides tend to bulge in or out. If you don't like that, put the carton in the sink with water and the walls will be straight. Metal and glass molds will give a shinier and smoother wall finish if you put the mold briefly into cold water right after pouring. To help get the wax out of the metal molds, there is a silicone spray release, but I haven't found that it is really necessary. Most of the molds are quite tapered, and the shrinkage breaks them free. If you do have trouble getting a candle out of the mold and it's not one that you want to destroy for the sake of the candle then usually dipping the whole thing in boiling water for a little while will soften the wax just enough to let the candle slide out nicely. With glass, such as liquor bottles and so on, all you have to do is break them gently. If you bruise the candle while breaking, you can cover the "shattered" spot by dipping in hot water or torching briefly. Or hold over the gas stove and let the burner briefly wash the wax. Mixing bowls, dog dishes, anything goes. Clorox bottles and the other plastics are OK, but sometimes you will get a strange effect when the heat from the wax starts to make the thing melt and sag. If it looks like you're going to get into trouble, lower it into the sink to quench it.

Glass is especially nice for different colored layering because you get some idea of what you're doing. It's also very cheap, and just a little messy. I find that when making the layered ones, I like to wait until just after the wax has skimmed over then add the next layer by pouring into a spoon held close to the surface of the underlayer. Otherwise, the new hot wax will puncture the old and you get nothing. By doing it as soon as possible you aid the adhesion too. There are plenty of things to do besides just filling the molds up. Try pouring in just a very little wax at around 160°F. and tilting the mold in all directions as you go. Then dump it out the same way. This will give lacelike tracings on the outside. Do it several times with different colors, or once with solid or layered center bodies. This is a popular item right now, but not too many are very well done. The trouble is that with the commercially available molds, you just can't see what is happening. Don't forget that once you've laid this delicate stuff down on the inside of the mold (the outside of the candle) that too hot a core-pour will wipe the whole thing out.

TRICKS

Ice from the refrigerator in a milk carton does kind of an interesting thing. The wax will fill up the spaces between the ice and of course will melt it a fair amount at first, but will still give a very lacy structure. You can then either call it quits at that or dump out the water after it has melted and the wax hardened and refill with clear or a different color. An easy way to solve the wick problem with the ice casting is to put a commercially-made taper in the middle of the mold first. Or you can put in one of your lumpy hand-dipped ones.

Dipping consists of building the candles up by repeatedly lowering them into a pot of wax at around 145°F., allowing them to cool and dry between dips. You can dip in several different colors and maybe carve into the finished item, revealing hidden layers. Or you can dip in one color enough times so as to get a reasonable thickness; then dip in another color, leaving some of the previous color exposed, etc. You can make more than one at a time by bending a strand of wick in half and dipping both ends into the wax--making two candles--or you can drape the wick over a stick, along with as many other wicks as you want and make many candles at once. Don't ask me how to get these hand-dipped numbers perfect, because I haven't the foggiest idea. Mine always came out pretty bumpy and crude, but I kind of liked them that way. There has to be a way to make them perfect, but I'll leave that up to the Black Forest experts.

Another favorite trick used to be to whip the wax as it was freezing and produce a thick air filled foam that can be kind of gopped around like a frosting. A friend of mine once made a really nice candle by casting different colored layers in a milk carton and then cutting down through the layers from top to bottom afterwards and reassembling by heating the two surfaces over the stove and resticking them together. This produces separate color cubes that look great and have no relation to the pouring process, so it's

very different. Here's another version of the same idea but even more frag-
mented. Go back to your childhood and try blocks again. Make up some
batches of different colored waxes and cast them into flatish molds like
pyrex baking dishes and bread tins so that you get wax around an inch deep.
After they have cooled and you have removed the slabs, cut them up into
blocks about an inch on a side. By stacking the different colored blocks up
you can make something really nice without having a molded look at all.
The wick on this can either be put in afterwards, or you can make the candle
in two halves and lay the wick between and stick the pieces together sandwiching the wick in the middle.

Glued together types have a tendency to look a little poor around the
joints so it is a good idea to torch them. Gently wash the bad areas with
the Bernzamatic torch, and with a little care you can fix it right up. The
wax that the torch melts will run, of course, so you have to keep the piece
moving to prevent drips.

Another idea for things to do with the torch is the partial destruction of
the candle after it has been removed from the mold. For instance, you
could make a layered one that alternated high- and low-temperature waxes.
Then by torching carefully you could melt out some of the softer wax which
would run and cause nice drips. This would give the finished product a nice
eroded look.

Should you want to improve the gloss of any candle that has become dull,
either by torching or because of a poor mold surface, there is an easy out.
Heat the entire surface of the candle to around the melting point or just be-
low, either by washing the candle with the torch or by dipping in hot water.
Before the wax has a chance to cool and cloud, dip it in cold water and
SHAZAM! Super Glowcoat Johnson's shine.

This just leaves a tip or two about colors and scents. If you wait until
all of the wax has melted before you add the color, it's easier to see how the
melt is coming. I generally just keep basic colors and mix my own non-pri-
mary colors like paints. This is easier on inventory, but you can just buy
the different colors or crayons. Keep separate pots going for different
colors and it will give you more variety and chance of unusual expression at
the time of pouring. If you want the candle body to glow from the light of the
flame, then you will have to go easy on the color. A transparent effect is
needed here, and too much dye will prevent the light from coming through.
With scents, add them at the very end, so that the aroma will not be cooked
off.

If you want a glue to fasten things onto the wax, shellac seems to be the
best. All my big candles used to go out with a felt bottom on them with a
woodcut inked design on the bottom giving the whole product a slightly more
finished quality. This hides any uglies you might have on the bottom too,

<u>COOKBOOK #6</u>

This candle will not be substantially different from Cookbook #3, but will look quite different. For a mold this time we are going to use damp sand. You can get a bucketful from the beach, local golf course, or highway department. Construction firms that handle cement will have it too. Obtain the same materials that are required for #3 and use a scent, too, as in #5. Let's use only one wick and keep the candle the size of a grapefruit so that there are no undue problems. Melt down in the double boiler a substantial amount of extra wax, say, two grapefruits and add color and scent. Of course, you have already prewaxed and prepared the wick. Make sure the sand is damp--not wet, and not dry, just damp--so that when you make your grapefruit-sized, round-bottomed hole the sides will stay in place. Take your finger and poke it into the bottom of the hole three times about an inch deep in the sand forming a triangle, so that the finger holes are about two inches apart. Now you must heat the wax to 200°F. Use a deep-fat or candy thermometer to check this. Plus or minus five degrees won't hurt. Arrange and support the wicks in the center and, when the wax is ready, pour it in. Keep topping off the well as in previous candles and then give at least six hours to cool. Dig out the candle and brush off the excess sand. Get a pot of boiling water and dip the whole candle in (holding by the wick) and hold for about three or four seconds then dip into a pot of cold water. Trim the feet so that the upper surface is parallel to the table and trim the wick half a paper match high (a half inch, naturally).

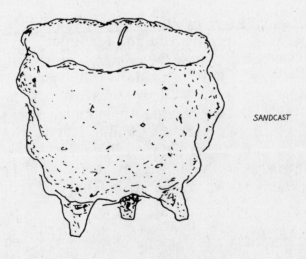

SANDCAST

like trouble with the wick. At first I stuck them on by just using the iron and having the heat melt a bit of the wax so that the wax grabbed the upper fuzziness of the felt. Too much heat would just have the molten wax saturate the felt which looked awful. Trouble was that the felt would come off pretty easily, until a friend put me onto the shellac bit. Elmer's glue etc., just won't work at all because it won't stick to the wax. Decoupage and all sorts of stuff become possible knowing this trick, but just remember that this is not wax work, but after-the-fact cosmetic stuff, which really doesn't have much to do with candles.

ON TURNING PRO

If you get into the wax at all, it is very likely to happen without your having very much to do with it. By the time you've given away all of the first slab, there'll be someone who wants to pay green. By the end of the second or third slab you'll have discovered the kind of stuff that appeals to you and the direction you want to go. Can you make a real thing of it? If your stuff is good, and I don't mean just professional and slick looking, it will no doubt sell--providing you have nice scents. All shopkeepers want scented candles, so don't waste your time taking them around if they're not scented.

But selling in the quantity that you need to do in order to quit driving cabs and stocking at the Radio Shack, that's a whole 'nother number. There's consignment and outright sales. Consignment means that you only get the bread if they sell, nothing if they just sit there, and most likely this is the way you will begin if you live in a smallish community. The price break for commission is two to three. If the shop buys outright you get 50 per cent. It's tough to wholesale after you've sold to a few friends at retail prices, but don't sweat it. Chances are you've been selling too cheap anyway and you'll get more than you think. Besides, the material investment is so low that you're not being squeezed. Bigger and more established shops in the suburbs will buy outright if they are interested at all. Don't be discouraged if they won't talk to you. Remember, they're into a pretty heavy money scene with mortgages, insurance, predicted first-quarter sales volume, and all that jazz.

Another thing is to go to the gift shows where the buyers come, or find an agent. This means a little less bread but in many cases it's worth it to eliminate the hassle of sales. You can then put your mind to making the stuff and actually produce more and make more. Breaking in is the tough thing. Once inside the magic circle, no sweat. You'll find out the type of thing that's moving and who is selling it and how much. I know a guy that was doing OK stuff in Aspen, but it wasn't really moving at three bucks. Just for kicks, the shop guy moved the price up to $5.50. They started to go. Weird things happen! Don't knock it if it pays the taxes on the farm, the tractor repairs, and the fencing for the goats.

As for producing in greater volume, the first thing is to get a better source of raw materials. First, apply to the State House for a tax-exempt sales number. This puts you formally in business and allows you to buy direct from the places that say "wholesale and trade only." Suddenly the wax is down to 15 cents a pound and the scents and colors drop accordingly. Maybe you'll want to get your accessories directly from a chemical supply outlet. A good one is McKesson Chemical, 5353 Jillson St., L. A. They have an office in New York too. The only problem here is that they have minimum orders in the neighborhood of $50. Most wholesalers have this policy. McKesson will sell scents in big bottles and powdered uncut dyes that are fantastic. As much powder as you would put sugar in your tea (none I hope, but some of the honey when you pick up the beeswax) will literally cover the entire inside of a good-sized room. Wicks you'll get by the spool and the whole thing will fall together. With larger volume, you'll have to set up a studio out in the old carriage shed. Don't use the barn, 'cause it's not fair for the animals with their better noses to have to hack the scents and wax smell. Get a hood over the stove if you can afford it. I don't know what paraffin vapors do to the lungs, but I'm sure it doesn't help them any. Buy a $15 thirty-six-inch gas range with at least four burners. If you're lucky, you can find one with six or eight. Put a shut off valve on the main gas supply line that can easily be reached and get a couple of heavy-duty fire extinguishers.

I got an old gas hot-water heater from which I cut the top with the welding torch. This thing is beautiful, for it has a thermostat on it and it's impossible to overheat the wax. The other thing is that you don't have to frig with the sheets. Just put them in as they come from the carton. A thirty-gallon hot-water heater cut down so that the inside is about twenty inches deep will be perfect. This will melt 150 pounds of wax and keep it at whatever temperature you set it at. Generally the range of the thermostat is from 140°F. to 180°. Do Not try this with electricity. First of all, it is bad ecology, as it takes four times as much world heat reserves to do the same job as gas. Also, wax shrinks when it cools, remember? Therefore it expands when heated again. If you have a full heater of cold wax, the electric element, which is in the middle of the tank, will not give the molten wax any channel to expand into. In other words, an explosion of hot wax, which is not too cool a thing to experience. Gas heaters have a chimney coming up through the middle which gets hot and melts the wax surrounding it. This provides an expansion channel from the bottom. Thirdly, if the level of the wax should get below one of the electrical elements, it would just burn up and probably ignite the whole mess in the process.

You'll have to put a couple of bricks or something in the bottom of the heater, because the temperature-sensing element for the thermostat is a thin tube that is raised off the bottom. Should you drop in a full sheet and have it hit this relatively delicate item, you'd be in trouble. Just build up some bricks on either side of it to protect it. When you want to make a

COOKBOOK #7

This candle will not be cast, but will be constructed. Gather the standard materials and pour some scented wax into ice trays with the dividers in. These should be metal, with metal dividers, and each tray should be a different color. After the trays have completely cooled remove the wax by lowering the tray right side up into a pan of hot water for about fifteen seconds. Remove the individual cubes from the divider by dipping the whole thing in the boiling water for about five seconds and then carefully wiggling the metal and teasing the wax free. Try again as it may take more heat, but be careful that the wax cubes don't just fall off and go floating around in the hot water. Next put a little melted wax into a shallow pan double boiler. This is your glue. Begin assembling by taking a cube and dipping the surface into the glue that you want to stick to another cube. Push together and hold for a few seconds. The thing should have about the same width as a quart milk carton when finished, so the bottom should have four or six cubes in it. Use your imagination and mix the colors and don't try to keep the sides flat, let the different cubes stick out different amounts. Also, don't worry about gaps, because as the flame melts the wax, it will run down and clog up the holes. When it is all assembled, heat a number eight knitting needle directly on the burner and push it straight down the middle of the candle as far as it will go. Take it out, wipe off the melted wax, heat again and push in again. Keep doing this until you get the hole all the way to the bottom. Insert your stiffened wick, add a little new melted wax around the hole with a spoon, and trim the wick. If you managed to pull this off you can do anything mentioned in the text, and I'm sure some others besides.

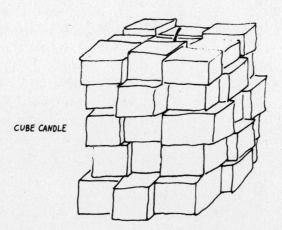

CUBE CANDLE

candle, all you have to do is just draw off some wax, add color, scents and you're home. I like to keep just unadulterated wax in the heater and add my stuff later. This way I can control colors and temperatures on a manageable scale on top of the stove.

My only other gimmick is a sandcasting table. This is, roughly, a table with the bottom twenty-four inches off the floor, sides that are fifteen inches high, and about twelve feet long. The whole mess is about three feet deep from front to back and is divided into three different sections for different types of sand.

EQUIPMENT

This is one of the beauties of wax. All you really need is something to pour it into and something to melt it in. The thermometer that I talked about before will help a lot too, but even that is not really a must (but be careful!). Pots and pans can be just the regular kitchen ones to start. Since the wax can easily be cleaned out, it really doesn't hurt anything. Just use plenty of hot water and some soap. If you get into it very deeply, you'll need a separate set of junk because you'll want to leave the pots half full, ready for the next session sometime. It's kind of a messy deal if you get to doing wild things and so I recommend newspapers on the floor. The Berkeley Barb works fine. For pots and pans, the local thrift store or Salvation Army or Goodwill store is the place. Anywhere from a nickel to a quarter for pans. I like three- and four-quart saucepans. One bigger one is good for the larger stuff. If you're pouring much, it is nice to have coffeepots because of the spout. Aluminum water pitchers work well too, although I paid a whole nickel for one only to find it had a leak where the handle was fastened on. In any case, don't use the coffeepots with a strainer type spout. If they have that, just take a pair of metal shears and cut that part out including the rim and that point in a V. If you are pouring cool wax it will freeze in the strainer and then you have no more spout. A big campfire-type enamel coffeepot is great, but they are getting rather scarce. So much for melting gear. For pouring into, you need molds. These are dealt with under the how-to heading and so I won't go into them here. If you really feel the need for commercial molds, and I can't talk you out of them, the local hobby supplier will be able to help you out. They come in all sorts of ugly shapes and sizes. Could you really dig a sixteen-inch, tapered, star-shaped mold?

I'm sure you'll come up with some neat inventions, but don't get too gimmicky. I know potters who have great studios, but don't make any pots. Remember, the craft is subservient to the art. Technique never produced any great art.

Crochet
Shelagh Young

"A propensity for crochet work has kept many ladies from the streets and the river. . . ."
Aleister Crowley

Crocheting always seemed a great mystery to me. I wanted to learn a long time before I actually did. I would sneak furtive looks into newsstand magazines and instruction books, only to find sentences like: "2 ch 1 tr 3 ch 2 tr into 3 ch sp at corner, 3 ch 1 dc sp. . . ." This mystical language would make my palms sweat, and I would slip quietly back to the sidewalk. One of the things that I've found out since is that anyone can crochet.

This is the craft whose versatility knows no bounds. With almost any material, using different combinations of a few simple stitches, one can go on to make practically everything. Crocheting provides the quiet pleasure, under the guise of concentration, of being alone with oneself. And, of course, there are so many pockets of time in a normal day--little spaces that can be spent productively: waiting for a turn in the outhouse, coffee breaks, waiting for the phone to ring, the bread to rise, the snow to melt, or the ambulance to come, not to even mention the time riding on buses, cars, and trains. Crocheting can be an aid in giving up smoking. It is totally portable. One hook, a supply of yarn, and the work in progress can always be tucked somewhere into one's trappings.

Crocheting in public always arouses friendly curiosity in all kinds of strangers. All this, for an initial investment of less than one dollar!

The basic requirements are the following:

1. Two willing hands. (These instructions are aimed at right-handed people. All others will have to be more resourceful. Hold the book to a mirror, or something.)

2. One hook, fairly large to begin with. About a size G would be good.

3. Some yarn, or other suitable material. (Two- or three-ply wool worsted, or soft string would do nicely.) It is best to begin with some substantially thick string or yarn, strong enough to bear the beginner's inevitable pullings-out. It will be faster and easier to work with, and you won't feel as if you're fussing with knots of microscopic importance. This preliminary yarn should also be of a uniform thickness, without exaggerated lumps or bumps. Later on, uneven textures become easier to handle.

And while on the subject of yarns: Department stores generally have nasty, uninspiring yarns. There is usually a poor selection of baby-bland or aggressive colors, and they are often expensive. Sometimes shops have bins of odd balls. It is wise never to pass one of these by without exploration, because often something unusual, some weird yarn that nobody else would buy is tossed in there at a reduced rate. But the absolutely best sources of yarns are the companies that do mail-order sales to weavers. They will send out samples charts and prices. You buy yarn by the pound, which is much cheaper. These companies come and go, but the most solid ones I know are:

The Village Weaver
8 Cumberland Street
Toronto, Ontario, Canada.

The Lily Mills Company
Handweaving Department
Shelby, North Carolina, 28150

Ayotte's Designery
Centre Sandwich, New Hampshire, 03227.

Yarns are cheerful friends. They are never wasted. Every project that is, for some reason, abandoned, can be undone and reused. Even a hopelessly tangled mess is good for wiping up spills.

Plenty of people tell me they have no trouble with patterns. I can't say. I can't remember using one myself. These instructions will equip anyone to follow a pattern, though if you can devise for yourself, so much the better.

A journey of a thousand miles begins with a single step.

Hands

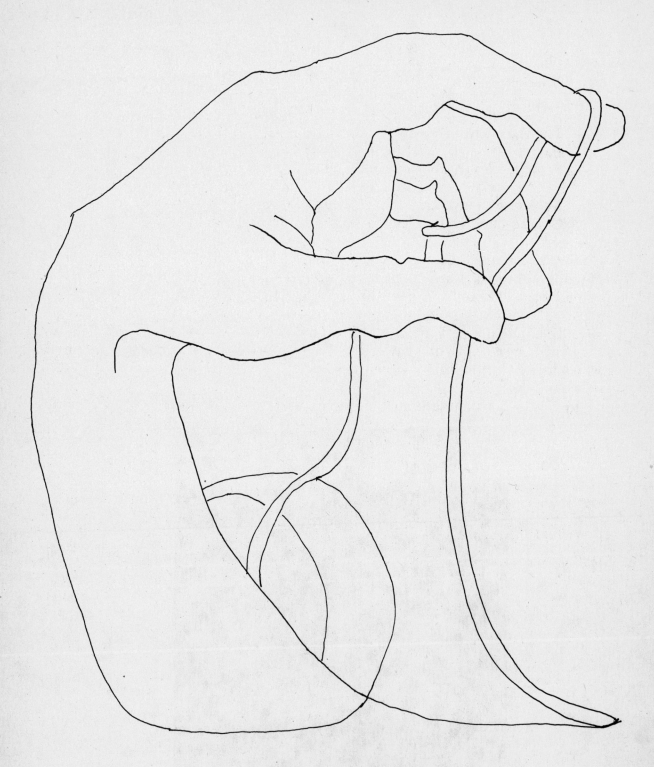

Working

Working

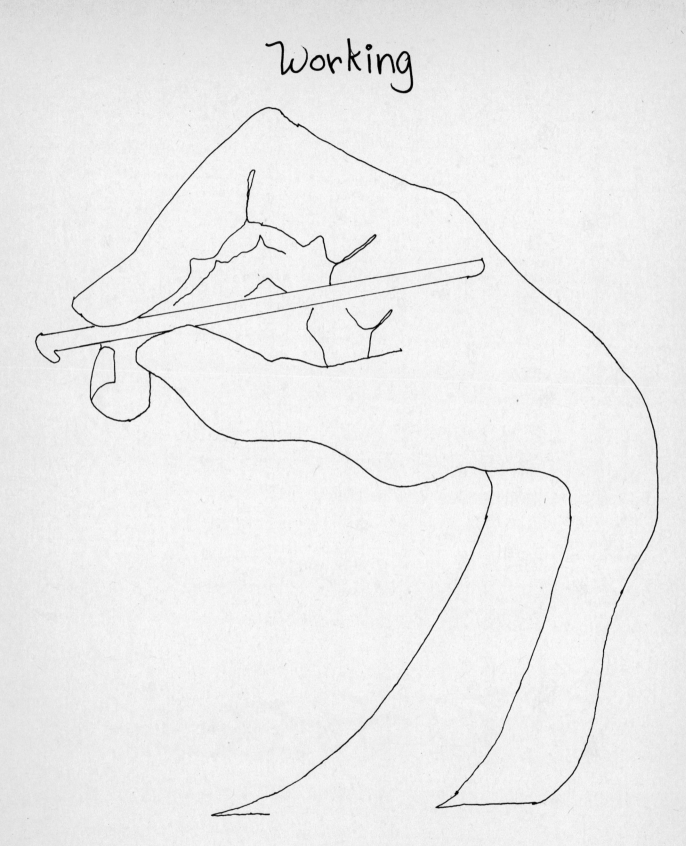

Hands

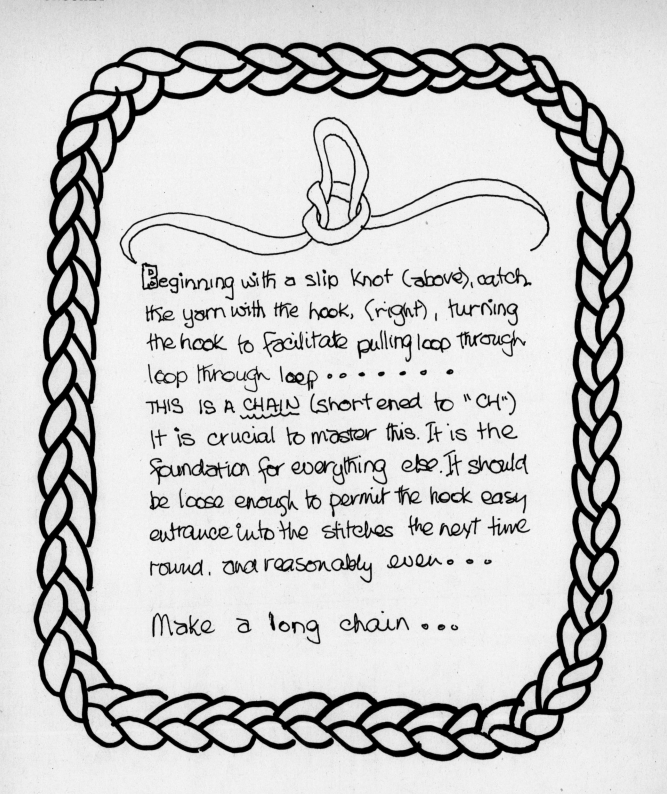

Beginning with a slip knot (above), catch the yarn with the hook, (right), turning the hook to facilitate pulling loop through loop through loop • • • • • • • •

THIS IS A CHAIN (shortened to "CH") It is crucial to master this. It is the foundation for everything else. It should be loose enough to permit the hook easy entrance into the stitches the next time round. and reasonably even • • •

Make a long chain • • •

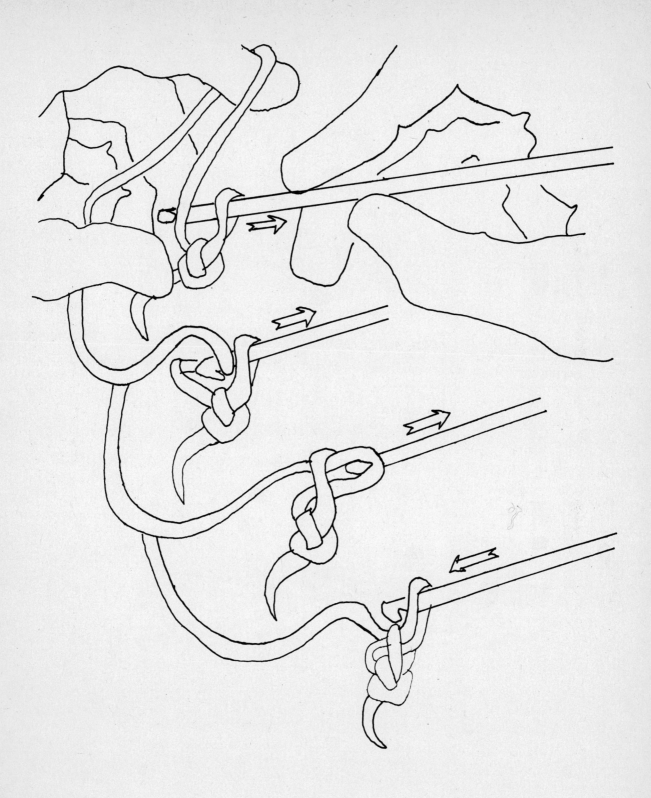

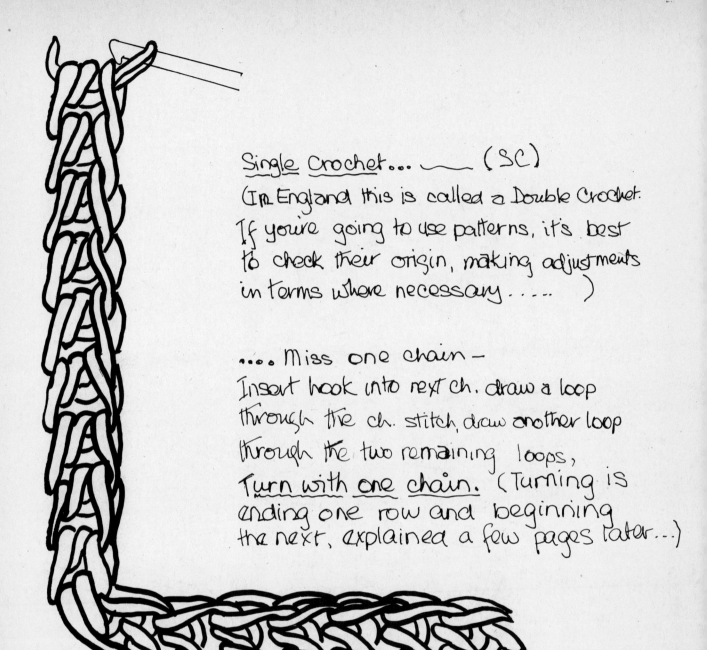

Single Crochet... ⌣ (SC)
(In England this is called a Double Crochet.
If you're going to use patterns, it's best
to check their origin, making adjustments
in terms where necessary.....)

.... Miss one chain —
Insert hook into next ch. draw a loop
through the ch. stitch, draw another loop
through the two remaining loops,
Turn with one chain. (Turning is
ending one row and beginning
the next, explained a few pages later...)

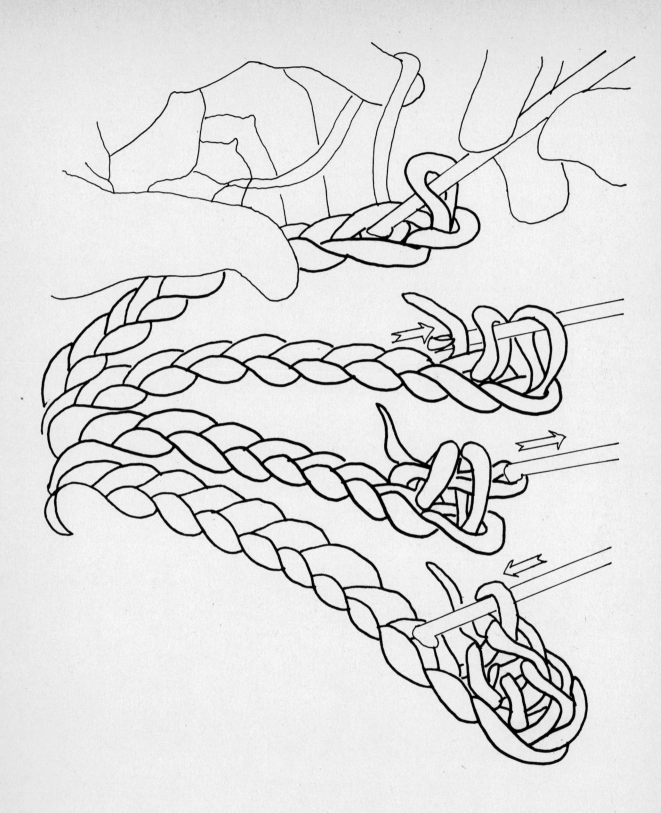

Fish-net Stitch...
Make a long chain.
Single crochet (sc) into the third ch from the hook.
Chain 5.
Miss 3 chains, sc in the next,
At the end of the row, chain 5, turn.
1 sc into the centre stitch of the 5 ch loop, chain 5,
1 sc into the centre of the next 5 ch loop, etc...

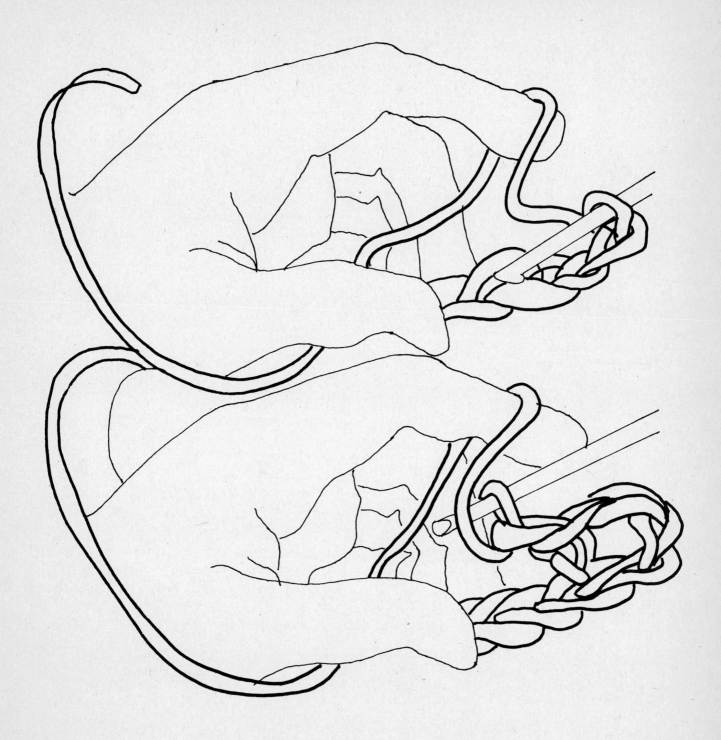

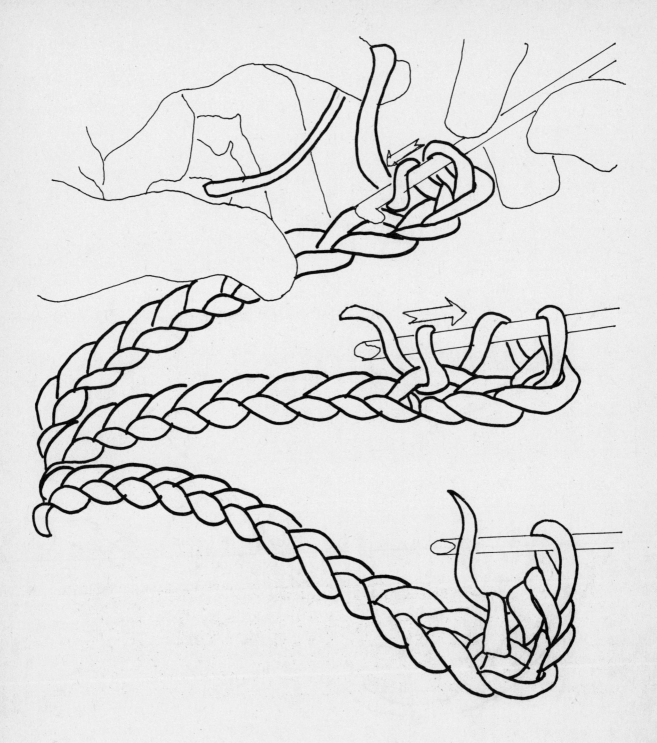

Half Double Crochet (HDC)
(English Half Treble Crochet.)

Miss 2 chains.
Draw a loop through the next chain stitch.
Draw another loop through the three loops
on the hook.
At the end of the row, chain 2, to turn...
(This is explained further next page...)

Turning

At the end of the row, chain two.
(For a row of single crochet, you would chain one.)
The idea is to bring the beginning of the row up to the
   level of the row. These two chains form the first
"stitch" of the second row.
Turn the work.
Now a regular stitch is made into the top of the previous
row, one into each stitch . . . . .

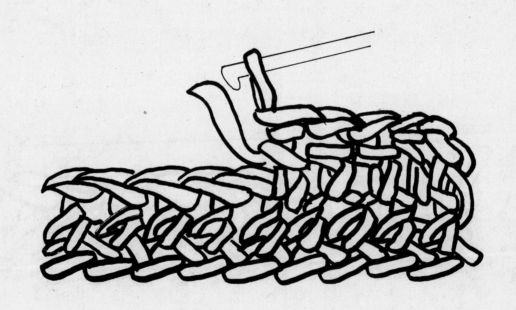

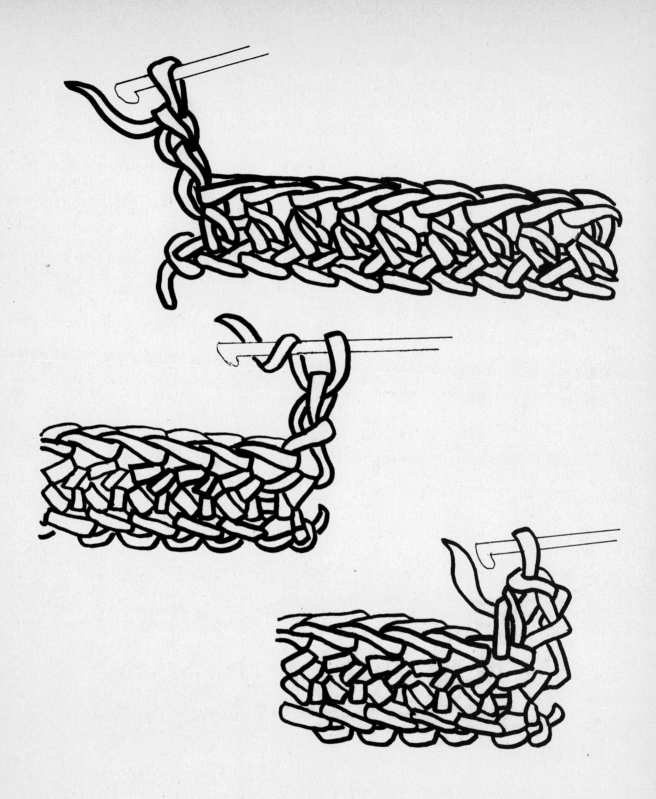

Double Crochet (DC)
(English Treble Crochet)

Miss two chains.
Draw a loop through the next chain,
another loop through two loops,
and another loop through the last two.
Chain 2 at the row end, turn.

This stitch is invaluable.
In infinite combinations and groupings,
literally everything
can be made with it...

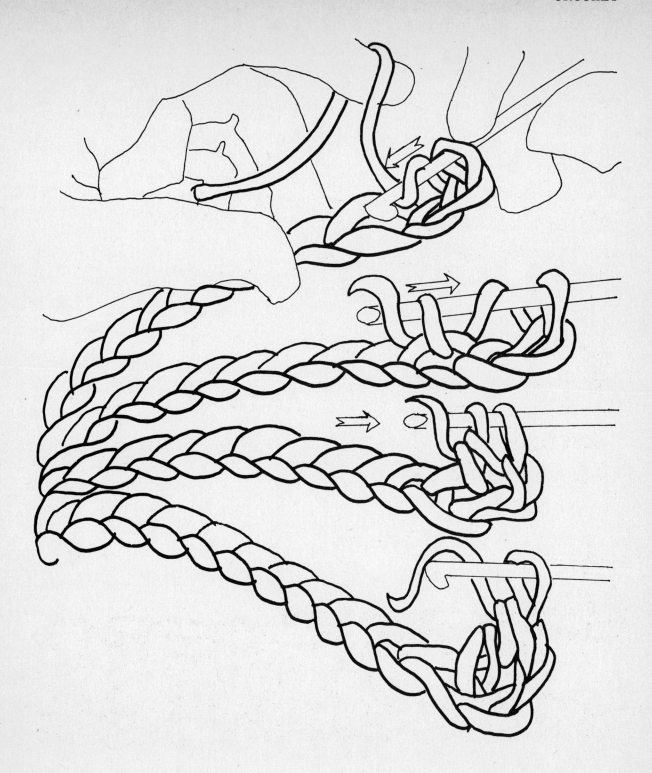

Clusters.

Miss two chains.
Do two double crochets into the next ch. Stitch.
Miss two chains.
Do one sc into the next ch. st.
Miss two chains.
Do three dc into the next ch. miss 2, one dc, miss 2, 3 dc.
into the next ch, etc. . . . .
Chain 2, turn, Make 2 dc in the first st, join with a sc into
the centre dc of the previous row, 3 dc on the sc, etc . . .

Finding this basic pattern was like Discovering a Great Truth.
I went about applying it everywhere, making everything with it.
It wore well.
It is still one of the pillars of my repertoire.

There are infinite variations on this.
Experiment with some, 2 TR. 1 ch, 2 TR 1 ch, etc.

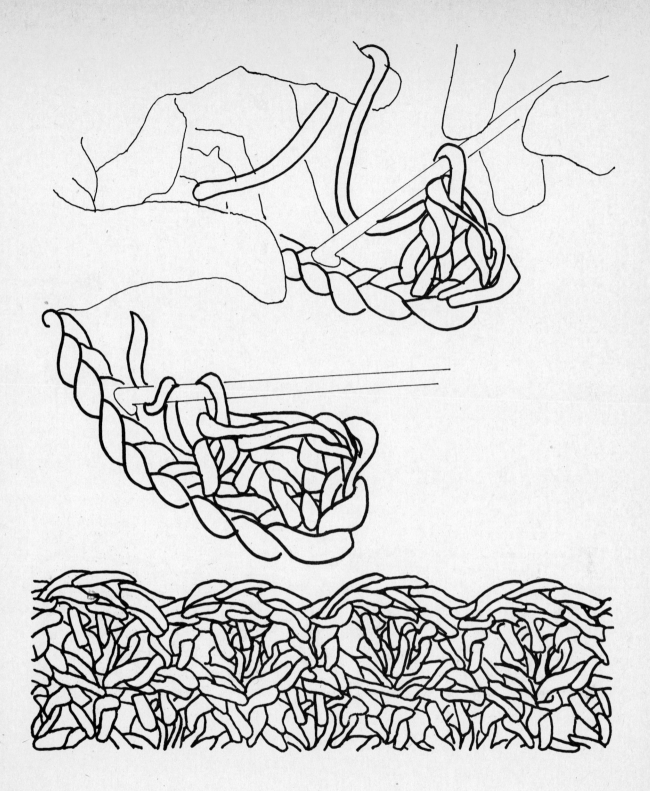

Treble Crochet. (TR.)
(English Double Treble.)

Miss 3 chains.
Wind the wool around the hook twice.
Insert the hook into the next chain,
Draw a loop through.
Draw another loop through 2 loops.
And another loop through two loops.
Then another through the last two.

At the end of the row, chain three to turn.

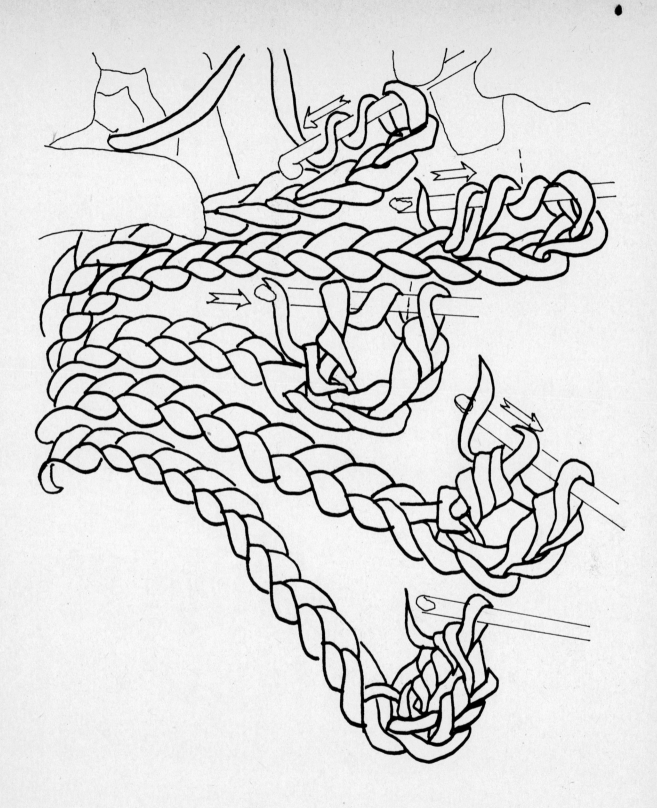

Flowers.

Chain 5. Join the ends of this chain together with a stitch
to form a ring. Chain two, make 15 double crochets into the
ring, joining the last double crochet to the top of the
chain "stitch" with a loop pulled through.
Chain 6. Skip two chains, double crochet into each one
back to the centre, skip one stitch, join this "petal" to the
centre with a loop pulled through. Chain 6 again,
continue all the way around—

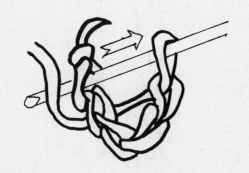

circles

Begin as for a flower, making a small chain ring.

To make a fishnet circle:

Chain three, join to next stitch, chain three, join to next,
all the way around once.

This can be done in a spiral, rather than in rows...

Chain three, join to the centre stitch of the previous loop.

When the circle starts becoming a cone, increase the number
of stitches per row by spacing the joins closer together,
(chain three, skip one, chain three, etc...)

This can be the beginning of hats, circular shawls, and doilies.

For hats, stop increasing when the crown is large enough,
and it will begin to turn down.

For shawls or what have you, keep increasing...

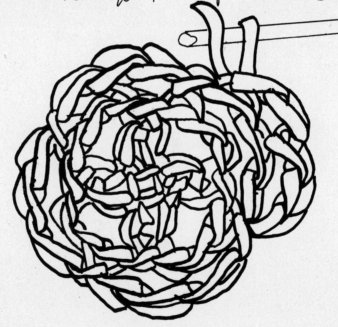

Squares.

Chain 6, join into a ring as before,
Chain 2, 2 double crochet into the ring, chain 3,
make three doubles into the ring, repeat this twice more.
Join with a loop pulled through to the first 2 chains.
Next row: Do 2 single crochets to reach the 3 chains of the
previous row. Chain 2, make 2 doubles into the 3 chains
space, chain 3, 3 doubles into the space,
Chain one, make three doubles into the next space, and so on —
Go around four times, making corners with 3 chains between
two trebles o o o o

These can be sewn together for afghans,
different stitches and groupings can be used for
different effects ——

Organic Leather
Phil Havey

Working with leather is . . . Ever since man began to wear clothing, he has worn leather. But during the mechanization of the twentieth century, especially in the U. S., the craft of skilled leatherworking has slowly disappeared. Efficiency through mass production became the criterion of clothing manufacturers. But with the coming of the New Age, with its emphasis on hand work, fun, and beauty, the craft of leatherworking has sprung to new life with a naïveté of its own which is worth mentioning. Today we no longer have trades and skills passed down to us from our forebears, so whatever "specialized" skill we decide to master, we turn our hand to it unaided and unhindered by our past. This is especially true for leatherworking. With traces of Puritanism still in us, it's hard for us to accept the fact that anything goes. Don't be afraid of leather. Have respect for its specific limitations as a material (it stretches, it is thicker than cotton, and doesn't take very well to darts or gathers) and its particular beauty. But reverence does not mean fear. It is fear that keeps us from everything, including the fun we can have from working with leather.

It is most helpful, when beginning to experiment with a new medium, to know a few tricks of the trade. This can make the difference between enjoyment and discouragement. On the other hand, too much instruction inhibits the imagination. In the following pages, then, I hope to describe to you some of the tools which make leatherworking easy, without limiting you to the particular style which I have evolved.

THE WORK TABLE

You can have a good solid table constructed for you by a carpenter out of unfinished lumber. The surface can be left unfinished because you never work on the naked wooden surface itself. Don't get stuck paying a large labor fee because, if you can't work a labor exchange deal, it is much cheaper to go to a secondhand furniture store and buy one of those massive dropleaf dining room tables that no longer fit in small modern houses. They are a glut on the market. The last two that I picked up ran me $8 and $10. They are usually the right height and width for the work you are going to do.

THE CUTTING BOARD

Although other craftsmen use durable and long-lasting types of composition board, such as pressed sawdust, I have great respect for my fingers and use simple and less resistant upson board until it begins to show signs of wear. Then I cut it up into smaller panels and use it for punching. Usually the standard 4-by-8-foot piece cut in half covers the work table surface that I have described. Upson board can be purchased at lumber- and building-supply outlets. It comes in varying thicknesses. I use a board three-eighths of an inch thick, which costs about $2 a sheet.

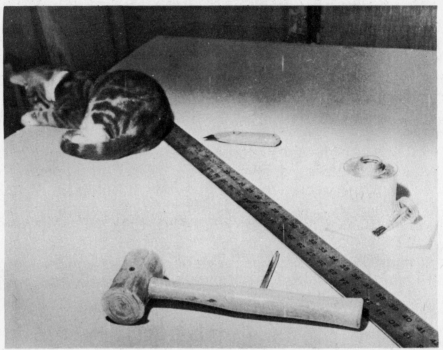

1   Supplies

I keep separate fringing boards of the same material so that no one spot on the cutting board is overworked. This may seem like a lot of precaution, but feeling your way along with a knife, alert for the bad spots where you have to work carefully, is a drag on both time and energy. I don't forget what I am doing, but can still work with the confidence that there are no flaky disaster areas lurking under the skins that I am cutting.

A smaller, rubber "pounding board" (as small as 12 by 12 inches and a quarter-inch thick) is even better for punching than upson board if you plan to pound a hard punch with a mallet. The reason for this is that rubber won't splinter or flake at all, and will muffle the noise of your hammering. If you can't find a solid sheet of rubber to use, a craft shop should be able to sell you a pounding board for a dollar or so.

LEATHER

Most of the sources on the subject of leather rightly assume that the reader is a beginner, so they send him to a high-priced retail outlet. If you want to work on anything of size or quality, you will have to deal with wholesalers. Even for small hobby-type work you are still better off if you go to leather wholesalers and buy their assorted scraps, rather than approaching retail stores or hobby shops. You can always pool your resources with another leatherworker so that it is worthwhile for the wholesaler to deal with you. In any coffee shop in the large cities, you will find half-a-dozen people seriously working with leather without doing anything like the type of thing that you are into. The medium is extremely flexible and personal (in fact, it becomes very hard to make a person that you hire reproduce exactly what you want him to do: leave him on his own for one week and you'll hardly recognize your original design). Make sure you are the one who makes the trip to the tannery.

Rarely have I been located where a tannery or wholesaler was not less than a three-hour drive from my shop. You only have to go once a month, so that is no great hardship, and you can always resell good leather at a price that makes up for its cost and the time you have spent picking out. But you can also have them ship your leather to you.

Information about wholesalers is hard to find. In New York I would suggest Gloversville, where there are at least two good tanneries that will wholesale (Cayadutta Tanning and Eton Leathers). Once you realize how tightly the big leather shops sit on the names of their wholesalers, you'll know that this little bit of information alone is worth the price of admission to this book. To many people in the trade, this problem is like the New York Times's Defense Department issue. The people in the big leather shops will give you a lot of technical aid, but when it comes to explaining an overall design that is exclusively theirs, or a materials source, just don't bother to ask.

When you get to the tannery, you'll find graded stacks of skins. With enough time on my hands, I have found skins in the 45-cents-per-square-foot stacks that were either misgraded or so close to the 55- and 65-cent skins that they downgraded them to avoid a hassle with some finicky buyer. The price differential is principally based on faults and scarring. If you have a fairly well-organized way of laying out your patterns, you can see right away which skins will work for you. This personal inspection of the skins will enable you to see all the new colors and textures being produced by the tanners. Even when there are no new colors, there is a wide diversity in dye lots, and the same standard colors can vary widely. I've seen colors like the dark blues that I don't normally like in leather come out of some dye lots so electric that they demand to be worked with. This variation in dye lots is one of the reasons that I always cut my laces from the skin that I am working with, rather than use prepared laces.

There are a lot of technical terms about skins--slunk, kip, belly cut, and so forth. These are more meaningful to the tanner than to the craftsman; however, there are one or two to know just so that you'll understand the possibilities of what exists.

<u>Cowhide</u> is the sandalmaker's stock-in-trade. It's good for tooled work and durability. On the retail market it runs from 70 cents to $1 per foot. I never work in it and have no idea of wholesale arrangements. It is not uniformly thick, for it thins out the farther you get from the animal's backbone.

<u>Suede</u> is leather with a nap. It runs up to almost $2 per foot in calfskin, but people expect to pay well for anything in good suede. You can, however, use the reverse side of glove-tanned cowhide (see below) for the same suede effect at far less cost.

<u>Shorthaired calf or cow</u> is hide with the hair still on it. The American Indians are always running around in it in those bad movies that take place in the southwestern United States. It makes arresting vests and beautiful handbags and belts.

<u>Splits</u> are skins with a suede surface on both sides.

<u>Glove-tanned cowhide</u> is very flexible leather more suitable for garments than its stiffer, less processed cousin that I mentioned first. One side is smooth, the other sueded. Most of my work is done in this leather. It runs from 45 cents to 52 cents, depending on how often the steer brushed up against a barbed-wire fence in his lifetime or had a case of bovine acne.

DESIGN AND PATTERNS

Forget the brown-wrapping-paper approach that most books speak about

2 Tracing a pattern
on the leather

and use poster board. It won't fold up on you or require a lot of pinning. Just lay it down on the skin, holding it fast with one hand, and run right along the edges with a slightly greasy colored pencil or chalk. You can transfer your basic pattern to posterboard by pinning it down on the board and cutting around it. If you don't already know a little about patterns either, buy some standard shirt and jacket patterns at the sewing store or carefully take apart some old clothes. Remember to pick simple patterns that do not require gathers or many darts. Bantam has a little pamphlet on patterns for 50 cents. Minor adaptations will be made in your work as you progress beyond the more conventional ways of doing things.

CUTTING

Use a matting knife or an Exacto-cutter and just face the fact that you're going to have to change an awful lot of blades, especially if you do fine fringe work. (These tools can be purchased at a hardware store. A mat knife costs about $1.50. Exacto-knives can be purchased for 70 cents.) Some people use a whetstone or some other sharpening device to rework their blades. The same time could have been used at their work table and they would have come out way ahead. I've often worked a deal with friends who are house painters, for my used blades are just right for scraping spots off windows. Friendship made the difference, otherwise that too would have been a bother. You'll probably find that a good, sharp scissors will work just as well on the thinner leathers. I cut a number of pieces at one time, following the old Zen adage "Do what you are doing." Be as social as you want while tracing and lacing, but cutting calls for concentration. There is a declining scale of catastrophes that runs like this: 1) cutting--you can make an irreversible mistake on the leather or on your own fingers; 2) punching--you can make a usually salvageable mistake on the leather; 3) tracing and lacing--you can rework anything as long as your blood pressure holds steady.

FRINGING

3 Cutting fringe

Fringing is a special kind of cutting that can make or break a jacket. I've seen some pretty slipshod work zipped right off the counter because the fringe was so well executed: I don't want to encourage a shoddy way of going about the work, but I do wish to doubly stress the care that should be taken with fringe. I cut fringe on separate panels from the main cutting board so that I can change them frequently. Fringe can be repaired by skiving the cut pieces so they can be glued. This consists of paring down some of the thickness of the leather so that there can be an overlap without a lump. You should glue these mended areas with an especially strong epoxy resin. A metal ruler or straight-edge can be purchased in the hardware store. Be very careful when fringing that the knife does not slip up onto the ruler and fringe your thumb.

GLUING

The reason for gluing edges under is purely aesthetic. If you are using thick leather, forget about it. Assuming that you will be doing a bit of gluing, I want to explain a little trick about the glue pot. You can buy a glue pot with a brush fixed through the center of the lid in any engineering or blue-print-supply shop. It is worth the little extra effort, for you don't have to worry where you are going to set down the brush every three minutes or the lid every ten minutes. Neither the brush nor the glue in the pot cake with the rapidity that happens otherwise. Take a square of scrap leather somewhat larger than the mouth of the glue pot and cut a hole in it about three-quarters the size of the opening. After stretching this over the mouth of the pot, fix it with a thick rubber band. This protects the threads around the neck of the jar from being smeared with glue. If you think this is much ado about nothing, you've never been around a leather shop on a Monday morning when the sloppy pots have had all weekend to harden. You can buy gallon cans of glue for as little as $5. For small projects, the rubber-cement glue sold at hardware and stationery stores will do quite nicely.

For a half-inch turn-under, paint the under edge of the leather an inch wide with glue, wait five minutes, or until the glue is crackly-tacky, fold

4 Cutting corner off after
   gluing down edge

the leather back a half-inch, and hammer with a regular carpenter's hammer. Make sure the hammer strokes overlap slightly. There will be a small piece of leather at the corners that has to be trimmed off (Fig. 4). Large sheets of simple brown wrapping paper can be used over and over again to protect the upson board while you work.

PUNCHING

I suggest a standard hole punch with a rolled rawhide mallet as the best means of making holes. You can get a nice rhythm going for you once you are into it and work out a whole array of tensions. I've never understood

5 Punching

the physics of it, but using a metal hammer instead of the mallet makes you feel like you are working on soggy blotting paper. Old pieces of cutting board or rubber board serve much better than the wooden blocks that some books recommend. Avoid a spring punch and its big brother the rotary punch (the kind you scrunch with your two hands) unless you have hands like John Henry or are intending to enter the international grasp and squeeze contest. If you are caught in one of those situations where you can't make a sound or your Aunt Tilly will blow a gasket, you have to use a spring punch and a small roller to press together glued leather. A rawhide mallet can be found at most hardware stores for about $5. The hole punches come in various sizes. Hobby stores like Tandy Craft on Fourteenth Street in N.Y.C. carry them for about 85 cents apiece.

LACING AND SEWING

There are a number of possible ways of putting the pieces of your pattern together. The most obvious method is with a sewing machine, but the standard machine will only work on the thinnest leather. With the better model machines, where you have a strong power source, you can use a heavy-duty needle and fifteen- or thirty-weight thread on any soft leather garment. You can also sew by hand. If you don't care for machines and you like more roughhewn stuff, you can also lace the pieces of the pattern togeth-

6   Stitching by hand

er with leather strips. This is also decorative and can be done in as leisurely a fashion as knitting. The lacing for a shoulder seam is shown in Figure 7. Just remember that the upper sleeve sets <u>into</u> the armpit hole and then the sleeve and body seams are laced together. To avoid lacing shoulder seam right on top of the shoulder, choose a pattern with a yoke (a shaped

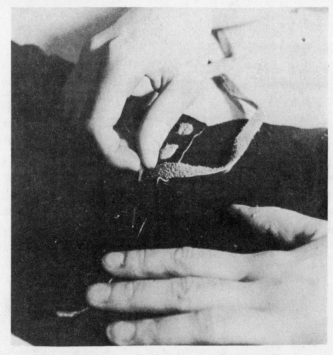

7   Lacing

piece) to add over the shoulder and back of the neck. Lacing is something that I'm tempted to touch on very lightly, for I've seen people who knew very little about leather invent fantastic new methods for lack of prepared instructions. Some things stay vaguely stable because they are so broad in principle.

I have found that a single knot at the end of a lace usually pulls through a lacing hole with wear. I use a knot that takes one extra turn around before going through the loop. Rather than knotting laces together when they have to be extended, I have found a rather nice way of lacing one through another

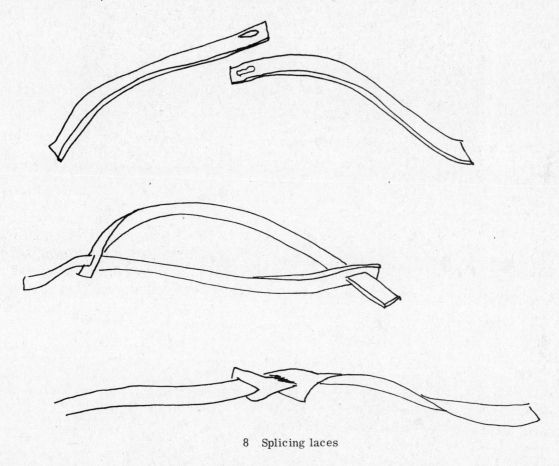

8   Splicing laces

(Fig. 8). Needless to say, the trick is done on the inside of the piece. Another basic is that front panels, pieces, and so forth overlap the back pieces.

It is often easier to draw the laces through the holes with a large needle, as in sewing. I always just slice the lace thin for about four inches and run it through the eye like a thread (Fig. 9). The needle itself should be mentioned in passing, for if you don't know that the ruggers needle comes in plastic, you'll end up inside on those nice spring days because of the way the sun flashes off a metal needle. I usually lace on a board the size of a portable draftsman's drawing board so I don't have to rearrange things if I have to set the work aside.

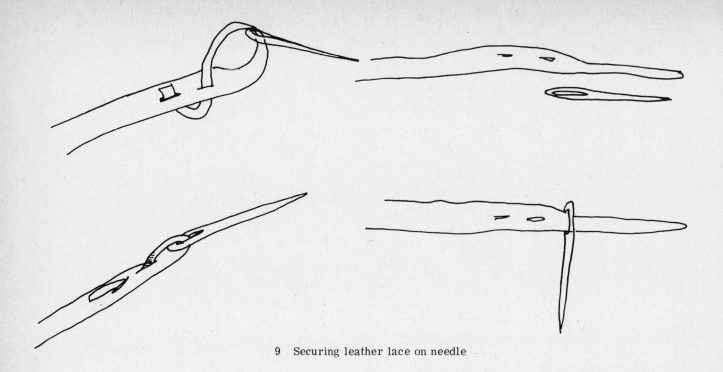

9   Securing leather lace on needle

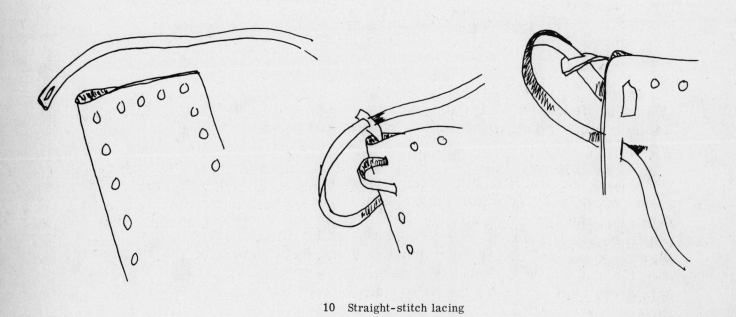

10   Straight-stitch lacing

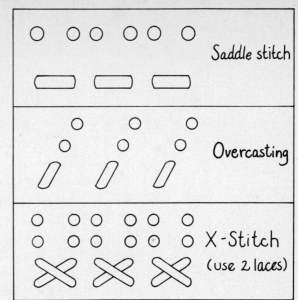

11   Other lacing techniques

MOSAIC AND PATCHWORK

Most patchwork garments aren't commercially profitable. That's why one that is well done is such an eye-catcher. Unless you really like to do patchwork the way some of our grandmothers enjoyed quilting, your return will be marginal if you sell your work.

The Eskimos and the natives of Liberia have done some excellent work by setting scraps of uniform thickness against a cloth background. As the glue is drying, the pieces of leather can be stretched slightly to make up any small gaps between them. These pieces can also be stitched together if more than normal wear is expected, but most of my designs were too expensive to work in and not cut for heavy winter sports; however, even in some of the high-fashion pieces, I did take the precaution of tacking down the panel corners.

When you want to fit pieces into each other with fancy curved lines, simply overlap the pieces and cut any kind of line that you want through both pieces. They'll knit right into each other.

To get a very primitive effect, take strips of leather about an inch and a half wide and run a line of glue three-quarters of an inch wide down the center. Pinch the strips together down the middle and you'll have a little leather ridge with wings flaring out on either side. Sew squares of scraps to these pieces that flare outward. This gives the same effect that leading does in stained-glass work. Remember, because leather cannot be eased (that is, led into curves without crinkling), it is better to keep to square designs. The corners are a small problem. Stick to sewing and lacing the squares together. You can also skive, or pare down the thickness of a piece of leather with a knife until you have a strip along both edges of the patches to be joined that is half the original thickness of the leather. This means that there will be no bulging seam where they join. I've heard of garments that have been skived and glued holding up well without lacing, especially if they have been glued with the new epoxies.

DECORATION

There are many ways of decorating leather. Besides using an interesting lacing technique and fringes, you can add beads (see Melinda's note on page 78), paint beautiful designs (best done with good-quality acrylics) or try actually embroidering on the leather. As far as what or how goes, it would be best for you to experiment and discover for yourself. You should have plenty of scraps of leather left over to experiment on. As with picking or designing a pattern, if you don't know too much about what you can or can't, should or shouldn't do, anything is possible, and whatever develops will at least be your own creation.

Te amo

Philip

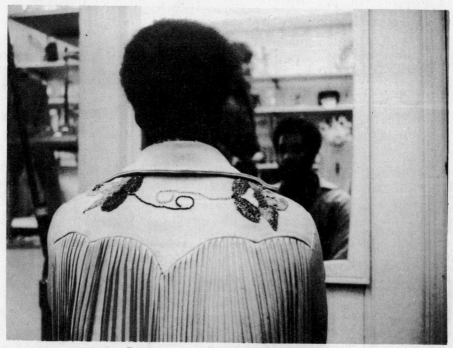

Dennis in a beaded jacket by Melinda

LEATHER BEADING

Beading on leather requires, first of all, great patience. There are several ways of applying beading, such as first beading whole parts on a loom, then sewing them onto the leather. For people, like myself, who simply sew, sewing directly on leather can produce textural and color effects that are just as satisfying.

Start by turning the piece to be beaded right side down and, on the back side, draw your design as it will be when it is finished. Using a number seven crewel embroidery needle (the smallest eye possible), thread it with Tandys heavy-duty, fine-weight thread, double, and knot. Cut the thread about a quarter-inch below the knot to ensure its holding. From the back, pierce the starting point of the design with the needle, draw the thread through to the front, pick up four beads on the needle, making sure the last two have large holes. Lay the beads on the right side of the leather and go down through the skin with the needle on the line of the design. Measure half way back down the line of the design you've already beaded and come up and pick up those last two beads. Pass the needle and thread through them.

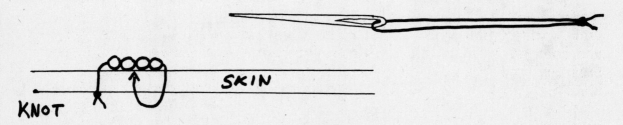

Start over, picking up four more beads, being sure the last two have large holes . . . , and so forth. The picking up of the last two beads ensures strength of hold and unity of line.

Love,
Melinda

In and Out the Hoops: Embroidery
Carol W. Abrams

Imaginative needlework design died with Mary, Queen of Scots and it seems no one has had the impetus to do anything about it. It's about time the "old lady in gingham and shawl" syndrome was phased out of the contemporary scene. I'm not saying those sweet little scroll-and-flower motifs are useless--just you-less. I think that what you make should say what you are. Individual expression in embroidery as well as in any other media, makes it vital.

We are a product of the kit-generation. Designing your own personal piece of embroidery can be as easy or as difficult as you want to make it. Start with joy and with simplicity; however, if you are absolutely desperate and completely without experience in anything aesthetically inspiring-- meaning trees, water, rocks, grass, machinery, the alphabet--then use a kit. Sigh. But if you've ever experienced a moonscape, or examined the surface of a rock, or wished the Easter egg in your head really was, then you sure as hell don't need a kit! And if you're saying right now that you can't draw straight lines—use your name, or trace shapes you find around you--ashtrays, cups, feet, cookie-cutters--anything with a strong outline. Check out those pre-European American Indian embroideries and those marvelous early American samplers, and some of those contemporary East Indian designs, and then say you can't design your own piece!

Embroidery is a phenomenal medium; I can say that although, naturally, I'm prejudiced. You have available to you colors ranging from antique yellows to electrifying magentas and nearly an infinite number of textures: wools, cottons, silks, blends, synthetics, metallics, and on, and on, and on. Being mainly a linear medium, almost any two-dimensional design adapts well to fabric and threads, yielding a fairly substantial product. I get a real sense of well-being with embroidery; it's warm--warm with wools, and cloth, and wooden hoops, holding an aura of peace that only fireplaces and home-made bread have.

Anyone with eyesight, a steady hand, and a bit of patience can do it. And you don't have to do chair covers or adorable little owls either. The equipment is fairly simple and can be very cheap. All you need to start is a hoop, a length of fabric, some threads, scissors, and a needle.

A HOOP IS A HOOP IS A HOOP

Beware: there are all sorts of fascinating hoops and frames with nuts, bolts, rivets, carving, holes, stands, gorgeous wood finishes, springs, and gadgets. Unless you are an <u>experienced</u> needleworker, these things are a waste of cash. Also those metal frames and hoops will bend, rust, lose their tightness, stain fabric and generally fall apart. Even if they are cheap, avoid, avoid, avoid. Most needlework shops, five-and-dimes,

Different-sized hoops

and department stores carry hoops. I prefer a ten-inch-diameter, lap-standing, wooden hoop now, but until I became more proficient with stitching and fully convinced that I liked embroidery, I found a three- or four-inch-diameter wooden screw hoop the greatest. It's small enough to hold in your hand and manipulate with ease. Anyway, if I hadn't liked embroidery I wouldn't have felt as guilty for putting aside a fifty-cent hoop as I would a twelve-dollar investment. Your hand-size hoop may seem a little puny when you bring it home, but once you work with it a while you might want it bronzed.

FINDING A SURFACE: A TWO DIMENSIONAL FEELING

Now you have to have a piece of stuff to work on. A good linen is your best beginning, though any hefty, closely woven fabric is fine. It's senseless to start with a sleazy fabric that's uncomfortable to handle and won't take to lots of throwing around. For all you know, you'll like your completed piece and regret the fact the fabric stinks. Homespuns, Belgian and Irish linens, and smooth-finished upholstery materials are all good bases. Select the fabric as you might select drawing paper or canvas--so that its color and texture coordinate well with your design. I prefer linen because it's solid stuff with a good substantial feel, takes a lot of handling, has a neutral color and a variety of textures that are pleasant, and lets the embroidery do its thing. By the way, linen does not need to cost nine dollars a yard--go somewhere else if it does. It shouldn't run any more than a decent dressmaker's fabric.

LET IT SHRINK

Buy six inches more of the stuff than you need to allow for shrinking and straightening. Wash the goods to soften the texture and to pull up that beautiful grain. Let it shrink now, before stitching. If you prefer a stiffer positive feeling between you and your medium, then add a little starch to the rinse.

WARPS AND WOOFS

If the salesman cut your fabric as straight as I've had mine cut, you'll have no choice but to straighten it. If you don't, your finished piece will disappoint you by coming out lopsided and distorted after blocking and finishing. You will probably find the edges that were cut were not cut along one single thread of the fabric, but rather many threads were severed in a seemingly straight line. You must, therefore, pull out the first thread or so, that runs completely from one selvage to the other. The selvages are the finished edges that don't unravel when picked at. Find these threads by following a single thread from one selvage across to the other, and seeing if it runs a complete course from edge to edge. To do this, clip it at the ends, carefully, and gently pull it until it is completely removed from the fabric. On some pieces of fabric there may be only one selvage or no selvages at all. In that case start with the single selvaged side and repeat the process on all the cut sides, or pick any side and use the same process on all four sides. The goal here is to have a piece of goods with four right-angled corners. Once the threads are pulled, cut away the excess fabric following the pulled thread line carefully. It's a real drag and takes up time, but if you do it to music it's not so hard to take. Just think, if Da Vinci had been a little more concerned with his

Pulling the thread to straighten the fabric

surfaces, maybe then his immortal paintings would not have proven to be so painfully mortal.

After all this thread pulling is over you will notice that the fabric's threads are running at right angles to one another, more or less. Find or draw a true, old fashioned ninety-degree right angle and lay a corner of the goods on it--if it doesn't line up perfectly then pull the opposite corners and edges diagonally, gently and firmly, humming a pleasant tune. Keep stretching the fabric in this manner until the fabric's corners and edges <u>are</u> at true right angle in keeping with the one you've drawn. Be careful not to unravel the edges that you've just so lovingly and painfully straightened, unless you like to work on postage stamps. Hem, whip or machine-stitch down folded narrow margins on all unselvaged edges. This prevents fraying. Would you believe, your fabric is ready for the application of your design! Whew!

DESIGN YOUR OWN THING

If you are still dry for sources of design, then open your eyes, baby, it's all right in front of you--in your knuckles, the grain of wood in a table top, the shape and shadows of that coke bottle in front of you, ice-coated trees in moonlight, a cross-section study of a molar, a camera lens, your signature, random patterns--embroider! Don't get graphic, that pansy need not come out looking like the real thing--it's a pattern, a source, a taking-off point, that's what really matters. You are celebrating forms, rejoicing in color, feeling the warmth, the textures of threads and cloth. Touch, enjoy, let your needle wander, be rhythmic, be free! If you <u>feel</u>

like rearranging an established pattern then, by God, do it! Beg, steal, borrow, copy, but always, always make it your own. Most of all--enjoy-- never settle for someone else's joy.

It seems the only thing offered to a prospective needleworker is kits. A kit is great if you really don't care if you are the technician at the end of a long line of people--the designer, manufacturer, merchant, etc.-- along with those fifty thousand other people that are doing the same kit. If that's your bag, love, then do it.

LAYING IT ON

Getting your design out of your head and onto the linen can be simple. There are many techniques. I've taken watercolor not too unlike the color of the fabric and drawn it on with a fine brush in freehand. Block out only the basic shapes--leave the detailing to the embroidery. Always keep in mind that you might want to change it, and too many unwanted painted lines are tough to get rid of.

Another technique I like, that doesn't mar the surface in any way, is to use regular sewing cotton and in basting stitches, using your needle as a pen, sew the design to the surface. Again it's best if the thread you use is also a similar color to the fabric so that if there are any threads left showing after embroidering they are unnoticeable or easily removed. This way, too, if you decide to eliminate or modify large sections you can just pull the threads out.

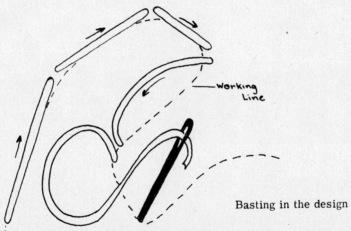

Basting in the design

Let's say you have a complicated design, one that you just don't want to change at all during the transfer onto the fabric, then this same basting technique can be used with modification. Draw or trace your pattern on tracing paper, gauze, chiffon, or any other sheer, fine material with a felt tip marker, watercolor, fountain pen or whatever suits you best. With basting stitches or even masking tape, tack this pattern on the back-side of your fabric. This way it will come out the right side up on the front of your fabric. Logical? Using basting stitches sew through the paper or material pattern and the fabric beneath, following the design carefully. Use small stitches in the more complicated areas so that when you are finished the pattern isn't lost in a myriad of stitches that mean nothing.

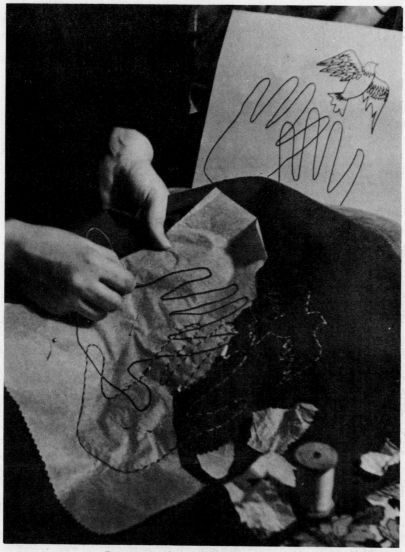

Basting in the design through paper

Changing the color of your threads may make it easier to distinguish the pattern later. Remember, though, that some of these threads will remain behind after you embroider over them, even when you've pulled out all the excess you can after completion. That's the reason for keeping the threads in shades of the base fabric or linen.

It's still best not to get too involved with the pattern's detail in the transfer--small changes are inevitable, and the transfer is only a guide for your needle's freedom. Keep the drawing or whatever else your pattern came from next to you always, so you can refer to that for the real details.

FUSSY

(This is necessary for those who feel it's necessary, and sometimes it is.)

Another technique for pattern transfer is the Holy (as in hole) paper-and-charcoal method. Tack thy fabric down on a board with thumbtacks or carpet nails, being sure all the corners are at right angles. Then lay a paper pattern made of wrapping paper from the butcher or heavy drawing paper on the fabric. Center it. Tape or thumbtack the paper pattern down. Better yet, use some books or bricks so that it will be easier to lift the paper up and see the progress on the fabric. Prick holes along the pattern's lines carefully, using a needle mounted in a cork or pencil eraser, or a small awl (which is like an ice pick).

Once the pattern is pricked, rub powdered charcoal in firm circular movements over the entire pattern with a blackboard eraser, a piece of wadded-up cotton, or a few layers of felt. Peek under the pattern every now and then to see if the charcoal is falling through the holes, adjusting the amount of charcoal or the size of the holes if necessary. The rubbing must be done in firm movements and with care--the charcoal shouldn't be too heavy or it will smudge.

I used to crush my own charcoal in the belfry at midnight on Bedlam Boulevard where I once lived, but you can buy powdered charcoal, or "pounce," in a pharmacy.

Be sure the pattern is complete on the fabric before removing the paper pattern. Imagine the job you'd have to realign the pattern if the transfer didn't work. Lift the pattern <u>carefully</u>. With watercolor and a brush follow the dots (remember the game "dot-to-dot" in comic books?--same technique), being careful not to smudge the charcoal with your hands. Air the fabric out on a nice breezy day or throw it in a dryer on the 'air cycle' for a few minutes. This should flap out all the loose charcoal. Thus ends the Holy Order of the holey-paper-and-charcoal method.

This whole thing, as far as I'm concerned, is too messy and too much trouble, and it places you in the irreversible position of not being able to change your pattern without a great deal of difficulty. But, if there's something that you really revere and it <u>has</u> to be exact, then this is a good way to do it. I say, though, freedoms all the way, and this is not one of them. Thus spake Carol, daughter of John and Ginny. Rest in Peace.

THE OTHERS

You can also use dressmaker's carbon found in a notions department, or wherever sewing supplies are sold. Follow the directions on the packet, using a blunt-pointed instrument instead of a dressmaker's wheel, which might be suggested on the packet. They are not worth the investment. There's also a thing called a transfer pencil. I understand that you draw with it on tracing paper, turn the drawing over onto the fabric and press with an iron. It's not supposed to give a very fine line, though, so it's best for larger, simple patterns than for very complicated, tiny patterns.

With all transfer techniques, be sure to leave an excess of at least a half-inch of fabric as a border all around the area your pattern covers, so you will have some room to work with when you mount it.

Don't--believe me-- use pencil to draw your pattern on the fabric. It smudges the cloth and the yarns, giving a gray murky cast to everything. You'll have to redraw the pattern many times, as the lines tend to dust off with handling. Also, avoid typing carbon--that can be disastrous! Felt-tip markers are not advisable either, the lines being too broad, and, unless they are positively waterproof they will run when you wet the fabric for blocking later. All of these methods are not worth the convenience they offer.

So now that you've got a good piece of straightened and hemmed cloth and a pattern transferred onto it, you are ready for the joyous part--the threads and the stitches.

STRINGS

You're in for a fantastic trip when you find your threads! The colors! The textures are indescribable--smooth shiny silks, nubbly synthetics, metallics, cotton flosses, yarns in wools and blends in a good variety of weights, tapestry wools, crewels in earthy shades. Touch them, smell them, rub them against your face, lay them next to one another. Revel in their presence, their substance. Any and all threads should come under your scrutiny. There's nothing more delightful than placing the polished brilliance of silk against the rich deep pile of wool. Imagine, play with, the threads, carefully choosing the ones you really like. A mountain of threads can be very frustrating, though, as can too many colors, so try restricting yourself in quantity at least. A little discipline is good for the soul. The stitches add dimension and, by combining threads, you can add to your spectrum of colors and textures. If you dig purple, then for Pete's sake, use purple!

I found the best threads to start with--and you may too if you are a raw beginner--were the very inexpensive cotton embroidery thread and crewel wools, a wool used specifically for embroidery.

Embroidery cotton (cotton floss) comes in six-strand skeins and in bulk quantities. The skeins are easiest to get, usually in dime stores and almost

86

every other sewing department. Each thread in the skeins is made of six strands, and you usually work only with three of those strands at a time. Experiment by using all the threads or fewer--depending on the effect that you need.

Crewel wool is wool made for embroidery. The best is from England and comes in shanks of one color or plaited in a flat braid in shades of one color. The texture is fine and strong by comparison to standard knitting wools and the colors are usually in heathers, antique tones, and soft muted shades. The manufacturers are slowly realizing that there is a demand for more modern colors like the ecstatic reds and purples and cool, vibrating greens and blues that are so contemporary. Unfortunately, dyeing the threads with commercial dyes can be disappointing, though very tempting. They are usually not colorfast, which can be disastrous when you block. I have no experience, as of now, with the natural dyes that are becoming popular, and don't know if any or all of them are colorfast. I would assume they must be to some extent, as the colonial women used natural dyes almost exclusively.

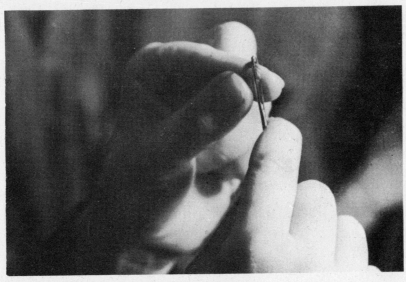

Threading the needle

Many places don't carry loose crewel wool, except that in kits, ugh. Root around in yarn shops and craft places, asking about them. If they don't or won't carry these wools for some reason, maybe the people can tell you where to get it. Friends of mine order their own.

When using crewel wool, use only one strand to start, doubled through the needle. Thread the needle as illustrated above. Doubling the thread over gives a richer effect and adds strength to the stitches. This, like everything else is no cardinal rule . . . follow your own head.

Tapestry wools are easily gotten because needlepoint is so "in" today. You'll usually find it in places that deal in yarns and rug-hooking equipment.

These wools have a heavy texture and are very strong by comparison to knitting wools. They also come in a fairly limited range of colors similar to the crewel wools--heathers, antique shades, and a greater selection of more contemporary shades than the crewels, but even so, not as many as I would like to see. You'll have to use a blunted tapestry needle or an embroidery needle with a very large eye, as this thread is tough to sew with otherwise. I find using single thread easiest to handle (rather than doubling it through the needle). Because it is difficult to handle at times, I prefer using it for surface stitches such as couching and the raised stitches. It's also easily split down into two or more strands (as in floss) that can be used very successfully.

Knitting wools and rug yarns have a more exciting range of colors and textures than either tapestry or crewel wools, and are much more available in most areas than either of these. The only real problem is that you can seldom buy less than one-ounce skeins (a skein is a quantity of thread usually measured out by length or by weight). One ounce is usually an awful lot of wool for usual embroidery needs. The stuff shreds easily and should be used in shorter lengths than other threads. It's very easy to work with and adapts well to almost all embroidery stitches.

I have found in some really complete knitting shops, something called mending yarn, used by knitters to make argyle socks, mend knitted goods, and embroider on sweaters and stuff. The texture is very fine and soft, not as hairy as crewel wool and the colors are usually soft and classic. The great thing about this thread is that it comes in lengths of only a few yards and it adapts beautifully to embroidery on fabric.

Silk thread is the queen of all embroidery threads, and is probably the most temperamental. I have found an almost unlimited range of colors. I've been told that you must rub beeswax on the ends of the threads but find this unnecessary if I work slowly and rhythmically, using threads no longer than the distance from my wrist to my elbow, doubled. Silk comes in threads of multiple strands like embroidery cotton and can be split in whatever configuration you want. It snags on any rough skin on your fingers and hands and it really doesn't hold up well on pieces that will be handled a great deal, but as far as I am concerned, it's worth all the trouble. I'm really hooked on silk.

All the silk I have has been imported and is relatively expensive compared to the other threads, so I make a point of not using stitches that leave a lot of thread on the wrong side of the fabric. I'm cheap.

DOODLE CLOTH AND OTHER STUFF

You'll need a good set of embroidery needles that have smooth long eyes and sharp points. Get them in assorted sizes if you are using a variety of different weight threads. A set of different size tapestry needles with blunt points is good to have if you are using heavier wools. If you are having difficulty pulling the thread through the fabric then the needle eye is too small. If there are obvious holes left around the stitch then the needle is too large. Having a set of needles in assorted sizes makes it easier to adjust them when you need to. Right?

If you don't already have a pair on hand, a good sharp pair of manicure or embroidery scissors, or any small, sharp-pointed scissors is absolutely essential. Large paper shears and such are clumsy though not entirely impossible to use. If you have to buy a pair of scissors this will probably be your most expensive piece of equipment for the whole project.

Along with everything else I also keep a notebook or journal with a fairly substantial binding so I can lug it around with me easily. In it I draw diagrams and notes on new stitches that I find in all those expensive stitch dictionaries. That way it's free. It's also great to have around to jot down ideas and sketches for projects, addresses of equipment and yarn shops, titles of relevant books and articles and anything else relative to my work. When I think I'm dry for ideas or have forgotten a stitch that I need right away, then I just consult my little old notebook.

A foot-square scrap of cloth of similar weight and texture to your fabric's is handy to have to doodle around on with new stitches. This way you also have a record of the stitches that you've learned and see what they can do with the threads you are using. It gives you a chance to mess around with the stitches, playing with them to find different effects and deciding which ones you want to use or not on your piece. It's terrible to anticipate covering any area, spending time and energy with a stitch you don't like. Don't settle for anything. Time is not relevant unless you are doing something you don't like.

TWO RINGS AND A SCREW: NOT BY TOLKIEN

To mount the fabric in the hoop, remove the inner ring from the outer ring and lay the area of the fabric you are to work on over the inner ring. Adjust the outer ring's screw so that it will fit firmly over the fabric and the other ring. You shouldn't have to adjust the screw again until you change the area you're working on. Press the outer ring down onto the fabric and inner ring, working with your palms and fingers all around the rings until the fabric is taut. I like to have the threads of the fabric in the ring running at reasonable right angles to one another, adjusting them visually. It's not that important. Pull the excess fabric evenly all around the rings until the fabric is drum tight. Remember, you will not be sewing as you would a seam, but punching your needle up and down through the fabric. A few stitches, like large areas of satin stitching and some knots, crush and dent under the hoop's edge as you move about from area to area. My suggestion here is to do these stitches last if you can.

The hoop and fabric are now prepared for the application of the stitches. Hooray!

ANATOMY OF A STITCH

Use the stitches, distort them as it suits you. Try them as linear stitches and fillers, next to one another, over each other, isolate them--do what you _feel_ like doing.

I'm only including in the following section the stitches that I enjoy the most and find the most versatile. They are easy to modify if you just think of the possibilities--try weaving a thread in and out a running stitch or placing a raised stitch over a trellis. Experiment, enjoy.

Follow the diagrams slowly and carefully, working it out in your head first. Take up your doodle cloth and get into the rhythm of the stitch and watch it grow. Touch it, inspect it closely--really look at it from all possible angles. Think of all the possibilities the stitch has to offer you. Even though you may have decided not to use it on your piece, note it anyway in your notebook. It might be just perfect for something later, and memory is not reliable.

To thread the needle, first loop the thread over the needle and pull the needle away from you and the thread toward you. This flattens the thread so that it will easily pass through the needle. Pinch the thread, grasping it tightly and slip the needle out. Push the needle eye against the pinched thread. It usually takes a few tries to get the thread through at first.

KNOTTING OFF: Knot the end or ends (depending upon whether you are doubling or leaving the thread as a single strand) of the thread and punch the needle down through the top of the fabric a bit off to the side of the working line. Follow the diagram (next page) carefully. After completing the area of stitches, cut off the original surface knot (A on the diagram). That way there are no bunchy knots on back of the piece and all the stitching is done on the front of the piece. Theoretically you shouldn't ever have to turn the hoop over during the whole process of embroidering, which is a good goal to work for if you like games.

FINISHING OFF: It's the same process as starting off. Tuck the two little stitches used for knotting off under the last set of stitches completed, pulling F off to the side of the work. Cut the thread close to the fabric surface at F.

KNOTTING OFF/ FINISHING OFF

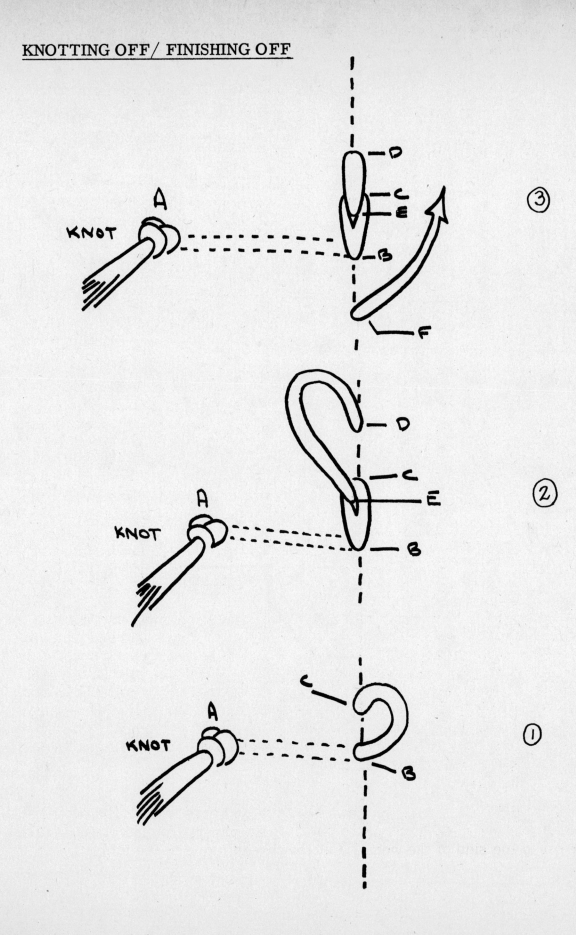

RUNNING STITCH: This is probably the simplest stitch in the whole conglomerate of stitches. It can be used readily for a linear stitch and can be modified for filling in an area.

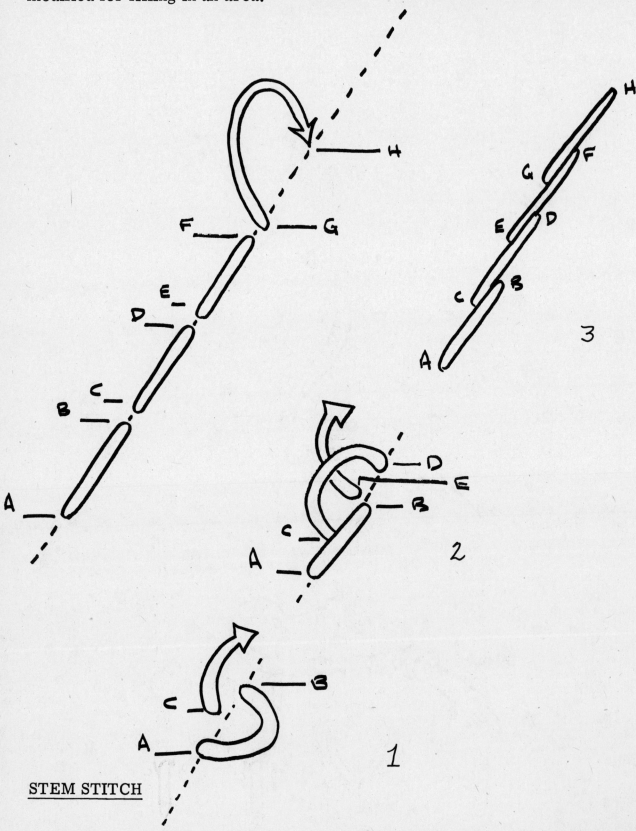

STEM STITCH

COUCHING: This is a great way to show off beautiful threads without much loss on the underside of the fabric. It's also an effective linear stitch.

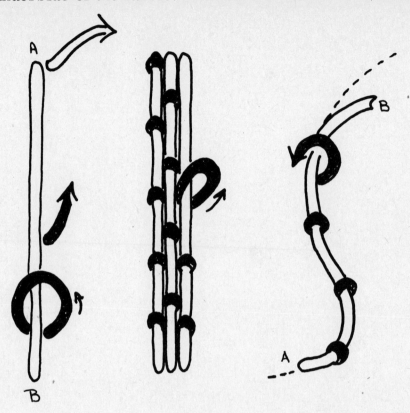

BOKHARA COUCHING: This is used mainly as a filler in classical embroidery. Because it uses only one thread, I have found it difficult to use as a linear stitch. That's a challenge.

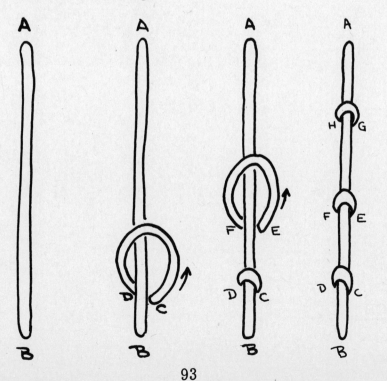

93

CHAIN STITCH

TWISTED CHAIN STITCH

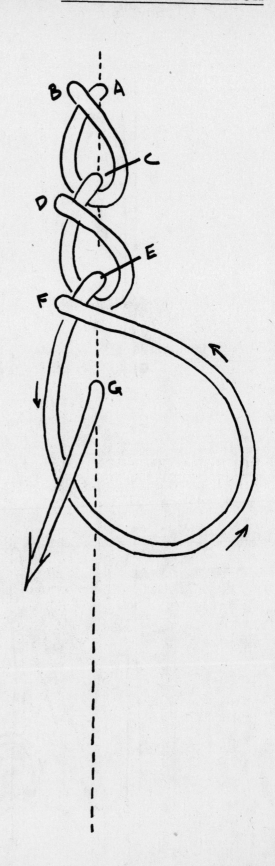

BUTTONHOLE STITCH

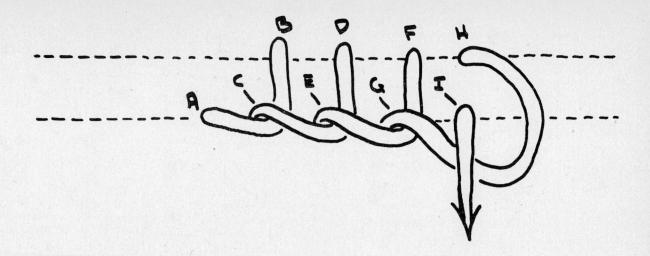

FRENCH KNOT: If you pull up on <u>B</u> it will be a lot easier to complete.

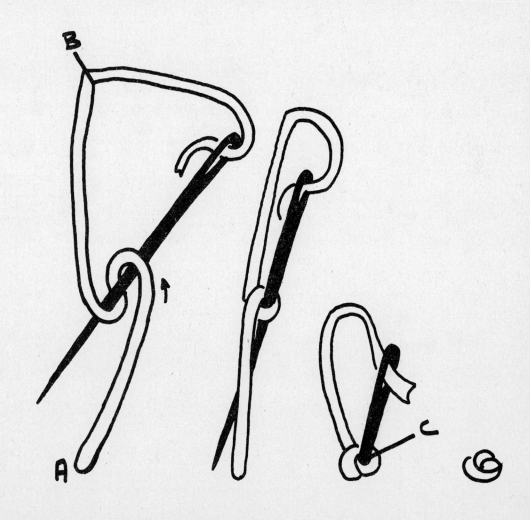

<u>CORAL KNOT</u>: Hold your thumb down on <u>D</u>.

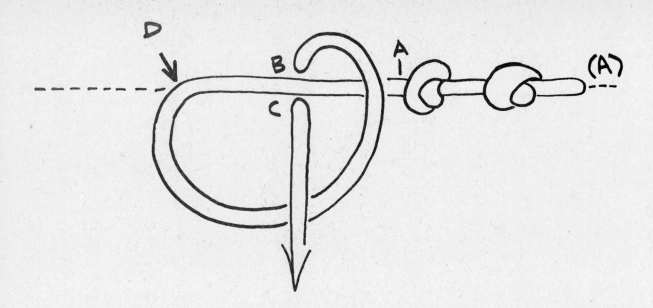

<u>SCROLL</u>

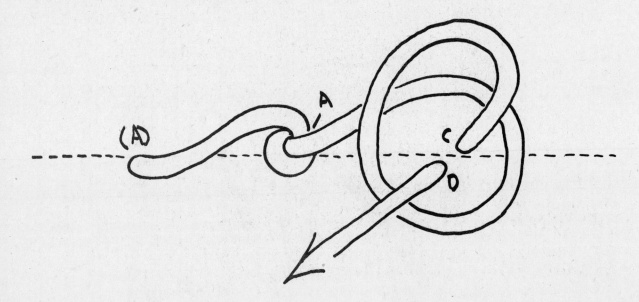

DOUBLE KNOT: This is my favorite stitch and is especially effective when the knots are spaced a short distance away from one another. Use D as if it were A to make the next knot, and repeat.

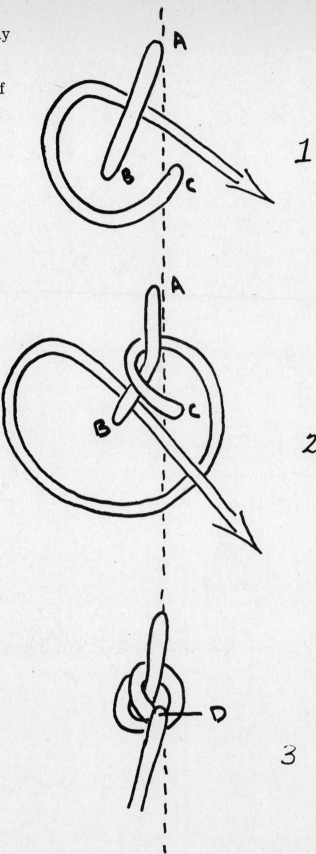

1

2

3

CLOSED FLY STITCH: With a name like this it has to be a good stitch, right? I've shown you the classical method of using this stitch, as it's easy to draw this way. If you think about it, the closed fly can be very versatile--in embroidery, that is.

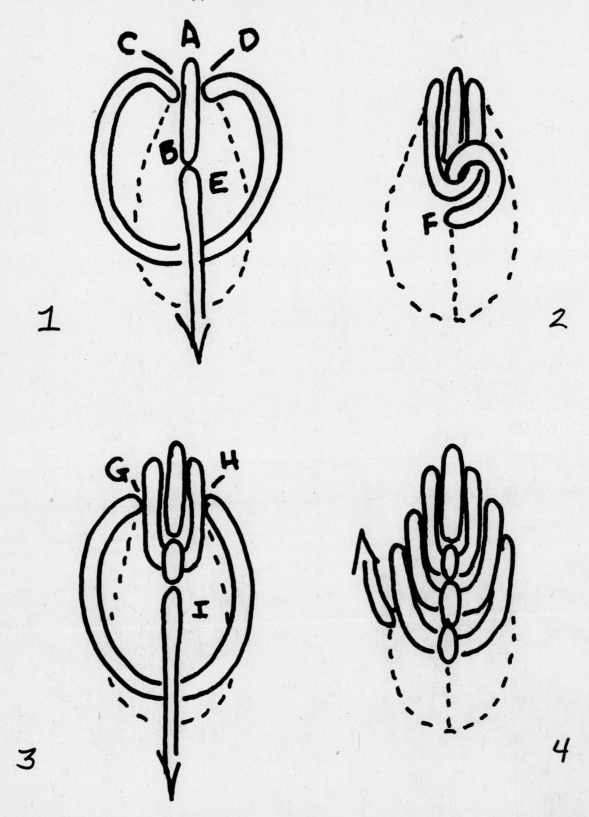

SPIDER'S WEBS: Always use an odd number of spokes, five minimally. This spoke-like structure is used for both the whipped (right) and the woven (left) types of webs.

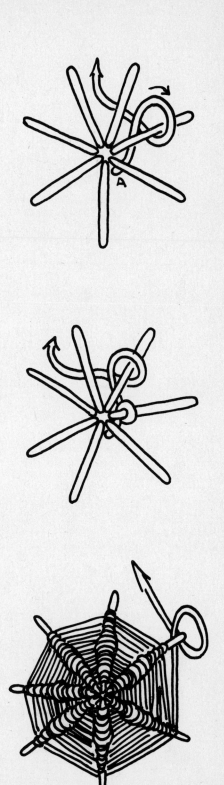

<u>TRELLIS FILLING:</u> Parallel lines and perpendicular corners are the usual order. The corners of the squares produced should be tacked down as shown, or in any way you can think of. The trellis lends itself very well to filling with other stitches. When filling an odd shape with the trellis, use the method illustrated at the right.

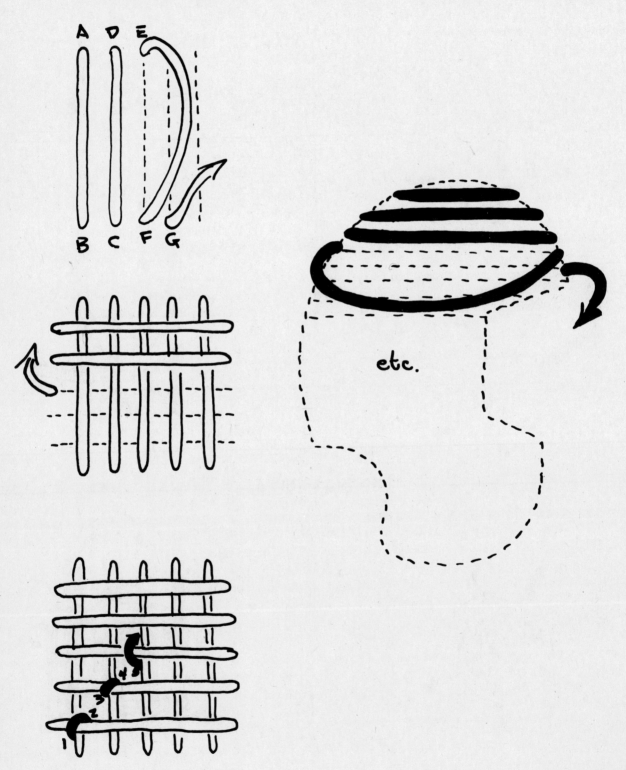

RAISED BUTTONHOLE STITCH: This, like all the raised stitches, can be used as a filling, or for a linear stitch if the parallel stitches used for a base are made one raised buttonhole stitch wide.

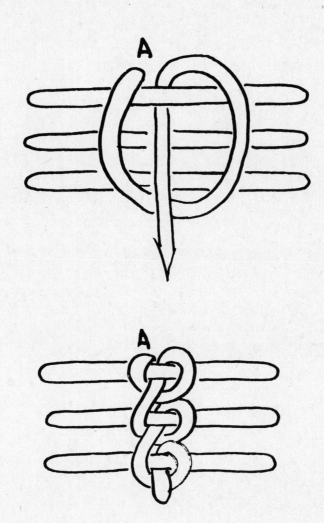

RAISED ZIGZAG STITCH: This stitch is a variation on the raised buttonhole and gives an intriguing knitted effect when used as a filling.

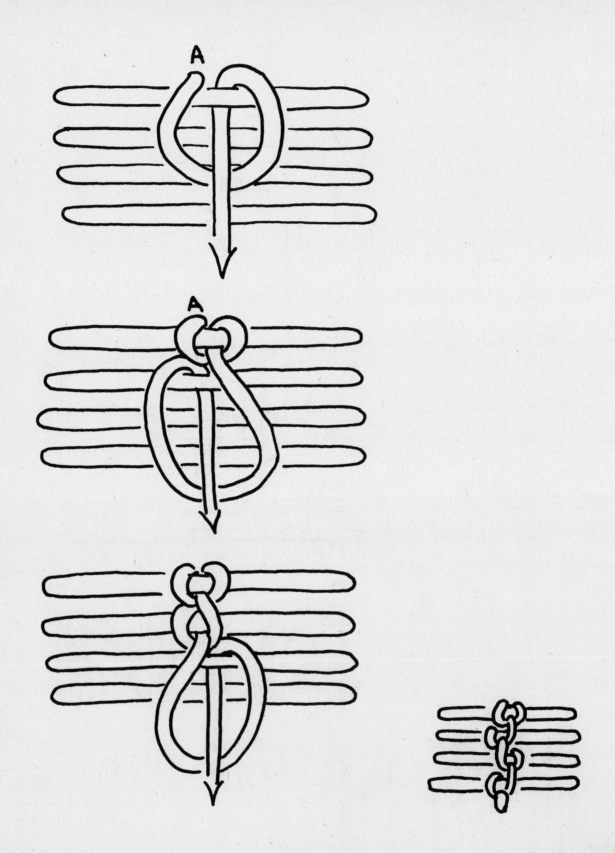

RAISED CHAIN STITCH: Pull up firmly at the arrow in order to get an even, symmetrical stitch.

To use all the raised stitches as filling stitches in odd shapes, use the same principle of filling in the parallel lines as in the trellis stitch, eliminating, of course, the perpendicular lines.

SATIN STITCH: Outline the shape to be filled with a very fine chain stitch or stem stitch and fill with long running stitches. Keep the satin stitches close together and at even tensions to one another. The back looks fairly much like the front.

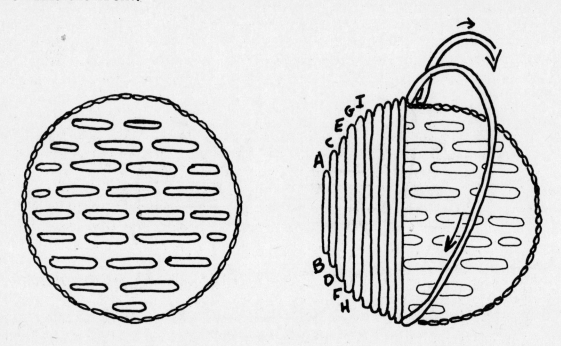

FALSE SATIN STITCH: There is very little difference, as far as I'm concerned, between the net result of this and the "real" satin stitch. The "real" satin stitch has more thread covering the back of the fabric. Some people say the false satin stitch looks flatter. It's up to you. I use it because there is very little thread waste on the back. As I have already said, I'm cheap. Use the same method of outlining the shape first and filling in with running stitches.

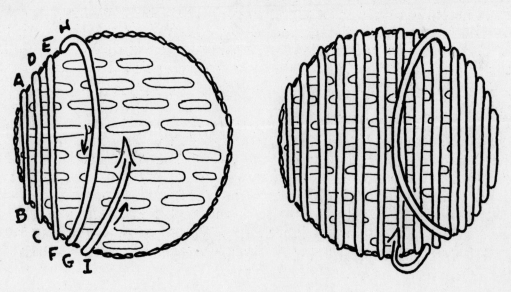

WRINKLED, HUH?

After completing your piece, you'll lay it out and it will probably be all wrinkled and hoop marked--not at all like the smooth finished thing you pictured. That's why you block it. You could press it, placing it between two or three damp towels and using a hot iron. The only drawback to the pressing bit is that it is difficult to prevent the fabric from becoming lop-sided. It's fine for small items but becomes tougher to handle on larger pieces.

The best method is blocking the completed piece. You can have this done by a professional (who is usually someone with more guts than his client). Find a reputable needlework shop, and attempt to see the caliber of work they do. Be fussy--after all this is the last bend in the long road to completion and now is no time for disaster. Most professional mistakes, though very few, are usually due to lack of concern. Don't be discouraged about doing the blocking yourself, you've done everything else so far.

You'll need cold water, a box of carpet tacks, a hammer, an old piece of cotton cloth or sheet (that's larger than your piece), and a wooden surface such as an old table or board that you can staple or hammer nails into (also larger than your piece). A pair of blunt-nosed pliers or, better yet, canvas-stretcher pliers.

Lay the sheet over the wood surface. Dunk your embroidery in cold water until it is soaked and spread it out, dripping, on the sheet. You did use colorfast threads and fabric, right? I like facing the embroidery up so that the stitches on the finished work will reveal their full textures. Facing it down flattens the stitches, which is good if you want a smooth, flat effect.

Smooth your piece out and measure the distance between each top to bottom and diagonal corner in order to make sure that the distance top to bottom on one side of the piece is the same as top to bottom distance on the other side of the piece and that the lengths measured across the piece to diagonal corners are the same. A carpenter's right-angle or a protractor would be handy to be sure the corners form right angles. This is most important.

Pull the fabric really tight, starting from the centers, using the pliers. Tack at even intervals working from the centers of the sides out, until there is about a one-half to one-quarter inch interval between tacks. Check the measured distances between diagonal corners and be sure the corners form true right angles. Let the fabric dry completely. (I hope you are not using your kitchen table.) If you don't plan to mount it right away after it's dry, then roll it up in tissue paper around a cardboard tube, rolling so the embroidery faces out. This prevents creasing of the fabric and crunching of the stitches.

PUTTING IT ALL TOGETHER: MOUNTING

There are several ways of mounting the completed piece. The most convenient for me is using canvas-stretcher strips which can be bought in almost any decent art-supply shop. They should be smaller in length and width than the dimensions of your fabric. As you can see, allowing for excess around the area of your fabric is a very bright idea. Canvas pliers or large blunt-nosed pliers, a staple gun (or hammer), staples (or carpet tacks), and time are the rest of the equipment you need. If you are using a hammer and tacks you had better have someone help you, as I understand most people don't have three hands yet.

Assemble the strips, being sure the corners are at solid right angles. Lay one side of the fabric along one stretcher strip, leaving enough cloth to fold over the strip along the back. Follow a thread running from one corner to the other, much the same way you did when you straightened the fabric. Lay this thread along the front top edge of the stretcher strip. This will help in keeping the threads running at right angles during the whole process. Start from the center tacking down the fabric on the top of the stretcher strip. Work your way out to the sides being sure that thread you've chosen as your guide is running on the top edge of the stretcher strip. On the opposite side pull the fabric tight, starting also from the

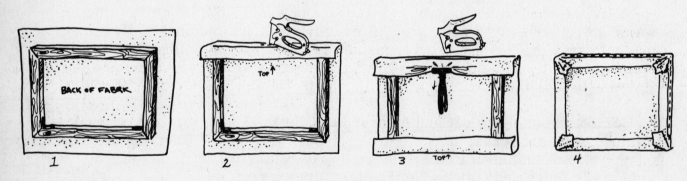

Mounting with tacks or staples

center using the pliers for better grip, and tacking as you did the top. You will probably find staples easier to use, pulling the fabric with one hand and stapling with the other, unless, as I mentioned, you have someone willing to work with you. Try having the threads of the fabric running as parallel as you can to the edges of the stretcher strips, throughout this whole procedure. If the blocking came out well, there should be little trouble with this. This avoids possible distortion of the whole piece when finished. Repeat the process on the remaining sides; find a thread, run it along the front outer edge of the stretcher strip, staple the fabric down working from the centers out. All along be sure the fabric is very taut and smooth on the front surface. Check the thread angles at the corners of the stretcher strips and get them as close to right angles as possible. It should resemble a fine stretched canvas when complete. There should be no puckering or odd pulling. The corners of the fabric on the back should be manipulated so that they lie as flat as you can get them. Staple them down.

Certain fabrics such as linen twill are nearly impossible to line up perfectly, so in a case like this, stretch the fabric so that it is smooth and the embroidery looks good. That's the whole point behind mounting, anyway.

The classic method for mounting is to whip the fabric onto a frame of thin board or stretcher strips with linen thread. I don't care to use this method, but someone might want to try. The board or the stretcher strips should be cut smaller than the fabric, as in the previous method. A thin piece of masonite or plywood is good. Heavy cardboard can be used for small items. It warps too easily to be used on larger pieces.

Use linen thread, which, unfortunately, is difficult to find. Try shoe repair shops or upholstery shops. Maybe a place dealing with weaving supplies will have it. Also the thread used for sewing braided rugs together might be good. Buttonhole twist or the other heavy cotton sewing threads at the sewing counters in department stores are not strong enough, and one broken thread can ruin the whole thing. What you want is a thread that's super-strong.

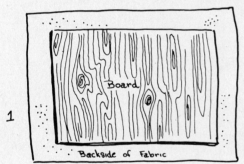 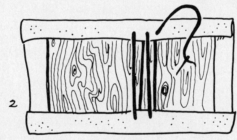 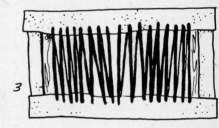

Mounting by whipstitching

Lay the fabric face down on a table, lay the board (or stretcher strips) over the fabric, centering it. There should be enough fabric in excess to fold over on all sides in a minimum of one and a half inches. With a doubled length of linen thread and a heavy tapestry needle, starting from the center in the same manner prescribed in the previous section, catch up about a half-inch of the fabric. Also find a thread running from one side to the other and have it run along the top of the board, so that there is a much easier time getting the threads to run at right angles to one another later.

Fold up the excess fabric on the bottom of the board. Bring the threads

down to the edge of the fabric you just folded up and catch another half-inch.
Pull the thread tight. By whipping the fabric this way, the front is pulled
tight and relatively smooth. Keep checking the thread you chose to run along
the edge of the board to see that it stays in place. Repeat this process on the
other two sides. The spaces between the stitches vary, depending on the
weight and substance of the fabric, but on the average they should probably
be about one-half to one-quarter of an inch apart.

Check the threads on the front surface to see if they are running at right
angles and that the fabric is smooth and tight. There should be no puckers
or pulling on the front at all.

Now, using either method you can frame your pieces as you please.

"LET ME MAKE THIS PERFECTLY CLEAR..."

I have restricted myself to embroidery "picture-making" just for the lack of space. The possibilities of this craft are vast if you just put your mind to it. As with life, it can be all encompassing or just a passing gig. As a crusader for self-expression and total individuality in media, I believe that embroidery is not only an expressive craft, but a completely contemporary means of personal communication. Anyone can take this craft as far as he wants to go. There are those who paint old mailboxes in order to enliven their environment, and then there is Picasso. The range between is infinite. Infinity is awesome in its possibilities. Embroidery, as with any other means of self-expression, is what you make it and can go as far as you want to carry it.

Hopefully, I have outlined a basic "vocabulary" of stitches and techniques that will get you started in new directions. Maybe I've introduced you to possibilities you've never considered. The point is not whether you've chosen embroidery as your means of expression, as your thing. Being a media snob is not my style. What is vital is that you express <u>yourself</u>, however it suits you. Do it with joy, with life!

Being is celebration.

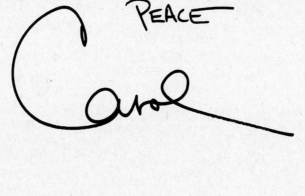

PEACE

Carol

Getting Into Pottery
[NOTES FROM THE UNDERGROUND]
Jean Young

Just remembering the cool, smooth, and sensuous feeling of bare feet in mud should get your head moving in the pottery energy field. That was really a feeling for the material, as they say; yes--however elemental it sounds. It'll be the same when you begin rolling a piece of wet clay around in your hands. Remember doing that with mud? There are other feelings to groove with when you think about doing pottery. Like a feel for form. A feel for design and color. The whole point is to get it all together into some kind of unity that your finished piece will reflect.

Start out by making something you really dig. Something you need. Then you'll be closer to expressing yourself.

A few people have been lucky enough to find clay ready to use in their own gardens. Some tools can be found or made at home. A knife and a sponge might be all you need. But whatever you feel you need can be found at the ceramic-supply shops. The best tools are your hands.

SUPERIOR CHEAP TOOLS, SOME HANDMADE

WIRE: Anything will do--an electric-guitar string, or even a nylon one. Tie each end to anything that you can easily grasp.

WIRE LOOP TOOLS: These have wooden handles and a wire loop at one or both ends. Several different sizes are needed. They cost from around 60 cents to $1.75, depending on size.

WOODEN MODELING TOOLS: These are all wood. There are any number of sizes and shapes. Choose a selection. They run from around 30 cents up, depending on size.

PIN TOOL: This is a pointed tool for scratching in designs and for trimming. A needle with the eye end pressed into a bottle cork will work for some things.

SPONGES: A sponge shaped like an elephant's ear is best. It's flat and thin with plenty of surface area.

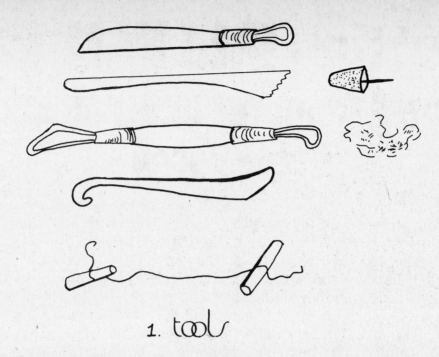

1. tools

PLASTER BATS: These are usually pie-shaped pieces of dried plaster. They support the objects you are working on, and they are used for moving your piece around without having to touch it (clay won't stick to plaster). Bats are only 70 cents to $2.00, but if you have a number of pots going at once the cost does add up. To save bread some people like to make their own bats. Buy some plaster of paris at the lumber yard. Enough for making four or five bats and a wedging table should cost under $3. Mix it up using directions on the package. Use paper pie-plates, aluminum pie-plates, or, for a square, you can pour it into any cardboard box. Coat pans with soap or vaseline to facilitate removal when dry. Just make sure that the form you're pouring into is on a level surface. A good, easy-to-use bat measures 6 by 6 inches across and 1 inch thick. Be sure to tape the corners of the cardboard box so the plaster won't run out. It'll take about twenty minutes for the plaster to harden.

WEDGING TABLE: This is a plaster slab used for throwing down moist clay to force out any air bubbles trapped inside. If you don't plan on going into pottery in a big way, at least right in the beginning, you really don't need a wedging table. Instead, you can tack down a piece of canvas to a sturdy table or floor (clay will stick to most everything not plaster or canvas). A wooden box 30 inches long, 20 inches wide, and 4 inches deep will make a wedging slab for every need. Perhaps you have one that size or smaller around the house. But if you have to make one, use the least expensive quarter-inch plywood and one-by-fours. Then mix up the plaster and pour it into the box or form. (Remember, the box should be on a level surface.) Scrape the surface of the wet plaster with the edge of a yardstick or straight board until smooth. When the plaster is dry, break away the box and move the slab to your working table.

2   Working on a big plaster bat

If you don't have a working table you can stack some cement blocks (also available at the lumber yard) against a wall which will hold the wedging slab and keep it from slipping.   The holes in cement blocks make good places to store equipment.

A BIT ABOUT COOKING POTS

I have to rap about this now even though it is one of the last things you do in the pottery process.   Reason is--so you'll know what I'm talking about when we come back to it again.

All clay is fired (baked) in a kiln (oven) for permanence so it won't leak or crack.   These kilns are ovens made to reach very high temperatures, a minimum of 2000º F.   Different clays are fired at different degrees of heat, sometimes referred to as "cone temperatures."   That's because in order to check the oven temperature you place small cone-shaped pieces of glaze and clay (dime a dozen in the craft shop) inside the kiln in a pat of clay.   Usually, cones are used in sets of three or four, and they are made to melt at a definite temperature.   Most kilns have a peephole on the side through which the cones can be watched.   This chart shows you how the cone numbers increase

113

as the Fahrenheit temperature increases.

$$06\text{--}1859^{O}$$
$$05\text{--}1905^{O}$$
$$04\text{--}1940^{O}$$
$$03\text{--}2039^{O}$$
$$02\text{--}2057^{O}$$
$$01\text{--}2120^{O}$$
$$1\text{--}2120^{O}$$
$$2\text{--}2129^{O}$$
$$3\text{--}2133^{O}$$
$$4\text{--}2174^{O}$$
$$5\text{--}2201^{O}$$
$$6\text{--}2246^{O}$$

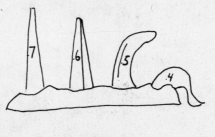

3. cones

Ceramic wares are classified as earthenware, stoneware, china, and porcelain. The two types most made are earthenware and stoneware. Earthenware is fired at low temperatures, around 1700°F. to 1900°F. (or cones 09 to 05). When fired, it is porous and will not hold liquids unless it is glazed. The clay color is red or buff after firing. Stoneware is harder and more vitreous (glasslike) than low-fired clays. It holds water even when not glazed. It won't scratch or break as easily as low-fired clays. It fires at cones 5 to 11.

There are many types of kilns: electric, gas, oil, wood, etc. (The Indians put their ware into a pit and burned firewood over it. The earth itself was the insulation.) Before you choose a clay you should locate someone in your area who has a kiln and will fire your things for you. This may not be easy. The YMCA and YWCA usually have kilns. Public schools and craft shops may have kilns or they may be able to turn you on to individuals who will fire your stuff. There is always a charge for this because kilns use a lot of gas or electricity. Daniel Rhodes's book Kilns costs $10, but if you are thinking of getting a kiln for yourself it would be worth the reading. The Golden Press book on pottery shows how to make a kiln for raku (used only for pottery that is glazed in ten minutes) that is relatively simple. However, their description on how to light it is rather vague, and I was told by someone who had gone through a course on how to make this kind of kiln that lighting it should be approached with caution. Craft shops and art stores will show you their catalogues of kilns, and they can order for you.

4 Opening an electric kiln for loading

THE GOOD EARTH

Almost everywhere there are spots where you can find clay for the digging. It's usually red clay. What you find might need a lot of cleaning because natural clay will have rocks in it or other stuff. Sift the clay through a screen to get out this unwanted material. It also might be too sticky or too sandy, and when this happens other clays can be obtained to add to it to make it a good working clay. For instance, a "ball" clay is too sticky to use by itself, but it may be what you need to hold together what you've found. If the clay you've dug up is too sticky then a "fire" clay which has tooth and texture can be added.

Workable clay (called "clay body") usually contains a combination of different clays. The good clay body should be plastic enough to be rolled into a coil without showing lots of cracks. It should have enough coarser clays or it will shrink too much when it's fired.

Clay also comes ready-mixed, with fine or medium grog (grog is a clay that has been fired and ground down. It gives texture and tooth to the clay). These ready-mixed clays come wet in quantities as small as a five-pound box for $1.25. I suggest you buy a twenty-five-pound quantity for around $3.75 to give yourself enough to work with. Five pounds isn't as much as you think. Clay weighs a ton. A fifty-pound tin which holds two separate twenty-five-pound batches in plastic bags costs around $6.50.

Gray clay is called different names by different companies. It's anywhere from pink to buff after it has been fired. Red clay is also called by different names such as Terra Cotta, Red Mexiclay, etc. The gray ready-mixed, though, has a wide firing range (cones 06 to 9). Red clay has a firing range of cones 08 to 9. These are the cheapest kinds to buy. Because of its weight, I suggest picking bought clay up in a car to save shipping costs, which are almost double the price of the clay.

Sometime you might want to mix your own clay bodies. This is much, much cheaper. Combinations of dry clay are mixed. Decide on the amount of dry clay you want to mix up. Weigh it (use a bathroom scale). Then measure out 35 per cent of the dry clay's weight in water. Put water in a plastic or galvanized garbage can. Then add the dry clay to the water. This you have to let cure for at least a week. (The older the clay the better. The Chinese used clay a hundred years old. One generation stored it for the next generation. They in turn stored it for future generations to be used many, many years later. That's old clay!) Then knead the clay like bread. Some people step on it like making wine from grapes.

CLAY CATHARSIS: WEDGING

This is a good way to use your action muscles and/or take out aggressions. The purpose of wedging is to remove all air bubbles and holes which might cause a piece to explode in firing. It has to be done before starting to make your piece. Cut the clay in half and throw one half onto the plaster wedging table. Then slap the other half on top of it. Keep this up until you can cut the clay in half and don't see any holes. If you haven't gotten down to making the plaster wedging slab, tack the under side of oil cloth or canvas on a firm sturdy surface. This way, the clay won't stick. Also, if the piece of clay is small enough, wedging can be done by pressing the clay through your fingers. The larger the piece of clay the more it needs wedging.

MOTHER, MOTHER EARTH

Take care of your clay. It should be kept in tightly closed, heavy plastic bags or containers with tight-fitting covers. Clay can be worked over and over again until it is fired. To get it back to the original plastic state, just add water. While you are not actually working on your piece, keep a damp cloth covering it, and wet the plaster bat it is sitting on.

SOUP TO DUST

Different steps in the drying of clay:

Leap 1: GREEN CLAY. Clay in the wet, pliable stage. Also clay that hasn't been fired.

Leap 2: LEATHER-HARD CLAY. Clay which is no longer pliable because its moisture has evaporated somewhat. It has not yet changed color. In this stage it can be carved, decorated, etc.; handles, etc., can be added.

Leap 3: BONE-DRY CLAY. Most of the water has evaporated and the clay feels warm to the touch. All clay should dry slowly so it won't warp or crack. When it feels dry you can put it near some artificial heat to let it dry more. When it is really bone dry it can be put in the kiln.

Leap 4: BISQUE OR BISCUIT. Clay that has been fired. For all kinds of clay this firing is at a low temperature--about 1800°F. It makes a pot easy to handle for glazing. It is still porous.

CLAY ON CLAY

"Englobes" and "slips" are used interchangeably in ceramic books. They sound as if they could be used interchangeably in comic books too! Slip is simply liquid clay--about as runny as heavy cream. "Englobe" means to cover; that is, with any material; however, slip is usually used.

Slip is applied to a wet or leather-hard unfired piece to color and decorate it. Always make your slip from the same clay you're using for your piece. Just add water and appropriate color until it is the thickness of heavy cream--or heavier. The reason for this is that various clays shrink at different rates and your slip is apt to peel off the pot if you don't use the same clay that you used to make the pot.

Problem is, if you want to put a white englobe on a red clay pot you have to use different clay. Try buff clay slips on test pieces of red clay to see

how it goes. Usually ceramic shops have a white commercially mixed englobe that suits all kinds of clay. Slips come in colors and cost as little as
85 cents a box. If you plan to use white englobe in a big way you can mix
your own. Daniel Rhodes's book Clay and Glazes has a chart for finding
ingredients for different firing temperatures. Ceramic stores can put it
together for you too. Usually six different ingredients are needed (cost,
about 35 cents a pound). Colors can be added that cost anywhere from 35 to
85 cents a quarter-pound each, depending on the color.

All color is made from oxides. If cobalt oxide is added to your slip,
you get a light to dark blue, depending on how much you use. Usually that
will be anywhere from 1 to 5 parts per 100 parts of slip. Chrome oxide
gives a green, uranium oxide gives a yellow. To get a jet black, which
looks good on red clay, you need to mix 10 per cent each of these three
oxides: chrome oxide, iron oxide, antimony oxide. Slip looks dull after
firing. You can rub some soft wax on the outside of a fired slip piece to
protect it and give it some shine. A transparent glaze over the englobe
protects it from eventually looking dusty. I'll talk about this further in the
Glaze Menagerie section. Slip fires at the same temperature as your clay,
but since it is a clay, it must be bone dry before it is ready to be fired.

HOW TO APPLY SLIP (this is not a put-on): Pouring on is the best bet,
usually while your piece is still wet. This is so slip and pot body will shrink
together. Two or more applications should be applied on top of each other
rather than using one heavy coat. It is best to do the second pouring soon
after you do the first. If the first coat is too dry it might fall off when you
pour a second one.

To fashion an area with forms and design, paint wax on your pot over
the area you don't want the slip to cover. The wax will burn out in the firing
and leave the original clay surface. Candle-melt will do, but better yet, get
some wax emulsion at the craft shop (about 75 cents a half-pint) because it
remains in the liquid state. Melted candle wax will have to be kept warm to
be liquid and clogs the brushes. Wax can be painted on in a precise manner
--sponged on for a lacy pattern, or spattered on, etc., etc.

SLIP INLAY: Slip inlay is a groove. Really! Groove out horizontal,
vertical lines (or shapes) with a pin tool, saw blade or anything else at hand.
Utilize this technique when pot is in a leather-hard stage, or just before.
Larger incising can be made with a corner of a wire loop tool. Pour on the
slip while the clay is still leather-hard. When the pot dries the surface is
scraped, leaving alternate patterns of slip and clay body. In most cases,
use a clay with less grog because it makes the piece easier to scrape.

TRAILING: Another fulfilling way to decorate pots is trailing. Fill a
plastic bag with slip. Then cut a smallish hole in the corner so you can

squeeze out lines or dabs onto your pot like a baker uses in decorating a cake. Another little number is to squeeze out line designs on wet newspaper. Pick up the paper with the slip pattern and press it against the side of a leather-hard piece. This is called slip trailed transfer.

SGRAFITTO: This is a good technique. It means "to scratch." You can scratch through englobes or opaque glaze, or directly onto leather-hard clay. The lines expose the clay body underneath an englobe. Wait until the piece is leather-hard before you englobe, and don't wait until the englobe is over-dry before you scratch through, otherwise it might flake off as you scratch. Pencil marks will fire out, so you can draw a design on the englobe first before using the sgrafitto technique. You can carve out whole shapes and forms with a wire tool where you want the clay under the englobe to show through.

POT COOKERY, CONTINUED

I have to go into two different kinds of firing so you'll dig what happens when I get into glazes. Firing is done at a temperature that depends on what clay and glaze you use. There are two stages in firing: 1. maturing, or bisque firing, 2. fusing, or glaze firing. (Stage three: If the glaze over-fires, it flows off the pot.) I already mentioned bisque firing when I talked about clay. It is low-temperature firing of bone-dry clay. The result is clay that's easy to handle for glazing. The pot, or whatever, is still sufficiently porous to absorb glaze. In order to hold water the bisque pot must be refired at a high temperature, either with or without a coat of glaze. One potter I know reverses the usual maturing-fusing stages of the firing process. For the first firing she fires high so the pot becomes vitrified and can hold liquids. Her second firing is low so that the glaze she applies over the fired pot can be either a low or high fire glaze, and she has no problems with this. There are no hard and fast rules.

THE GLAZE MENAGERIE

A glaze when it has fused is glass. There are so many different glazes that I want to tell you about some--so you'll know what's happening when you make selections at the craft shop. I'd advise purchasing ready-mixed glazes rather than mixing up your own formulas, etc. For one thing, most books on glazes seem to be written for the MIT student. My first pottery teacher was working on her Ph.D. in ceramics at Southern Cal when she was offed by all the weird chemicals.

Time was when there was a mystique about mixing your own glaze. It was secret knowledge, with everyone holding on to his private (he thought) little discovery. But the word is out, and has been for some time: commercial glazes can give you consistently a better glaze than you can obtain through random experimentation. Many potters with years of work behind them do not mix their glazes. I don't really put down getting into mixing your own recipes. It takes know-how, and eventually you may want to do it. I'm just happy that ready-made glazes are no longer referred to as the means and ways of little old ladies in hobby shops. There is plenty to do in concentrating on the essence of the item you're making, its form, color, size and whether you want a design or not and if so, what kind.

To give you an idea of what's involved if you _were_ eager to start mixing your own glazes, you'd have to start with the knowledge that all glazes are composed of THREE BASIC INGREDIENTS: 1. Flux: any chemical which makes the glaze flow at a certain temperature; 2. hardener: used to stabilize the flux so it won't flow beyond a certain temperature; 3. fixative or adhesive, which will make the glazes stick.

These combinations form a transparent, non-colored glaze. Add color and you get a colored transparent glaze. Add an opacifier (such as tin oxide), plus the base glaze makes a white opaque (chalky) glaze. Clay, plus a colored transparent glaze makes a dull or mat glaze. Course, there's lots more to it than that. You'd also need a gram scale for measuring out dry glaze.

TYPES OF GLAZE: Basically there are three types of glaze (they're ready mixed at ceramic shops): 1. shiny; 2. semishiny; 3. dull. Shiny glaze can be transparent or colored-transparent, which allows the whole body of your piece to show through. It should be the consistency of milk, should you have to mix it with water. Glossy is also shiny but allows only slight traces of the body to show through. It should be heavier than milk. Semishiny glaze, such as enamel, is less shiny than the above. It's applied in a heavy-cream state. It is a bit more opaque (chalky) and hides the item. A thin coat however, will act like gloss. Dull glaze has a mat surface and is always opaque. Antique glazes are dull but have the habit of changing continuously and sometimes leave shiny spots. Mat is applied thicker than heavy cream. The ceramic shops will probably have preglazed tiles to look at to help you select a glaze. Ready-to-use liquid glaze is most expensive. Powdered forms have to be mixed with water (about 50 to 65 per cent), and sometimes the directions on the package tell you to add a mixing solution and screen the wet glaze through a 80- to 100-mesh screen (also in your local ceramic shop). The mix may have to stand twenty-four hours before using. But, powdered glaze is the least expensive way to buy and, should you buy a colorless base glaze, you can add your own colorant and water.

No single glaze will always react the same way. There are too many variables such as temperatures, different kinds of clay, etc. One glaze can be put over another for different effects. If you have your own kiln it is easier than having to take your pots somewhere else if you want to put them through many firings. Each slightly higher temperature changes the look of the glaze.

WAYS TO GLAZE: There are four methods of glazing: pouring, dipping, brushing, spraying. There's not much to it. You'll probably pour if you don't have a big supply of glaze to dip into. Brushing should be done with a large soft-hair brush. Dab, don't stroke. Brushing is all right for small pieces, but for large ones it might come out unevenly. If you have to spray, do it outside with the breeze going away from you. Otherwise you get into protective masks, ventilation booths, and all that jazz. Everyone's hip that nothing is healthy to breathe but clean, fresh air--when you can get it.

Bottoms of pots shouldn't have any glaze. If they do, they stick to the kiln shelf. Paint some wax on the bottoms of pots so the glaze won't stick there (I talked about wax in the section on how to apply slip).

To glaze the inside of pots, pour glaze (it could be thinned here a bit) inside with a cup. Swish it around to the top edge. Pour out excess. All pots should be glazed on the inside if not on the outside. It makes for easy cleaning. To pour on the outside, place the pot on some chickenwire, a couple of boards, or the cooking rack of an oven over a pan. Pour evenly. You may have to adjust the thinness or thickness of the glaze. See what you can do with it to get what you want.

GLAZE DERMATOLOGY: Since doing pottery is complicated, there are many variations to what happens. You're always experimenting. Don't let any puritan pieties get in your way. A farmer once told me that if you like a plant, then it's a plant; if not, it's a weed. So if you like the way your pot comes out of the kiln, then it's not a defect. If you don't like it, then you can call it a defect. One of my first pots is still a favorite to me even though what happened in the glazing would theoretically be called a defect. It is a red clay pot with blue and white opaque glazes sort of running down from the lip. But the white part bubbled in the kiln like lace and the blue stayed put. What an accident for me--I thought I was favored by the gods!

Here are some things your glazes could do. Crawling: the glaze pulls away from the body in small areas and exposes the clay body. Sometimes firing at a higher temperature will make it flow back. Flowing: dig this; if the glaze is fired beyond the right temperature it may flow right off the pot! Crazing: if the glaze contracts more than the clay while cooling, it will have small cracks throughout. This isn't the best result if your piece was meant for food items. But sometimes you might want this effect on the outside of the pot. Crackle glazes are sold ready-made for this purpose. Potters in China used to color the cracks and then refire the new color into them. They really had it down to something like the space control. Cracks can be heightened by rubbing in shoe polish, ink, or acrylic colors. Peeling: Slip might have been applied to a pot that was too dry, or it could have been put on too thick. Peeling can also happen to a glaze when it is not right for the clay used. Test beforehand when you are unsure, if you want to see if you like the look of some "accident" firing. Commercial glazes are reliable and you shouldn't have any problems.

STACKING AND FIRING A KILN

If you don't buy or build a kiln of your own right off, it would still be a good idea to know a little about the firing process.

There are two ways of stacking a kiln: bisque and glaze. Bisque is easy because the pieces are really stacked. You don't need shelves. You can put one pot inside the other with the heaviest on the bottom. An evenly stacked kiln heats the best. About 1750°F. or cone 07 is high enough.

Stacking glazed pieces is more difficult, for the pots should not touch or the glazes will fuse together. Place at least an eighth-inch apart. Glaze firing takes more time.

The larger the kiln, the longer it takes to heat. The kiln is heated slowly with vent holes open to let out moisture and vapors. Whoever is watching the kiln is given a warning that the kiln has reached the right temperature when the first cone bends over. A half hour later the next one starts to melt. Then it's time to turn off the kiln.

If it takes eight hours to reach your cone number, it will take twice that time to cool. The door should be cool enough for bare hands before it's opened.

A LITTLE EARNEST PREACHING [PLEASE FORGIVE]

A misquote from somewhere goes: "The fashioning of shapeless matter, like clay, shows man's drive to impress himself upon the external world."

Remember, you are free to choose your way to do a piece of pottery. For the past thirty years pottery has gone away from decoration--shape and glaze and texture have been everything. Also, muted colors have been preferred because they are believed to be more natural to the clay itself. Pottery books imply this is the "modern" way! Another taste dominating this modern trend is for the crude look. But don't be intimidated or you won't be awake to all the possibilities of contrast or even to the current changes in the pottery world itself. Thinking in terms of opposites helps.

Picasso did drawing on pottery and he is a painter. Some potters think drawing should be seen on paper only, never on pots. If that's true, then why is there so much elaborately drawn-on pottery in the Egyptian, Greek, and Oriental rooms of the Metropolitan Museum in New York, not to mention the Museum of the American Indian?

Currently, a few potters are breaking away and doing pottery with clear geometric designs and pure color. The designs suit the shape and size of the pots. These potters feel that scale, shape, and color are amplified by their choice of decorated patterns. All modes, thank Allah, are open to you unless you're working a production-line number and don't have time to get deeper into your own thing.

WAYS TO MAKE THINGS-OR-HOW TO WORK YOUR WORK

SLAB-HAPPY: Making slabs is a method of building a piece. First, wedge the clay you're going to use, then roll out with a rolling pin. To get an even thickness, use two pieces of wood as thick as you want the clay slab (three-eighths of an inch thick is good) as in **Figure 5**. Cut shapes out with a knife (these will be joined to make a complete object later on).

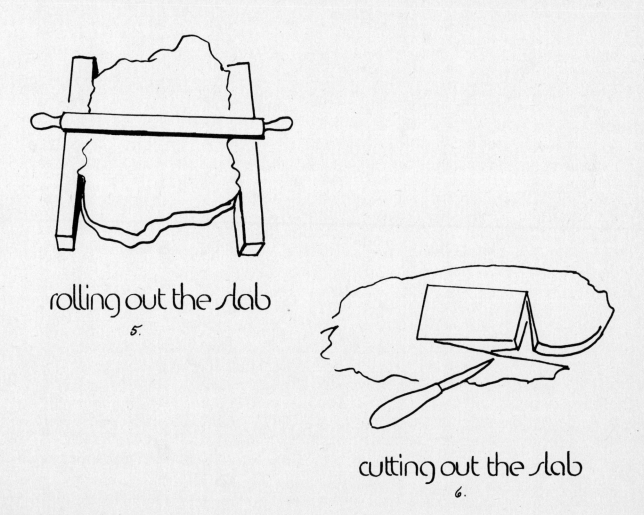

rolling out the slab
5.

cutting out the slab
6.

Decoration? Anything can be pressed on a slab of clay to make impressions. Use the end of a ruler or the side of a piece of wood or a glass to stamp out circles. Anything goes. For textural effects, slab work is a natural.

Put the cut out parts (say, of a box) on a plaster bat to stiffen. Weight them down with bats or the parts will warp. No air gets underneath, so turn them over once in a while. This will take from twenty minutes to two hours. In the leather-hard state they can be lifted in the hands without bending.

7. scoring two slabs

Joining pieces is done by scratching grooves into the clay with a fork (scoring). Loose runny clay (slip) is put on over the scored joints. Then the joints are fitted together by working both pieces with your fingers. Reinforcement is done by pressing a smoothed coil, not leather-hard, into the joint.

8. reinforcing corner

A simple lid for a box can be made by using a slab of the same size as the one on the bottom. Add slab strips to the underside of the slab top. Make sure they are indented in enough from the edge to fit inside the box lip.

Rather than have just the flat piece for the bottom (called "foot"), you might want it raised a bit. Strips cut at right angles and put on flat by welding is one way. Welding is done by putting some water on each part to be joined. Then rub that area until the surface loses its shine and becomes tacky. All you have to do is press them together and they stick. Beautiful!

The example of making a box (Fig. 8) is only here to show you the method of using slabs. It can be varied greatly. It can be combined with the coil method I'm getting to. Figure out what you want to make with slabs and build your own construction.

COIL (A LONG AND WINDING ROAD): Start with the amount of wedged clay you think you'll be using. Coils can be any thickness or length. The smaller the piece the thinner the coils, generally. Twist and roll a piece of clay in your hands until it becomes a coil the size you want. Then finish it off by rolling it with your fingers on a wet piece of canvas, a bat, or wedging table. Cover coils with a wet cloth so they won't dry out until you use them.

Coils can be joined any combination of ways. Welding is especially good if your clay is starting to dry a bit. You can also pinch the inside wall of the coil to each previous coil.

A base can be either coil or a piece of slab. If it is a coil, just wind the coil flat on the table until it reaches the size you want. Then add the first coil on top of it. To make the shape slope in, put coils slightly towards the inside edge of the previous coil. To make the form curve out, or become wider, add the next coil to the outside edge of the previous coil.

Coil work can be completely smoothed over both inside and out. The American Indians did pots that were so smoothed over that they almost look like wheel-thrown pots. Sometimes they simply left them unworked for a decorative effect. Scratching a design, with vertical and horizontal strokes on the horizontal unworked coils, produces interesting effects.

To make open coilwork pieces such as hanging lamps (so light can shine through) or a fruit bowl (so air will reach the underside of fruit), just wind coils into circles and undulations.

If you happen to like the shape of anything you have around--glass, tin can, a cottage cheese carton, or a museum piece you found in a rummage sale, you can use it as a form for open coil work. Turn it upside down.

First cover it with wet newspapers and then cover it with a lace design of balls and open circles laid out flat and joined together on the form. The top can be of one coil. Leave this until firm, but remove it from the form as soon as you can before any real shrinkage begins, which will cause it to crack.

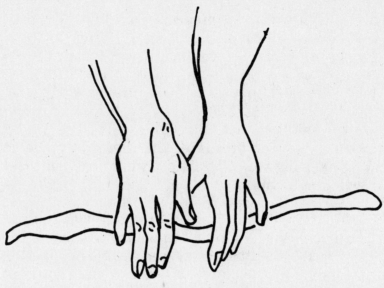

rolling out the coil

9.

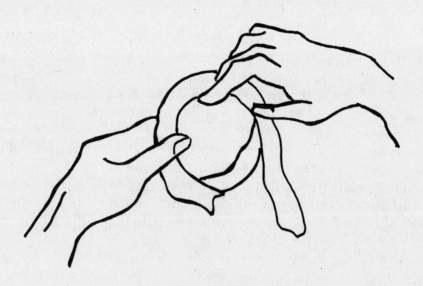

ring of coil on base

10.

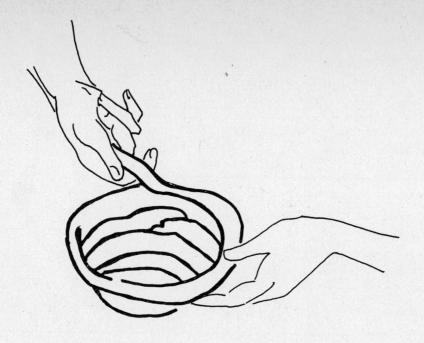

11. building the shape with
the coil

12. coils stacked

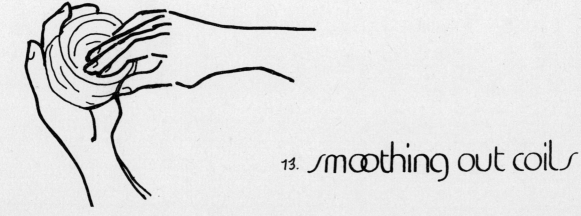

13. smoothing out coils

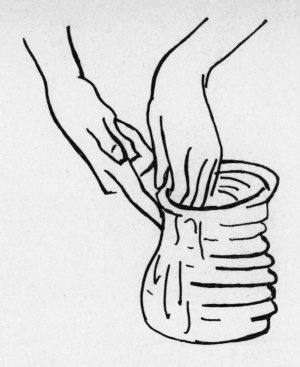

smoothing out coils
14.

open coil work
15.

REVOLUTION AT THE WHEEL

One has to have a wheel in order to do a wheel-thrown pot. When you feel the urge to start you can always find wheels in ceramic workshops. High schools usually have adult education classes that cost little--and they have the precious items necessary like wheels and kilns. There may be a private work shop going on where you can do wheel work, or maybe you have a friend who will let you use his.

There are many kinds of wheels you can make or buy. In almost any area there is usually someone who makes wheels. Individuals who make wheels advertise in craft magazines as well as the commercial factories.

Someone told me about the most ingenious self-made wheel. His friend had found a front car wheel in a junk yard with all the brakes and springs and junk attached. He dug a hole in the ground and filled it with cement. It was deep enough to push all the stuff in back of the wheel in the cement. The wheel was then in a raised horizontal position. He also took off the tire and filled it with cement for the kick wheel. After it hardened he put the wheel back on. Next he removed the hubcap and carefully filled the center part of the tire with plaster so it was level. He uses this in much the same way primitively built wheels are used: He kicks the cement wheel and gets it going the speed he wants and uses the center plaster part to throw his clay on. It is low, so one advantage is that he can stand up over it and work on very tall cylinders.

Buying a wheel involves a lot of decisions: whether you have the room for one, cost considerations, and what type you want. Assuming you have access to a wheel, I'm going to describe how to throw.

CENTERING: This is the first phase. Throw down a wedged piece of clay about the size of an orange or grapefruit. The wheelhead must be dry. Clay won't stick to wet metal. To work on a plaster bat, pour runny clay on the wheelhead, wet the bat and stick it on the wheelhead. Clay will stick better to a damp bat. The bat can later be removed from the wheel-head with the pot still on top and left to dry, which is an advantage. The orange-sized ball of clay must be thrown with enough force to make it stick. This is why working at the potter's wheel is called "throwing." Pat and push the clay to get it more on center. If the throw was way off, do it again. A small bowl of water, plus sponge, plus modeling tools should be near you. Wet your hands so there won't be any friction between your hands and the clay. Now get the wheel going at maximum speed. Brace your elbows against your body and press on the side of the lump with right hand while the left hand presses down on top. Another method of centering is to put your hands around both sides of the clay, forcing it up into a cone shape. Then press it down--up and down until you feel it is centered. No one way is the "right" way.   Whatever feels "right" for you is the way to do it.   Clay is tested to see if it's centered by supporting your arm in a stable position and holding a pencil toward the spinning clay.   Your hand and arm are rigid. When the pencil lightly touches the spinning clay wall, watch to see if the pencil jumps on the edge.   If so, the clay is not on center.

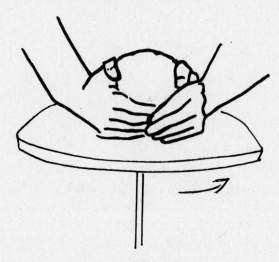

centering the clay on the wheel

16.

OPENING AND RAISING: The speed of the wheel is slightly slower than in centering.   Both thumbs are pressed straight down in the center of the clay lump.   Don't press all the way through the bottom.   You need clay there when you build the foot.

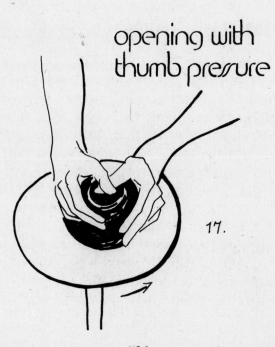

opening with thumb pressure

17.

18.

raising the wall

Thumbs move toward the fingers which are on the outside. Place your left knuckle or fingers outside the pot. Push in and up. With the inside fingers of your right hand press outward and up the wall opposite your outside fingers. Try to make the walls thin but not so thin they will collapse. Also, try for straightness. You will discover the whole thing is pressure and sensitivity to what is happening. If the wall goes out too much, choke in, use both hands on the outside to force it in. A bottle is made this way.

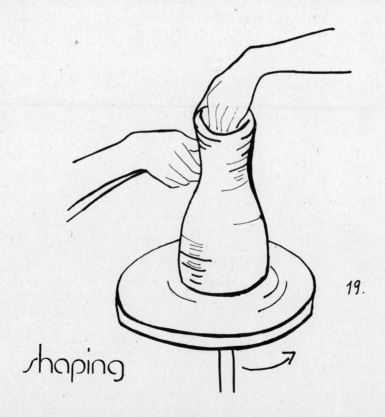

19.

shaping

removing excess
water

20.

A bowl is made by more pressure on the inside. Sponge off excess water.
Use a sponge attached to a stick for inside cylinders (the wheel is kept going
when you do this no matter how slowly). Too much water weakens the clay.

If the top is uneven, don't worry. This is common. With the wheel
going slowly, cut it off using a pointed tool. Finish with a piece of paper
towel or sponge. The walls can be smoothed with a sponge instead of
fingers.

While the wheel is still turning, trim off excess clay from around the
bottom of the pot with a wooden tool.

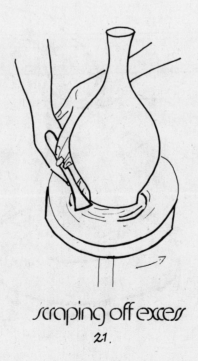

scraping off excess
21.

132

Remove the piece from the wheelhead by running a wire between the pot and wheelhead. If you use a bat, simply remove both bat and pot at the same time. Put it away to get leather-hard. Then you can begin to finish the bottom--or foot.

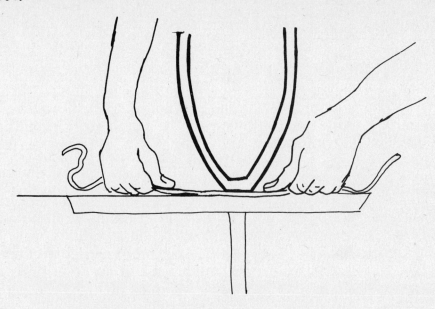

22. removing pot by passing wire under

23. shaping base

FOOT RIM: When the pot is firm enough to be turned upside down on the wheelhead, make the pencil test to center it. To secure the pot, support the rim with small globs of clay. Wire loop tools are used to get the rim going. Press the tool down slowly until strings of clay are cut away leaving a raised area. Hands should be supported above the working area on some kind of rest to keep steady (Fig. 23).

SOME MISCELLANEOUS NUMBERS

A thrown pot is symmetrical and it's round. If you want to flatten the sides, press a board against either three or four sides. Paddling the sides with a textured surface of board into a square form is one variation. Corners can be raised by squeezing with fingers or the edge can be smoothed over.

Handles are usually made after the rim. The area on the pot where the handle is to set is dampened with a sponge, and a piece of wet cloth is laid on that part. A pulled handle is one that is drawn or pulled vertically from a lump of clay. Then it is bent over to form a half circle. It stiffens in ten or twenty minutes. The part to be used is pinched off. To attach: score the pot with a fork where it is to be fitted. Then use some slip. Blend it into body with your fingers. If you need more clay around the joints, a small coil can be worked in. When merging clay together, keep one hand braced inside of the pot pressing outward against any pressure on the outside. This prevents distortion. A handle can also be cut from a slab and hand shaped.

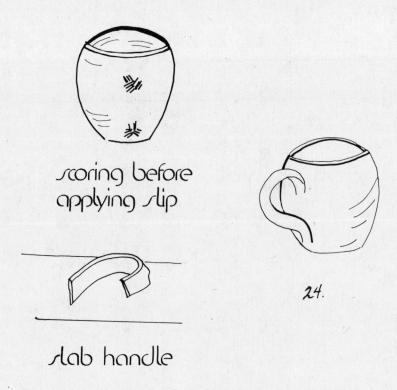

scoring before
applying slip

24.

slab handle

A simple pitcher-like spout is made by pressing with both hands on the outside of the pot towards the area for the spout. While one hand is pinching the side together, the other is pulling out the spout at the edge with a finger so that it has a downward curve leading outward.

THE END—BUT ONLY THE BEGINNING

Go to the museums. If you go on weekdays the vibrations you get from items there are strongest. These good vibes are not being absorbed by all the bulk of body weight on the weekends!

Worrying about being influenced is a waste of time if not a vanity. Rather than have a sense of bad design, I think it's best to hit the museums and absorb the best. Roger Fry's Last Lectures is in paperback now and is the best thing I've read on sensitivity and vitality in art works. In the section called Vitality he says, "But the pride of the craftsman as such will always urge the suppression of sensibility in an art-object." That's a heavy thought but also a liberating one if you want to concentrate on developing your sensibility, as much as developing your craft.

BOOKS

J. B. Kenny. The Complete Book of Pottery Making. Chilton House. $7.50. The longest sections are devoted to molds. It gives some glaze and clay formulas.

Bernard Leach. A Potter's Book. Transatlantic Arts. $8.75

Daniel Rhodes. Clay and Glazes for the Potter. Chilton House. $7.50. Included are many formulas for earthenware, stoneware, and porcelain bodies.

Daniel Rhodes. Kilns. Chilton House. $10.

Weaving

Sandy Sprinkling

Weaving is a groove if you love color and texture. And if you love allegory it's even better. History and mythology are full of weaving metaphor: "the warp and weft of life," "the tapestry of history," . . . You dip into a very old and deep stream of human experience when you get into weaving, not to mention the fact that you will make beautiful things to use and look at.

This chapter is an introduction to very simple kinds of weaving. If you really get "hooked" you can look into more complex weaving processes such as are done on floor and table looms. You will find plenty of good literature available on those subjects.

I got into weaving the hard way: first I learned how to use a floor loom, then a table loom. After I bought my own floor loom I had to wait several months for delivery and, at that point, I looked into what could be done with simpler materials. I found that essentially the same activity goes on with all looms: yarn is strung back and forth in parallels across a space or board as "warp," and yarn is picked over and under the warp threads as "weft" or "woof" (Fig. 1). Different combinations of warp

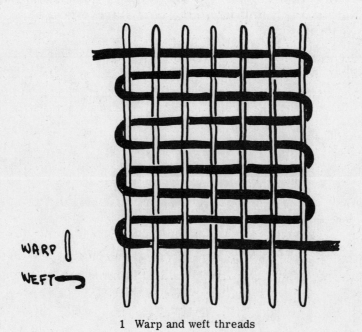

WARP

WEFT

1 Warp and weft threads

threads can be picked up to make patterns and textures in great variety. Several looms are described here: cardboard, frames, board, and frozen warp. A few basic weaves are introduced to start you on your way.

I've used the looms introduced here mainly to make small tapestries or wall hangings. You can try these out, making "samplers" to get the feel of weaving. Consider that each method you explore opens the way to hundreds of variations. Besides being a craft with which to make useful and durable items, weaving is a plastic art and needs loving attention to line, texture, form, color, filled and open space, and materials.

As for rules, well, anything you love and find works out, goes; you will find that if it doesn't work it will probably fall apart. Experiment. If you don't like what you're doing, tear it apart and start over. Be a perfectionist and you sharpen your tools and your perception, and your experience as well as your product will be of high quality.

CARDBOARD LOOM / BASIC WEAVES / USE OF EQUIPMENT

The first piece of equipment that you need is a piece of cardboard-- shirt cardboard, illustration board, or chipboard. Chipboard is a special cardboard that is flexible and strong. It comes in different weights, so you have a choice, but I recommend the medium. Art-supply stores usually sell it. You also need yarn, a large tapestry or stole needle, scissors, ruler, pencil, a wide-toothed comb and a long, narrow, flat stick or bamboo skewer.

A cardboard loom is a small project, and a small investment. You can use leftover yarn you haven't finished off in knitting, crocheting, or rug hooking projects. And cardboard is readily available in the form of shirt boxes, cereal boxes, cardboard boxes, etc. Cut a piece from any cardboard box you have around. It shouldn't be too much larger than 8 by 10 inches, or 10 by 12 inches; anything bigger gets unwieldy. The finished project will be about one inch smaller all around than the dimensions of the board.

If you want a symmetrical piece of weaving, measure off half-inch or quarter-inch intervals along the top and bottom of the cardboard. These will be the points at which the warp will be wound; the space between intervals that you have chosen will determine the density (closeness of weave) of your piece. Warp threads that are very close together will produce a closely woven piece, and those farther apart will produce an open weave. Warp intervals of one inch or wider will result in weaving that may be too loose to hold together; quarter-inch to half-inch spaces are best for this size piece. If you want to cover the warp with the weft, use larger spaces between warps. If you want the warp to be part of the overall design, use close warps.

Cut notches (V's) about a quarter-inch deep at each point you've marked. Slit the first and last notch on all four corners of the cardboard so that the ends of the warp yarn will not slip out easily.

The best yarns to use for this and most of the projects following are any of the softer wools and knitting worsteds. I don't recommend tapestry wool because it isn't very resilient, and elasticity is an important quality of weaving yarn. Also, weaving uses up quite a lot of yarn, and tapestry wool comes in very small quantities.

The cardboard is prepared and you have the wools with which to begin warping the loom. Make a knot on the end of the yarn and slide the knot into the upper lefthand notch, pulling the yarn down into the slit. The knot should be flush with the back of the cardboard, where it should remain secure. Wind your yarn around the cardboard from the top to the bottom notch, around the back to the next top notch and down again, wedging the yarn firmly into the notches. On the front of the cardboard you should be forming parallel vertical lines of yarn. Don't pull the yarn tight; it should be firm but not stretched, as it will then bend the cardboard and "kill" the yarn. The weaving process tightens the warp as you go. A general rule to bear in mind throughout your weaving is to keep everything looser than you think it should be. This seems to be one of the most difficult operations in weaving to remember. In teaching I found I had to remind students over and over again to "keep loose." So if I keep mentioning it, it's because you'll probably keep forgetting it. Tuck the end of the warping yarn into the last slitted notch and it should remain secure.

Thread a long or short tapestry or stole needle with a foot or two of yarn--you must use a blunt-tipped needle so that you don't split or pierce the warp threads. You can find these needles at a good notions counter or in shops that deal in needlecraft supplies. If you don't want to bother with a needle use your fingers.

With your threaded needle go over the first warp thread, under the second, over the third, under the fourth, and so on. Don't pull the yarn tight! Leave at least three inches of yarn before the first warps, and, if you've used yarn only a bit longer than the warp is wide, leave at least three inches after the last warps at the end also. These ends will be woven into the back of the fabric when the piece is complete and will strengthen the edges (selvages).

The next row of weaving is alternate to the first, the weft going under the warp thread previously gone over (Fig. 2). The third row should repeat the first row, the fourth row repeats the second, and so on. This "over one, under one" is called Tabby, or Plain weave. Once you get into the rhythm of the weave, experiment with different weight yarns, adding beads or whatever turns you on. Most important of all, enjoy, and let your

138

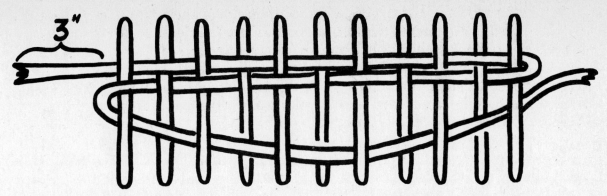

2 Tabby or Plain weave

mind run loose (like the yarn!).

I repeat, don't pull the yarn tight across the warp, as natural as it may seem. This can only lead to distortion of the selvages (side edges) and pinched, tight weaves whose textures and subtle patterns are lost. Stay loose and the resultant piece will be plush and the patterns will lie together naturally, softly. To help achieve this, what is called "bubbling" is done with the weft yarn: arch the weft yarn across each row so it is longer than the row is wide and push it with a wide-toothed comb or your fingers against the preceding row. This action is called beating in, and the comb, or whatever you use, is the reed or beater. An Afro comb is an excellent beater, though any wide-toothed comb can be used. A kitchen fork works, too, and so do your fingers. Both beating in and bubbling the weft are universally

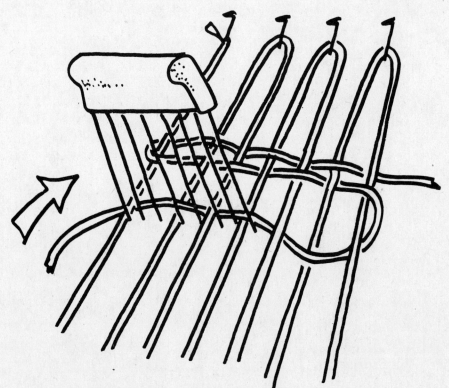

3 Beating in the weft

done in weaving whatever the size or complexity of the loom. If you want the warp to show through--that is, to be part of the design--beat loosely. If the warp is to be completely covered, beat harder. Try both ways to see which suits the yarn weight and your requirements best. As mentioned earlier, you must suit the warp intervals to the weave--that is, for a covered warp, greater intervals between warp threads; for warp as part of the overall design, lesser intervals.

While weaving, you must pull up the warp yarn that you have passed the weft under to avoid splitting or piercing the warp (which can lead to all sorts of problems, such as inability to beat the weft down, weakening the warp yarn, and so forth). To insure the safety of the warp yarn, and, incidentally, to make life easier for you, you can do this with a narrow flat stick, a narrow ruler, tongue depressor, one of those flat sticks that you find in some clothespin packages holding them together, or a bamboo skewer. Whatever you decide to use, it should be longer than the warp is wide. I've tried them all and, depending on the yarn and what I'm doing, each has proved to be useful. The bamboo skewers are handy for a lot of things. I buy them in markets that carry Oriental foods. Next time you buy sesame oil, pick up a bundle of skewers. They're also good for staking up philo-dendrons or as spare knitting needles. I understand they're even good for skewering.

4 Use of a shed stick

Using the skewer (or stick) as if it were the weft, pass it under and over the warp, sliding it straight across the width of the warp. (If you like the way it looks, leave it there as part of the weaving!) Pull the skewer up and away from the cardboard to form an opening through which you can easily pass the weft without damaging the warp yarn with the needle. The space or opening that is formed this way is referred to as the shed. Any stick that is used to make this opening is called the shed stick. A flat stick, when used as a shed stick, may be turned on its side, leaving both hands free to pass the weft through. You must remove and replace the shed stick for each row of weaving, since the weft goes over and under different warps each time; however, you can leave one stick in for one shed permanently, and that will save having to go over and under for one of the two openings. Just flatten it. Then insert another shed stick to make the second opening. Bubble the weft after the stick is in place, remove, if necessary, and beat the yarn into place. Such is the weaving process.

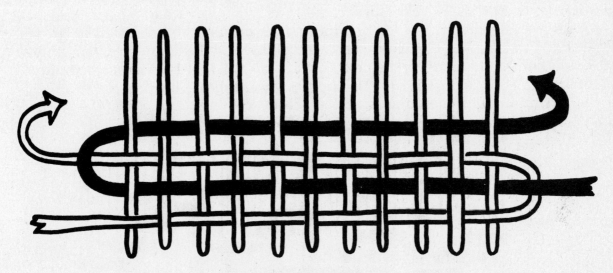

5 Vertical stripe Tabby weave

There are many variations of the Tabby weave. One is the weaving of horizontal stripes. You simply change colors of the weft yarn every few rows of weaving. A vertical stripe in tabby is possible also. Thread two tapestry needles with two colors, weave "over one, under one" (Tabby) all the way across the warp with one of the colors, leaving a three-inch excess as usual. With the second color, weave Tabby beginning at the side of the warp where the preceding weft ended (Fig. 5). Repeat, weaving every other row with the same color. The same color weft will always cover the same warp threads in alternate rows and, if you do enough of them, you will discover you have vertical stripes. Follow the diagram carefully, being especially aware of how the ends of the wefts loop over or under the next. This alternate color tabby is a technique used in native weaving all over the world.

Tabby is by no means the only weave available to a prospective weaver. Barely introduced here are basket-weave, twill, knotting, and wrapping. Each will lead you to fantastic discoveries, I'm sure. By passing the weft over two warp threads and under two, and so on, reversing each second row by going under the two that have been gone over previously, you will produce a basket-weave.

Twill is a strong, attractive weave commonly used in the production of yardage for clothing and upholstery. There are hundreds of variations possible and, when used for small pieces on the looms described here, they can add good surface excitement: diagonals, herringbones, arrows, zigzags. If you follow the diagram for the basic twill technique very carefully (Fig. 6), you should be able to get the knack of it with a little practice. The diagram does not show the weft that passes under the warp; the weft drawn is just that which passes <u>over</u> the warp (the spaces being the weft <u>under</u> the warp). Every two warps are passed over and under until the width of the warp is covered. The second row is shifted over one warp, then two warps are covered over, the next two under, and so on, until four rows, each shifted over one more than the last, complete the pattern. The lower design in Figure 6 can be made by weaving four rows and then reversing the pattern for the next four. Try twill with contrasting colors for background and pattern. Background would be Tabby. A great many of the variations in woven material are achieved by taking up different combinations of warp threads.

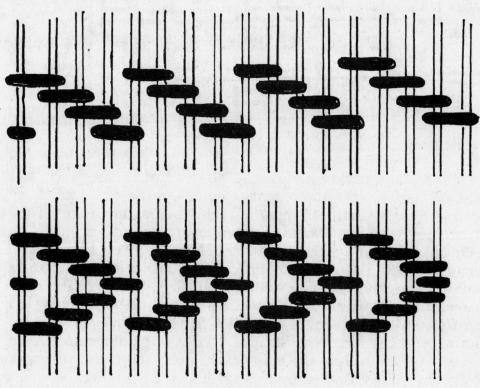

6 Twill weave

Soumak weave is one of the wrapped-warp techniques and provides an interesting contrast to the preceding weaves. Tie the weft yarn onto the first warp thread on the left side of the loom. You don't need a shed stick for this weave, as each warp is covered in each row. Pass the weft over the second warp, turn under the same warp and over to the next warp and repeat. Soumak can also be made by going over four warp threads and back under two of them. You are actually encircling the warp with the weft, and this weave is similar to the stem stitch in embroidery. If you wish to have the Soumak weave's diagonal texture run in the same direction in succes-

7 Soumak weave

sive rows, weave alternate rows of Soumak and Tabby (first row Tabby, second row Soumak, third Tabby, and so forth). Soumak is a very sturdy weave and is used extensively for rugs. It can also take on many faces without any variation in technique. By using soft, elastic wool you will develop a flat and linear weave; if a springier, stiffer yarn is used it will produce a raised coil-like weave.

The Rya knot or Giordes knot is another way of wrapping the warp. It is used in a type of Scandinavian rug weaving where a strong plush pile with graduations and soft blendings of color are characteristic. It can be used as pile, long or short, or loops if you don't cut between the knots. There <u>must</u> be several (two or more) rows of Tabby between each row of knots or they will not hold. These knots are best done on closely spaced warp threads. Upon completion of the areas you want to cover, clip the crest of each loop for a pile or fringe texture, or leave loops. Very, very long fringe as a part of the design, with beads or even macrame decoration, can be quite beautiful when combined with plain flat weaves and different heights of knots.

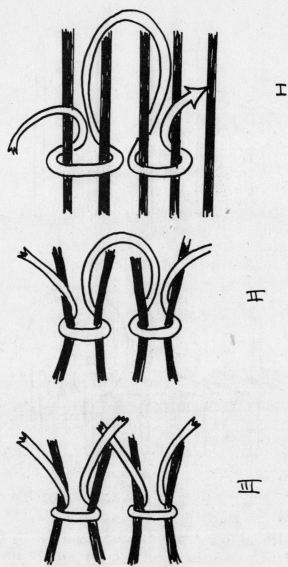

8 Rya or Giordes knot

So far we've covered weaving with wefts from one side to the other, and there are many possibilities for further exploration. Making forms with color, adding color, developing different shapes within the piece, all add to the surface excitement of the basic weaves.

To weave wide vertical stripes, of the same or different widths (vertical being the direction of the warps, horizontal being the direction of the wefts), follow Figure 9. Pass each weft yarn over the other as in the diagram and weave in opposite directions beneath the row where the joint was made. This is called Interlocking. Repeat this each time you wish the colors to join. This can also be done for shapes that aren't geometrical, by joining the colors at the edge of the shape to be filled. You need to work with two needles--or bobbins (a half skewer with yarn wound round) if your piece is big enough to warrant carrying more yarn than you can put in a needle. Actually, if you have three or four colors going across one row, you need a needle or bobbin for each color. In Figure 4, I am using a bobbin.

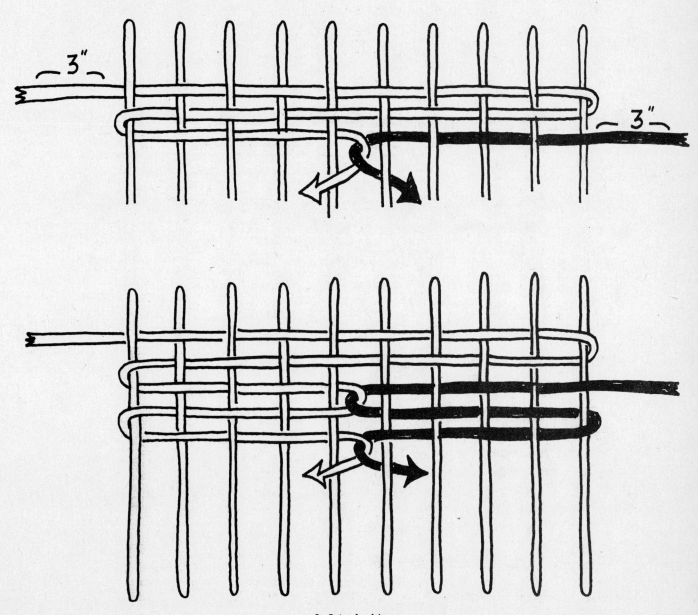

9 Interlocking

Another way of working with separate color areas is the Slit-tapestry technique. This is a very ancient method used for rugs and textiles as well as tapestries. The two color areas fall adjacent to each other but do not join. This technique also works as a part of a design within areas of a single color. Follow Figure 10 carefully, being certain that the two colors meet on the same weft row. Each must continue in pattern as the same weft. Note how the second color (left) maintains the "under, over" pattern of the first color as if it were the same weft. Slits can be opened for a different effect by pulling the weft tighter on each side of the slit (an exception to the general "keep loose" rule!). Holes and open patterns can be achieved with this technique. If you want to use slits within the same color area, you will still need two or more needles or bobbins for each area.

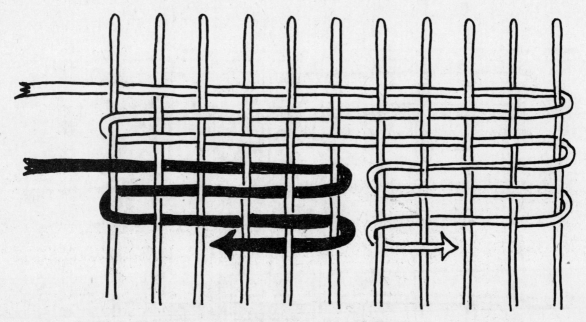

10 Slit-tapestry technique

For the looms described here you can easily fill in one shape or area at a time by using the Dovetail technique shown in Figure 11. (When using a floor loom you won't have the luxury of being able to fill in one shape at a time, as the woven section is rolled up as you weave, and each row must be completed before going on to the next.) A gradual diagonal can be achieved with this method of joining colors, as shown in Figure 11B; a more extreme one appears in Figure 11A.

All of the techniques and weaves covered so far should be experimented with freely, and you should cater to your whims. If it doesn't work, you won't like it, or it will fall apart, or both. That shouldn't be considered a loss--you've learned something.

11 Dovetail
technique

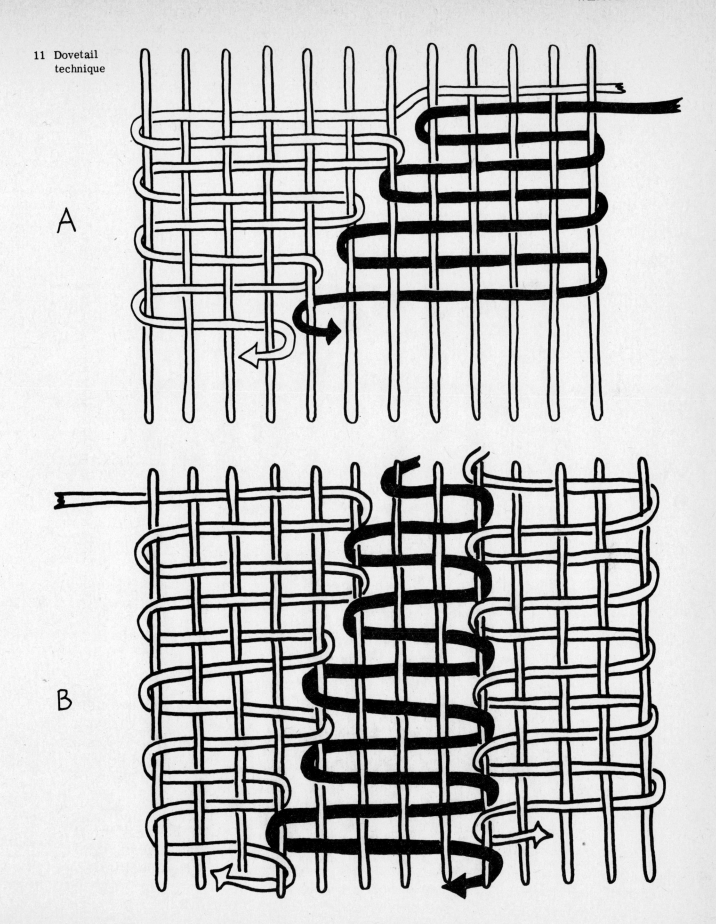

A

B

To remove the piece you've finished from the cardboard, turn it over and cut the warps in the middle for fringe that will be of equal length on both top and bottom, or cut shorter on top or bottom as you prefer. See Finishing and Hanging below for special touches. Turn the piece over and with a tapestry needle or crochet hook tuck and weave in the ends. If you like them hanging out--leave them!

BOARD LOOM

The method of warping is the only real difference between the various looms covered here. The cardboard loom has its warp wrapped around it, front to back. The board loom has the warp wound around nails or T-pins

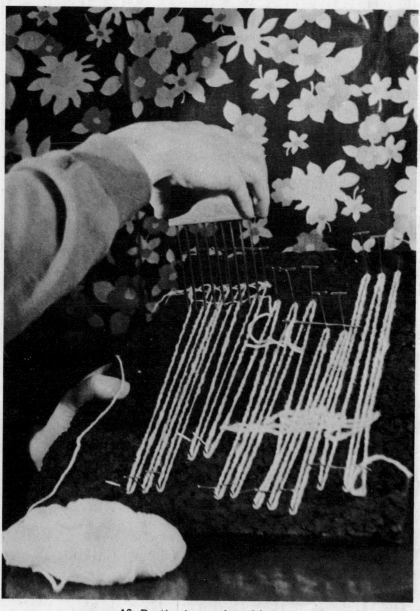

12 Beating in on a board loom

on one side of the board. For this loom you'll need a piece of cork, celatex (a thick, light fiberboard found in lumberyards), or plywood. The size of whatever you decide to use should be an easy size for you to handle. Anything larger than 18 by 24 inches will probably be too clumsy to work with. Have on hand finishing nails (if you are using plywood) or T-pins (for cork and celatex) and all the rest of the equipment listed for the cardboard loom.

You can make irregular woven shapes on a board loom, as you are free to place the pins or nails in various positions around the board (Fig. 12). T-pins can be found in macrame and art-supply stores. The pins should be pushed into the cork or celatex at a slight angle--the top of each pin pointing toward the outer edge of the board (Fig. 13). This will prevent the pins from pulling out when the warp is wound around them. Remember to place the pins close enough so that the piece will hold together when woven.

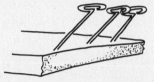

13 Angle of T-pins on a board loom

At the end of the yarn for the warp, tie a slip loop (Fig. 14) onto the first pin in the upper lefthand corner and proceed to lead the warp down to the first pin on the lower edge. Bring the warp up and around the second top pin and down, repeating and forming somewhat parallel lines, until the last pin is reached. Be sure to keep tension even and firm, not taut. Tie a thumb knot (Fig. 15) around the last pin, and it should keep the warp secure. To change or adjust the warp threads, pull the pins out and place them elsewhere. Do it now, it'll be difficult later. Weave on!

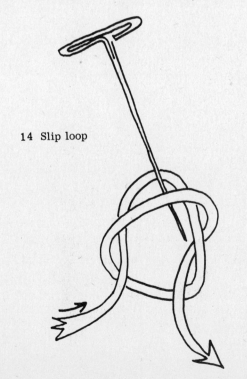

14 Slip loop

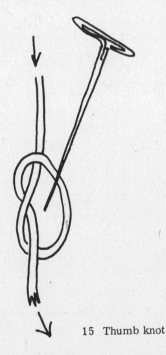

15 Thumb knot

Remove the finished piece from the board loom by pulling the pins, or sliding over the nails if you're using a plywood board. Weave all excess ends into the back with a tapestry needle and finish the top and bottom as you like (see Finishing and Hanging).

FRAME LOOM

To warp a frame loom you must first have a frame--either one you've nailed together from lumber scraps (1 by 2 inch board is good), an old picture frame, or canvas stretcher bars that come in different lengths and are sold in art-supply stores. The last are quite easy to put together but are not rigid, so you might need some kind of reinforcing at the corners to keep the rectangle from going askew. Finishing nails (nails with small heads), a hammer, yarn, beater, shed stick, scissors, needle, and whatever else you'll be using for the actual weaving complete the list of supplies.

Hammer nails in a row along the top and bottom of the frame, as close together or far apart as you want, remembering you want the piece to hold together; it's probably best at a quarter-to a half-inch apart. The warp is wrapped over the opening in the frame, so there should be at least two inches of space between the two side warps and the inner edges of the loom (frame) so you'll have room to work in, begin nails at that point. Hammer nails at a slight angle away from the center opening so the warp won't slide off the frame when wrapped around them.

Tie a slip loop on the first upper lefthand nail (as done on the T-pin on a board loom) and wrap the warp carefully, following Figure 16. Keep the tension even and firm. End the warp with a thumb knot (Fig. 15) around the last nail reached. You are now ready to weave, and the weaving process is the same, though the loom is slightly different. On this loom you will be more aware of the open space you cover or weave around, and the loom itself is lighter in weight.

Remove the piece from the frame loom by sliding it off the nails. Do not cut, as there will be no way of holding in the end rows of weaving if you have woven right to the nails top and bottom. If you want fringe top and/or bottom, keep the weaving in the center of the frame, slip the warp off the nails, and then cut the loops. Knot to hold as described in the finishing and hanging section below. Weave in excess weft ends.

A frame loom with a laced-in beam is a device for weaving a hanging bar right in as a part of the design. To do this you'll need a frame (stretchers, lumber scraps) about three inches wider all around than the size of the piece you wish to complete. (Actually, I usually match the size of the piece I'm weaving with available frames, or boards, or whatever.) Other supplies are yarn, a dowel or twig, or whatever you want to weave in as your hanging bar (which must be shorter than the width of the frame),

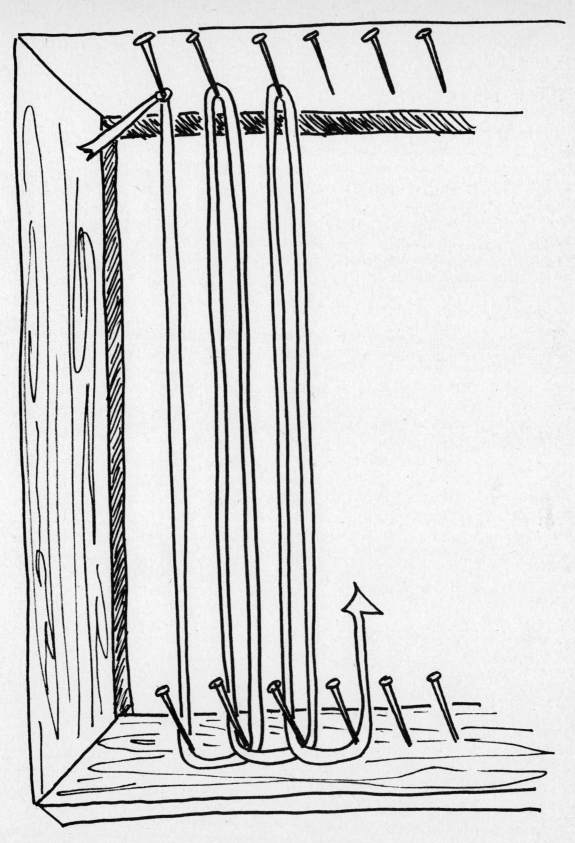

16 Warping a frame loom

and beater, shed stick, needles, as for the other looms. In addition, you will need a chair or two to wind the warp around.

Measure the height of your frame. Then look for a chair, or two chairs, doorknobs, two C-clamps (hardware store items), around which the yarn can be wound the same length as the frame height, and slipped off easily. Begin wrapping the yarn for warp around the back of the chair, circling it half the times the number of warp threads you'll need (each complete circle around the chair back will make two warp threads). The way to determine how many warp threads you want is the width of your piece--that is, if you should want it 10 inches wide, with warps a quarter-inch apart, you will have 4 warps per inch, or 40 warp threads or ends. Wind carefully-- even, firm tension is more difficult to achieve when winding a warp in this way. When finished, slide the yarn off the chair and slip the dowel or twig (referred to as the beam) into the loops of uncut yarn at one end, allowing the yarn to hang from it.

Another piece of yarn three or four times as long as the length of the beam will be used for attaching or lacing the beam to the frame. Tie a slip loop (Fig. 14) onto the lefthand end of the beam--the warp still hanging from it. Distribute the warp yarn over the beam evenly. It's probably a good idea to do this with the frame lying flat on a table so you won't lose the warp by having it slide off the beam. Gravity is a basic problem here. Lace the length of yarn over the frame and under the beam carefully, following the diagram (Fig. 17), suspending the beam two or three inches beneath the frame. Separate the warp threads at fairly even intervals between lacing points. This procedure is done so the beam will be stable and suspended between the frame sides for weaving and the finished piece will hang without distorting or slipping to one side. The space between the beam and the top of the frame can be adjusted for tension. As you weave, the warp gets tighter, so you may want to loosen it; or, if it is very stretchy yarn, you may want to tighten it. Make another slip loop at the end of the lacing on the beam.

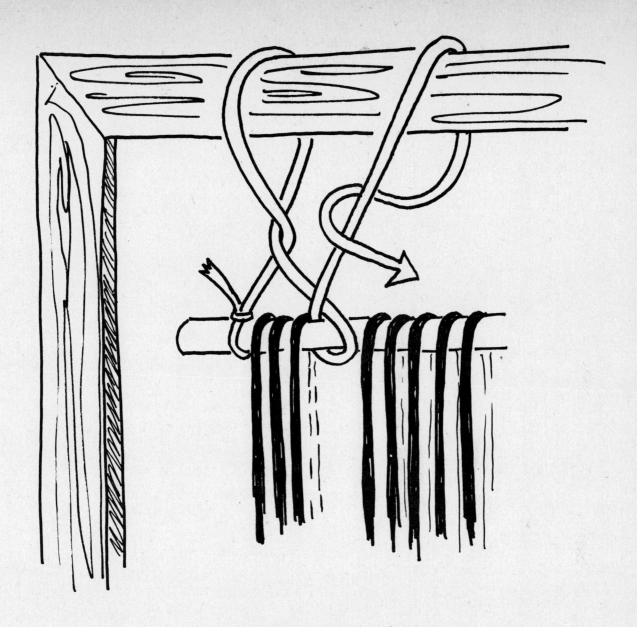

17 Lacing a beam to a frame loom

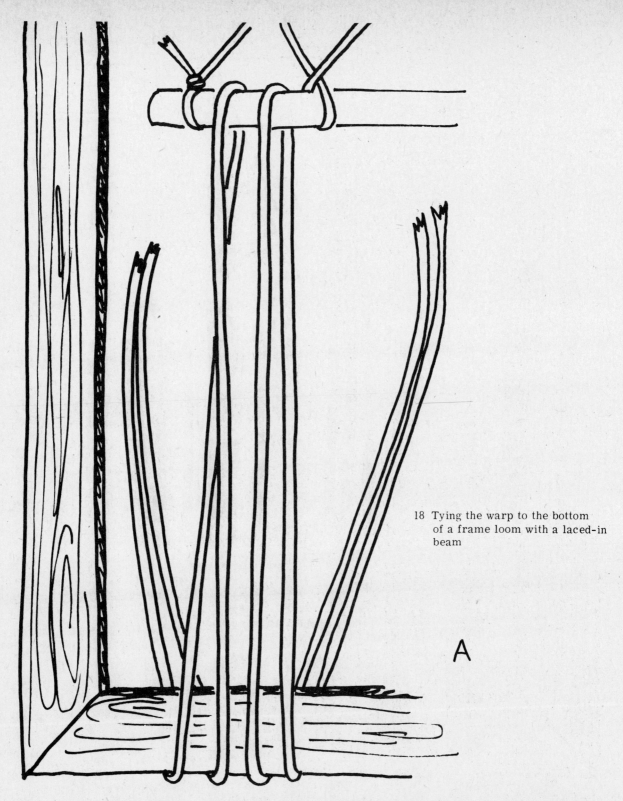

18 Tying the warp to the bottom
of a frame loom with a laced-in
beam

A

Now that the beam has been suspended from the frame, and the warp threads have been distributed over the beam at even intervals, clip the bottom loops of the warp. Bring all the warp threads (ends) forward over the front of the frame. Separate them into bundles so that they will be evenly

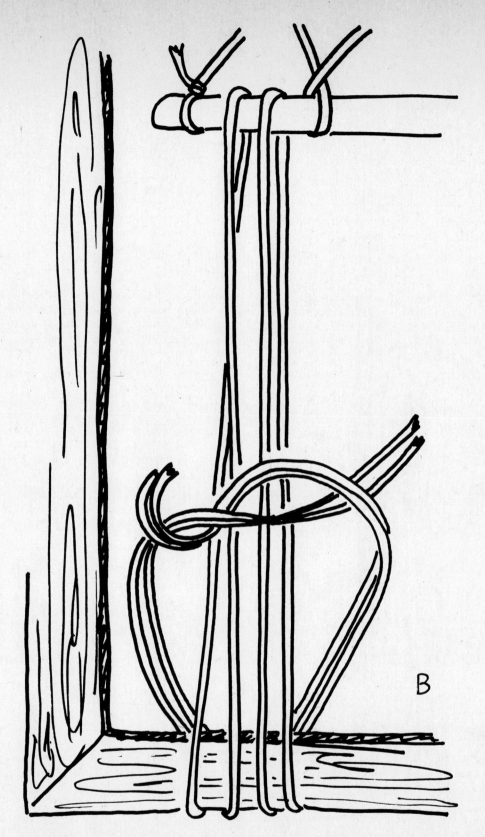

B

placed over the bottom of the frame. They can be the same bunches separated by the lacing on the beam. Take each bunch and wrap it around the bottom to the back of the frame, dividing the bunch in two at the back. Following the steps in Figure 18 <u>A</u> through <u>D</u>, tie knots, as described, close to

155

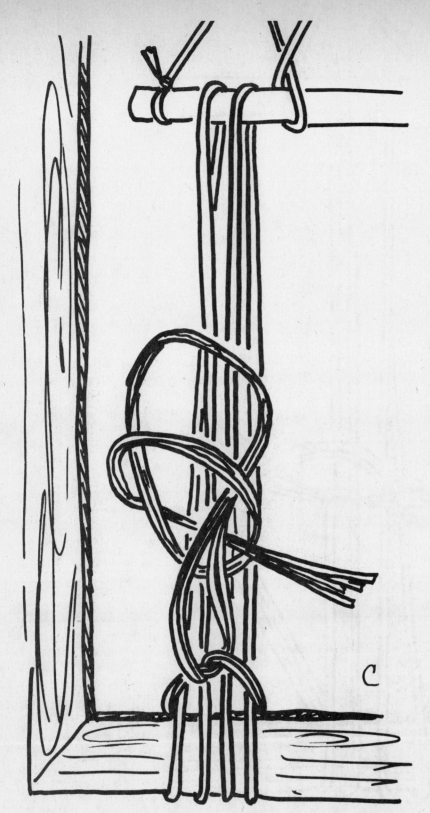

C

the frame at the bottom. These knots (slip knots, or half-bows) are used
so that when the piece is finished they are easily loosened. The overall tension can be adjusted by loosening or tightening the lacing on the beam; the
tension on individual threads can be adjusted by retying these knots.

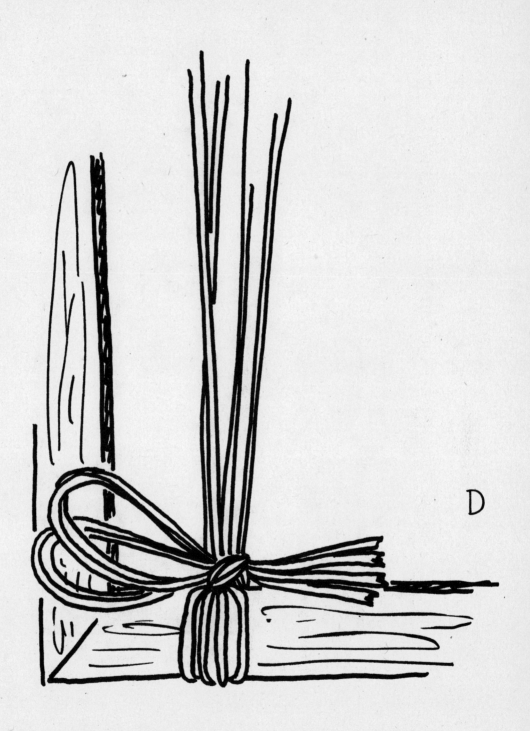

D

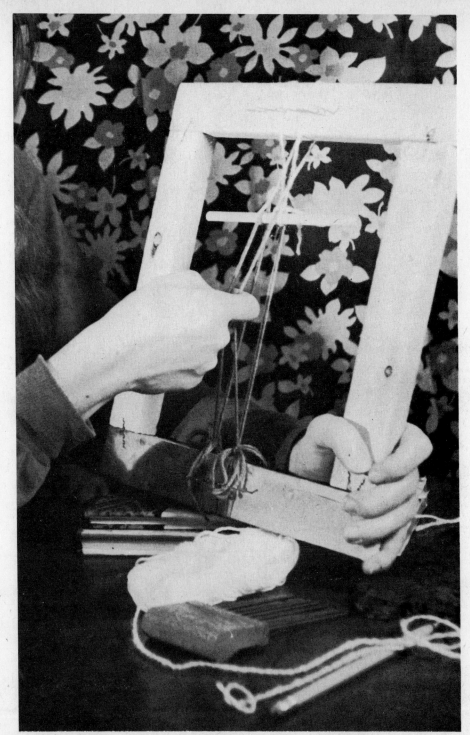

19 Warped frame loom with a laced-in beam. Notice the space
   between warps; these will be brought together by twining
   first weft

When each bunch has been securely tied to the bottom of the frame, the
warp threads are spread evenly over the beam and evenly across the bottom.
You will notice that the beam has divided (spread) the warps forming spaces
(Fig. 19). Closing these gaps by pulling the warps till they are more nearly

20 Doubling a length of yard across a frame loom with laced-in
beam in preparation for twining

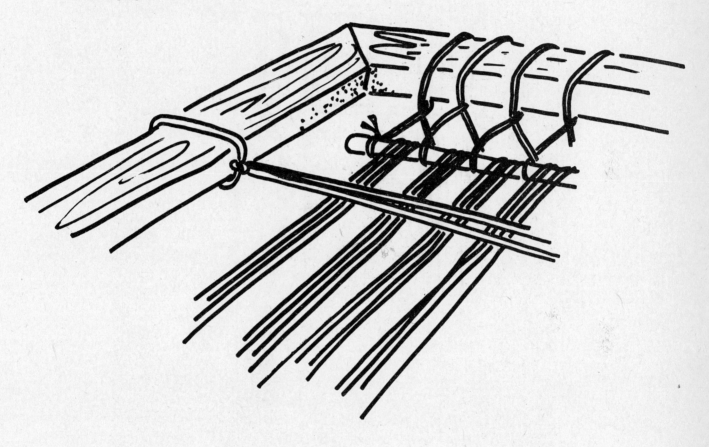

parallel will make the weaving neater. Twining (another wrapped-warp
weave) will bring the warp threads that are behind the beam forward and
place them all on the same level or plane. Take a piece of yarn at least
twice the width of the frame. This will be woven into the top of the piece,
so plan it as a part of the design. Double the yarn around the lefthand side
of the frame and tie both ends into a square knot very close to the inner
edge of the frame (Fig. 20). Pull both ends over the warp so they lie
straight across it, and determine where you want to start your weaving
(right up close to the beam or with a space between the weaving and the
beam). Slide the yarn up to the point where you will start, and proceed to

twine the yarn around the warp threads. Follow Figure 21 and work the weave straight across the warp, tying the two ends to the frame on the other side. Pull the weft threads tight every six or seven warps and be sure they are evenly spaced, or spaced as you want them. Once you've tightened them it's very difficult to realign the warp, as I've found out, without redoing the whole row.

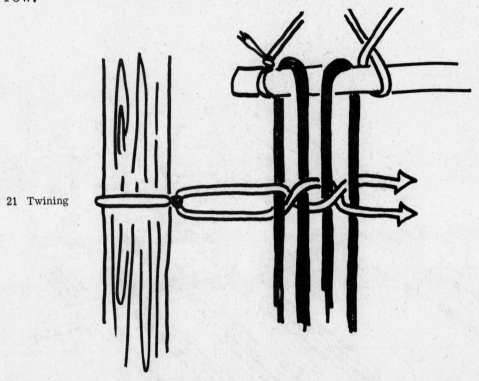

21 Twining

If you will be using a lot of one kind of yarn try using a bobbin (as mentioned before, a half-skewer, pencil, orangewood stick--with yarn wound round it). Use it as you would a tapestry needle by unwinding enough yarn to go across the warp, and pass the bobbin through the shed. This is also a good way to keep the yarns you're using in order.

Untie the slip knots along the bottom of the frame and finish however you'd like. Unlace the top lacing, attach a cord for hanging, and hang the piece up.

FROZEN WARP METHOD

The frozen warp method is a way of weaving without a loom. This technique eliminates the loom by incorporating the tension that a loom would produce into the warp itself. This is done by stiffening the warp with a white glue solution before weaving. The possibilities this technique offers are virtually unlimited and tremendously exciting. The weaver can produce unique shapes, even work in three dimensions or on freestanding pieces, without the use of outside support.

22 Sandy with a frozen warp piece

Relatively little equipment is needed for working a frozen warp. A bottle of white glue, which can be bought in almost any hardware, houseware, department, or art-supply store. Groceries sometimes carry it, too. Along with this--yarn, string, scissors, push pins, needles, a big pan or bowl, and a piece of strong cardboard (heavy clipboard's the best) or plywood, half again as big as your piece—are all that's necessary.

Mix approximately ten parts glue with one part water in a bowl or pan. Wrap the warp (string, cord, yarn) around the back of a chair or chairs (see the earlier section on frame looms with wrapped warps for more detailed instructions). Slide it off the back of the chair and dip it into the glue solution, mushing it around until it is completely soaked. I usually do frozen warps outside or in a studio, so I don't mind the mess, but you can cover your floor with newspaper, or a painter's dropcloth for protection. Remove the warp from the glue solution and spread it out on the cardboard or hang it on the wall (which you have previously protected with newspapers, I hope). Arrange the wet warp in any shape you want, leaving spaces and areas to weave in. Try to maintain some parallel warp threads for strength and diversity from the open spaces. Allow the warp to dry.

When the warp is dry, it will be stiff and you can weave all over it. Throw yourself into it. Use colors that you love, try some textured yarns. The finished piece can be very expressionistic and exciting. When you are finished weaving, hang it up.

The choice of a loom is mostly a matter of individual preference. However, the board loom and frozen warp are freer, more expressive methods, while the frame and cardboard looms are more suitable for traditional weaves, patterns, and shapes.

FINISHING AND HANGING

After your weaving is completed remove the piece from the loom-- whichever loom you've chosen. Cut the warp at the back of the cardboard, if you've used a cardboard loom. Pull the T-pins or slip the piece off the nails, if you've used a board or frame loom. Untie knots and undo the lacing of the frame loom with wrapped warp.

Fringes are most usual on woven pieces. If you want fringes on pieces woven on the board or frame looms, you'll need to attach them after you remove the piece. Use the macrame mounting knot (Fig. 23) for attaching fringe. Otherwise, of course, the fringe is just the unwoven warp. Some way of keeping the weft from sliding off the warp must be devised. Beads can be slid up to the weft and knotted in place, macrame knots can be used and are very beautiful as part of woven pieces. A common knot (Fig. 24) is a simple, effective way to finish the piece. What is most important is that the finishing should be an integral part of the design of the weaving as well as hold the weft in place. Try different methods.

The wrapped-warp method of weaving has a built-in hanging rod, and you can also add a hanging rod (or rods, to top and bottom) to pieces made in other ways. One method is to take the warps hanging from the top of the piece and tie the ends around a rod (dowel, stick, branch, or whatever).

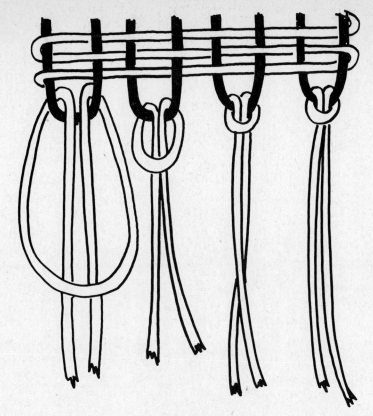

23 Attaching fringe

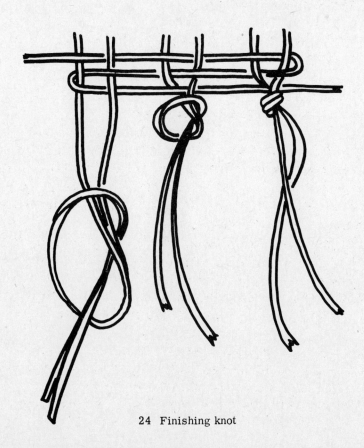

24 Finishing knot

It's a bit tricky to get all the knots even, so the stick hangs in properly, but keep at it and you will get good at it.

To apply a hanging rod to a piece woven on a board loom or frame loom, don't clip the warp loops at the top (after slipping them off the frame). Lay a dowel, or whatever, along the top of the loops and, one at a time, tie the loops to the bar with another cord (Fig. 25). Don't clip these loops if you have woven right up to them--the loops hold in the weaving.

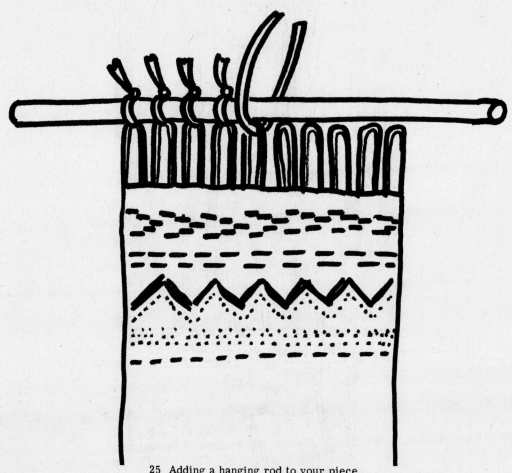

25 Adding a hanging rod to your piece

Most of all, you must use your imagination and sense of design to determine how your piece will best be displayed; there are no rules--if it works, use it.

PROBLEMS

If your weaving exhibits any of the following characteristics then you might consider tearing it apart and starting again. These are all typical mistakes, but if the mistake works as design you might want to keep it. The fabric strength will be diminished by most mistakes, so don't fall into sloppy habits and pass off their effects as "art."

SHRINKING SELVAGES (edges or sides). This comes from pulling the weft too tight. The yarn should be bubbled loosely and beaten into place more carefully.

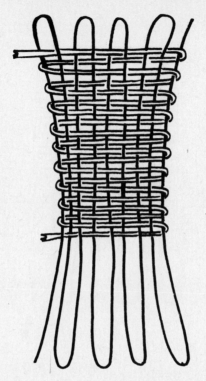

BULGING SELVAGES. The weft is too loose. It should be wrapped against and around the end warp threads, leaning comfortably. Each row should maintain the same tension if even edges are desired.

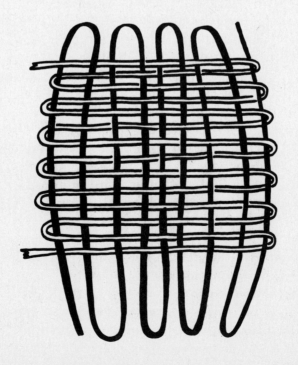

<u>WOBBLY WEAVING.</u> This comes from uneven tension over the loom to begin with.

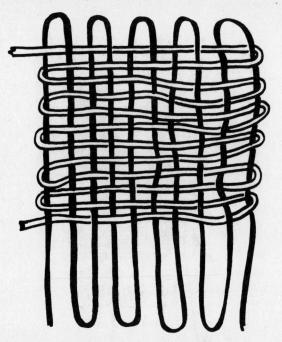

As you may have noticed, I have mentioned tension quite a few times. From this you may deduce that, while tension in daily life is not so desirable, it is a cardinal facet of weaving. So respect and use it with care.

CONCLUSION

Finally, it's your time, your materials, your aesthetic investment-- make something you love making. I haven't mentioned any "useful" projects here--most books on weaving do that. Even so, on these simple looms you can make such things as purses, pillow covers, headbands, belts, ponchos, curtains, afghans, and many other things. Pieces can be made separately and sewn together to make larger items. My own predilection is for tapestries and wall hangings. One of the reasons for my preference is that you are much freer to experiment with different yarns and materials such as dried grasses, weeds, leaves, bark, seaweed, metals, whatever turns you on. It's amazing how you start noticing your environment in a new way when you are looking for weft materials. Warp is less flexible, but try different kinds.

Don't be intimidated by what's been done, or being done. Just take it on, one step at a time, getting as big or complex as you choose. There is always further to go, more to learn, more to do. But you can stop anywhere (if you can, that is, once you get into it). Don't worry about being good. If you love doing it, that's the reason to do it.

Tie Dye and Batik
Shelagh Young

Tie dye and batik are related in principle. They are both methods of resist-dyeing, which means that parts of the fabric are protected from absorbing any dye during the dyeing process by the application of wax (batik), or by tying the cloth tightly in a pattern (tie dye). The design is made by the resistance of these parts to the colors, and, with the use of more than one color, by the overlaps and color contrasts.

These are probably the oldest and most primitive methods of printing designs on fabrics. Their origin is probably central Asia, the period of their invention as remote as the art of dyeing itself. In old Japan there was a technique called Kyochi Zome: silk was clamped between two boards with a pierced design through which the dye was applied--a tedious process, but the results were magnificent.

The most popular patterns in tie dye now are done by folding the fabric and binding it with elastic bands to make diamonds, and sunbursts, and freeform splashes of color.

WHAT YOU'LL NEED

FOR TIE DYE:

A good pair of heavy rubber gloves.

A large metal cooking spoon, for lifting and stirring during dyeing.

A box of Ivory Snow detergent. A little added to the dye solution will help the colors seep in.

A turkey baster, one of those long pointed glass, or metal, or plastic tubes with a squeeze bulb at the end.

A large box of thin, medium-sized rubber bands, for tying.

Some bleach.

An endless quantity of newspapers, and an old sheet.

These things, if not around the house already, can all be found on the shelves of any department store or hardware store, and can be had used from most thrift stores.

Good dye is essential. After all the time and effort invested in doing a piece, the result should be worth it.

Cheap dye is a horror. The kind you can buy in drugstores and super-markets--without mentioning brand names for fear of lawsuits--is terrible. The colors fade quickly, wash out, and actually end up being terribly expensive, if you're considering doing more than one piece, since you're paying around 35 cents for about a tablespoon of dye.

One brand of packaged dye is very good but, again, it would be expensive to use in volume. These dyes are made by W. Cushing & Co. They aren't available everywhere, but are worth looking for, if you want to experiment with some things before sinking a lot of money into bulk dye. The address of the company on the package is: W. Cushing & Co., Dover-Foxcroft, Maine, U.S.A.

Bachmeir and Company, in New York, sell the best bulk dyes I've found. They seem a fairly large investment, running from about $8 to $14 a pound, but they really go a long way, and the results are beautiful. You might be able to find some friends interested in dyeing, and the group could split the cost. Bachmeir makes a different dye for each fibre, the colors are fast and dependable and mix well. Their address is: 154 Chambers Street, New York, New York, 10007. They will send price lists, and each color must be ordered by name and number, and can be sent c.o.d.

Other companies make cold-water dyes. These are necessary if you are going to use any wax (batik) in combination with the tie dye (wax will melt away in hot water).

And finally, you can explore the possibility of using natural vegetable dyes. There are many pamphlets on the subject, most libraries have some information. You can get beautiful, subtle, earthy colors by foraging for dye-producing plants and roots, like chickory, indigo, sumac, and even onions. (Vegetable dyes are only viable if you have much more time than money, since the process of dyeing becomes more involved; as a matter of fact, it becomes a major procedure.)

You will also need several large, deep washbasins, preferably enamel. They are durable and easiest to clean. The size of the basins depends on the size of the pieces you will be doing. There should be enough room for the fabric not to be crowded, but not so huge that a lot of dye would be wasted each time.

Dyes are poisonous and messy. Bear this in mind when you are setting up your work area. The kitchen should be a last resort. The gas company will hook up a small gas burner that sits on a table, with a tank of gas (you use very little) for around $14. If you have a basement with washtubs for rinsing, so much the better. The gas burner can be installed there. If this is all impossible in your particular circumstance, cover everything with newspaper. Bleach will remove dye from almost everything, including you.

FOR BATIK:

A double boiler, for melting the wax. Wax is inflammable, and should never be heated directly over a flame. If you can't get a double boiler, a small pan resting in a larger pan of boiling water will do.

For dye-pots, you'll need washbasins or plastic pails, since the dye doesn't have to be heated.

And rubber gloves, cooking spoons, mountains of newspapers, lots of paraffin wax, some cheesecloth, an iron.

Some thumbtacks, a piece of smooth plywood, and a scraper of some kind to take the wax off the board.

An assortment of brushes. Watercolor brushes are best, sable if you can afford them. (Good brushes generally last longer than cheap ones.)

There is a tool which is good to have, although certainly not an absolute essential. It looks rather like a metal pipe with a wooden handle and has a fine tube extending out of the bottom end. You might be able to get one at a batik studio in a large city, or at a hobby or craft store; otherwise one can be made quite easily with a stick or piece of bamboo, and two pieces of copper tubing. On the next page is an illustration, showing how one can be made and used. The advantage of having one of these tools is this: the wax must be kept very hot for batik, so that it will penetrate the cloth completely and not form a crust on the surface of the fabric that the dye can seep beneath, where you didn't intend it to go. Wax cools very quickly on a brush. You have to keep dipping the brush into the wax to keep it hot enough. This tool, being metal, stays hot longer. You dip the pipe into the wax; it fills; the copper heats up, and you can draw on the fabric with more ease. It makes a finer, clearer, and more precise line than does the brush.

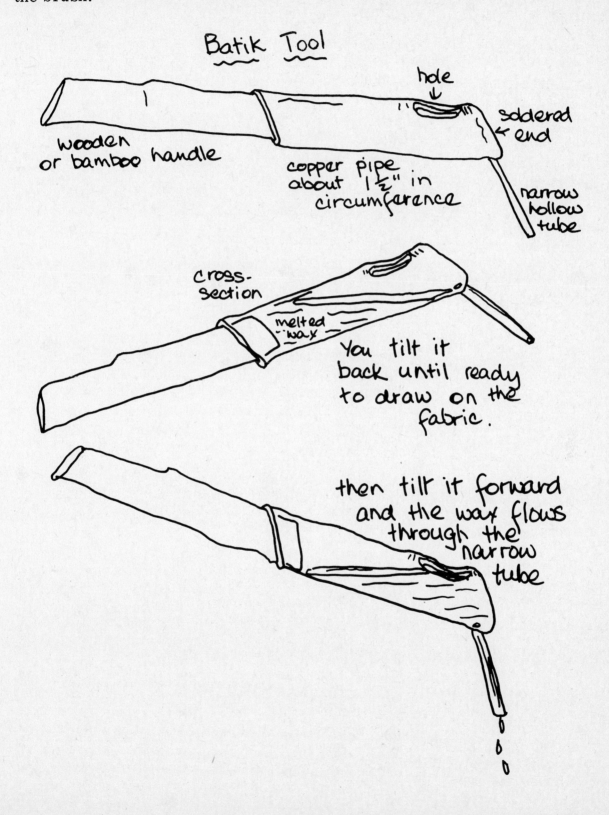

Batik Tool

hole

wooden or bamboo handle

copper pipe about 1½" in circumference

soldered end

narrow hollow tube

cross-section

melted wax

You tilt it back until ready to draw on the fabric.

then tilt it forward and the wax flows through the narrow tube

Cold water dyes are hard to find. Batik studios are good sources, if you can find one. I really can't recommend any as reliable sources, since they seem to fold up and slip off into the night so quickly and so often. Try hobby and craft stores, too.

There is, of course, the selection of fabrics. For tie dye, I like working best with velvet (especially old velvet), silk, silk chiffon and satin. The lustre and light-reflection of satins and velvets give a whole beautiful new dimension to the colors. Unmercerized cottons fade. So does nylon. I'd say they aren't worth your time and energies. White acetate satin would be a good starting place. It is inexpensive enough for experimentation, and looks fantastic when done. And it can be used for millions of things--satin sheets, curtains, pillows, clothing, and wall hangings, to name a few.

I like to use different textures in materials, like velvet and satin, in patchwork. And combinations of batik and tie dye are endless. If you do any sewing at all, you can cut out a shirt or a dress, sew together the shoulder seams, sew on the sleeves, leaving the underarm seam and the sleeve seam open so that the material lies almost flat, and then batik and tie dye a pattern to follow the shape of the garment--maybe a pattern that swirls around the neck and drips down the sleeves. Beautiful.

Each fabric reacts differently to the dye. There will be subtle changes in every piece you do. I have never tried to batik on velvet. The wax would interfere with the nap, or the nap with the wax. It would probably be very difficult to get the wax out of the fabric without destroying it. But then, I've never tried. What are good are fairly heavyweight lining silk and medium silk shantung, linen, and mercerized cotton. Very lightweight materials don't hold the wax well; very heavy ones are much harder to penetrate with wax.

THE DYEING PROCESS

BATIK:

Batik is a process of painting with wax on fabric, then dyeing the exposed parts to make a design. You melt the wax in a double boiler or similar contraption (never over direct heat, to avoid fires). It must be kept hot. Remember to keep adding a little water to the bottom pan; it boils away.

Thumbtack the fabric to a board. You can draw your design very faintly on the cloth with a light pencil, then start applying the wax, with a brush or with the batik tool already described.

If you are using brushes, the wax should be applied hot enough so that it will penetrate the cloth fairly evenly, and not just spread out over the surface of the fabric in a crust or the dye will seep through it. This is very important. And remember that every part of the piece not protected by the wax will absorb color. You have to think almost in terms of negatives: you cover one area, but the areas all around it take on the color. Design possibilities are as infinite as your imagination. You can begin with free-form "action" batik, Jackson Pollock-style, loading the brush with wax and letting it drip onto the cloth in streams of droplets and lines. This looks fantastic when combined with tie-dyed crunches--like ocean waves with bubbles. And you can do very precise designs, even realistic paintings. Since the colors are protected from each other by wax during the addition of further colors, the number of colors on one piece of work can be limitless.

The fabric is dyed in cold-water dye, the instructions for which vary, according to the source. Sometimes you have to add your own mordants, or substances to "fix" the color. Sometimes these are pre-mixed.

The fabric is dyed and hung to dry with newspaper under it to catch drips.

Cover the ironing board with newspaper and, while the piece is still slightly damp, lay it on the newspaper on the ironing board, put a layer of newspaper over it, and begin to iron very carefully. The iron should be fairly hot, so that the wax melts and is absorbed by the newspaper. Keep changing the newspaper, discarding the wax-saturated sheets. Keep ironing until no more wax appears to be coming out on the newspaper and the fabric is only very slightly stiff. Now, sink the fabric into enough boiling water to cover it well, and hold it well beneath the surface. The last remaining little bit of wax will float to the surface, and can be skimmed off with cheesecloth.

Now the fabric is hung to dry again, and is ready for the second waxing, then the second color. This seems to be an appropriate place to mention color. In batik you have more control over colored areas than in tie dye. If the wax is applied carefully, you can plan exactly what colors will develop and exactly where they will be and where they will overlap to make new colors.

TIE DYE:

In tie dye there is always a certain element of surprise, a certain amount of the unexpected. Basically, though:

Where red and blue overlap will be purple.

Where red and yellow overlap will be orange.

Where yellow and blue overlap will be green.

AN EXAMPLE OF OVERLAP

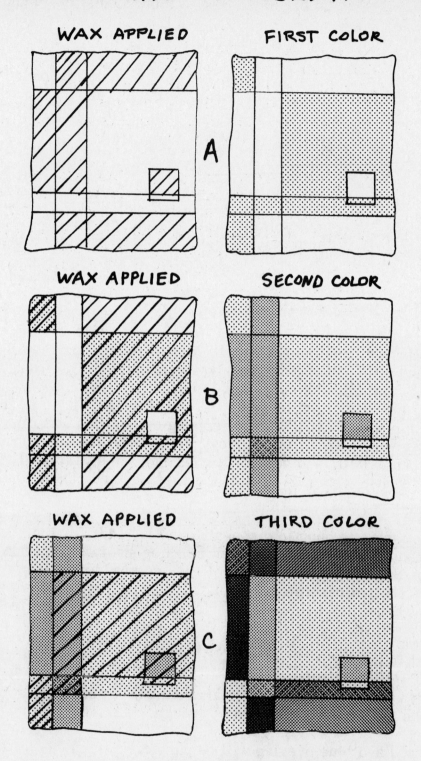

WAX APPLIED   FIRST COLOR

A

WAX APPLIED   SECOND COLOR

B

WAX APPLIED   THIRD COLOR

C

Where red and green, or green and orange overlap will be brownish . . .

Different shades make different tones of colors, of course. Turquoise and yellow most often make lime. Pink and turquoise make a shade of fuchsia. Depending on the brands and shades of dyes that you will be using, you will arrive at your own favorite and most successful combinations. There aren't any rigid rules in tie dye, everything is very loose and approximate. Don't be afraid to experiment.

Three colors per project are usually plenty. More than that and they begin to get a little muddy. Again, remember that depending on how the fabric is tied the colors will meet and mix and overlap to make new colors. The dyeing itself depends on the tied pattern: The fabric can be totally immersed in the first color, rinsed, retied, and placed in the second--and so on, for a complete overlap of color over the whole piece. The fabric can also be dyed in sections in different colors, then put in an overall color. Once again, be willing to experiment.

THE DYEING PROCESS

Wear rubber gloves. Fill the basin about halfway up with water. There should be enough to allow the fabric easy movement. Heat the water to a light boil and keep it approximately at that heat. To every gallon of water add two heaping tablespoons of dye and two tablespoons of Ivory Snow.

Wet the fabric. Sink it into the dye and leave it there from thirty to forty-five minutes, lifting and stirring often.

Take it out and squeeze out the excess dye. Put it on a newspaper, and squirt a few drops of bleach on each elastic with the turkey baster. Wait ten seconds and drop the whole piece in a basin of cold water.

Take off all the rubber bands and rinse until the water runs clear. It is now colorfast, even in the washing machine.

Wring it out, and iron it while still damp. An old sheet over the ironing board will help in the ironing by absorbing a little water. If the iron sticks at all, it's too hot. And now for the folds. After you have mastered these basic folds and patterns you will, no doubt, go on to invent ones of your own.

Have fun.

The fabric can be
simply
tied in knots

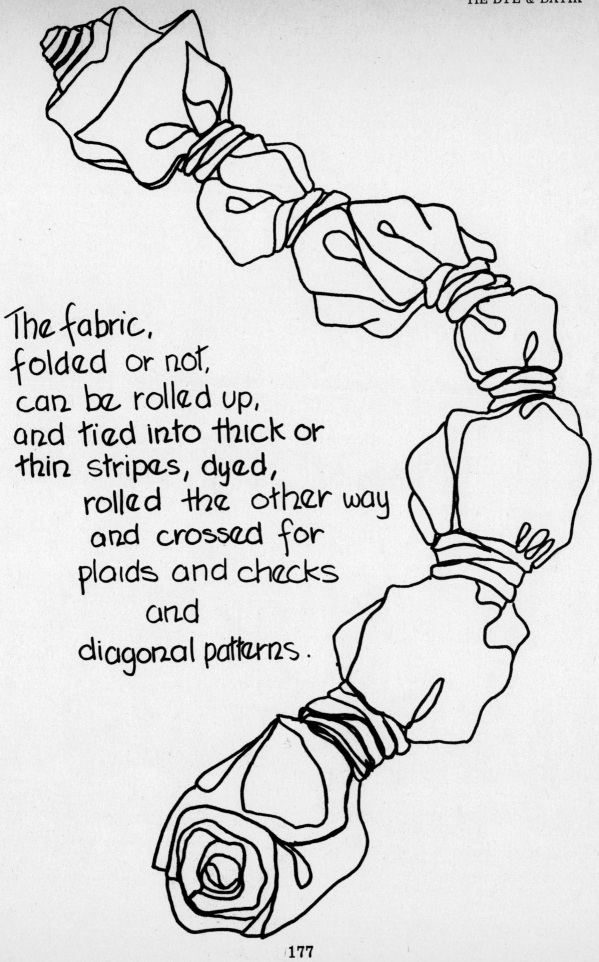

The fabric,
folded or not,
can be rolled up,
and tied into thick or
thin stripes, dyed,
 rolled the other way
 and crossed for
plaids and checks
 and
diagonal patterns.

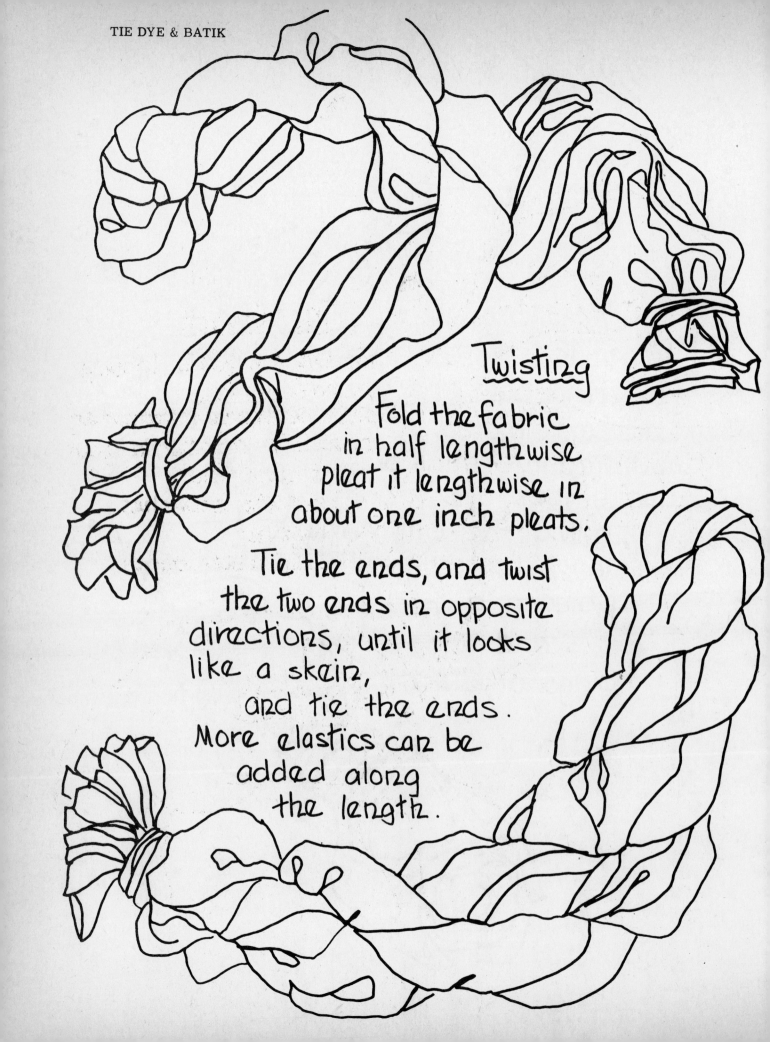

Twisting

Fold the fabric
in half lengthwise
pleat it lengthwise in
about one inch pleats.

Tie the ends, and twist
the two ends in opposite
directions, until it looks
like a skein,
and tie the ends.
More elastics can be
added along
the length.

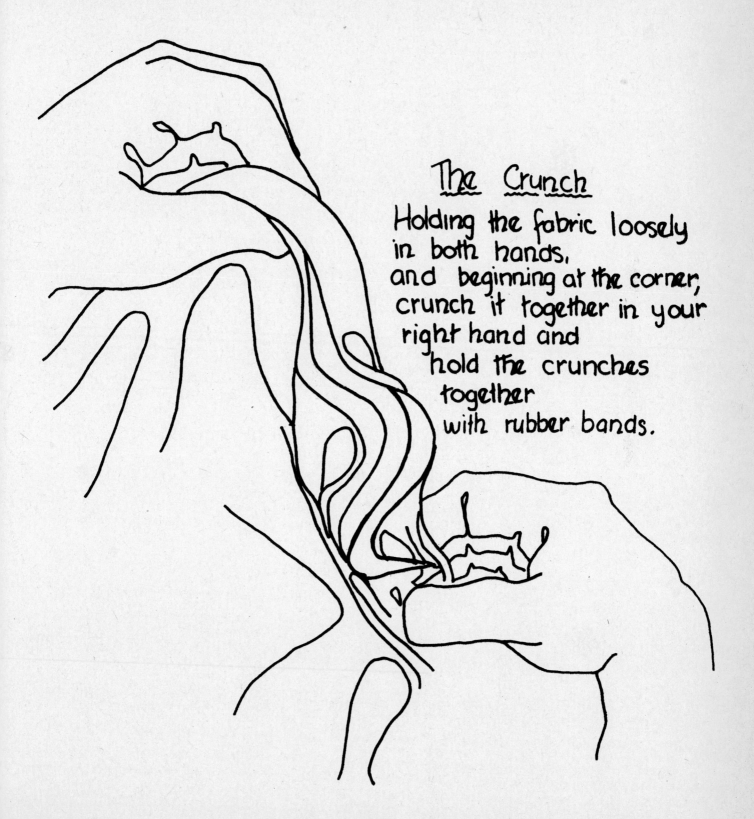

The Crunch

Holding the fabric loosely
in both hands,
and beginning at the corner,
crunch it together in your
right hand and
hold the crunches
together
with rubber bands.

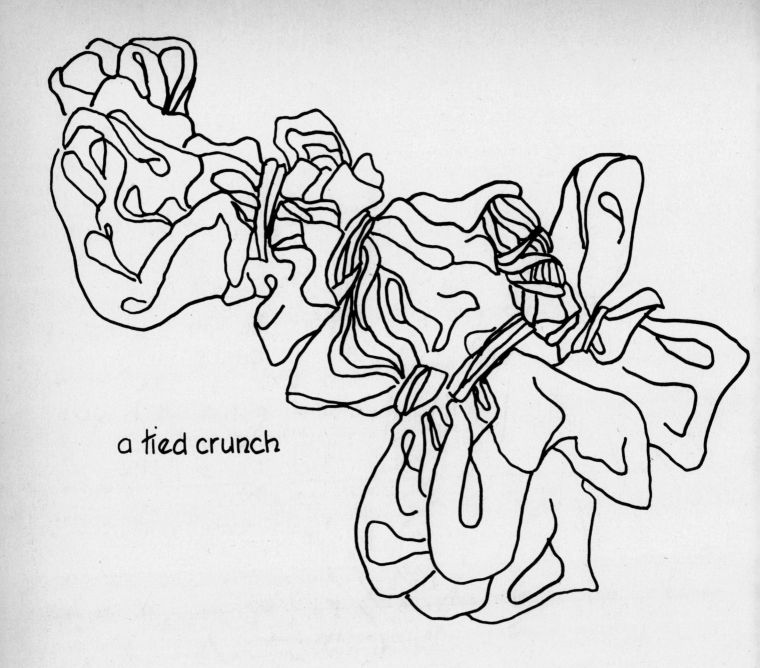

a tied crunch

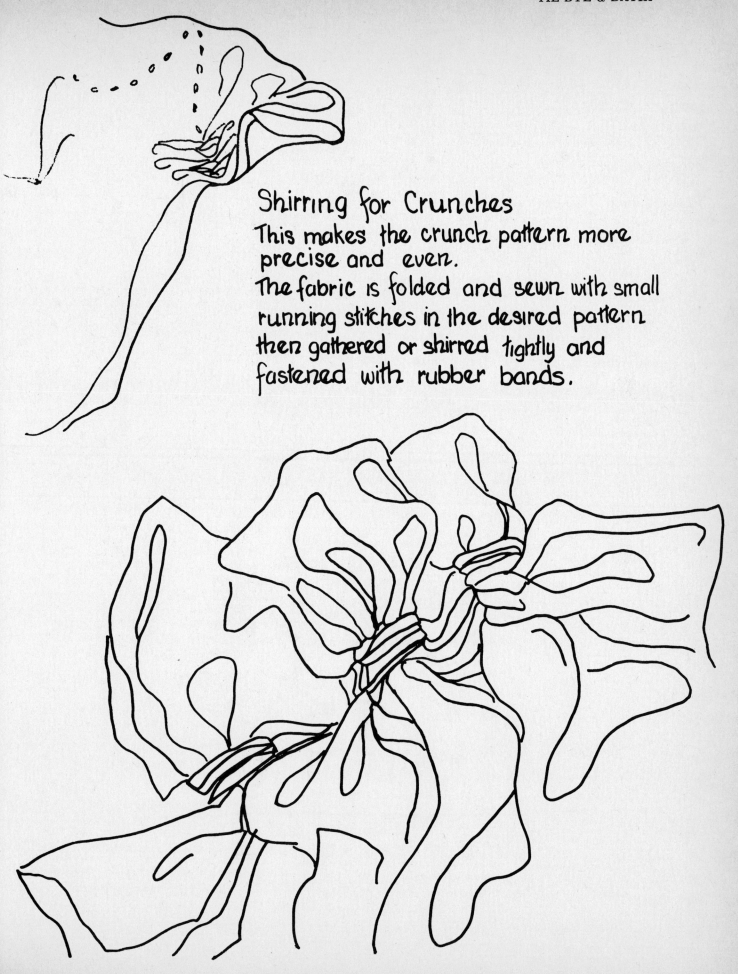

Shirring for Crunches

This makes the crunch pattern more precise and even.

The fabric is folded and sewn with small running stitches in the desired pattern then gathered or shirred tightly and fastened with rubber bands.

Nail-head Patterns.

Finishing nails are driven into a board,
in a pattern or shape or outline.
Knots are sewn and tied around the nail tops,
then the fabric is pulled off the nails and
dyed.

(It looks like smocking.)

This method is best in combination with
batik, with a little melted wax painted
around the ties for better color
delineation.

With the use of wax, use cold dyes.

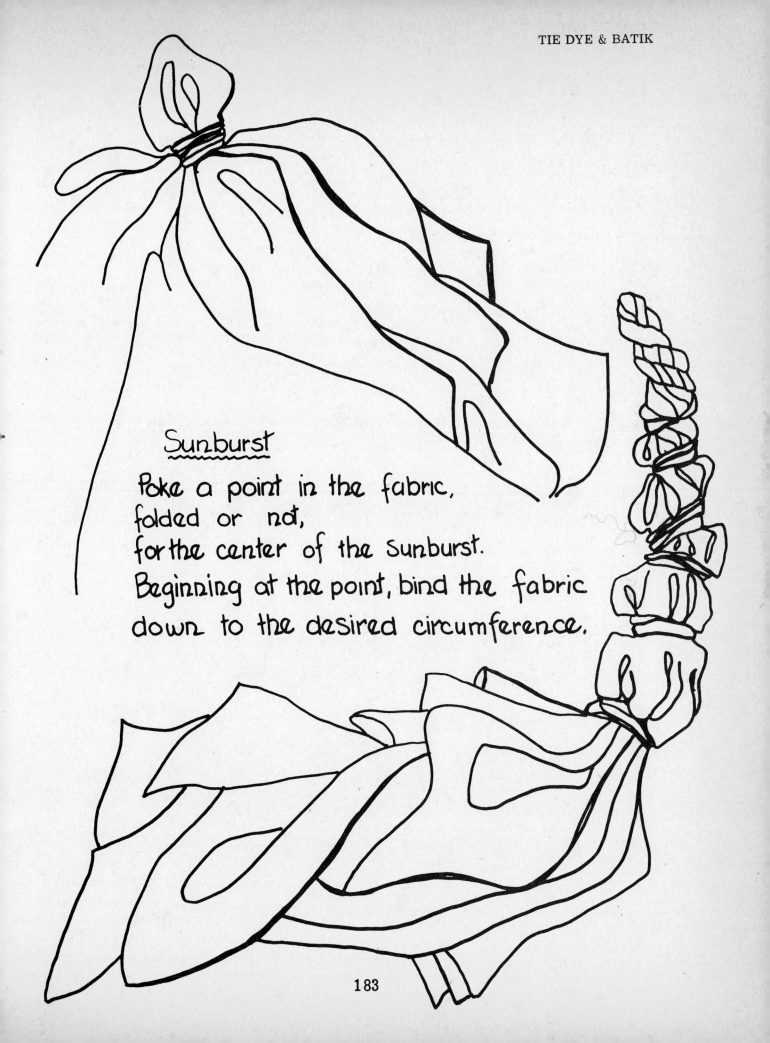

Sunburst

Poke a point in the fabric,
folded or not,
for the center of the Sunburst.
Beginning at the point, bind the fabric
down to the desired circumference.

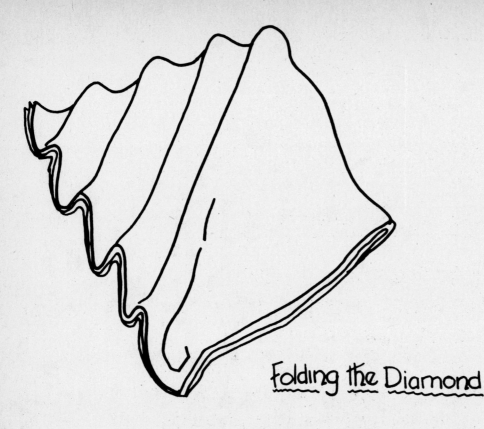

Folding the Diamond

Fold the fabric with the selvages together,
with the right side up.
Fold again in quarters.

Pleat diagonally, corner to
corner, binding the pleats
with rubber bands
about an inch apart.

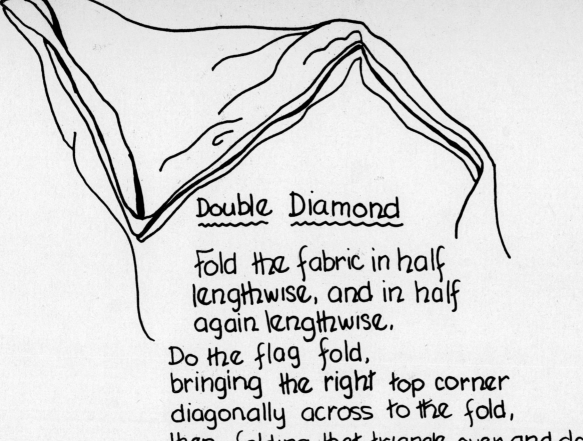

Double Diamond

Fold the fabric in half
lengthwise, and in half
again lengthwise.
Do the flag fold,
bringing the right top corner
diagonally across to the fold,
then folding that triangle over and down,
and so on, until the whole piece is folded into
a triangle, the points of which are
tied with rubber bands.

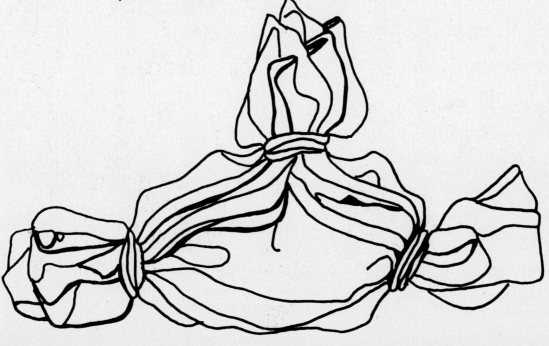

Silkscreen
Roger Sessions

Silkscreen is probably one of the most versatile of all art forms. The fact that anything that lies flat and doesn't move or talk back can be printed on by this method is attested to by its successful use everywhere from the designs on Kellogg's cereal boxes to giant replicas of tomato-soup cans. The silkscreen has a subtle influence on all of our lives, and even perhaps on history--where would we all be if some bright boy at Harvard had not had a silkscreen to print the fist symbol with? It may not even be an exaggeration to say that behind every successful revolution, there are two people down in some basement pushing squeegees. As one can see, silkscreeners come in all shapes, sizes, and colors.

For this reason, I dedicate this chapter to everyone who at some time in his life will have a love affair with a squeegee, whether he be revolutionary, artist, or boy scout.

Silkscreen is based on the following simple principles. Silk is placed over the surface to be printed. A stencil is placed on the silk. Ink is forced through the silk and is blocked at certain spots by the stencil. Where the ink is blocked, a blank appears on the printing surface. Where there is no stencil blocking, the ink goes through and prints. The squeegee, a rubber blade with a wooden handle, forces the ink through the silk.

In setting up shop, I've found the following items essential. Almost all of them can be found at a good art-supply store. The few exceptions are either hardware store specialties or easily found in obvious places.

BASIC PRINTING UNIT: a sturdy frame of wood with tightly stretched silk securely stapled and taped on. The frame is attached with removable hinges onto a wood base or backboard. Paper is then fed on top of the base, the frame is let down, and ink is forced through the silk.

SQUEEGEE: As described before, the squeegee is run across the surface of the silk, forcing ink of all colors through the silk and onto the printing surface. The squeegee is the last link between you and your finished product. A word of warning: squeegees have personality and can produce slightly unpredictable effects.

INKS: You need the three basic colors (red, yellow, and blue), plus black and white. From these, using your imagination, you can mix just about anything else. Try to visualize colors you can get by mixing yellow with red (oranges), red with blue (purples), blue with yellow (greens). Any addition of white with pure color gives you tones going towards soft pastel, and any black gives you your color in darkish form. A mixture of black and white with any pure color "grays" that color. Interesting things can happen in mixing; you find them by mixing samples: for instance, a bit of black with yellow will mix to a yellow-green or avocado color. More about applying color later.

Also under this heading comes what is known to silkscreeners as "base," a mystic substance that smells horrible and is used to thin down the inks that are bought much more concentrated than even you real fanatics could hope to use.

GALLON OF WINE: This lubricant to your creativity may be cheap but make sure it's drinkable. An inexpensive chablis can serve the purpose handsomely. True, there are those who feel silkscreen is a "fine art," best done without the intoxicating friendship of wine, but these purists are rather scarce and unlikely in any case to effect any lasting social changes.

CLOTHESLINE AND PINS: or any other suitable drying arrangement you can think of. Paper clips can be strung on a wire hanging device. Drying time may range from five minutes to five hours.

DECENT-SIZE PLATE OF GLASS: This is the best palette you can have (and the cheapest) for mixing inks. A lot of other things can be used in an emergency, such as plates, pans, wood surfaces, and so forth.

A LOT OF CLEANING FLUID: such as white gas, turpentine, paint thinner. Used for all the obvious reasons.

SHARP CUTTING KNIVES: used for cutting stencils. They must be very sharp. Exactos and similar brands are fine.

STENCIL PAPERS: I'll go into this later.

SILKSCREEN TAPE: special tape that is resistant to water, ink, and cleaning fluid. This is used for taping the silk to the frame.

MANY GLASS JARS: for storing ink that you mixed and then didn't need. Whatever you do, don't use plastic because ink eats right through it.

CLEANING SETUP: a good sized washtub will give you years of satisfaction for this purpose.

MASKING TAPE: you'll use it for everything.

PRINTING PAPER: Almost any paper prints. Choose a type that suits your purpose.

SILK: Most art-supply houses carry silkscreen silk. Start with a relatively inexpensive (but not the cheapest) type, and as you continue you can try different qualities.

MAKING YOUR OWN PRINTING UNIT

Your first major project must be making your printing unit. They can be bought ready-made at many art-supply stores, but then again, so can TV dinners, which are about equal in personality, content, and uniqueness. Prices for these units vary according to the size. Assuming that you would like to "roll your own," follow these steps:

> Determine how large a printing area you need and how large you may want your prints to be. Remember that small prints can be made on a large screen, but large prints cannot be made on a small screen. Let's say, in a hypothetical way, that we want a printing area of 12 by 18 inches. The frame must be large enough to give this much area for a stencil, plus enough room to put the stencil on, plus enough room to tape the silk to the frame (the silk is both stapled and taped to the frame for additional support). Stencils are taken off the silk and new ones put on, but the silk is only changed in extreme circumstances).

> We have determined that it is necessary to be able to place a 12-by-18-inch stencil on the screen. An additional 2-inch border is necessary on all sides of the stencil to allow for proper positioning and a little maneuverability. This brings the area necessary up to 16 by 22 inches (adding 2 inches on all sides).

> You will need an additional 2-inch area on all sides for taping the

189

screen to the frame (by the way, "screen" refers to the silk, not to the stencil). Now the total area is 20 by 26 inches (adding another 2 inches on all sides).

This, then, is the total amount of empty space you must allow within the frame to accommodate a 12 by 18 inch printing area. Note that the necessary additional space is not proportional, and is the same for a small frame as it is for a large frame.

Now that we have an idea how large an area we are working with, the actual building can begin. Keep in mind that the finished frame must be very rigid to support the great tension put on it by the stretched silk and also that it must be very level (in other words, it cannot rock when put on a flat surface). Test the wood for bendability at the length you are planning on using. Wood that is quite suitable for a 20-by-26-inch screen won't support a 35-by-45-inch screen. Standard 1-by-2-inch board should work fine for our hypothetical frame.

Cut two pieces 30 inches long (the length of the inside plus 2 inches on either side for the wood) and two pieces 24 inches (ditto).

Cut the ends so that they fit together.

Fit them together, and fasten with corner braces securely, checking for levelness and snugness.

Cut a piece of silk about 3 inches larger all around than the frame.

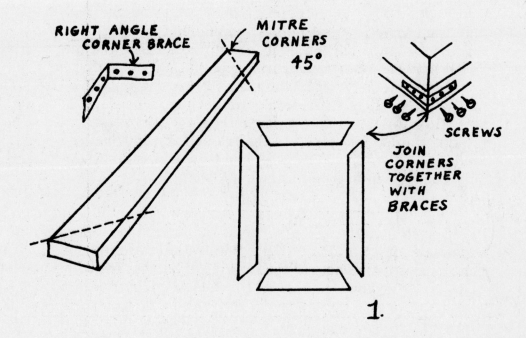

RIGHT ANGLE
CORNER BRACE

MITRE
CORNERS
45°

SCREWS

JOIN
CORNERS
TOGETHER
WITH
BRACES

1.

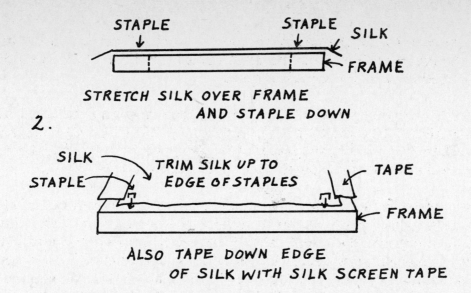

STAPLE STAPLE SILK

FRAME

STRETCH SILK OVER FRAME
AND STAPLE DOWN

2.

SILK — TRIM SILK UP TO
EDGE OF STAPLES TAPE

STAPLE

FRAME

ALSO TAPE DOWN EDGE
OF SILK WITH SILK SCREEN TAPE

Begin stapling the silk onto the frame with a staple gun. Start at
the corner of one edge and put staples in at an interval of about 1
inch. Before stapling at each point, pull the silk tautly
away from all other staples. Try to achieve a uniform tautness,
like the top of a drum. Staple opposite sides, first starting from
the center and working outwards. When finished, the silk should
be just tight enough to give about a half inch.

When the stapling is done, trim the silk almost up to the staples.
Then tape each edge with your silkscreen tape.

Turn the frame over, with the silk side down, and tape the inside
edges.

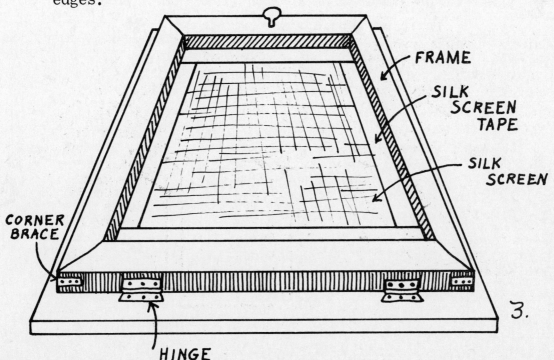

FRAME

SILK
SCREEN
TAPE

SILK
SCREEN

CORNER
BRACE

HINGE

3.

191

Hinge the frame onto the straight backboard (three-quarter inch plywood is best for this). It shouldn't be warped, and pick a size 6 inches or so bigger all around than the frame (Fig. 3). Figure 4 shows a good way to keep the screen propped up.

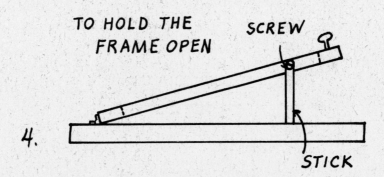

TO HOLD THE FRAME OPEN   SCREW

4.

STICK

OK. The groundwork has been laid. If you have gotten this far, you can sit back and take it easy. If (much more likely) you got hung up on some point, then now is the time to bring out the wine. Relax. Have a glass, then try again. It usually goes a lot easier this time.

STENCILS

Once you have gotten your printing unit finished, you can start making stencils. This is the most creative part of your venture, and therefore, to many people, the most fun. There are three important types of stencils which I'll discuss in turn. In general, each stencil represents one color, and a finished print may involve any number of stencils and printings, depending on the number of colors used. There are, however, some short cuts. A two-color, blue-yellow print is going to need one stencil for each of the two colors, but a three-color, blue-yellow-green print may be done with two stencils also. (Yellow and blue mixed or printed together make green.) In the latter case, one stencil would be cut for blue and green, and another for yellow and green. The two stencils would overlap on the green site only. Both yellow and blue would be printed separately but they would combine on the "green" sites to create that color. This overlap technique can be carried quite far, giving up to seven different colors from three printings of the basic colors (red, blue, yellow).

GLUE STENCILS: Water-soluble glue is used for glue stencils. The glue is applied with a paintbrush directly on the silk in every place where you do not want color going through. When the glue dries, it forms a hard film which the ink cannot penetrate. The ink is spirit-soluble, and, as such, will not dissolve the glue (nor will cleaning fluids). Basic law of chemistry: two things that are not soluble in any of the same substances will not dissolve each other. A glue stencil can literally be soaked overnight in turpentine with no ill effects; however, a few drops of water can destroy the stencil in a matter of seconds. If you add a few drops of food coloring to the glue just before applying, it will be much easier to see the work, since the glue is normally almost invisible.

After the stencil is dry (usually from one to three hours, depending on humidity and other factors) it must be held up to a light and searched carefully for "pinholes"--that is, any place where there was not a sufficient amount of glue to form a solid film. Ink will come through any of these places. A few more dabs of glue will prevent spotty prints.

Glue stencils can also be made by applying spirit-soluble touche with a paintbrush every place on the screen that you do want the ink to go through. After the touche dries, the entire screen is coated with glue. When this dries too, the screen is washed vigorously with spirits. Since only the touche is spirit-soluble, only the touche (and whatever glue is on top of it) is washed away in the spirit bath. This has the advantage of not requiring negative thinking when painting the stencil.

Glue stencils give more of a painted look to the finished print, with less definite lines than other methods. Clouded effects can be achieved with light glue painting. Since it is difficult to get well-defined lines, this type of stencil lends itself with difficulty to the overlapping techniques discussed before, which require very precise coordination. However, far be it from me to say it can't be done.

"STENCIL" STENCILS: The "stencil" stencil is the more traditional approach to stencil making, especially in overlapping, and, like most traditional approaches, it is one of the less rewarding ones. It involves the use of specially prepared stencil paper (again, your friendly neighborhood dealer will be happy to supply you). The "paper" has two layers. One is heavy plastic and serves as a backing for the extremely thin layer of film which is the actual stencil. The film is made to adhere to the backing just enough to allow it to be peeled away when you are ready, but not so much that the two parts would become separated under accidental conditions. The stencil is prepared by cutting away the outlines of the open sections (open, is of course, where the ink is to go through) and then peeling these sections off the backing. In cutting, only enough pressure is applied to cut through the thin film, and the backing is left intact. The screen is then placed, silk side down, directly on the film so that they are touching. The film is dabbed with acetone through the silk and begins the process of dissolving. Film is soluble only in acetone. Too much acetone would completely eat the film up, and it must be carefully applied so that only enough to make it adhere to the silk is used. When the film has completely adhered to the silk and the acetone is dry (a matter of one or two seconds), the backing is very carefully peeled off, leaving a ready-to-print stencil.

The advantage of "stencil" stencils is that fine, well-defined lines can be made and put exactly where you want them, which is necessary for fine color-coordination. The disadvantage is that this is extremely difficult to perform, since there are about six places where you might easily destroy the stencil. This method also requires the use of large amounts of acetone, which is more inflammable than turpentine and a potentially serious health hazard if not used in a properly ventilated area. It is probably one of the commonest types of stencils now in use. For me, I find it much more of a drag than it's worth.

PAPER STENCILS: Although paper stencils have an almost nonexistent use right now in the silkscreen world, I think that they hold by far the greatest potential, especially for the amateur who is not interested in runs of several thousand prints. The paper stencil is extremely simple to make. Cut a piece of paper a little larger than the outside edges of the frame. The paper that you use for this stencil should ideally be about the thickness of newsprint, but of a consistency that will not as readily allow ink to soak through. Even newsprint will work for a run of less than twenty. Cut your design out of the paper (Fig. 5). A very sharp knife will make your

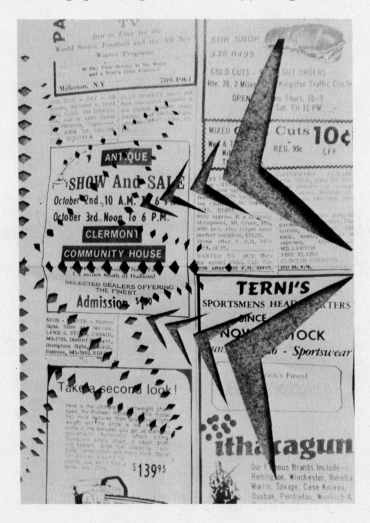

5.

burden incomparably lighter here and is guaranteed to reduce your ruined stencils by half. When your stencil is completely cut, ignore it. Get everything else ready for printing. When you are all ready, lay a sheet of newspaper (instead of printing paper) on the backboard, and the stencil on top of that. Let the screen down (Fig. 6). Center the stencil so that it overlaps a little on all sides. Then put some ink on the screen, and squeegee it through (see section on printing). The ink will provide enough cohesion to bind the stencil to the screen, and the stencil will remain in place until it is purposely peeled off or until the ink is washed off.

6.

The disadvantage of this technique is that the stencil is only good for one run (a run being as long as you continue printing consecutively).   The advantage is the ease and maneuverability of working with these stencils. You can even peel one off and put another one on without washing the screen, as long as both printings are of the same color.

The alert opportunist may see great possibilities in this method. For example, the same cohesive force that holds the stencil to the silk will hold leaves and god only knows what else to the silk, allowing for interesting and original effects.   Yet this technique is all but ignored by the silkscreen textbooks.   It is rarely mentioned, and its possibilities are only superficially explored.

COLOR MIXING

In technical jargon, there are three types of silkscreen colors; transparent, translucent, and opaque.   These terms refer to the different degrees of transparency that each gives when printed.   For example, transparent blue printed on transparent yellow gives green, as mentioned before.   Transparent colors are prepared by diluting the raw color (from the tube or can) several times with base.   (Proportions of ten base to one color are not at all unreasonable.)   Opaque color completely blots out anything printed underneath it.   It is made by mixing raw white with raw color. Translucent color is prepared by adding both base and raw white to raw color.   A translucent blue printed on transparent yellow gives a very bluish green.

Exactly what proportions you want must be determined by your own experimentation, keeping in mind that base is a lot cheaper than color and that a little color can be made to go a long way.

In time you may find yourself building up a collection of particularly appealing colors in the same way that other people collect vintage wines. There are literally hundreds of different silkscreen colors on the market for you to choose from.   Never, of course, buy a color that you can mix yourself; you will, however, occasionally find some wonderfully pure, high tone that you could never duplicate.   There is one particularly beautiful fuchsia that I regularly stock up on after endless failures at mixing it myself.

PRINTING

Your frame is built, your stencil cut, your color mixed and your wine is poured, so you are now all ready to print.   This is a very joyous occasion, and your dress, manner, and mood should reflect this fact.

7.

You have by this time already devised a way of drying your prints. Close at hand you should also have cleaning stuff (rags, etc.), printing paper, scrap paper the same size as your printing paper; the printing set-up; squeegee; the colors; and any other unmentionables that you find necessary to do your best. Realize that any clothes you are wearing will never look the same, so plan your attire accordingly.

Lay some color on the screen as shown in Figure 8 in a column perhaps an inch or two thick, and center the dummy printing paper underneath the frame as best you can by eye. Hold the squeegee at the angle shown in Figure 9 and firmly run the squeegee the length of the printing unit, stopping two or three inches short of the opposite side; then turn the squeegee around and do it again in the opposite direction (Fig. 10). Lift up the printing unit and remove the printed dummy. Notice whether you have centered it well or not. Position another dummy and print that one. Keep going through this trial-and-error procedure until you decide that you have found just the right spot to place the paper to get the proper margins. Border that spot with some very lightweight cardboard and masking tape so that you can easily feed paper into the unit without fumbling.

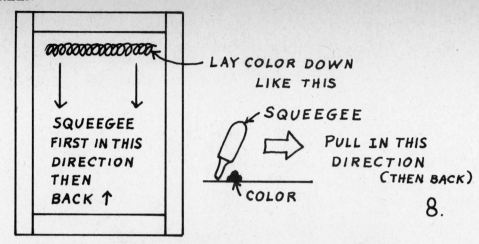

LAY COLOR DOWN
LIKE THIS

SQUEEGEE

COLOR

PULL IN THIS
DIRECTION
(THEN BACK)

SQUEEGEE
FIRST IN THIS
DIRECTION
THEN
BACK ↑

8.

9.

10.

11.

Just go though exactly the same procedure with your <u>real</u> printing paper and you have your first print (Fig. 11). If you are planning on doing a job using more than one color, you'll find centering much easier on subsequent prints, now that you have a printed reference on the paper to look at. Make sure that you print enough extras to allow for messups later on. After that, what can I say?

When you're done for the day, cleaning up is a drag, but it must be done. If any ink at all is left on the screen, it will dry and permanently block out parts. On the other hand, be careful that in your enthusiasm you don't rip the fragile silk.

Use for cleaning fluid whatever the particular solvent is for your ink--white gasoline, turpentine, paint thinner are the standards. Keep in mind how flammable these substances are when you dispose of rags. It would take very little to turn a pile of turpentine- or gasoline-soaked rags into a major disaster area.

SPECIAL EFFECTS

As you continue silkscreening, you will undoubtedly discover new techniques for creating your own special effects. I'll describe two of my favorites to help get you started. The first is open-screen technique. The stencil, if used at all here, is simple, and may serve no other purpose than to create a border. The effect is created by placing the ink before you print as shown in Figure 12 and causes the illusion of one color fading into another. The other technique that you might be interested in is printing on wet objects. Just before you print, get the object good and wet in whatever solvent you use for that particular kind of ink (water for water-soluble inks, turpentine for oils, etc.) and then just print normally. You can get some nice blurred effects that you can learn to control with varying

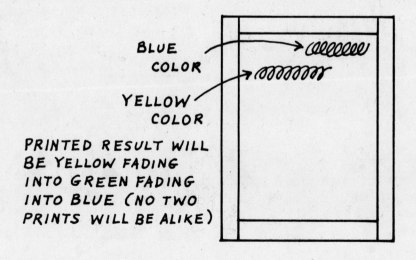

BLUE COLOR

YELLOW COLOR

PRINTED RESULT WILL BE YELLOW FADING INTO GREEN FADING INTO BLUE (NO TWO PRINTS WILL BE ALIKE)

12.

amounts of wetness. Don't limit yourself to one or two techniques but experiment with them as much as you want. If all of this brings visions of sugarplums dancing in your head, fine. Think creatively and feel free. Your silkscreen studio is your castle.

PRINTING ON CLOTH

Before I leave you to your printing, I'll add a brief note on printing on cloth, which is slightly different than paper printing.

First of all, you will need special cloth inks, which may take some tracking down. The printing itself is basically the same, except that when you're all done, you must fix the ink to the cloth. Ideally, this is done with a large oven contraption that costs about $5000, plus $200 for shipping; if this is beyond your means, an iron will do. Heat does the fixing, so the more you iron the finished fabric, the better the end product will be.

You will be better off using a variation of the basic printing unit rather than the same one. I use a table made of a full 48-by-72-inch sheet of three-quarter-inch plywood with a full 48-by-72-inch sheet of soft board on top. Some sort of padding on top of that will probably be worth the effort. For the printing unit I just use an unhinged and unattached frame and silk. The fabric is pinned to the table, and the printing frame is placed freehand on top of the fabric. Using this method, you sacrifice the ability to do any print requiring a fine color coordination, but you gain in ease, cost, and maneuverability. If you are going to go seriously into cloth, it will be well worth your while to learn something about batik, since batik and silkscreen can be combined most profitably.

Silkscreen, then, is at the least an experience, and at its best an art. Its limitations are many, though these same limitations can be manipulated until they seem far less formidable than they first appeared. Use both your mind and your body. Your equipment is just an extension of your self, so consider it as such. Most of all, of course,

Love your squeegee,

Roger

Let's Knot: Macrame
Paul Schwartz

Macrame is decorative knotwork that first appeared in
the Middle East as fringe on shawls and towels. It was
developed in Spain, France, and Italy through sailors'
and fishermen's knots until, by the sixteenth century,
European lacemakers were creating designs of great
complexity.

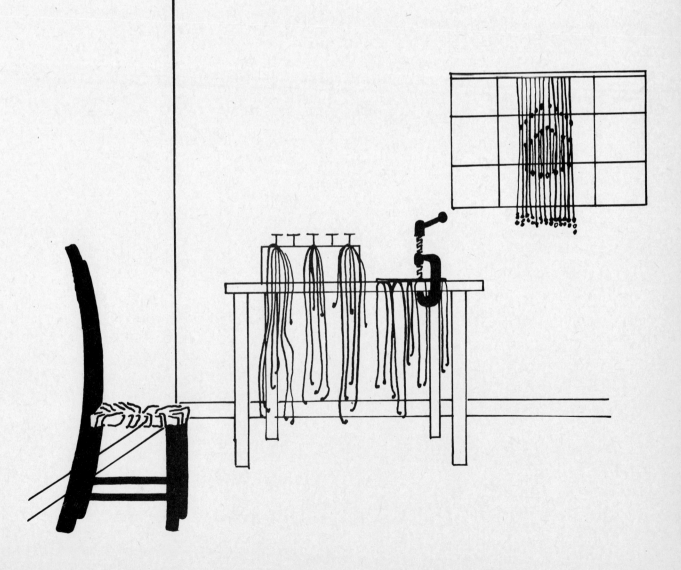

As a craft it's great fun and can be learned by mastering a few simple knots that have a great variety of applications. Some of the things that can be macramed for the home are wall hangings, curtains, hammocks, hanging planters, free-form sculptures, screens, and room dividers. Wearing apparel, such as vests, chokers, shawls, bracelets, headbands, borders for clothing, pendants, and even bathing suits can be macramed.

Its emphasis on rhythmic control has a stabilizing effect that has led some of the world's foremost statesmen like Churchill and De Gaulle to find soothing relaxation in both knitting and knotting. It can be satisfying therapy for those who see their larger problems in terms of confused strands and loose, fraying ends.

TOOLS

Most tools in macrame are simply designed to give you a third or fourth hand to hold the stationary cords; therefore, these easily rigged gadgets are essentially a wide selection of clamping and pinning devices.

STOMACH CLAMP: The stomach clamp is a small rectangular piece of wood with two grooves to hold the strands of the material being knotted. To prevent the material from slipping, rubber bands are stretched around the sides of the grooves. Drill a hole in one end so that it can be snugly attached to your waist by a cord. It may feel awkward at first, but after a while its value becomes evident.

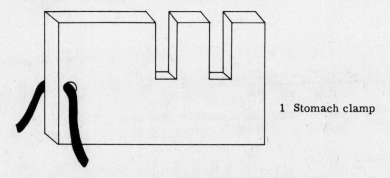

1 Stomach clamp

C-CLAMP AND FLAT BOARD: These are devices to hold the material to a table or to another board so that tension can be applied to the lines as you knot. (The strands you work on are clamped

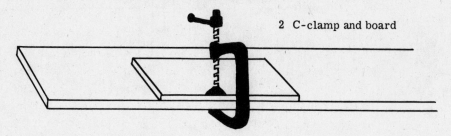

2 C-clamp and board

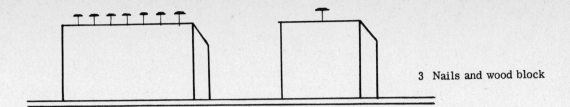

3 Nails and wood block

under the board). Or: Instead of clamping, you can also take a heavy block of wood and drive a row of nails into it as shown in Figure 3. (If it's heavy, it won't slip off that table in front of you.) The nail method works best when you are using thin cords or only a few strands (as when you are making a belt or straps) because you can't wrap bulky cords around a nail.

ROD OR STICK: A knitting needle or long glass stirring rod fastened to a cork or polyurethane board by U-pins (which you can get in a sewing-goods store) does somewhat the same job as the clamps. Since the moored-down knots are able to slide across the rod, adjustments in the beginning are easier.

In addition, you'll need a scissors and ruler for cutting and measuring. You also need hands, eyes, and other sensibilities. These tools are an abstraction but only until they become extensions of the hands. With that, the manipulator vanishes and the creative process flows. The true experience of craftwork is the abandonment of the Great Manipulator and the acceptance of the Great Body.

MATERIALS

The basic materials are anything that can be knotted--cord, twine, rope, and yarns of various weights. The material must be flexible enough to tie, but not so elastic that it leaves misshapen knots. For example, most leather lacings don't knot well because it is hard to maintain tension and control the strands. Certain kinds of yarn tend to curl up and disappear. But don't give up on yarns, for some relatively smooth yarns can show off knots very nicely. The best materials are those closest to the ones that the sailors originally used, such as butcher's twine, jute (an unusually coarse cord that works in well with butcher's twine), rayon cords, rattail (a rich-looking satin cord that seems to offer the widest variety of colors), tubular (a rayon and cotton cord), and chalklines. Most of these materials can be obtained at any hardware store. For others you may have to canvass the nearest urban garment district. You can find other usable materials by trying them out. Some may give more resistance than others. Some may fray more than others. It's your choice. Often different materials combined in a piece add diversity and interest; this technique, however, can present problems. Some materials will not knot securely with others. You become aware of this when knots work loose without too much difficulty.

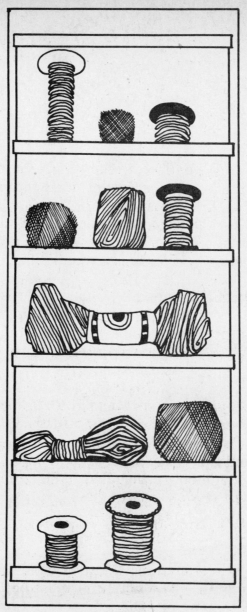

4 What you'll use

If it takes a great amount of tugging to get a secure knot, it generally won't remain tight for long--especially if you are making an item of apparel like a belt. Oftentimes you may have to double material to get a proper knot. Linen seems to combine well with other materials. Rattail and tubular do not work well together. It is best to experiment with many types to develop the faculty of determining how best to execute the macrame piece.

ACCOUTREMENTS

Once you have beads on your mind, you will see them everywhere from the five-and-dime store to your mother's closet. The list is long--antique beads, beads from old jewelry, macaroni, and feather-quill; in short, anything with a hole in it large enough to accept the thickness of the material

206

you want to wiggle through. Rattail is best for beading projects due to its slick surface. Yarns and threads of less density can be pinched together at the ends and made to go through beads with ease. An especially good thing to know is that a bit of Elmer's glue or Sobo glue on tips will dry and make these ends stiff like a needle. The glue also helps condense the pinched ends even more to narrow a point for beading.

In most cities there is a bead district in or near the garment districts. For instance, there are entire warehouses in New York City that sell nothing but billions of beads. Clear or opaque glass beads run about 90 cents per hundred--so that gives you an idea of what to anticipate if you want quantities. Some dealers try to force large purchases if you seem the least bit unsure of yourself. Make sure you tell them what you need.

PLANNING AND PREPARING

Bow to the East. Select your materials with a careful eye for the weight, color, and texture that are called for by the nature of your project.

As a general rule, the cord should be from two to four times longer than the anticipated finished length of your project. The amount of the material varies with the length and breadth of the piece, the type of material being used and the complexity of the knots. A twelve-inch piece of macrame work with a glorious network of half-hitches in chains or half-knot sinnets (a sinnet is a long cluster of knots) could require more material than a twenty-four-inch piece with evenly placed square knots. Narrow and flexible material will knot tighter, leaving more to work with than heavier cord. Some ropes or line will not draw tight no matter how hard you pull, so you need to allow for such situations ahead of time. These combined factors must be considered before starting unless you want to let it all hang out by clustering knots very spontaneously for a free-form type of approach. It is best to overestimate than to run out and have to tie in cords nine-tenths of the way through a project. If you find that you need more cord, an easy splice is made by applying glue to the unraveled ends of each cord and twisting them together. Be sure to allow for proper drying time or they may pull loose.

When mounting strands on rings or dowels or other strands, the cords are halved in such a way as to create a reversed double half-hitch. Don't worry if this sounds like a sophisticated football play, for the procedure will be explained in the next section on knots. It's important to note here, though, that if the cords are mounted in this manner, a double length of material will be required for each strand, and only half the number of long strands will be necessary. For example, should you want to make a rather simple two-foot wall hanging of twenty-four strands, you cut twelve eight-foot strands, measuring them with a yardstick or using a device called "two nails to a measure," which is simply two nails struck into the wall four feet apart. You tie the material to one nail and wrap it around the other and back twelve times to give you a dozen eight-foot lengths. Cut the material where you originally tied in. When a lot of material has to be cut, you may find strands popping off the nail, in which case a friendly hand may be necessary.

MOUNTING THE STRANDS

It is easiest to clamp the strands under a board with a C-clamp or tie them on a nail (refer to Figures 2 and 3). These are the methods used by professionals who must produce a volume of specific work, a belt for example, in a short time (it is hoped that the reader's thoughts are directed towards aesthetic creation through craft rather than knotted with exploitative intentions).

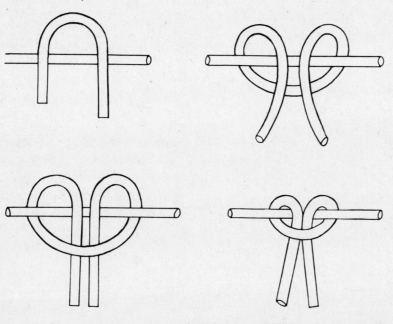

5 (A) Reversed double half-hitch

(B) Mounting on a buckle

A more sophisticated mounting method is halving the strands and tying them to a dowel, rod, or buckle with a reversed double half-hitch (Figs. 5A, 5B). The horseshoe loop of the first step should be in the middle of the strand held in your hand. This is the "hand strand." The horizontal line in Figure 5C represents a dowel or holding strand, which is either fixed

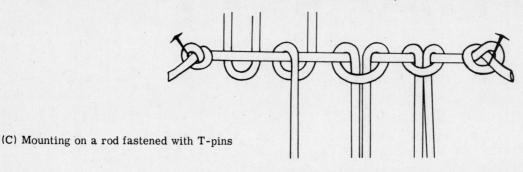

(C) Mounting on a rod fastened with T-pins

tightly between two nails or knotted and T-pinned to a board. (A T-pin is shaped like the letter T and can be purchased in art-supply stores and sewing-goods shops.) Bend the horseshoe over and slip the two hanging strands through the loop as shown in the picture. Using this knot, you can mount almost anything.

USES OF THE STOMACH CLAMP

Either by using the reversed double half-hitches or the nail or C-clamp method, anchor the ends of four strands and sit down in a straight chair with the stomach clamp tied around your waist. The middle strands are held together and brought through the left side of the groove in the clamp, then down. Lock them in place by wrapping them tightly around the clamp once. There should be no slack between you and the mounted end. If there is, re-groove a little higher and tighten up or move the chair back a bit. You have to wrap some of the more satiny materials through the groove a second time.

THE HALF-KNOT

With the two middle strands clamped taut, take the two outside strands and make a half-knot: take the left strand and pass it over the two grooved strands, making a small figure 4. The right strand is then passed under the grooved strands and through the center of the 4. When tightened, this is the completed half-knot. If this is repeated four or five times, you have a sinnet of half-knots.

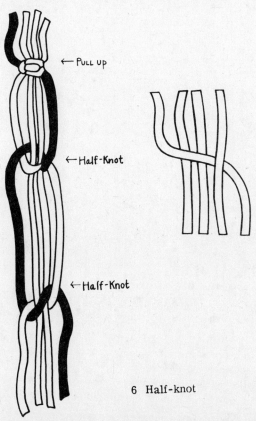

← Pull up

← Half-Knot

← Half-Knot

6 Half-knot

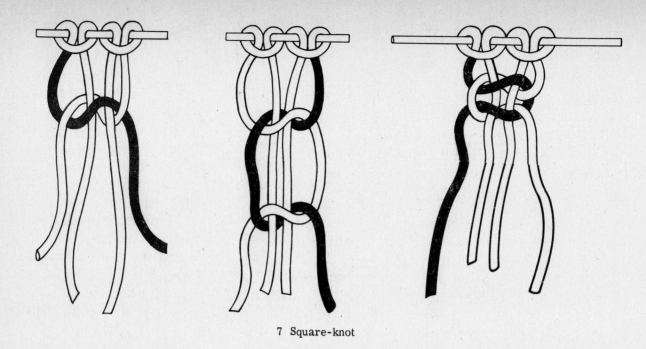

7 Square-knot

THE SQUARE-KNOT

A square knot is simply two half-knots. This second half-knot is added to the first by bringing strand number one back across the grooved strands, strand number two over it, under the grooved strands, and up through the loop. By tightening each one of the knots separately from both the top and the bottom, the knot is completed. Practice a sinnet of square knots (Fig. 8).

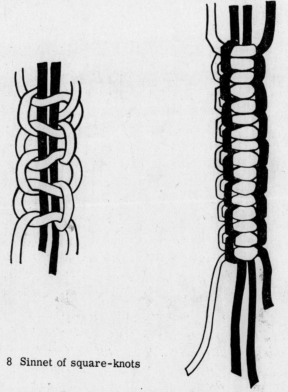

8 Sinnet of square-knots

THE HALF-HITCH

This knot with its many variations can create an almost unlimited variety of effects. The two middle strands are clamped, and the outside cord on your left is looped over the two grooved strands; then back around again and through the resulting gap. Since the knot is only used along with other knots, don't worry if it seems loose by itself. Just loop the right strand over the grooved strands and make a half-hitch under the first one. By continuing these hitches with two strands, first on the left and then on the right, you make a chain of alternating half-hitches.

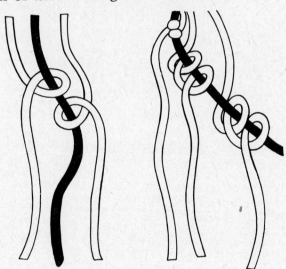

9 Half-hitch (left) and double half-hitch (right). (Only one grooved strand is being used here)

DOUBLE HALF-HITCHES

As you may have guessed, this is a series of two half-hitches made one after the other about the same strand or strands. By interworking these knots some of the most interesting macrame is made. Changing the angle of the knot-bearing strand can lead to a vast variety of designs. Try a vertical line of double half-hitches. With four strands you can make two vertical rows with each middle strand as knot-bearer for the outside strands on either side, or you can have one knot-bearer for two strands. Another possibility is a double knot-bearer in the middle. For horizontal and diagonal rows use more than four strands. Let's say there are twelve strands hanging loose. The one on the extreme left will be the knot-bearer. The bearing strand is stretched across the others at a right angle. Then, using each strand in succession, a series of half-hitches is made. They are brought under the knot-bearer and over to the left, so make sure there is a little slack still in each knot before it is in its final place. Then you can fix it with a tug. For a diagonal effect let the knot-bearer angle downward and tie in without changing the angle. Pay attention to the proper degree of tension and adjustment of the knot-bearer. As you work with diagonals, you will accidentally discover ellipses. Make them work for you at a later time.

Elements of Design

1. Pattern — Total; specific

2. Shape — of piece; within the piece

3. Texture — materials, knotting

4. Color — strands, beads, bones, shells, etc.

5. Line — amount, directions

6. Contrast — color, types of materials

7. Variety — knots, patterns

8. Density — of knots

9. Space — openness; between knots

10. Repetition — knots; pattern; lines; color

Repetitive square-knot patterns can be made by immediately tying the loose strands of one square knot into another knot. When a square-knot is to be made over two strands, the two working strands come through the middle and the two component strands hang on either side of the knot. One of these hanging strands can be used with the hanging strands of an adjacent knot to form another square. This can go on as long as you wish to continue the design. (Another approach is to use the square knot over a single strand.) Through the use of double half-hitches, knot-bearers can be made to converge and diverge, creating diamond patterns (Fig. 10). By varying the spacing and alternating the knots and grooved strands, other patterns can be brought about. For example, with four strands a conventional square knot is made by tying the two outside strands about the two inner ones. Fix these outside strands to a stomach clamp and start a square knot about an inch away from the original one and a new alignment begins to appear.

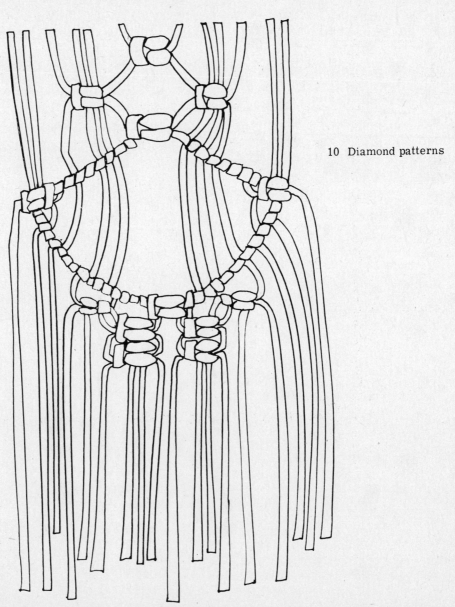

10 Diamond patterns

When two diagonal double half-hitches converge, a double half-hitch is made by one knot-bearer over the other. Vertical or horizontal rows of double half-hitches placed beside or below each other can angle off in different directions by alternating the strands being used as knot-bearers. For example, a twelve-strand row of eleven horizontal double half-hitches can be made by using the first left strand as knot bearer. Under that, a row of ten double half-hitches can be made using the second strand as bearer, and so on until the system is played out.

I don't want to give you blueprints for working in macrame, because most of the gratification of any craft comes from working it out on your own, but some of the concepts below are pretty basic and good to know when you start working out a design. They are technical considerations that can be picked up with little or no effort.

Series of knots can be worked into patterns that are either anticipated or arrived at spontaneously. Often while working one pattern, others will emerge. One day's error will be another day's plan.

An example of a pattern is the alternating square-knot triad, which can be made once the square knot is understood. As you know, a square-knot consists of two parts: the middle strands held by the stomach clamp, and the two outside strands, which, as the components of the knot, are tied around the middle ones. An alternating pattern is formed by using the component strands from the knot already tied as the middle strands for the next knot. Practice this with eight strands first, by working with two groups of four strands (Fig. 11). Make two square-knots beside each other, taking care to keep them as horizontally true as possible. Now use the right com-

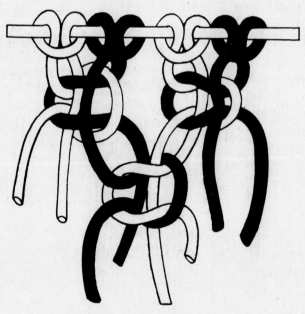

11 Alternating square-knot triad

ponent strand from the left knot and the left component strand of the right knot as the middle strands of a new knot: what was the right middle strand of the left knot becomes a component in the third square knot when it is worked in with the left middle strand of the right knot. This third knot forms a sort of inverted triangle familiar to all you junior achievers as the symbol of the Great Earth Mother. The triangle can be expanded as you become used to working with more and more strands. Make three rows of alternating square knots and you have engendered that little diamond shape within a circle that is the subconscious key to alchemy. Through silent contemplation of the horizontal, vertical, and diagonal members of the pattern, the essential energy of the universe is manifest.

Variations appear everywhere. For example, two knots (or a double square-knot) can be tied side by side with two more placed directly beneath them as if to make sinnets. When a third element such as two square knots is tied in below, the point of a triangle is made. No jive, this is how the molecules gather. Another pattern of square knots can be made with six strands using two groups of threes. One strand is used as the middle strand and the square-knot is tied around it; the second elements are made in the same side-by-side fashion. The third and final element is made by using the right component of the left knot as the middle strand. The components of this knot are the middle strand of the left element and the left component of the right element. Expand, experiment, and change this as you will. Patterns of infinite variety will come to mind. You've only to close your eyes.

Double half-hitch patterns are determined by the position of the knot-bearer. Since the double half-hitch can be drawn tightly on the knot-bearer, repeating rows of close knots can be made, to create a mat effect. A diamond pattern can be made with half-hitches by using two middle strands as knot-bearers. They diverge in opposite directions up to the last hitches at the widest point, after which they converge until the diamond is completed (see Fig. 10). Rows of double half-hitches can be placed beside and below each other for a warm, bulky effect. They also can be used to separate patterns within a whole design. Different colors can be introduced to the design with contrasting and bold effects. Materials of different color and gauge can be mixed together to create a variety of textures.

FINISHING

Loose ends can be left as fringe or tied off with a gathering-knot. (Fig. 12). On pieces like a belt, the long ends can be left for braiding and then secured by a noose-knot (Fig. 13). Ends can be further secured by placing a small knot at the tip of each strand to prevent fraying. If you're neat conscious, these knotted ends can then be cut to a uniform length. Loose ends can also be finished off by knotting sinnets (Fig. 14).

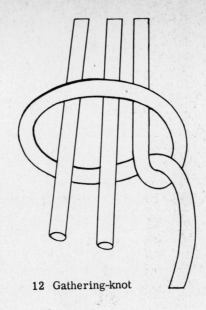

12 Gathering-knot

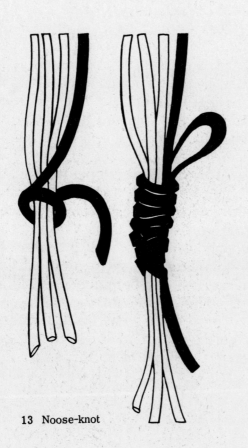

13 Noose-knot

14 Sinnet

WOODSTOCK CRAFTSMAN'S MANUAL

2

Woodstock Roots 2

Here is an extension of the first Manual, written by craftspeople who live in Woodstock, New York. Their voices are fresh with the spirit of a new age in crafts. For them there are no academies, no sexist his and her crafts, no trite projects. They have done much to eliminate the psychological block of thinking in terms of beginning, intermediate, and advanced.

The freedom is here, I think, to allow you to get together with the people and close to their crafts. They don't harness you with designs to copy; they encourage you to find your own feelings so you have the concentrated satisfaction of making something real. All you need is the ability to read to get on with these authors.

My reason for putting together these books with more crafts is that today our vitality demands more than an unquestioned allegiance to a single pursuit. It used to be that a weaver was a weaver was a weaver, but today a weaver is a songwriter, is a silversmith, is a tipi-maker, is a media freak. The whole earth is a whole life of multi-experiences.

Thanks to True Light Beaver/Alan Carey for the photographs in Making Media and the photograph of Sandee Shaw in Bronzeworking; to Arnie Abrams for the Needlepoint photographs; to Woody Woodriff, who is shown making sandals in the Sandalmaking chapter; to Glory Brightfield for borders in Tipi-Making; to Shelagh Young for illustrating Tipi-Making and Sandalmaking; to Terry Fowler for typing; to Bill Reed for his nine-to-five; to Peter Grant for his help with Stained Glass; and to Ellyn Childs, Ferol Sibley Warthen, Kyle King, Yvonne Outen, Jim Young, and all the authors who did their own illustrations.

Jean Young

Crafts

People

Patchwork Appliqué Quilting

Carol W. Abrams

Grandmother's quilt was a cave, warm and silent, hiding me from a fluorescent, clattering world where pimples, thick glasses, and big feet were unacceptable. There I would snuggle, flashlight and book in hand, succeeding often in extending the bedtime hour, invisible save for the massive lump in the center of the bed. Time never existed as I lay dreaming and toasting in the stuffy warmth of the old cover, the world outside a memory. Ah, that quilt—it wasn't a fancy patchwork delicacy, nor was it a marvel of appliqué and sewing wizardry. It was a solid, useful, heavy quilt, copper-colored on one side, functional brown on the other, six inches thick and very big.

Since then I have barely grown accustomed to the fluorescence, the noise, the masses of people. Like many poorly adjusted urbanites, I seek security in the past. Quilting has become a symbol of that past, that security. A quilt fosters a feeling of calm connectedness with people who had time to touch personally all that surrounded them. It is to these craftswomen I give my deepest thanks for giving me and others a chance to enjoy their labors.

There are many kinds of quilts and quilting techniques. The term "quilting" is misleading. It is a catchall word for appliqué and patchwork and is used in conjunction with these as well as on its own. Quilting is the final process of finishing a patchwork or appliquéd top and turning these humble pieces of cloth into plush, warm, rich blankets, feasts for the eyes and body. The simple sewing of a back, some stuffing, and a patterned top of scraps and pieces became a glorious and involving craft ... no, an art. Yes, art rivaling bas-relief. Patterns, scrolls, feathers, flowers, birds, geometrics, ropes, symbols, and signs have all been the subjects of the quilter's needles. The cold-fingered colonial and pioneer women, gathered in their fire rooms, gossiping and passing news, turned the dreary, necessary task of making bed clothing into an expression of beauty as well as welcome warmth on those bitter winter nights.

Piecework quilts, made of snips and chunks of discarded clothing and scraps remaining from sewing projects, were frugally cut and fitted into ingenious patterns with never a precious piece wasted. Some old patterns have pieces so small that many now would think it foolish to worry about such bits. In this age of inflation, we could learn much from those thrifty craftspeople: the idea of recycling material is far from a new one.

Patchwork, the technique most people think of in connection with quilting, is the same as piecework, except that instead of snips and scraps you use fabric specifically set aside for the purpose. Piecework and patchwork are actually so indistinguishable on any other level that it isn't worth the time quibbling—I will refer to both here as patchwork (you must admit it's easier than "patchwork or piecework"). Use both methods when you get involved—combine scraps you have around (finally you'll have a way to use that size-38, man-tailored shirt Cousin Isadora sent you for your nineteenth birthday) and fill out the collection with purchased stuff. Don't stand on ceremony, piece your patchwork or patch your piecework.

Appliqué is the ultimate in extravagance in quilting by comparison with patchwork. This technique is widely used by the Pennsylvania Dutch, who have perfected the art of quilting (though it's by no means the only technique they use). Sewing one piece of fabric onto another larger piece in a pattern is appliqué. Odds and ends from other sewing projects, or unworn pieces of old clothes, can be used as successfully here as with patchwork. Delicate scrolls and arches, circles and gentle curves, leaves, flowers, imaginative medallions, and other forms are all possible with appliqué, unlike patchwork, which is for practical purposes limited to straight seams. Though skilled patchworkers are able to handle very gradual curves, appliqué affords greater flexibility in design.

Both of these methods are exciting and offer possibilities that can harness the creative energies of even the most stubborn pragmatist. Imagine producing an object, useful and welcome, a grand addition to any lifestyle, adding warmth to rented flats far from home or adding that "personal" touch to professionally decorated places. Beauty and utility are interchangeable and indistinguishable when you surround yourself with a quilt of your own handicraft.

PATCHWORK

PATTERNS:

Forward, I say, and on to the nitty-gritty. Like everything else, if you haven't any experience but want to try, <u>start small</u>—a patch, a purse, a pocket—wherever your head takes you. Just whittle the following directions down to size. What shall I use as a pattern, you ask. Well, says I, anything as long as it fits into a square. There are many sources for patterns; dig out of those dusty library archives some Italian Gothic ornaments, Mohammedan designs, Byzantine folk-art patterns, Arabian floor and textile patterns. Go to your nearest toy box and take out the wooden blocks and play around with them—as tempting as it may be to build towers and go boom, try to use them as pattern builders for patches. There are many old books around of classic American patterns specifically for quilts. Maybe your grandmother has a few. You will soon want to design your own. If you're new at quilting, pick an easy pattern.

Random or Crazy Quilt patterns use schnitzels of fabric, all and any shape and size, sewn together to fit into squares. These may have been the first attempt by a needleworker to make a larger cloth from a smaller cloth. Maybe a blanket was so old and so patched that it inspired the "crazy" pattern.

By far the easiest patchwork is simply sewing squares of cloth in rows or brick-fashion. This is a very old "one-patch" pattern. Thin strips of cloth sewn into ribbons and laid in alternating light and dark stripes is an old pattern called Roman Stripes. Hexagons, rectangles, triangles have all been used for one-patch patterns. These one-patches produce soothing all-over textured patterns that were obviously the grandmothers of all the patterns in America. Great things can be done with color and fabric combinations here.

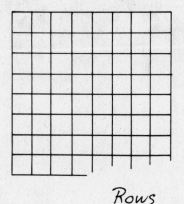

Rows

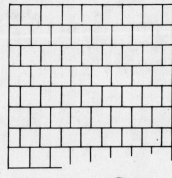

Bricks

Three-patch patterns are also simple, and the next step from one-patch. The striking (yuk, yuk) Streak o' Lightning, in which light and dark triangles are set together, is a form of this primitive pattern.

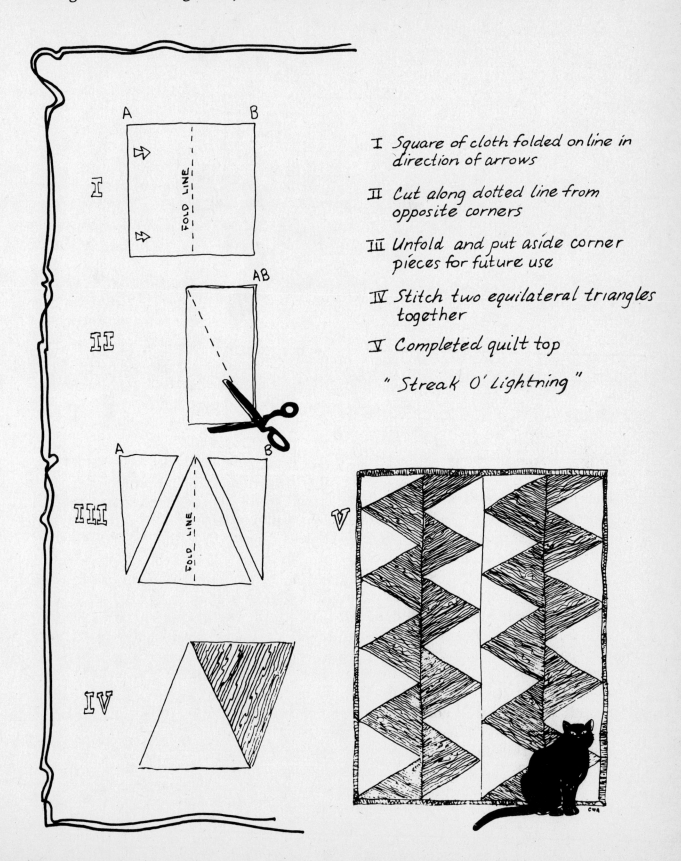

I   Square of cloth folded on line in direction of arrows

II   Cut along dotted line from opposite corners

III   Unfold and put aside corner pieces for future use

IV   Stitch two equilateral triangles together

V   Completed quilt top

"Streak O' Lightning"

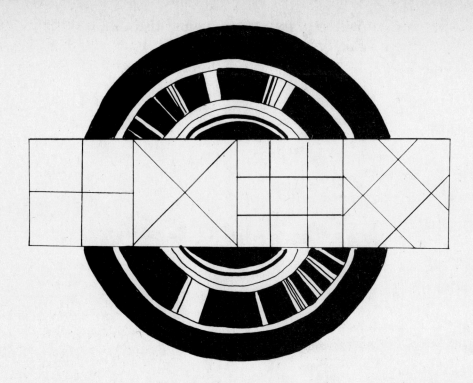

The most familiar and varied patterns for patchwork are the numerous four- and nine-patch patterns, all based on the folding and cutting of a square into three or four parts.

Diamond patterns can open up many more possibilities for effective and beautiful patches, though they are more time-consuming to make than plain squares. Middle-Eastern, Moorish, and Oriental geometrical designs have a very fine comrade in American diamond-patch patterns.

As kids we would cut from colored paper six- and eight-pointed stars, snowflakes, and lacy geometrics on dreary afternoons. We could create a snowstorm in July or a starry summer night on a drizzly November day. Little did I know these patterns, so easy and beautiful, were the basis for many, many impressive patches: Lemon Star, Carpenter's Wheel, Sunburst, etc. Here's a chance to mess around as if you were eight again, and have a productive time of it. Newspaper, construction paper, brown paper—whatever you have on hand—and a pair of long-bladed scissors are all you need. Using colored construction or two different kinds of plain paper gives you a chance to visualize colors in a completed pattern or relationship of light and dark. In the old days quilts made for the spring and fall had lightweight filling and a color scheme of spring white and fall colors. They have a nice dark-and-light effect.

The paper should be 14 to 18 inches square. A big square is more fun than a little square. The square you choose will be the size of one cloth patch when finished. Fold the square into three or four parts. Make straight cuts through all the layers of paper and see what you come up with.

Folds

Interchanging pieces

Cut two or three of the same shape from different papers and interchange the pieces with one another. This is the basis of all patchwork. If you don't like what you've come up with, try again until you do. Keep in mind that all the seams (cuts) should be straight, for ease in sewing, especially if you are a novice. Concave and convex forms are tough to fit to make the patch come out perfectly square later. Save the fancy curves for appliqué. There are many classic patterns relying on curves—Orange Peel, Drunkard's Path, Dresden Plate, Rob-Peter-to-Pay-Paul—so don't put them out of your mind completely. I am just advising discretion.

"Drunkard's Path"

"Rob Peter to Pay Paul"

Fold in direction of arrows along dotted line

Right angles, squares, isosceles triangles, equilateral- and right-triangle rectangles, and parallelograms are all pure forms, and any number of unique patterns can be worked up by using them in conjunction with one another. It's one great and fascinating puzzle.

Folding a square to make a six-pointed or eight-pointed star is easy. The eight-pointed star is a real gas to play with; as the angles between the points form a right angle they can be used easily with squares and right triangles.

Cut along "A-B" through all layers

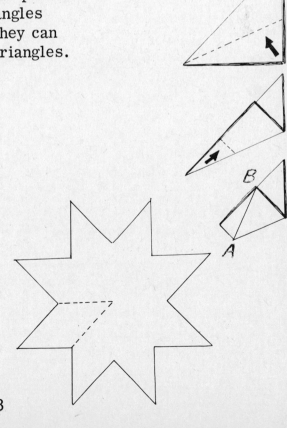

233

Once you find the forms you like, make pattern "templates" of them out of flexible bristol board, cutting them with precision. Record your patterns full size in a notebook or drawing pad as reference for future quilts and as an insurance against the loss of your templates. Write on each template the number of times you'll need to cut that shape out of cloth to complete each kind of patch you are planning to use. All the pieces must fit precisely together "as accurately as a baby's puzzle," one of my teachers has said. This is the time to assure yourself of that accuracy. You can build quite a collection of templates to use over and over again. Our grandmothers and great-grandmothers would exchange their patterns, each user adding her own touch. Histories can be written tracing familiar old European patterns as they moved through colonial, pioneer, Victorian, and turn-of-the-century changes, and there is always room for more; an original pattern is prized above all else. In this day of extended leisure time, and with the need to touch once again all that surrounds us, patchwork and all forms of handwork are welcome.

FABRICS:

Broadcloth, men's shirt fabrics (especially the new bright prints), muslin, fine linen, percale, cambric, polished cotton, good old gingham, and, of course, calico and chintz are fine for a washable, usable product, whether it be for appliqué or patchwork. Old sheets with bright patterns and colors are perfect. Baby clothes and old shirts and dresses are good for patches. Wools, silks, velours, velvets, and satins are excellent, and very plush for patchwork. These require some experience to handle and should be steered clear of by the novice. This age of permanent press can be a boon to the quilter, though many prefer to stick to the original natural cottons and linens and wools used by the early quilters. The rougher, wrinkly surface of these fabrics lend a certain charm that the synthetics can't offer. You must go where your head takes you. I use anything I can get my hands on that will work well with my patterns, as long as the fabrics are of comparable weight and composition.

If you are hard up for scraps, hunt through the closets and boxes

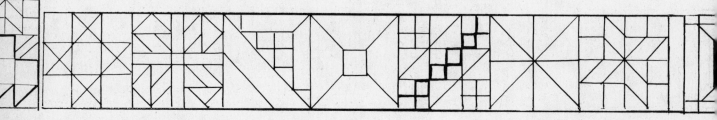

around the place. This is a good excuse for cleaning out the attic. One veteran quilter I know goes to the Salvation Army or similar outlets and buys old clothes to cut up for patches. Neighbors, friends, and relatives are also good sources. This was the way scraps were latched on to by the early quilters. It must have been fascinating to go over the patches: "This is granny's wedding dress, sister's christening robe, great-grandfather's best Sunday suit..." Imagine the future: "This is grandma's jeans she wore at her lib meetings, sister's workshirt she wore in the Chicago riots, great-grandfather's best meditation toga..."

If you are buying material for your quilt, measure the surface you anticipate covering (i.e., bed, pillow). Add a few inches for seams and translate into yardage. This will cover your backing. With full-size paper patterns of your basic patch blocks determine how many patches you will be using to cover the surface of your quilt; in order to complete the design, some blocks must be sewn side by side; others can be framed with strips of fabric or interspersed checkerboard fashion with plain fabric blocks (squares). Account for a border also if you want one. You should have an idea now of how much basic fabric you'll be needing to cover the back, and the borders and blank blocks if you are using any. Once these decisions are made you'll know the number of patch blocks. You have already marked each template with the number of times it will have to be used to complete each basic patch block. Trace the template that many times on a large sheet of paper, placing each tracing at right angles to the paper's edge as you would on fabric. Group those to be cut from the same fabric together. Leave at least 1/2-inch on all sides of each tracing. Repeat this process for all the templates to be used to complete the block. With a straight-edged ruler, measure the areas each set of templates occupies on the paper. Treat the templates of the same type that will be cut from the same fabric as one set. Multiply these sets by the number of patches required to complete the quilt. Convert the number you get into yardage. You will have the amount of fabric needed for each fabric used in all the patches. Be generous—better too much stuff than too little. This process may sound a little like the "house that Jack built." Take it slow and it will work every time.

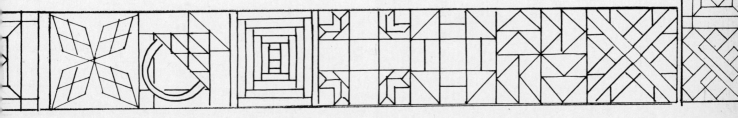

As an example, let's choose this block for the top of the quilt. We will use it six times to complete the design (this is an arbitrary number, the number of times you will use a block is up to you.)

It takes three templates to make up the block chosen. I have shown the templates cut out of cardboard and marked on them the number of times each will be used to complete one block.

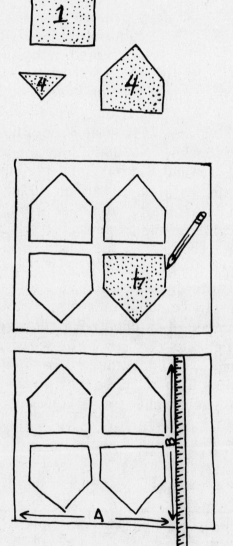

On a large sheet of paper trace one of the templates the number of times it will be used from one type of fabric (lay the templates, as you would on the fabric, at right angles to the sides, leaving a generous 1/2-inch between each tracing for the seam allowances).

With a ruler or tapemeasure measure the width and length of the area occuped by the template tracings. Multiply side A by side B and you will have the number of square inches of fabric one set of pieces from one template will require. Then multiply that number by the number of times you will be using the complete block on the surface of your quilt (in this case we decided to use this block six times, so multiply by six). From this you will derive the number of square inches of fabric you will need all together for all the pieces cut from the same fabric from one template.

Repeat this whole process for each template.

Convert the total number of square inches into yards of fabric you will need (see chart). I usually add a safety margin of at least 1/2-yard to give me room to manipulate the pieces and allow for errors.

There are:
1296 square inches per yard of 36-inch-wide fabric

1620 square inches per yard of 45-inch-wide fabric

1872 square inches per yard of 52-inch-wide fabric

If you are using scraps, there's no way to tell you how much of what cloth you'll be needing, obviously. But that's the fun of it. You'll still have to figure out your backings, borders, and empty blocks as before, though. Unless you are lucky and have enough stuff around, you'll have to purchase that much fabric at least. Group your scraps together by color instead of by pattern, as it is most likely you will have more scraps similar in color than in pattern. That way you will know what colors you have most of and which one will dominate. There are no set formulas for any of this, it all depends upon what you have available to you at the time. You can make each patch complete in its own color scheme, with the pattern determining how they will be coordinated; or you can disperse your colors evenly throughout the quilt. A quilt whose pattern is made of scraps is a lot like people; the pattern is the same but the fabric each individual patch is made from determines its character. Within one quilt each patch could be different— bold and bright, soft and quiet, crazily mixed up, darkly somber, subtly textured, or sunny and light.

CUTTING AND MAKING PATCHES:

Your templates are made, your fabric is together, and you are ready to begin. With these, a pencil, iron and ironing board, <u>sharp</u> scissors with long blades (notice the emphasis on sharp), and a lap-size board or table, with a good light, you are ready to cut your pieces. Whether you are making a bed-size quilt or a single patch you must organize yourself. Even though you are not instrument-flying, try and repeat to yourself "precision and accuracy," "precision and accuracy," "precision and accuracy," throughout this whole trip. This is where it counts. All pieces must be cut accurately so they fit precisely together to avoid unnecessary pulling and puckering later.

Wash all new fabric before you begin. It removes stiff sizing and shrinks it now—not later, after the quilt is completed. Check also to see if the fabric's color runs. Wow, could that be messy!

You had better have a reasonable relationship with your iron, as you'll be seeing a lot of it from now on. Press all fabric smooth. Spread the fabric, <u>front side down</u>, on the lap-board or table. With the longest part of the template running along the length of the fabric parallel to the selvages (the warp, or bound sides), trace the template as you did on paper once before. Use a sharp pencil, sharpening it as you go if necessary. A two-degree variation in some patterns can distort the entire quilt's surface. Repeat "precision and accuracy," as you carefully trace all the pieces you'll need. Leave 1/2-inch between each tracing—a generous 1/2-inch at that— as this is your seam allowance. If you are using a patterned cloth, make sure your template tracings are all running in the same direction to assure evenness and symmetry in all the patches. Repeat "precision and accuracy." Now, relax, go for a walk, flip on the FM, or just have a leisurely cup of tea before moving on to the next step. Have a friend over so you can brag about how well you are doing.

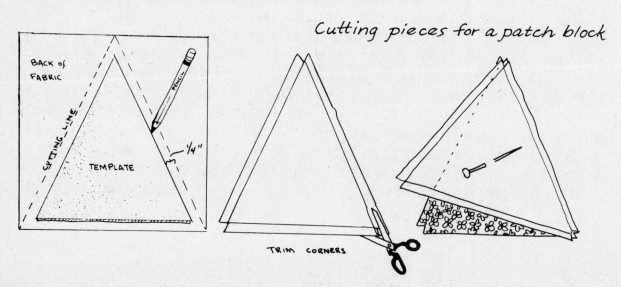

Cutting pieces for a patch block

BACK of FABRIC

CUTTING LINE

TEMPLATE

PENCIL

1/4"

TRIM CORNERS

<u>Carefully</u> cut around the pencil lines, leaving 1/4-inch excess as a seam allowance. The pencil line becomes your seam line. White blackboard chalk or French tailor's chalk can be used on dark fabrics if pencil won't show. The chalk should make a thin, fine line for reasons already stated. Use sandpaper or emery board to keep the chalk sharp. Pencil is better if you can possibly manage it. Remember "precision and accuracy."

Cut all the pieces for all the patches now so that, should you be short on fabric, you will have a better chance of matching it. Use a lap-size board while sitting in a comfortable chair. This makes cutting very pleasant, especially if the chair is on the front porch of an old farm-type house. Breathe in the good air (pretend, can't you?) and really experience this homely task. Consider the past, look to the future. Become one with yourself and the world. The board gives you a place to spread the fabric with its tracings out in front of you. Sort the pieces, either by color and shape or by complete patch. If you are using scraps but have definite ideas about what you want in color and pattern put the pieces for a whole patch together. Otherwise sorting by shape is convenient, so that you can grab a piece when you need it. Safety-pin them together whichever way you sort them. Just don't lose any. Man, that would be disastrous if you had no more fabric — just think.

After traveling along this long arduous road, you are now prepared to stitch the pieces together. You'll need your iron again, a short, sharp needle, and white (it's stronger) mercerized cotton. A good light, a comfortable chair, a crackling fire or your favorite "soap," or some good conversation with a good friend provides a really fine atmosphere in which to complete each patch. Remove two pieces that are placed next to one another in your pattern from their pins and press them if they are wrinkled. Put them face to face with the sides that correspond together. The pencil lines

Stitching the pieces

239

are the lines that you will be stitching on, using small, neat running stitches. Knot your thread to start and, at the end of each seam, backstitch once or twice to finish. Make sure your needle is piercing the pencil lines on both pieces of fabric so that they will fit perfectly together. Repeat "precision and accuracy."

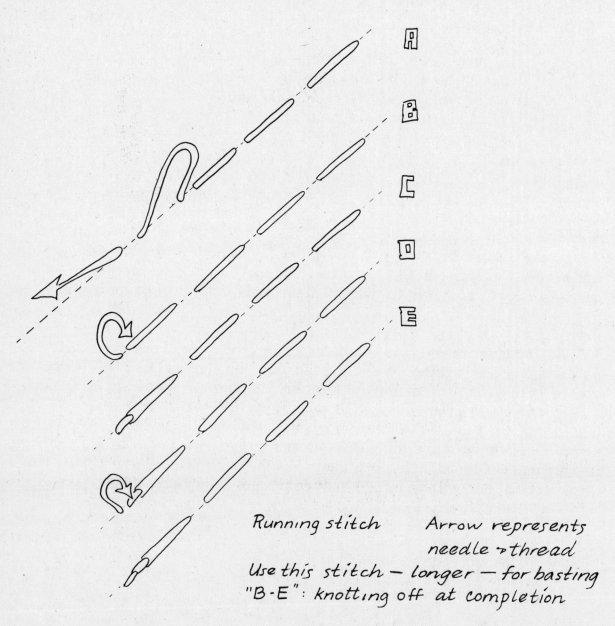

Running stitch   Arrow represents
                    needle → thread
Use this stitch — longer — for basting
"B-E": knotting off at completion

Press these pieces lightly, flattening the seam to one side. Repeat the stitching process with the next adjoining piece. Finish seaming various sections of the pattern first, then join them together, overcasting the corners where they join. Try to be accurate. "Precision and accuracy" is truer here than anywhere else. In no time your patch should be complete. Iron it lightly from the back, pressing all the seams over to one side.

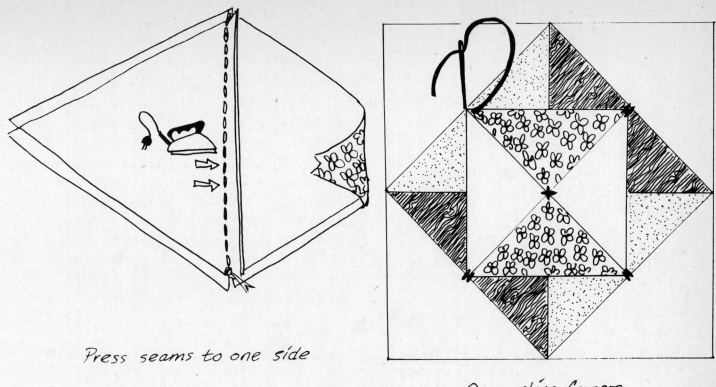

Press seams to one side

Overcasting Corners

BLOCKING:

Blocking means simply pressing the patchwork block so that it will lie square. You'll need, once more, your ironing board, or, better still, a table, or board larger than your block, with a couple of layers of towels and a sheet or pillowcase thrown over it. Pin down the patchwork block with the corners square. Use a right angle of some sort—a protractor or carpenter's angle; don't eyeball it, that's too inaccurate. Stretch and pin the piece securely and lay a damp cloth over it. Press smooth, starting from the edges and working to the middle. That way you don't stretch and distort the edges. Ironing the block dry is a no-no. Steaming is the key, and a steam iron is even better. You are only trying to set the block straight, not dry the living daylights out of it. Let the block cool off a minute before removing it from the board so it won't stretch while it is still damp and hot. Blocking will be the test for your "precision and accuracy" sessions. If you have laid and cut your pieces accurately, sewn precisely on the pencil lines, pressed the pieces all along—then there will be no problems. If not, then your difficulties will show. Doom and gloom—puckered seams (too tight stitching), pulling corners (inaccurate cutting, tsk, tsk), separating seams (too loose stitching or seams that weren't flattened to one side), lopsided fittings—doom and gloom. You've learned though, and should try again. Most likely none of these things will have happened at all (if you were thinking about what you were doing).

SETTING AND SEAMING:

Now the blocks are prepared to be "set" together. This is a quaint term meaning fitting and sewing together the blocks and any strips or blank blocks that are used to connect your patchwork blocks. When all your blocks of patchwork are complete, lay them out and admire them. Arrange them in the order that you want. Check out the total measurements again and adjust the borders and connecting bands, if you'll have any. If you had decided to lay out a checkerboard-type quilt with every other block blank, check to see if the blank blocks correspond in size to your patched blocks. Adjust the seam allowances now. Pat yourself on the back. Brag a little. You've come this far and the rest is a downhill trip, coasting all the way.

A few variations on quilt sets

I like to do all my seams by hand. I enjoy it. Seam the blocks together using neat running stitches, overcasting corners as before. If you've decided to use a sewing machine, adjust the stitch length to a bit longer than the one ordinarily used for the type of fabric you're using. The seams won't be so pinched after quilting. For a quilt with borders around each block, add the shorter borders, on the top and bottom first. For the long vertical borders connecting these strips of blocks and borders, basting first is recommended, even if you are using a machine. Stitch as before. Repeat until the top is done. Press the whole surface from the back checking that all the seams are secure and flat to one side.

HALLELUIAH! It's time to quilt.

But first a word about appliqué.

APPLIQUÉ

Lush primordial ferns, rich lazy feathers, weird birds, and all sorts of exotic flora and fauna have been spread over quilt tops in appliqué for centuries. Fantastic wreaths of roses, strawberries on vines of laurel leaves, eagles, farmhouses, grapes—almost anything the mind could conjure was used. Appliqué gives the needleworker a chance to experience long continuous curves, jagged shapes, tiny circles, and complicated forms. Things that patchwork couldn't offer.

The appliquéd top is usually worked in blocks, much the same as patchwork. But instead of building a block of fabric from smaller pieces, you sew fabric pieces cut in shapes onto a solid fabric block. Pattern inspirations are all around us—hands, kaleidoscopes, Busby Berkeley movies, your mother's old crystal, food, circuses, gardens, traffic signs—

anything can be converted into a pattern appliqué. If you've patched a pair of jeans you've appliquéd.

The principles, procedures, and measurements are almost the same as for patchwork—the pattern worked up, templates cut, fabric needs determined. The only real difference is that the templates do not have to fit precisely together, as you are not fitting a block from the pieces. One appliqué extra you may want to put on your shopping list is bias tape. More about this later.

Cut-paper patterns are fun, and those used for patchwork can easily be adapted to appliqué. Cut curves, holes, petal forms, snowflakes, old-fashioned hearts, Art Nouveau forms—see what you get. If you want geometrics or patterns that are symmetrical, fold paper and cut much as before. Don't get too terribly involved (especially at first) with intricacies, doodads, and tiny little shapes, as tempting as that may be (they are difficult to sew down, anyway). Bold simple shapes are easier to handle. Canadian multimedia artist Joyce Wieland designed a huge, wall-hanging quilt using the cool, sensual lines of Canadian landscapes, each block containing a different pattern and each block a different size. There are things that surround us that can be beautifully worked up into intriguing patterns. Look around, become aware, the world is beautiful.

When you have found something you like, trace it out on large sheets of paper. Paint or color it with crayons or cut it from colored paper and see what relationships develop (remembering, of course, that your fabric colors will only approximate the pattern's painted ones).

Cut your cardboard templates.

A review of what was covered in the previous section: First, measure the amount of backing material you will need, allowing for seams around the edges. Then, measure the amount of base fabric you'll need to cover the top. You can do this by simply doubling the amount you need for the backing, if you choose to leave it whole and appliqué over the entire top. This is especially effective for large bold central designs. On the other hand, you can cut the top up into blocks; if you plan to do this, remember to add extra for the seams you'll need to join them together. Blocks are easier than trying to manipulate yards of fabric all at once. I can't sit with an 8- or 10-foot-wide piece of cloth and try to stitch a 3-inch by 4-inch shape to it without a little frustration. Many needleworkers carry it off beautifully and with little trouble, so obviously it isn't impossible. Now, measure the amount of fabric you'll need for your appliqué pattern by again tracing all your templates and measuring the tracing areas for each fabric you'll be using. Record your templates in a notebook, as suggested for patchwork. I encourage this because more than once my cats have taken great delight in chewing up my templates and leaving their sodden punctured remains all over my work place. So rather than eliminate the cats, or lock my templates up, I simply retrace them from my notebook. (Cats, as I'm sure you realize, aren't the only threat to templates.)

So, you've designed a pattern, cut your templates, figured the fabric yardage you need for the back, top, and the borders and the pattern (avoiding stretchy or sleazy fabrics), and have your trusty iron, sharp scissors, table or cutting board, and sharp pencils on hand. You are now ready to begin. Make sure you are working in a comfortable well-lit environment. Baroque recorder music might be a soothing accompaniment.

Carefully trace the templates on the back of the fabric, leaving a generous 1/2-inch between each tracing. Cut and sort the pieces as described for patchwork. Mistakes made cost time and material. Once again, each piece should be ironed and this time the edges should be turned under 1/4-inch. If you find that you are singeing your fingers in the process then crease the edge under as you would fold paper, between your fingers. Most fabrics will cooperate, at least until you can press the edges down with the iron. Use the pencil line as the fold line so the pieces conform to the templates. On deep curves, convex or concave, clip the seam allowance to ease the strain. Don't cut through the penciled seam line or it will show on the piece's surface as a slash and will ravel and fray. Ugly, ugly. You might even run a basting stitch or a very long machine stitch right on the pencil line before folding the seam allowance under. This seems to ease folding. Baste the folded edge down with a contrasting colored thread and long running stitches. Keep your knots on top so you can just clip them off and pull out the thread when the appliqué is complete. Sort the pieces and pin them together with long safety pins, and move on.

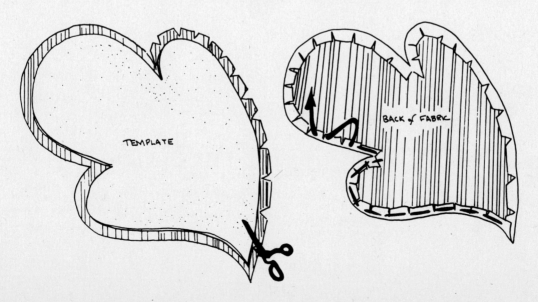

TEMPLATE

BACK of FABRIC

Find the center of your block by folding it into equal quarters. This helps lay out the pattern evenly, especially if it is symmetrical. Lay your pattern pieces out on the base block in the order you wish to complete the pattern. You may even wish to transfer an outline of the whole pattern onto the base block with transfer pencil, dressmaker's carbon, or chalk. Then all you have to do is stick the right pieces onto the right shape, sort of like the "cut and paste" stickers that Uncle Dan gave you for Christmas (even though you were almost eighteen). Baste the pieces down to the block in contrasting thread, overlapping sections appropriately (stems behind flowers, etc.). Then sew the pattern down with super-neat appliqué stitches, keeping the pieces and base block as smooth and flat as possible. Use white thread or a color to coordinate with the pieces. Most appliquéers sew the pieces down by hand with the base blocks in their laps or on a table. I like to use a 10-inch standing embroidery hoop or the larger standing quilting hoop, depending upon the size of the base block. You might want to try it. It gives a nice smooth finish and frees both hands for stitching. Mount your base block in the hoop so the surface is smooth. Don't over-stretch it by making the fabric too tight or you'll have just what you didn't want—puckering. Neatly appliqué the pieces to the surface and, if you didn't stretch the base too tight, you'll have a very professional-looking product. As you can see, I discourage very stretchy fabrics (though every fabric will stretch some), because there is less control of surface tension with them.

Basting

Appliqué stitch should be very tiny-- almost invisible.

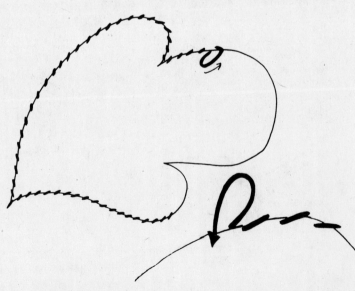

If you have a pattern with pieces less than 1 inch wide, then bias tape can be used very comfortably, giving you the chance to avoid having to cut such thin schnitzels of cloth. You can purchase this ready-made in any well-stocked notions department, or you can make it out of the fabric used for the rest of your pieces. I like making it. It's therapeutic. This way you wind up with a perfectly coordinated appliqué at less expense. Bias strips can also be used for binding the completed quilt's edges. You must account for these things when you purchase the fabric for your project. Gad, it is frustrating to have bias stripping that goes all around the quilt . . . almost. To make bias strips, pull a thread running from one selvage to the other on each cut edge of a piece of the fabric. (This ensures that the warp and weft of the fabric are at right angles to each other.) Fold the fabric so that the selvage of one side runs along the pulled thread line of the adjacent perpendicular side. With a long straight-edge (a metal-edged ruler is perfect) laid diagonally on the fold as in the illustration, draw parallel lines about 1 inch or 1-1/2 inch wide with a pencil. With sharp scissors cut the lines. Press under the edges of each strip to make the right width.

To use bias stripping or commercial bias tape on straight lines is easy; just baste down and appliqué. To use it on curved lines, baste the <u>inside</u> of the curve first, then appliqué, <u>baste</u>, and stitch the outside of the curve last. This way, the tape has a chance to stretch into place without the interior curves puckering. Believe me, it really works.

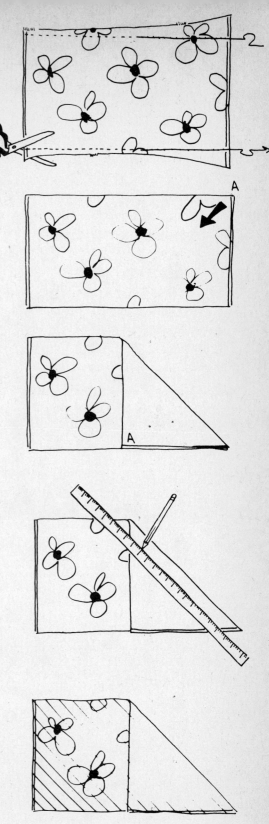

Making bias strips

247

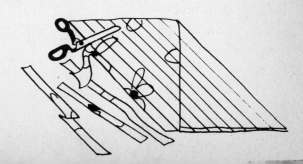

When the pattern is complete on a base block, you should block it by pinning it to the ironing board and pressing it with a damp cloth in the same manner described for patchwork. Work gently—avoid stretching. Press from the <u>center</u> out to the sides, unlike the sides-to-the-center method for patchwork. Appliqué presses much smoother this way. When all the blocks are completed and ready to be set together, lay them out and make all the necessary adjustments and considerations now. They will be breathtakingly gorgeous, right? Set and seam the completed blocks together, checkerboard, strips and borders, angles... whatever you feel suits your pattern best.

One more time: HALLELUIAH! It is time to quilt.

... almost.

If you have chosen an elaborate patchwork pattern with very little negative (empty or blank) space in it you'll not have to fuss too much with quilting patterns (the linear patterns the quilting stitching makes), as the patchwork becomes the major part of your quilting pattern. If you have chosen to make a top with alternate blocks of pattern and space (checkerboard), quilting patterns must be considered and chosen. Most appliqué tops have quite a bit of negative space. There again patterns must be selected. It is here your imagination can run wild. Quilting patterns are much like a pebble thrown in water. The many concentric rings form the pattern. Quilting patterns are just a stone thrown in water that refused to throw up concentric rings—instead there are concentric forms of all sorts, ropes, waves, feather forms, geometric forms, and so many more.

Quilting is simply the sewing together of a top, some stuffing, and a back or bottom. Sounds simple, right? Wrong. Sure, you can just stitch the three layers together so they don't slip, but if you are going to invest

Some quilting patterns

all that time in just stitching them together, why not make it an exciting creative experience? So far, patchwork or appliqué has been more than creating big things from little things or sticking one piece of cloth onto another. Quilting the top to its stuffing and backing can also become more than just stitching together. Some of the more expressive antique patterns for quilting were ferns, wreaths, feathers, feathers, feathers, plant forms, fan forms, geometric forms, and pineapples (yeah, pineapples), to name just a few. Early American quilters often traced around their kitchen utensils to make up their quilting designs of concentric circles, interlocking circles, waves, ropes, and vines. Almost any simple shape can be used— hands, feet, bird forms, flower forms, geometrics, some of those fantastic Art Nouveau shapes, symbols. Blow your grandmother's mind by quilting peace symbols all over a White House Steps quilt top. A Spirograph can be of great assistance in making your own designs, which can be transferred to the quilt's surface.

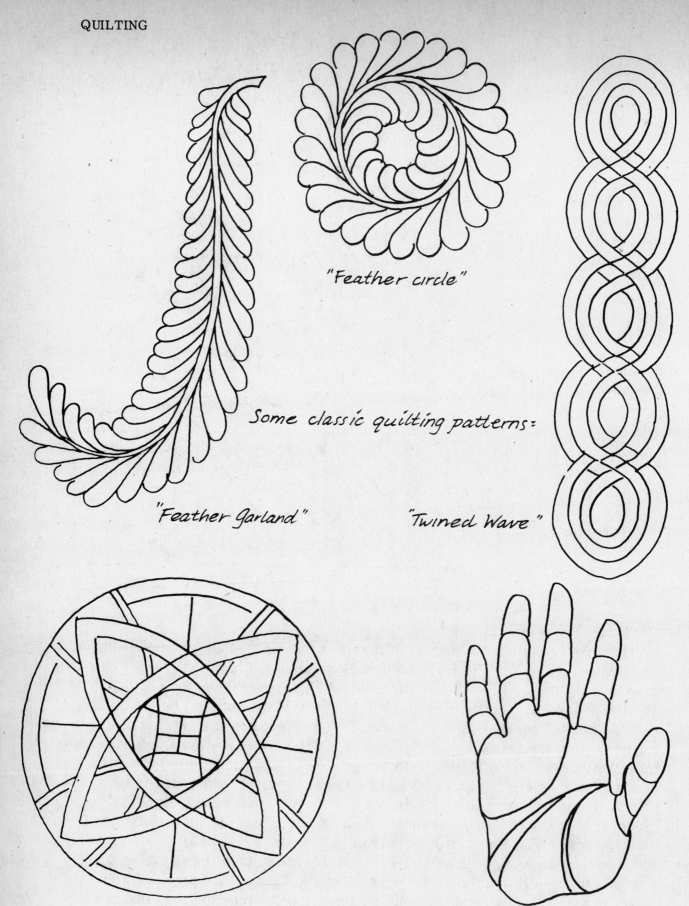

"Feather circle"

Some classic quilting patterns:

"Feather Garland"

"Twined Wave"

A compass and hand used as quilting patterns

The main consideration throughout this whole deal is to secure all three layers together so the stuffing doesn't shift; therefore, there shouldn't be wide expanses of space left on the quilt top when it is finished. Distances of not more than 2 or 3 inches of space are ideal if you are using a thin stuffing. Distances of 4 to 6 inches are acceptable for thicker stuffing.

As I mentioned, patchwork-patterned tops don't usually require very elaborate pattern considerations as the patchwork itself is the major quilting design. Appliqué patterns can pose very exciting challenges to the quilter as their patterns are usually very open, with lots of space. Theoretically, the back of the quilt should be as attractive as the top when the quilting is done. Keep this in mind when designing the quilting patterns you'll be using.

Draw full-size on newsprint paper the pattern or patterns you will be using. Trace them on tissue paper with a transfer pencil (found in good notion departments or needlecraft-supply houses) and press it out onto the quilt top. Or you can use a dressmaker's carbon and wheel—follow the directions for use on the package. Don't use typewriter carbon paper, it's not made for this purpose, and smears, and stains, and in general will spoil your disposition to quilt. You can use cardboard templates and trace your patterns with a sharp, hard-lead pencil. If you use this technique, be sure to sew on the pencil lines so they will disappear more readily. This technique is especially useful for repetitive patterns, as you'll only have to make the template once.

After you have put your quilting designs on the whole quilt top, using any one of the methods that you find most comfortable, you'll be ready to place the quilt into its frame for the actual quilting. If you are more existential by nature and wish to decide on pattern as you go along, you can do so right in the frames. This is especially effective for sampler quilts set in checkerboard fashion, with each patchwork or appliqué block containing a different pattern and alternating with blocks of solid colors with varying quilting designs.

Now can I quilt? Well...

THE FRAME

You must build a quilting frame (actually there are other options open to you here; see page 261) and prepare the top, stuffing, and back for the frame, which takes longer to describe than to do. Some people have been able to buy an old frame for a few $$$ in country used-furniture stores, but you can easily construct your own with very little understanding of carpentry. All you need are two 10-foot-long two-by-fours and one 8-foot-long two-by-four, a saw, a drill and 1/2-inch bit, 1/2-inch doweling, sandpaper, shellac or varnish, brush, staple gun, wide twill-tape (mattress ticking or heavy canvas strips will substitute nicely)—at least twenty feet of it—and four C-clamps (optional). This will make a frame that is adjustable, large enough to carry a double-bed covering, and flexible enough to do smaller projects on. Obviously, you'll need space to lay out your frame. Don't panic, though, if you get a closed-in feeling with the prospect of a 10-by-4-foot frame; the directions can be modified to make a smaller frame if you need one.

Drill holes about 2 inches apart for about 2 feet through either end of each 10-foot length of two-by-four. Saw the 8-foot two-by-four in half and drill holes 2 inches apart for 1 foot or so through either end of each half. Sand and smooth all the boards, smooth off the ends, and lay on a couple of coats of varnish or shellac. Cut the doweling into 6-inch-long pegs, sand them smooth. You'll need only four pegs at any time but cut yourself some extras anyway. There's no need to shellac these. You might have to sand them down a bit to fit.

Making a frame

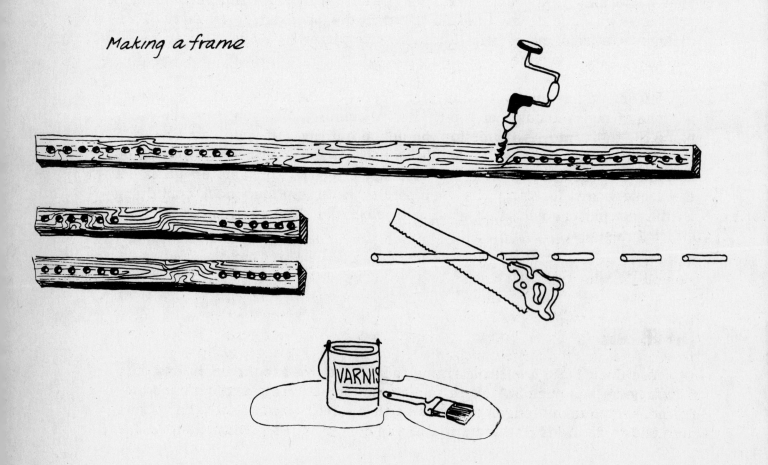

If you can't find twill tape that is at least 4 inches wide dig up some canvas or ticking that wide. (Either get it from an upholsterer or make it yourself.) Fold the strips in half lengthwise and staple them to the 10-foot boards, keeping the fold away from the wood and skirting the holes. The frame is done.

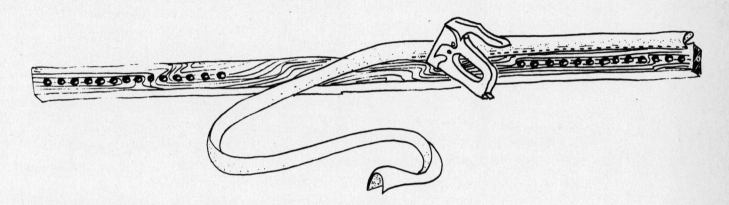

To use the frame you'll need four ladder-back chairs you can prop the frame on, or two sawhorses 28 to 32 inches high, depending upon how tall you are and the height of the chair you'll be using. Your chair should be comfortable and armless so you can slide it under the frame. For me, the best frame height is a bit higher than elbow height when I sit in a chair. Finding the right chair and positioning of the frame should be done carefully. You'll be spending many hours here, and cricked backs and numb elbows can be avoided with a little thought. Many quilters prefer their frames chest high. They feel they can see the stitching better.

MOUNTING

The frame is ready for mounting the quilt. The fabric used for the back should be seamed together if necessary. The filling, which should be of the highest quality you can afford, can be purchased from most good department stores and fabric shops. Also, many craft and needlecraft magazines have advertisements with order forms for stuffing. It comes by the pound or in sheets folded and rolled. Cotton batting is most easily available, but some of the synthetics are rapidly gaining in popularity. They are light and easy to work with and produce a beautifully puffed product. By the sheet (synthetic or cotton) purchase double the yardage needed to cover the whole quilt, plus a few inches all around. One-half pound of cotton stuffing is needed per square yard of quilt to be covered. Check with the manufacturer to be sure. You can also use blanket flannel or an old woolen blanket as a filling if you don't need quite so much warmth and weight. Many old quilts had this kind of filling if the quilt was to be used in the summer or in warmer climates. This quilting is not as plush, obviously, but just as effective if done well.

If you are fortunate enough to have a carpet bigger than your quilt, or a floor you can push tacks into, great. If not, wide masking tape will do. Lay the backing with the fabric right side down on the floor. Pin, tack, or tape it to the floor with the sides parallel and the corners at right angles. Spread the filling over the backing evenly. If you are using sheets, lay them down in one direction, overlapping the edges about 1/4-inch, and then spread another layer on top of the first in the opposite direction, overlapping the edges as before. This prevents hollows showing through the top after quilting. The filling should extend beyond the backing's edges a bit.

Baste the filling to the back with long running stitches; start from the center and work out to the sides, then work from the center to the corners diagonally and all around the perimeter. Use a long needle and butt it against the floor as you baste so you know that you have stitched through both layers. Slide a piece of cardboard between the backing and carpet so you don't sew the two layers to the rug. A curved needle might help with the basting—bend one in a vice or look for a curved upholsterer's needle. Bladelike canvas needles can slash your backing, making it useless, so avoid them.

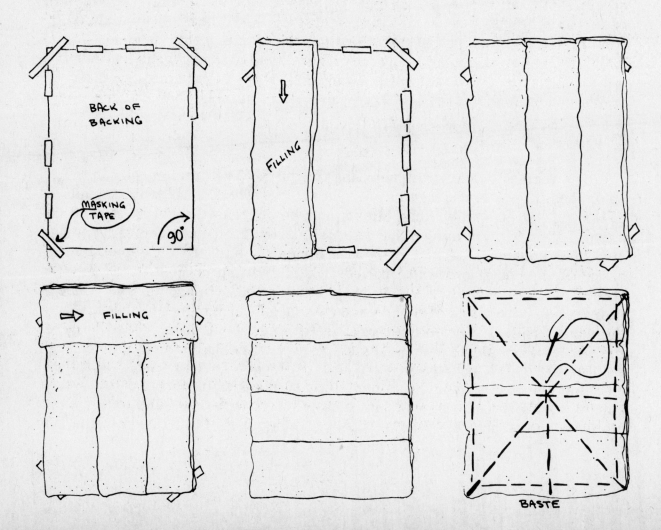

Iron the top again, smoothing all the wrinkles, and recheck to be sure that seams are all flat and to one side and all the corners are overcast. Be sure that all the surface basting stitches are removed. Lay the top down on the layers of backing and filling; it's sort of like one huge sandwich. All the sides should be parallel and coincide exactly with the backing; if not, there will be curling and sagging happening all over the place. Bad news. Trim the backing if it is too large for the top or vice versa. The corners should be at right angles to the sides. Use a protractor or a carpenter's right-angle. Baste the top down to the other layers, from the center out as before. Detach the whole thing from the floor. The entire surface should be smooth. The basting stitches should not be too tight or too small. The quilt stitching will actually secure the layers together; the basting is just to hold it together until it is mounted and sewn.

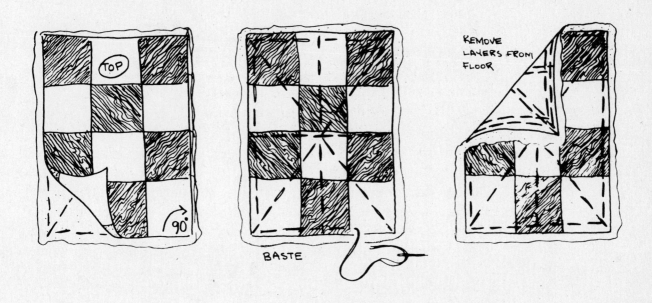

With the layers back on the floor, place the longest bars of the frame along the shortest ends of the quilt, facing the tape toward the quilt. Center the quilt on one of the bars by measuring and marking the center of the quilt's side and the center of the bar and matching the two. With the center marks together, stitch the quilt to the tape with even running stitches. Use strong thread (buttonhole twist or linen thread for braided rugs) and work from the center to each end. Repeat this procedure on the opposite side. The quilt must be centered or the surface of the quilt will be lopsided after you dismount it from the frame.

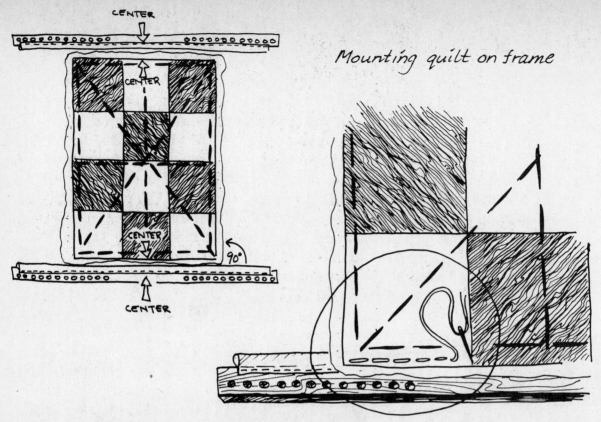

Mounting quilt on frame

With the help of a friend, roll the quilt under, carefully so that it is smooth and tight, an equal number of times on each bar. The top of the quilt is exposed. The two bars and rolled quilt should resemble the ancient scrolls of Jerusalem. The quilt is still on the floor. Slide the two shorter bars under the ends of the longer bars so that they are perpendicular to one another. <u>Carefully</u> unroll the quilt enough so that there are about 3 feet of quilt exposed between the bars. This is the area you will be quilting first. The center of the quilt should be in the center of the frame. Match holes in the bars and slip in a peg at all four corners. The corners must form right angles and the quilt must be suspended drum-tight between the bars; if not it should be rerolled. Again, the edges of the quilt and the blocks

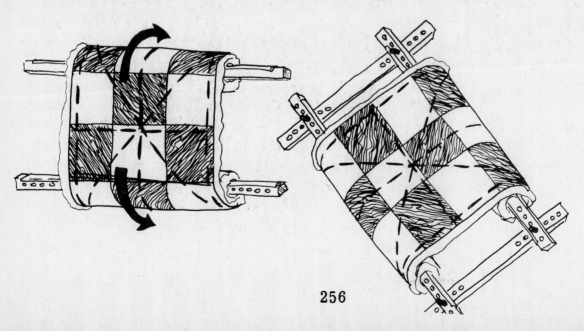

256

must be at right angles. Check it all out now. This is the foundation for the quilting, and it must be done well or the resulting product will be disappointing. Lift the frame onto the four chairs or the sawhorses and prepare yourself for a new experience. For extra security use four C-clamps to hold the frame down to the horses or chairs.

NOW, you can quilt...

Frame mounted on horses and quilt ready for stitching

QUILTING

Arm yourself with a pincushion liberally stabbed with sharp needles 1-1/2 to 2 inches long, an emery bag (usually the strawberry attached to a tomato pincushion) to sharpen your needles, a thimble if you can use one, otherwise a rubber filing tip (found in office-supply shops or stationery stores), or, if you are stubborn, develop a callus. A pair of sharp scissors, Band-aids for punctured fingers, some relaxing music, good light, your armless chair, and, last but not least, thread. White thread, standard mercerized sewing cotton #50, is good, though thread marked "quilting" is even better.

If you are ambidextrous you have been blessed with a quilter's most fond wish. If you are ambidextrous and very neat, so much the better. But if you are ambidextrous, neat, and patient, you have the whole thing licked. All of us can't be ambidextrous, but with a little effort we can develop neatness and patience, right? So my mother used to tell me.

Thread your needle with a double arm's-length of thread, knot both ends together, put on your thimble, and plunge ahead. With short, neat (there's that word again), even running stitches follow the lines of your quilting pattern from the center out. Punch your needle down at right angles to the surface, piercing all the layers, and then punch the needle back up through the layers almost at the point of entry. This gives a clean, fine line of stitches that won't shift any of the layers. Trace with the needle and thread along the edges of your patchwork or appliqué pattern about 1/16-inch from the seams. If the patch pieces or appliqué sections are large you may want to stitch a pattern within them.

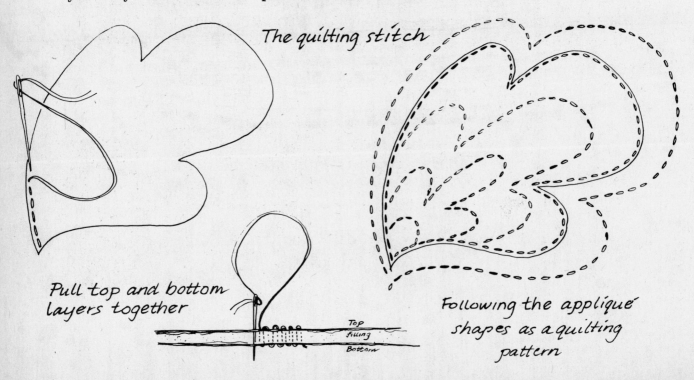

The quilting stitch

Pull top and bottom layers together

Top
Filling
Bottom

Following the appliqué shapes as a quilting pattern

Quilting along pattern seams.

(Black thread is used for clarity in this illustration)

Finish quilting the exposed area between the bars. Detach the side bars and carefully roll the completed area up on one of the long bars, exposing a new area to be quilted unrolled from the other bar. Attach the bars together as before. Repeat this rolling and unrolling, moving from one side of the center to the other, until the quilting is finished. Through the whole process be sure everything remains smooth and tight and the corner angles are maintained always at right angles. While quilting, if you find that the surface becomes flaccid (lower in the middle than on the edges), lacing the edges of the exposed area you are working on to the side bars with strong white quilting thread or heavy linen rug thread will maintain the proper tension.

Lacing quilt to frame

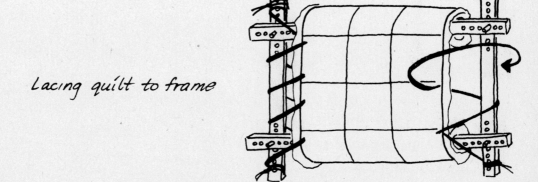

When the quilting is complete, disassemble the frame and remove the quilt. Isn't it a beauty? Won't the Joneses next door just flip out? Prepare the binding for the edges, in a length that will go a few inches more than all around the perimeter of the quilt. Use bias strip binding prepared as described earlier, or commercial blanket binding, bias tape, or wide ribbon. Lay the quilt out on the floor and trim any excess filling. By hand or machine bind the edges, as shown.

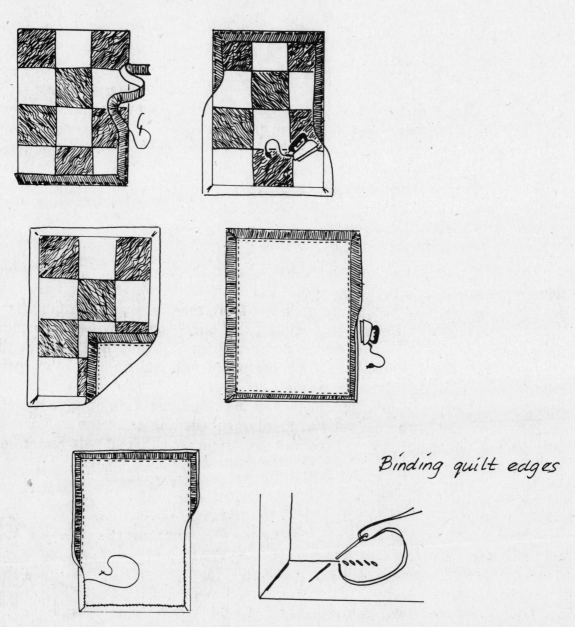

Binding quilt edges

FANFARE, MUSIC, APPLAUSE (clap, clap, clap, clap, clap, clap, clap): your quilt is done.

Phew!

ALTERNATIVES:

Quilting can be done on a sewing machine; however, I use a machine only when the seams are so boringly straight and long that I can't bear the idea of stitching it all by hand. The thought of trying to work a large bed quilt under the needle of my machine without someone else to hold up the quilt's weight does not turn me on at all. I want quilting to be a creative, involving experience for the quilter, and the machine just puts itself between the person and the quilt. See what I mean?

If you are crammed into a small place or hassled about messing up the decor with a 10-by-4-foot frame complete with sawhorses, you can readily quilt each block separately and quite effectively on a quilting hoop. The quilting hoop is simply a glorified embroidery hoop. Of greater proportions than an embroidery hoop, it is used in much the same way—by stretching the area to be quilted over the hoop and stitching the layers of back, filling, and top the same as you would for the larger frame. Many quilters prefer the hoop to the large frame because it is more portable and can be left standing in a room without taking up all that space. You can either quilt each block upon completion of the patchwork or appliqué, and stitch the blocks together later, or you can quilt the entire top as already described.

You can also manufacture a much smaller frame with the inside measurements corresponding to the size of the blocks you plan to make. Just carve the directions down for the large frame to the desired size. A frame like this is good for smaller projects—clothing, hangings, and such—and is certainly more portable for people who keep on truckin'.

All the steps described earlier for mounting in the frame and quilting should be followed, with a few modifications. Most likely you will not have to roll your project up on the frame, but if you do it's exactly the same procedure as for the larger frame. If you want to quilt each block separately, baste the sandwich diagonally from corner to corner and all around the sides and proceed to mount it in the hoop or smaller frame and stitch. To connect the separate blocks together to make a complete quilt top, lay the blocks that go next to one another face to face and sew the tops together where the blocks join. Do this with long running stitches by hand or machine. Don't stitch through the filling or the back. Turn the blocks out and lay flat. Press the back edges under 1/4-inch and sew together, by hand, as shown. Be careful of your iron's temperature, especially if you are using a synthetic filling. When you have all the blocks sewn together in this manner you can quilt along the seams between each block: stretch the quilt in any one of the suggested frames and quilt-stitch about 1/4-inch away from the seam lines. You can also do this in your lap or on a table without

Pre-quilted block with filling trimmed

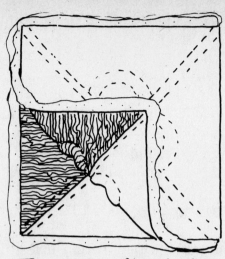

Two blocks face to face

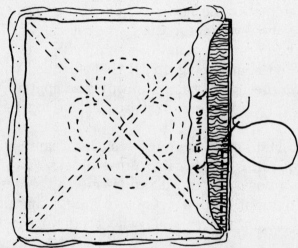

Stitching with running stitch

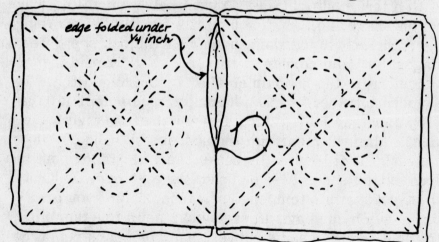

edge folded under ¼ inch

Seaming back of blocks together

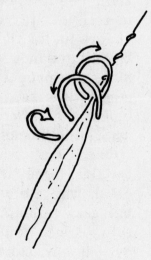

Joining the pre-quilted blocks

Quilting the unquilted seams

a frame, as it requires all straight stitching. A frame is necessary for fancier quilting. Bind the edges of your finished quilt top as already described.

If you are using a big frame and can't leave it set up in the middle of the room, prop it somewhere. Okay ... so your waterbed, Japanese screens, hookah, gas range, that old chest from the Salvation Army, your old man's easel, the parrot's cage, and your mother's snake plant are in the way, and you just can't bear to cover up Che's picture. Try the ceiling. Yeah, that's what I said. The ceiling. Attach eye screws from the hardware store to all the corners. If you can't do it yourself, have a friend who's into carpentry put a pulley system on the ceiling. With a set-up like that, all you have to do after a day's quilting is hoist it up to the ceiling. Fantastic for the acoustics.

Remember all the old cowboy movies when Gary Cooper would be a-courtin' his girl with fiddles and the dancing going on in the old ranch house? Everybody would be dressed to the nines, and a big feed was put up. Most likely this was a "bee" of some sort; nine times out of ten it would be a quilting bee. When a family had a few tops finished and ready for quilting they would throw a party that would last all day. Ten or fifteen needleworkers would start early and could finish a number of quilts by suppertime, working in shifts. It was a chance for an exchange of news and friendly conversation when casual visits would be impractical—distances and transportation time being what they were. Unlike canasta parties the bees would at least produce a usable product.

Think, if you had a quilt ready for quilting and had a few friends who knew how to stitch and you could manage to get them in the same place at the same time, you'd have a finished product in practically no time! In this day of social isolationism and super-mobility there is a need for tying people together, a chance to exchange views and relate to one another. The quilting bee is as good as any peace table, all parties working toward one goal in a mutual nonpolitical situation where generations can meet and talk. In our search for a road to the past and more peaceful days, or to a future where all people can work side by side happily, productively, and without hatred, as picayune an event as a quilting bee might also just put one more crack in the walls of despair and aloneness.

Sandalmaking

Betty Kusmin

There was a time when the fashion was to avoid facing feet. Feet were presumed to be the ugliest part of your body. As a kid I used to draw people standing in high grass so as to avoid having to capture that most difficult three-dimensional part of the standing figure. But the world turns and, ironically, I'm now a sandalmaker; and in the public sphere feet are in the spotlight. You now hear almost as many discussions about shoes and feet as you do about which car happens to be the safest and most economical. What kind of shoe is best for warmth? And which shoe offers the most freedom in summer?

In warm weather most of us are unhappy if we have to wear anything on our feet, and sandals provide the freedom of bare feet without any of the hazards or discomfort.

Custom-made sandals provide the most in the way of comfort and durability ... hand-wrought soles to protect your own natural ones. And some straps. No protection in themselves, it is interesting to remember that straps are there only to keep the foot on the sole. A string to tie the package.

These age-old devices are more similar to their ancient counterparts than any other single aspect of modern dress. In fact, all strap combinations are directly related to ancient strap design, which then, as now, was solely (sorry) concerned with simplicity, beauty, and comfort.

Custom sandals sell for $18 to $35 and even higher, and since to collect your supplies would cost about that, it is best to think in terms of learning a trade—making sandals for your family or community, on either a nonprofit or a professional basis. You certainly won't save much money just by making one pair for yourself. Handmade sandals are best, though, and are a good investment in the long run, for they can last fifteen years or more if they are resoled every few years. Improving with age, sandals take on the patina of old leather, and the markings from the toes become increasingly personal.

The time spent in learning sandalmaking is soon repaid because it's a craft there'll always be a demand for. A commercial sandalmaker friend used to scare beginners with lines like, "Go ahead and make your own sandals—get flat feet and stay out of the army." But that shouldn't deter; nobody gets flat feet from sandals, and the reality trip dictates that you take a look at a sandal and try to figure it out. And when you do, the mystery begins to evaporate quickly. Realizing that the straps and the top and bottom soles are the only major components, you'll see sandals can't be as complicated as some craftsmen make them out to be.

Most of us are a little awed by the craftsman's secrets. We're somewhat frightened of learning a new skill ourselves. This is even more the case when a craft is a functional one. If we attempt a leather wall-hanging and it's not quite right, that's o.k. We know we can alter it to suit our personal esthetic. We simply fiddle with it until it feels right, and in doing so we don't worry about whether we've weakened it structurally, etc. Even a handbag or belt, though utilitarian, doesn't have to fit a specific shape, like someone's foot. Knowing that sandals have to satisfy all the above needs, we become more concerned and anxious than we would with a wall-hanging. They have to fit and feel right.

Sandalmaking, then, only appears difficult because people usually fail to find out from sandalmakers the common sense behind much of the mystique. Practical underlying reasons for the process will become self-evident, for all the rules are there merely so the foot will be comfortable in the sandal. The beginner should be aware of certain things about sandals and feet before he begins. For starters, feet vary. Left foot differs from right foot. Walking habits vary. Leather has vagaries of its own, too, stretching and softening differently, according to tannage, climate, etc. All of this must be allowed for when you are constructing sandals. For instance, my own feet are flat and I need a sandal with more X-straps (to keep my foot anchored) than someone with good walking habits. A wearer with simple taste and good arches can manage fine with only two straps across the front, or else a simple T-strap, or a toe loop and arch strap.

TOOLS AND SUPPLIES

Leather suppliers should have everything you'll need for this new challenge. Look in the Yellow Pages for your area under Leather Suppliers. In Boston, The Berman Leather Co. and M. Siegel are two I deal with, and both Mr. Berman and Mr. Siegel are very helpful. In New York City I use A.C. Products. For good equipment, get the free catalogue from C.S. Osborne and Co., 125 Jersey St., Harrison, N.J. 97029. MacPherson Leathercraft Supplies, P.O. Box 395, San Francisco 94101, will send a free catalogue also. Tandy's is a chain of leathercraft shops located in Rochester, New York City, Albany, and who knows where else. This company offers a 10 percent discount if you purchase ten different items.

I let my leather supplier recommend what's best at the particular time I order. There are so many different names for grades and variations that I can't keep track of them all. Nor are the ones I want always in supply. Your supplier can really be a big help. Because he deals with other crafts-people and has the benefit of their combined experience and opinions, I have come to think of him as a headwaiter recommending the specialty of the day.

What you'll need:

SQUARE-EDGED LEATHER KNIFE: This is used to cut the soles out of the skin; it's also called a matte knife or four-way knife. Art-supply shops have this as well as hardware stores. It will cost 75¢ to $1.50.

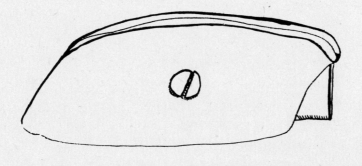

2.

LIP KNIFE AND SLOT PUNCHES: The knife is for trimming. The punch will make the slot holes through which the straps run. Since both are expensive, confine yourself to just one 1/2-inch punch. If you're going to make a lot of sandals, then get all sizes of punches from 3/8-inch to 2 inches. The latter size is used for wide arch straps. A variety of punches enables you to make a large variety of sandal styles with different strap widths—a must for business.

3.   4.

PLOUGH GAUGE: This ensures a straight line when you cut straps, since it has a setting device to keep the width constant. If you are only doing a few pairs of sandals it doesn't pay to buy this tool. You can use a knife and steel ruler for cutting straps. But for a sandal business the plough gauge is indispensable.

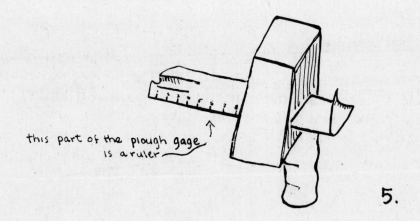

this part of the plough gage
is a ruler

5.

BONDING CEMENT: With this you join bottom and top soles. A cement like Barges, gotten at craft shops, is very good. You'll need a glue brush to apply it. Since glue is not enough, by itself, to hold the sandals together, they'll also be cobbled (nailed together).

6.

TACK HAMMER, COBBLING NAILS, AND ANVIL: Nails should be brass and about 1/8-inch longer than the thickness of top and bottom soles. Nails are driven in through the bottom sole, and the anvil is used so the nail will bend back on itself and form a V when it hits the metal. Any steel object can replace the anvil if you're only making a few pairs of sandals.

7.

RAWHIDE MALLETS: These are useful for hitting and bonding the bottom and top soles together after they're joined by the glue (before nailing). Any wooden object for pounding, and wood to pound it on, will do, though, if you're only experimenting or not going into business.

8.

A SKIVER is a tool that holds and curves razor blades. This costs about a dollar and is used to thin (skive) the strap tips to feed through the sole hole and the tips of straps that go around the buckle. It is also used to skive the underside of both top soles where the straps cross under: by reducing the thickness, the sole will be flat, without lumps from the sandwiched straps. Don't skive out the bottom sole, as this will only decrease its life as it wears thinner. A matte knife can also be used to thin straps.

9.

REVOLVING PUNCH, for making the buckle hole. Since this runs about $15, skip buying it and have a shoemaker put the buckle on for you.

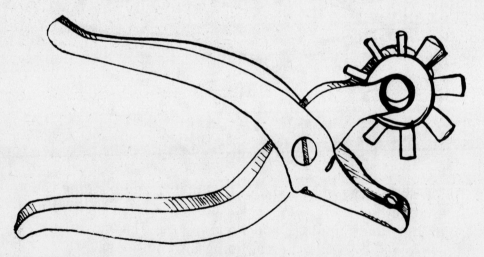

10.

RIVET SETTER: A shoemaker can also eliminate the necessity of buying this item, which is used for attaching rivets in buckle placement. Again, when you do a lot of sandals this tool will come in handy. You can avoid the need for the setter, however, by making sandals with ties, or the kind that are of the permanent nonbuckle variety.

11.

SANDPAPER: In finishing, the edges of the sandals must be ground smooth by using <u>coarse</u> sandpaper wrapped around a block. Then use <u>fine</u> sandpaper for continued sanding. Next, buff the edges with a soft rag or lambswool. For making sandals commercially, you'd best buy a motorized sander with interchangeable discs.

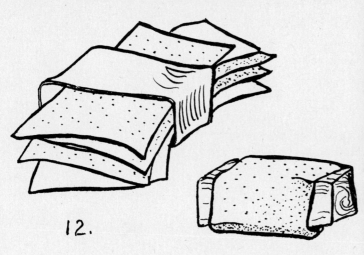

12.

13. Using a motorized sander

Sandals needn't be dyed, the oil from feet helps darken them naturally. Personally I prefer this look. For commercial production, however, it's best to have some aniline dyes handy. Most customers want their sandals dark when purchased, and customer education in this matter is more arduous than dyeing the sandals. Fiebing's Leather Dye shines up well and costs, at most, only 75¢. Use it on the edges of soles and straps.

14.

For finishing and preserving the sandals, use leather oil. Hardware stores, as well as leather suppliers, will have in stock Neatsfoot Oil and/or Lexal. By accident, I once drank some Lexal. It looks like stale coffee, and I was in the habit of storing it in a paper cup. When phoned, poison control informed me it was nontoxic. Nevertheless, I don't recommend it for coffee breaks. Come to think of it—it might be a good idea to label your liquid supplies. Tell the wearer to continue to use this oil when the sandals have gotten wet. Puddles and rain cause leather to lose its natural oils, and eventually it becomes brittle unless treated with preservative oils as a safeguard.

THE SKIN TRADE

Buying leather isn't all that difficult, even though there's a mystique attached to it. Sandalmakers can be overheard talking about the relative merits of chrome versus oak tannage, etc., etc. Since only oak-tanned leather can be molded into an arch, I always use a 12-ounce (or so) oak-tanned bend cowhide for the bottom sole and an 8-ounce shoulder cowhide for the top. Bend cowhide is from the back and rump of the animal, and large bend skins are available. Shoulder cowhide is not as strong. That is why it is advisable to use it only for the top sole. See your leather supplier for advice on different sole tannages.

I definitely prefer thick to thin bottom soles—not just for impressing customers or even for durability, although these are advantages, but because a thick sole acts better as a cushion against hard surfaces and sidewalks, and therefore is a good preventer of foot fatigue. (Somebody may want a thinner bottom sole, so a commercial sandalmaker would be wise to keep some around. Just in case.)

For straps I like horsehide. But since it can't always be gotten I use latigo (another tannage leather) for adjustable sandals. Latigo comes in some lovely colors and also takes a stain beautifully. But it has too much stretch for a fixed-strap sandal (this is one whose straps are attached permanently, with no buckle or tie for adjustment).

I find it pays to use the best leather available regardless of price because the difference in cost between fine and mediocre leather per pair never seems to exceed a couple of dollars, and in retailing this difference is readily and profitably absorbed.

Built-in obsolescence doesn't work in this craft. Generally, the longer a pair of sandals lasts, the more a customer should want to buy. He will feel more like a collector of various styles and less like a sucker forced to repeat his mistake. Discerning and appreciative people like custom-made sandals, and this is one of the major rewards that come from working in this particular craft field.

THE PATTERN

Both feet are outlined while the person you're making the sandals for stands on a piece of paper, feet slightly apart, weight evenly divided. It gets embarrassing rummaging around tearing apart old lunch bags. Mayonnaise twixt the toes is a drag. So have lots of oak tag handy. This is a lightweight board about as cheap as anything you'll find—about 7¢ a sheet. When tracing, hold the ballpoint pen or pencil vertically in order to get a true outline. The space between the first and second toes should be marked for the toe thongs. The arch is marked in depth by sliding the pen under the foot; both the length and highest point of the arch should be indicated. This will help in molding the bottom sole. Do this accurately!

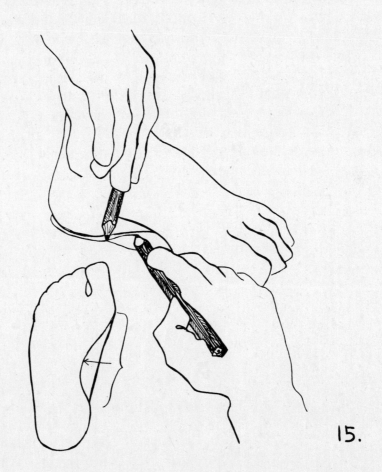

15.

There are four main bones you want to mark when fitting the sandal. These bones should be paid special attention to because straps must not go over the bones.

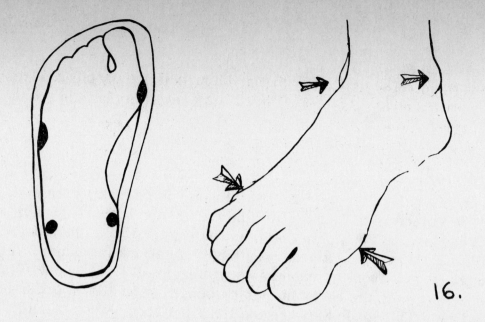

16.

Once the foot is outlined, draw an evened-out contour of the tracing about 1/4 inch outside the original drawing. This contour is, natch, the sandal pattern. I leave a bit more than 1/4 inch around the toes (toes spread after a bit of exposure to sandals). You need a margin for error mostly around the toes and also somewhat at the heel. This allows for changes in walking habits. Later, after the sandals have been worn for a while, any excess can be ground off. (I believe in lots of fail-safes.) You can create pleasing shapes for what may be a rather strange foot. Also, you can make these contours the same for the right and left feet, even though the actual contour differs. The outside line in the drawing of the sandal sole below is the outer edge of the top sole. The inner line (or exact contour) shows you where to place the straps. Here is one example of possible strap placement.

17.

The strap marks go <u>slightly on the inside</u> of the inside line so the straps will come into the sandal <u>under the foot</u>. Place straps <u>only</u> where there are no bone markings, since a strap will chafe and hurt if it rubs on the bone. You can punch slots in the tracing and weave the straps through to see if they look right. (More details on strap placement when we discuss different sandal styles.)

Once the straps are marked, put the pattern on the top-sole leather and cut flush with the outside contour of the pattern. Then punch the slots where they're marked for straps. Be careful, for this is a crucial part of the operation. Sometimes you'll perhaps punch those slots too far in. In this case don't use the leather for that particular sandal. But save that top sole! It can be pared down for a smaller size or else used as a sample in your sandal business.

If the slots are in the right place, everything else will follow smoothly and you'll have a well-fitting sandal. But even a slight error in slot placement will cause a poor fit. If you're unsure, seek some advice before proceeding with this operation. A look at the illustration below may help clarify things for you, however.

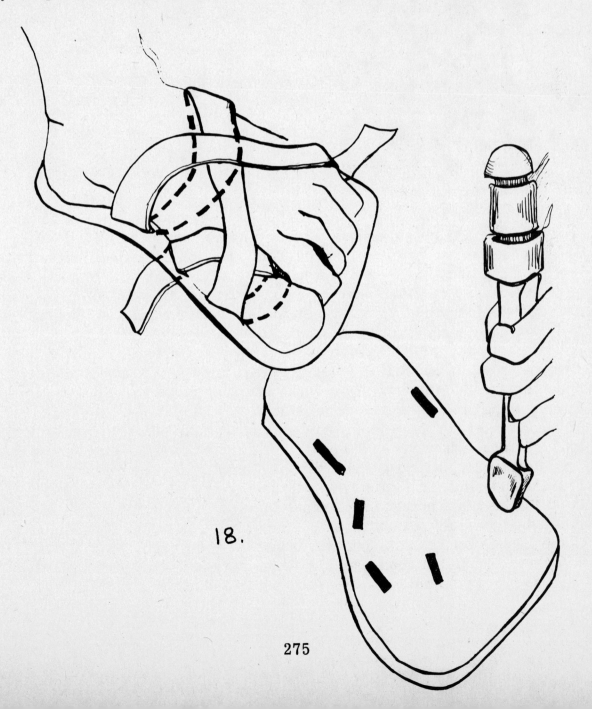

18.

The next step involves the cutting of the bottom soles. Cut them out of your leather 1/2 inch to 1 inch larger (all around) than the top soles. This allows for shrinkage in the next procedure, which entails molding the bottom soles to the foot. This is done after the bottom soles have been soaked in water for a half-hour or so and then left to partially dry for a few hours. (Too much soaking and the leather flops back to its original flatness.)

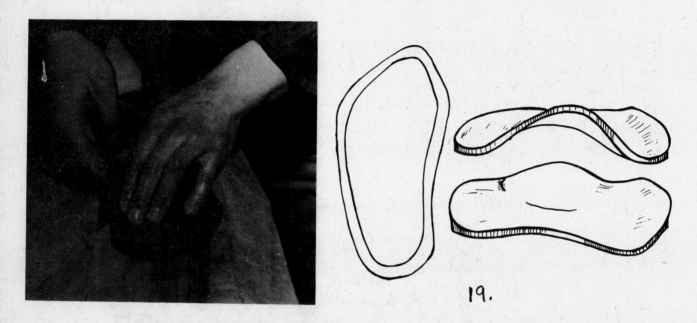

19.

After your bottom sole has lost much of its moistness, hold it to the foot and mold a fairly exaggerated arch, with a corresponding cupping or raised edge around the toe and heel. This will look extreme at first, but will soon sag into a more realistic shape. Arches always mold more easily to the wearer's foot if they start out too high rather than too low. If the arch is drastically high, just sit on it for awhile for a quick collapse.

The bottom sole will have to dry thoroughly before you glue it to the top sole, so allow several days for complete drying. Cloudy, damp days make for even slower drying, but you can speed things up a bit with a fan. This molding process is one of the main reasons for the notorious slowness of sandalmakers. There is one perfectly acceptable shortcut around this lengthy waiting, however, for professionals; a number of bottom soles can be uniformly cut and molded in a very large pattern. This premolding process underlines my belief that individually molded arches are not as important as many buyers and sandalmakers have come to believe. In actuality, the foot molds the arch, so the only drawback to this faster method is the waste when you strip off excess bottom-sole leather to fit the customer's foot. But it is a good approach to solving the problem of impatient buyers. This trimming is where your lip knife proves most helpful.

Instead of molding the heel, you can make a small heel for your sandal. This heel is merely the shape of the heel of the bottom sole, glued and cobbled onto the bottom sole. It can be replaced when it wears down, for it is the first place to show real signs of wear.

STYLES

Both fixed and adjustable straps keep the foot on the sole. With the fixed-strap style, the strap that prevents the foot from moving forward off the sole is the toe thong or toe loop. These go between the first and second toe or over the big toe and prevent the foot from moving forward. Some people find these loops irritating and uncomfortable at first, but it usually only takes a day or two to break in the sandal. Sometimes I use a clothespin to pinch that part of the leather thong that goes between the two toes. This helps speed up the breaking-in process.

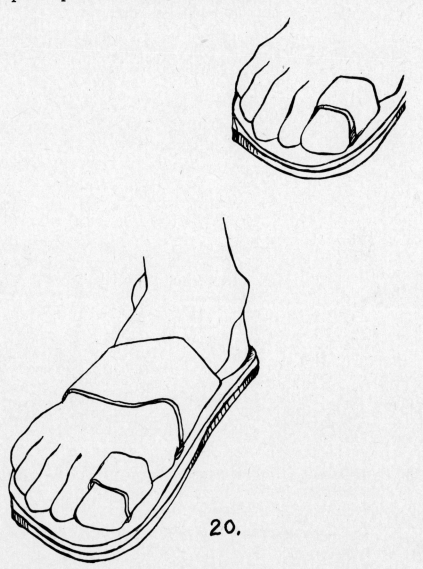

20.

An alternative barrier to the foot moving forward is a strap across the foot just behind the two front bones. The bones and straps keep each other in place. To keep the foot from sliding backward you'll place a strap that ties or buckles high around the heel. Unless you have long straps tied up the leg, gladiator style, you'll need side tabs to keep the heel strap high. To keep the foot from sliding sideways use either an arch strap (Fig. 22) or an X strap (Fig. 23). Both of these come across the instep of the foot.

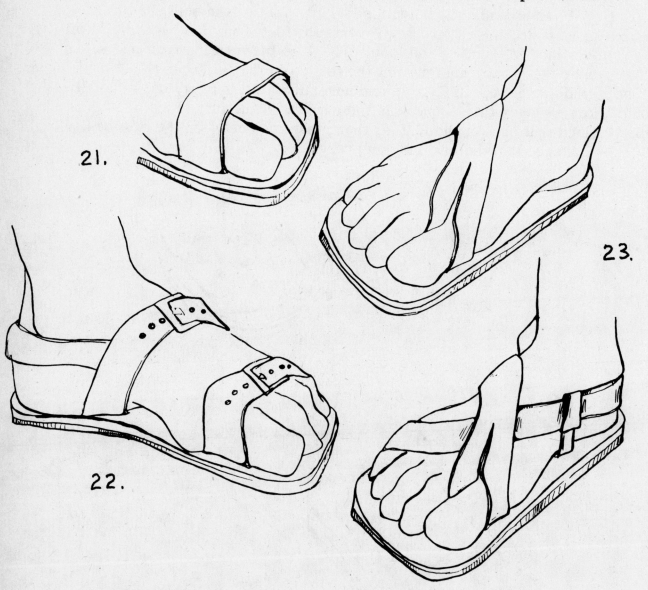

These are the basic straps, and all variations in sandal style come from combinations of them. You can experiment by winding straps around your own feet until you come up with something pleasing that works. The number of possible designs is endless, but keep in mind they must all work for the structural purpose intended: to keep the sole on the foot comfortably and gracefully.

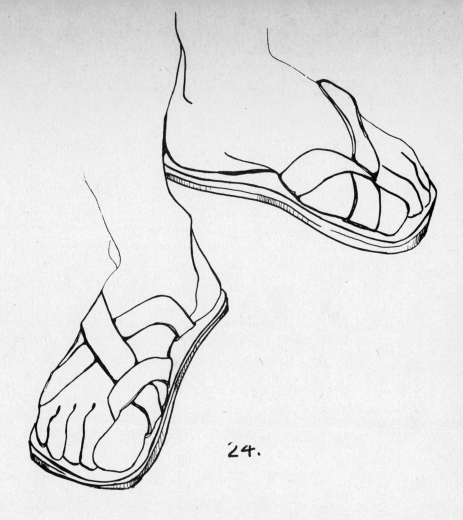

24.

Remember, no straps should feed into the sandal over a bone, or the wearer will be uncomfortable. The bones are useful as tension points, with the straps either in front of or behind them, depending on the way the strap functions. That is why bones should be marked carefully in the first place, and those marks considered when the slot marks are placed. Most sandal discomfort comes from carelessness in this aspect of sandalmaking.

Next, skive the flesh (under) side of the top soles where the straps lie. Some straps will loop under the top sole from one slot to another. This area, too, will need to be skived. For permanent straps, skive about 1 to 1-1/2 inches from the slot, or turn them toward the outside edges and don't skive at all.

25.

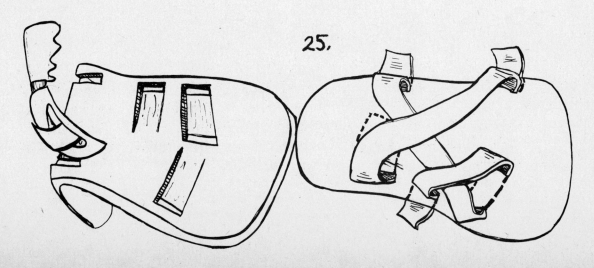

GETTING IT ALL TOGETHER

Now that the bottom sole is molded and the top sole is punched, cut the straps. As I say, horsehide makes for very nice straps, but, if unavailable, use latigo. Now you put that four-way knife and steel ruler or the plough gauge to use. To attach, feed straps through slots in the top sole.

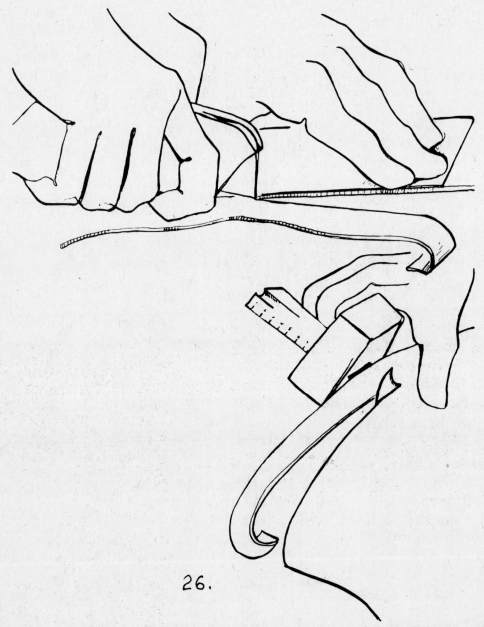

26.

If yours is a fixed-strap sandal, you'll first glue the straps down to the underside of the top sole after having achieved the required tightness (at a fitting) on the wearer's foot: when the foot slips in and out of the sandal with slight difficulty. Straps stretch. So don't worry about overtightness as long as the sandal can be gotten on and off. There is an alternative to gluing: you can turn one end of each fixed strap toward the center, and the other end toward the outside. This makes it easier to tighten later if the straps stretch. You'll be able to tighten without opening up the entire sandal. Both methods have their advantages, and fine sandalmakers practice each method. If yours is an adjustable style, simply weave the long single strap through the top sole but do not glue it. And be careful not to glue this strap when gluing top and bottom soles together. You want it to remain free. When gluing, be sure to follow specific instructions on your cement can.

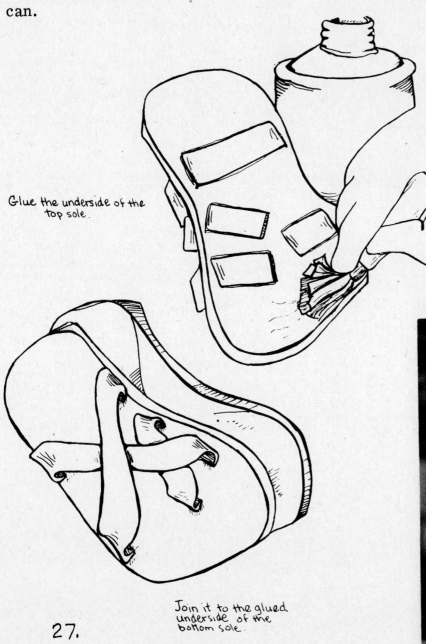

Glue the underside of the top sole.

Join it to the glued underside of the bottom sole.

27.

Now glue top sole to bottom sole and give it a once-over, all-over hammering job.

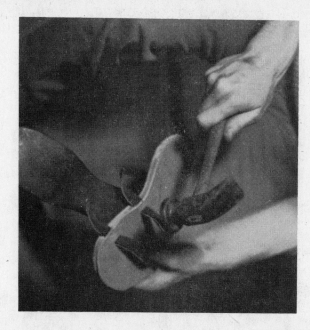

28. Hammer the glued-together top and bottom soles while the glue is still tacky

After the glue has dried, the next step is cobbling (nailing) around the entire edge of the sandal. This furthers the work of the glue and helps keep the sandal from coming apart. Place nails about 1 inch apart, and in from the edge about 1/4 inch. Remember to hammer against an anvil or metal object so the nail turns back on itself. (By the way, you're working the nails in alternately from the bottom and the top of the sole, for strength.) Be careful not to drive the nails through the adjustable straps, or, naturally, they won't adjust. Making small holes first helps when you're pounding in the nails.

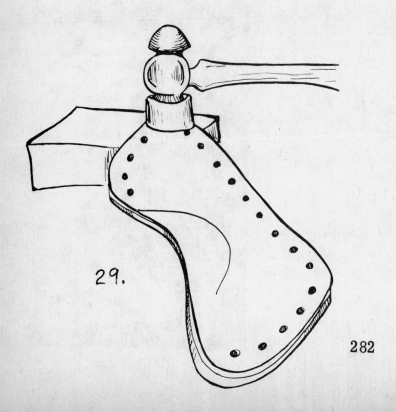

29.

282

Cobbling the arch helps it stay up longer. Drive the nails in perpendicular to the arch; this involves tilting the sandal on the anvil to get the angle right. About ten nails in the arch should be ample.

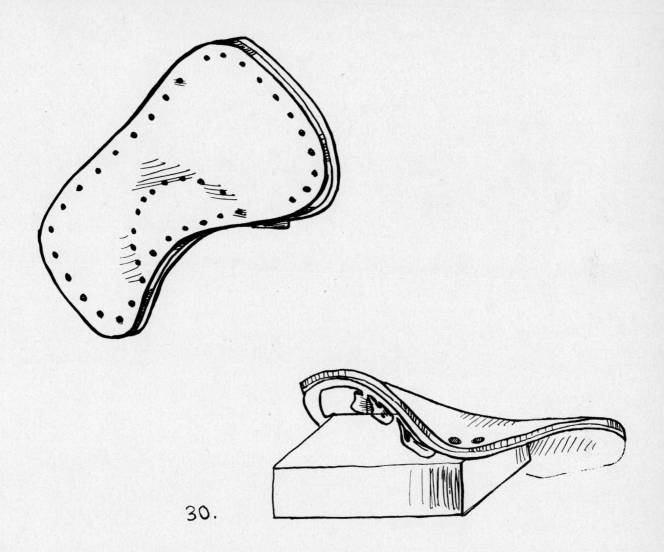

30.

Mention should be made here of an alternate method of bonding the top to the bottom sole—stitching. It is a process that is seldom used, for it is time-consuming, and only if applied with much exactitude is it as efficient and attractive as the cobbling technique.

TRIMMING, DYEING, AND FINISHING

If the edges are cut carefully there won't be much hassle in the trimming of them. After trimming go around the edges with rough and then fine sandpaper (as described under <u>Supplies</u>). Finally, buff with any soft cloth or lambswool.

Buckles get put on last. Remember! Heelstrap buckles fall on the outside of each foot in front of the heel, <u>not</u> on the bone. The buckle is attached by rivets to the strap that comes from the front outside of the sandal. Punch holes for closing the buckle on the other straps. Allow for stretch by providing lots of extra holes, about 1/2 inch apart. Either have this done by a shoemaker, or, if you've obtained the somewhat costly (around $6) rivet setter, follow the instructions that come with it for attachment of the buckle.

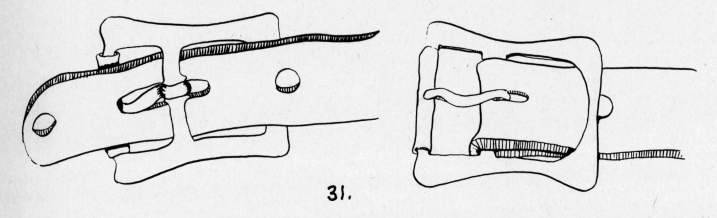

31.

Any dye, if desired, is now applied. The sandal gets oiled, rubbed, and hand-polished, and is then ready for wear.

Happy walking!

Betty Kusmin

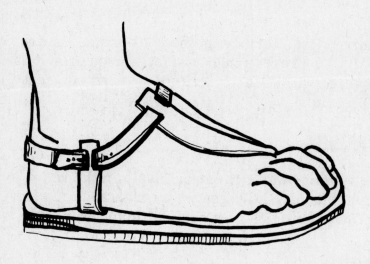

284

Woodblock Prints

CARDBOARD CUT

PASTE-ON CARDBOARD CUTOUT

MULTIBLOCK COLOR PRINTS

ONE-BLOCK WATERCOLOR WOODCUT

Jean Young

Woodblock is historically the earliest method of printing designs on paper and textiles. When ink is applied to one side of a block of wood, and paper is pressed onto the block, the ink is transferred to paper. I was soaking in the tub one day, thinking about how to describe the printing process, when it finally hit me that the water was cold. I climbed out shivering and jumped all over the bath mat and bathroom floor to warm up, and there they were ... a dozen or more examples of the printing method! Lots and lots of footprints. The whole scene down there looked like an Escher woodblock, with unfallen arches all over the place looking like some kind of solar primeval dance had gone down. There was one difference, which took me half an hour to figure out. The wet foot is placed on the bath mat,

and in woodblock, paper is placed on the wet block, and then it's turned over when you go to see the print. This means the print is in reverse from the way you executed it on the block—the left side will be on the right side and the right side on the left. If conceiving your design in reverse is going to create a mental block right away, there are ways to get around this, so don't cop out.

 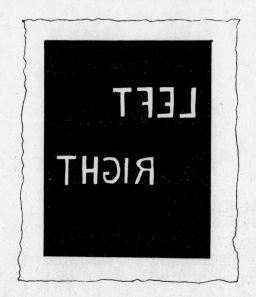

The Chinese, who discovered this process, used it to print the written characters of their language. They found that when they hollowed out a shape in the wood, the raised part, when inked black, would be the only part to print.

If thinnish lines are cut away from the block, black ink is rolled over the surface with a roller, and paper is pressed on the block, the lines will not print, and the image will be like a white line drawing on black.

White-line woodblock: <u>Ajax</u> (1932)

286

You can transfer a drawing to tracing paper and then to the block by turning it over (in reverse of the original), and, with carbon paper next to the woodblock, redrawing it. A carbon copy appears on the block. You also can use a pencil on the block as your beginning point; or you can start right off gouging out your design. (More later about tools.) Sensibility comes through direct this way. It also provides that immediacy for people who don't like to plan ahead, and the excitement that comes from the unexpected.

White lines are the easiest and most natural to the block-print medium. Integrated white and black lines can make the most of the woodblock technique. However, if fewer black lines and more white lines are used, the actual work will be easier than the other way around.

Woodblock by an early Provincetown printmaker (1916). Here white lines are preferred over black.

When a black line is wanted instead of a white line, you have to go to much more trouble. Draw on the block where you want it to print black, and then cut away all the surface around the line you want to print. When inked, the print will come out looking much like your original drawing on the block, dark lines on white paper.

Black-line woodblock:
A Medieval Herb Garden (16th century)

287

In the fifteenth century the dark line was preferred over the white line by European artists. Had preparing black-line woodblocks been a simple, rapid, and natural process, artists would have continued to make their own designs, cut their own blocks, and do their own printing. Imagine how much more time would have to be spent cutting a block if you wanted to make a fish-net pattern of black lines and the background white, instead of composing the picture so that the net could be of white lines and the space around them black. The more tedious woodblocking became, the more the artist did only the original drawing; a craftsman transferred it to the block and cut it, and a third person did the printing.

During most of the nineteenth century the poor woodblock had no real character of its own because everyone insisted that it must look like something else—drawings, etchings, charcoal drawings, washes, or even photographs. One medium imitating another is a sort of never-ending round robin, and the results are hypocritical because they pretend to be something they aren't. An emphasis on technique will cause the material you use to lose its identity. Anyone who gets to know woodblock, and loves it for what it is, will prefer those prints that remain true to the character of woodblock, and you'll notice they have more vitality, too. A lot of work by M.C. Escher is woodblock.

The idea you want to express is always preeminent, and craft secondary. Learning the craft is the easiest part of the trip. And there are many things you can find woodblock useful for: posters, decoration for catalogues, a total design for newspaper ads, birth announcements, greeting cards of all sorts, and wrapping-paper design; you can also print your own wallpaper using oil inks or acrylic paint.

ENVIRONMENT

It takes a while to build up to the level of being strung out on your own work. Start by concentrating on your working environment, which will help you get off. Eventually, you will have accumulated so many images and ideas you'll want to make into prints, you'll have no problem beginning. Your ideas will expand so much that the constant build-up creates a need to get them out of your system by getting them down on paper.

When you're beginning, and even later on, it's nice to go to a little trouble to settle in properly in a working area. Some burn incense, but a must is burning lights if it's not bright enough. Light is so good for the eyes. Some years ago, when I was material for the martyr-stoic syndrome, I thought a hard chair was good for hard thinking, but I've had to face the fact that I feel interrupted if it's too cold or too hot or a chair too hard or too low for working. Now I really notice it if it's too stuffy and odors from turpentine and paint fill the air or if my environment is too quiet. I like to hear human activity around. It makes me feel less uptight and more integrated with the world. The ivory tower is too remote and one can get twisted up there and trapped in a time warp, with only the reality of the sound of your own tools working the wood. Feel into it. Ask yourself what makes you more comfortable and free, and take some time out to put it together.

TOOLS AND SUPPLIES

MATERIAL FOR CREATIVE ENERGY: All I've ever needed, or gotten the habit of needing, are candy and coffee while working. They energize me and intensify my ability to zero in and get what I want done. Once I get into a project, I get stoned on the experience of doing it and forget the candy. Dylan Thomas was a candy-bar freak, too.

The worst part of being a sweet freak is that too much candy can be a real bummer. Sometimes I've really gone too far and sort of O. D. 'd on it. After a lot of bad anxiety about too much candy and too much coffee, I finally talked myself into modifying the whole creative energy consumption habit. Five years ago I was smoking too, and what with turpentine from all the oil painting I was doing, I was living at a near-toxic level. If you're a health freak, and you should be, try Fig Newtons and juices.

Music can also be a way to start the creative energy flowing. If you're a purist, listen to Mozart before you start your work. It is better for clearing your head than sweeping the back porch like some Zen monks do before they start their creative work. Mozart doesn't just leave you empty but full of vibrations moving out of pure clarity. Sometimes I work with a James Brown record on in the background, especially at night. The natural free wild energy and directness will keep you company, but you've got to cool it if you leave your work table dancing and exhaust your energy.

GOUGES AND CUTTING KNIFE: Woodblocks can be cut with one good knife. The bigger art-supply stores sell very good woodcutting knives and gouges singly. Try to buy the best, which would be of well-tempered steel. Small art shops will only carry sets of six, which run between $8 and $15. These include the cutting knife and gouging tools in V- and U-type shapes, and also a chisel to shave out larger areas of wood. Tools get dull fast cutting wood, and a sharpening stone is a necessary item (available at both art-supply and hardware stores, and relatively expensive—around $2). For

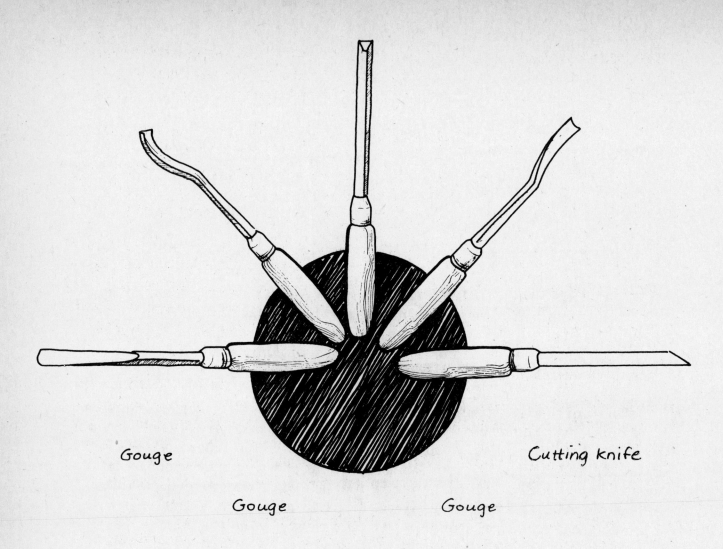

Gouge

Cutting knife

Gouge   Gouge

Chisel

this reason, I don't recommend getting the cheap Japanese set of twelve carving tools, which are only $2 or so. They will dull right away and won't take a new edge. Some people just use a pocket knife and find that's all they need. In any case, getting initial supplies should be the least of your worries because none will cost you any heavy bread.

If you are starting to cut for the first time, don't chew a Butterfinger because the name might have more power of suggestion than creative energy and you'll end up with a finger that looks like a Tootsie Roll.

PAPER: Try anything that is somewhat absorbent (most paper is absorbent if it is thinnish). A light cream newsprint paper is perfect, and people use it for pulling their first prints. One of the reasons newsprint is not used other than in the trial printing is that it can ruin your whole act because it doesn't stand up over the years, and anything you want to save for more than two years can't be counted on remaining in good condition.

Rice paper is the best and comes in sheets and pads at the art shops. Sheets can be cut to size for your block, but a smart way to buy is to remember the size of your block if you have one, and buy sheets or pads that will be 2 or 3 inches larger all the way around than your block. Most rice paper is white, but if you find a cream paper and use it, your print will have a richer effect.

Heavy paper, even if it looks absorbent, will not grab all the ink off the block as easily as the thinner paper. Another advantage of thinnish paper is that the ink or at least a clear impression comes through the back of the paper, so it is easy for you to see what you're doing when rubbing the ink onto the paper.

When using a water-base ink or watercolor paint, and if you want a softer edge to the shapes and lines on your print, heavier paper can be dipped in water, pressed between sheets of newspaper, and then used in dampened condition. Good lithograph paper is beautiful, substantial, and soft, and if you can find a way to use it in woodblock, so much the better. Use any color paper you want, but mostly you'll find white or cream.

THE WOOD: There are many nice things happening at the lumber yard. It's a world of big space devoted to a big natural resource. The smells of pine and cedar, the not altogether unpleasant sounds of the power tools, and the preoccupied shouts of the carpenters and workmen drown out your connection with the outside world. The fact that you are there with apparently wanton abandon, compared to those zapped heads paying heavy lumber bills and crazed goons taking away tons of lumber for more Levittowns, enables you to really enjoy the whole scene.

A relatively big section of the Woodstock Lumber Yard is for storage of the end pieces remaining from ordered-to-size jobs. It usually takes me a long time to adjust to so many choices. No one bothers me and I take my time. Just hanging around and getting familiar with the place has improved my attitude towards building. I'm not afraid of a table saw and have used it a lot for picture-framing and remodeling our farmhouse. There's nothing to cutting and cracking sheet-rock, and anyone can hammer.

I usually end up taking more pieces of wood for woodblock home with me than I need, and the lumber yard used to give them away. The relative freedom in picking these blocks up and getting into their various surfaces and feel started me out painting on wood. They've been charging for wood the last few years, but the cost is so little that you can count on this being the cheapest part of the craft supply.

Any size block can be used, as long as the paper you have will be more than enough to cover it. A convenient size is about 10 inches by 14 inches, and look for pieces that are at least 3/4 to 1 inch thick. This will help guarantee that the plank will be absolutely flat with no warpage—check this out before selecting. Also find pieces that have at least one side free of any knots. Ink will not adhere well to knots. If you find wood free of knots on both sides, you can use both sides for cutting. The best way is to know your paper size beforehand, and find a size (or else have a piece cut down to size) to fit the paper.

Any wood, providing it isn't too hard or too soft, can be used. Pine boards (soft wood) are good. Of course, if you can get ahold of pear wood, like Escher did, try that. And, if you feel like experimenting, try pieces that have been crosscut out of a small tree and sand them down.

INKS: Art shops sell block-printing inks for about 60¢ a tube. These come in either oil or water base. Water-base prints are matte (that is, the ink has a flat, dullish surface) and they dry faster, so you usually don't need to rig up something to hang these prints to dry on. Oil-base ink is thinned down with turpentine. There is also an extender available to give you more mileage. Oil-base has a slickish surface and will take a while to really dry, so these prints must be hung up in a clothesline situation with either clothespins or the Bulldog paperclips that dime stores and art shops carry.

The basic trouble with the lines of printing ink generally available in retail shops is that the choice of colors is too limited and they don't mix well. People who do color printing for the most part use the multiblock method (described later) and need a limited color selection in the first place—that's why manufacturers of the ink feel they don't have to provide a good range of colors.

When doing the one-block print, where you cover the entire block with one color, I suggest using black. Then your two colors will be black and white (if you use white paper). This still remains the color scheme most natural to woodblock printing. But I don't want you to be stuck on any theories! Matisse's collages of large sitting figures look great in the color he chose—a sky-blue placed on white paper—so you will want to psych out any color that will suit your purpose.

ROLLERS: These are called brayers in art-supply stores. They will run between $1.50 and $6. The most expensive is also the best because it is softer. An adequate brayer runs about $3. The cheaper ones are too hard: wood inside, a thin cover of rubber on the outside.

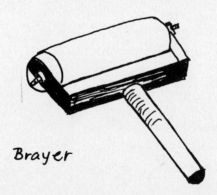

Brayer

PALETTE: Thick glass (or thin glass with a few layers of newspaper under it) is the best possible palette on which to roll the brayer in the ink, and the best possible thing for mixing all kinds of paint. Painting the underside of the glass with white paint makes a perfect white surface for seeing colors clearly. Placing the glass on top of white paper will also do the trick. Soft or hard paint and ink can all be easily scraped off glass with a single-edge razor blade. If the edges of the glass are too sharp, a quickie solution is to run some Scotch tape along them; however, paint will eventually get stuck on the tape.

DOING IT

CUTTING THE BLOCK: This is a woodchopper's ball, and one part of
the whole process is to SEE what you're doing. If you're wearing dark
glasses, take the lenses out first. The block should be cut with the knife
blade slanting toward the middle of the cuts, forming a V. Slanting the
knife toward the side of the cut will make an undercut, weakening the raised
edge, which may eventually chip off. The knife is used for cutting out
white lines, for cutting outlines of areas that will later be completely gouged
and chiseled away, and for cutting outlines around lines that will stay raised
and print black. Hold gouges so that the handle is up against the palm of
your hand for maximum pushing pressure. Your fingers guide the cut. It
is important, right off, to get into the habit of working the gouge away from
you, away from the hand steadying the block. If not, as you push the gouge
it could slip off the block, cutting or jabbing your other hand. If you're a
strung-out neurotic or nervous type, don't listen to hard rock or you might
end up with a cut Tootsie Roll. Just make do with a little light, lobotomized

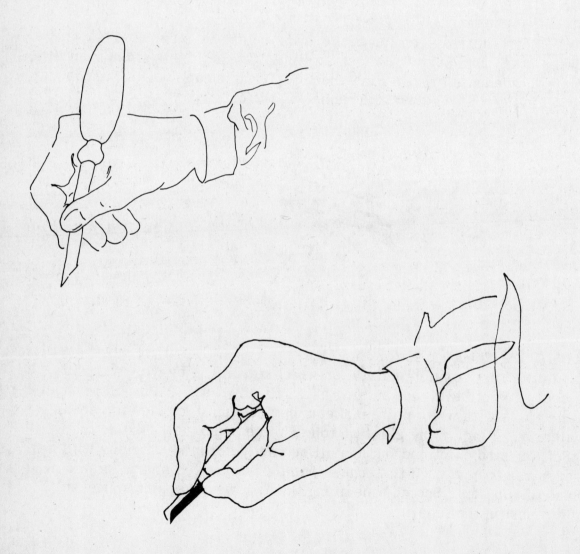

music, as long as it's good stuff. Nailing a strip of wood onto your working table and placing the edge of the woodblock against that while working on it will keep the block, but not the gouge, from slipping. (Large areas of wood can be chiseled away.)

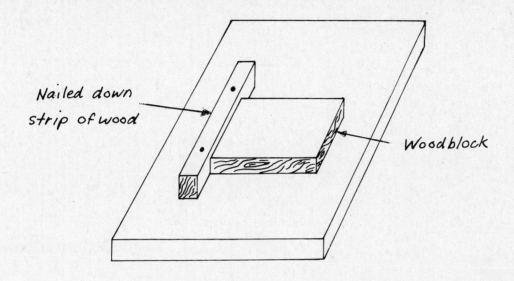

Nailed down
strip of wood

Woodblock

Cut into the wood at a depth that comes natural to what you're cutting, at least 1/16-inch deep as a rule. But narrow spaces are cut shallower than the wider ones. If a largish space is cut too shallow, it will be hard to keep the ink out of it when you roll ink on the block, and then it will print when the paper is laid down.

This is where you can work out any latent hostility. It is also the time to eat a Mars Bar. You are really attacking, and unless you want to cop back into the system, this part of the process is a good exercise in going against the grain.

Picasso said once that he destroyed in order to create. He would wipe out his own efforts to get something better. He also liked to work in a messy, cluttered room; it made him feel like creating order out of all the chaos.

Don't get me wrong, all this aggression shouldn't spill over into your philosophy of life, or influence your attitude about people—not like the ego-mongers' power-trip on the political machine that destroys in war, they tell us, in order to "create peace" and "make the world safe." In cutting the block you are putting human energy into the wood as you destroy it. Your energy in man/woman-made forms and structures can say what you want it to say through the impression of the wood pressed into your print. Nothing lost—everything ingrained.

PRINTING: When you are ready to print, bite off a chunk of Heath Bar and roll the brayer over the ink on the glass palette so it spreads even all along the brayer. Roll the ink on the block, then place a sheet of your printing paper on top of the inked block. Hold one hand down on the paper while rubbing sections of the surface with the back of a tablespoon until the entire surface has been burnished. Hold the spoon so that your thumb presses down in the center of the spoon. This is the part of the process that really uses some energy. (That's another advantage of eating candy now and then.) A clean brayer can be used and also a low-heated iron, and you can even stomp'n'rock on it, but nothing is as good as the spoon to bur- nish the paper so you won't lose consistency of pressure in all areas. A silver spoon, if kept polished, is best.

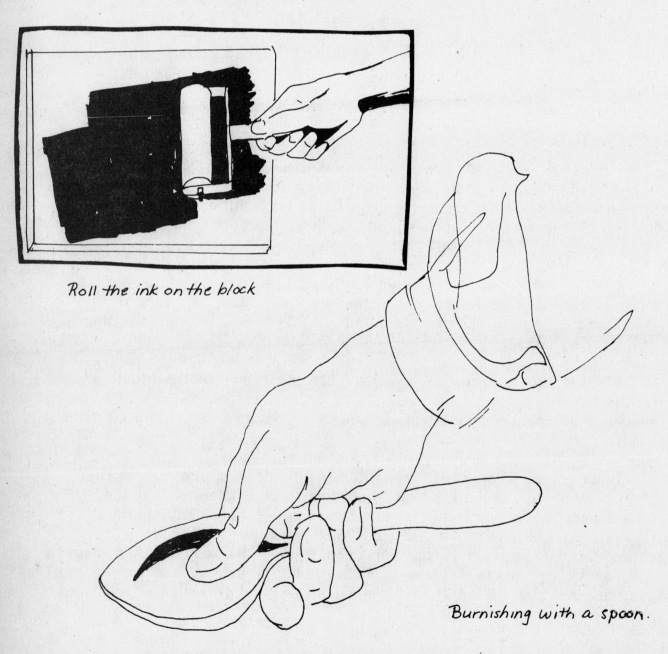

Roll the ink on the block

Burnishing with a spoon.

Finished prints will take a while to dry and should not be stacked on top of each other. If you do a few prints, you'll no doubt have enough floor and table space to lay them down on. But remember, oil inks take longer to dry than water-base inks, and you may need to hang oil prints.

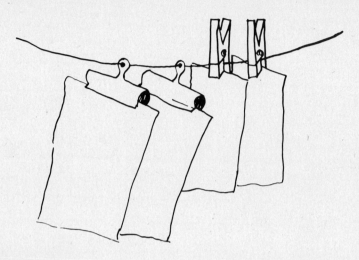

THE CARDBOARD PRINT

There are two ways to use cardboard for printing. Both are perfect, since they can be done quickly and, also, much experimentation can take place. (1) Shapes can be cut out of cardboard with scissors or knife with little hassle and arranged and glued onto a stiff surface;

(2) Cuts can be made in thick cardboard in the same manner as in wood.

MATBOARD: Single-thick costs around $1 for a sheet 30 inches by 40 inches and runs about half that price in the 20 by 30 size, at any art-supply shop. Generally, just small pieces of matboard will serve your purpose because you will be cutting out forms to glue onto a large surface. Since matboard is generally used to mat pictures for framing, perhaps you can get pieces (for free or for very little money) that the framer has cut out of the center of his mats. This way, you might get different textures to experiment with. Pebbleboard is speckled with little holes. A friend likes to put even more holes in pebbleboard with an ice pick.

Double-thick matboard is about double the cost of the single-thick, but it's necessary if you want to cut into it, as in the woodblock method. Little texture will come through on your print when you use cardboard and it is less expensive than matboard or wood. (Grayboard is cheaper but not so many shops stock it.)

A UTILITY KNIFE is best for cutting into cardboard or matboard. Blades can be replaced when they wear out. The cost is about $1 per knife, and they can be gotten at hardware and art stores. (It's also called a mat knife.)

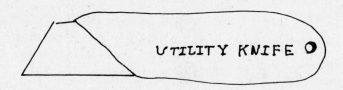

PAPER: Same as used in woodblock; thinnish paper is best (for grabbing all the ink) especially in cardboard printing.

DOING IT AS IN WOODBLOCK: Using a double-or triple-thick matboard or cardboard, make line cuts about 1/16-inch deep into the cardboard with the mat knife. Use the mat knife to outline any areas that are to be cut away. Then use the mat knife to pick into the cut and lift up the areas and peel them away (cardboard is composed of layers of paper).

When the cut is finished and ready to print, you must shellac the surface (even the cuts). Any other kinds of medium might dissolve oil or water inks, so be careful what you use. Polymer Medium, which you use with acrylic paints, might work, as might Sobo or Elmer's Glue, if you have any around the house. Although these are water-base, when they dry they won't be dissolved by either oil or water-base ink or paint. But varnish, for instance, will dissolve oil. Shellac brushed on is best for your health, unless it comes in spray cans. Who needs more toxic material in their body? Spray outside and get it done quickly, if you do spray.

If you need sugar-induced creative energy and drink coffee, more poison will matte your mind and fuzz you down. By the way, I've found that a good way to face up to commercial candy products is to chomp a chunk off your favorite bar and just let it float around in your mouth and melt; then analyze what it really tastes like. If your taste is like mine, it will taste like a lot of cheap chemicals. This is a moment for revelation.

DOING IT BY GLUING: In this method complete shapes are cut out of single-thick cardboard or matboard and glued onto masonite, plywood, or any other kind of stiff surface. This surface can be painted white so that its color won't interfere with your color design. Those who have done collage (pasting paper on paper) will like this number because the principle is the same. Cutting with scissors is easiest. The cut-out pieces can be arranged on the base surface with experimentation and spontaneity, balancing the forms, shifting them around, taking pieces out, putting another shape in, until you have them in positions you want to make permanent. Even then, when they are glued down, you can cut parts of your design away with the utility knife, then sandpaper the surface; you can always add to it, and cut in lines as in woodblock.

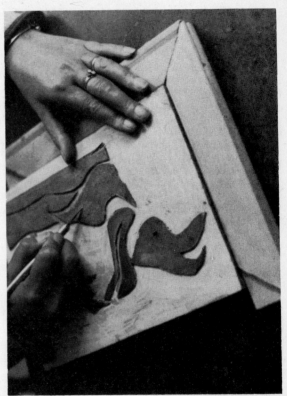

Cutting in lines after the cardboard pieces have been glued down

In doing abstractions, if you feel your arrangement or organization looks like the kiss of death—dried up and dull—just to show yourself what a totally uninhibited arrangement would look like, try throwing the pieces on the block and see how they fall. Also, try putting some pieces in reverse or upside down. There is great value in seeing what an accident or inverted thinking will do. If you want to print a trial run to see clearly how it will look when it is reversed, or if you're not sure you will like the arrangement tomorrow, glue it all down with rubber cement (which is a temporary glue), shellac, and print as a test. When you want the pieces to be glued permanently, use Sobo or Elmer's. It helps to place a heavy book on top of the permanently glued parts for half an hour.

Jim Forsberg, who discovered this cardboard method (when he came out of the Army in 1946), told me an easy trick. If you have a hard time thinking and working in reverse, arrange your cut-out forms on the size block you want, Sobo the top of the cardboard pieces, then place another block (any surface the same size) on top of the glued pieces. When you turn the block around, the pieces will be in reverse and glued in place. When you print onto the printing paper and turn the paper around, it will be like your original arrangement. Shellac and print.

With this kind of printing, edges have a softer quality than woodblock.

Another thing Jim discovered was that some people did not like the print cut away from the edges of the paper. (Collectors buying Japanese prints, for instance, are very careful to see that the original edge of the paper is intact on a print they want.) Because of this, he had to be careful and line the paper straight with the block because he couldn't trim down any off-center edges. Center by measuring with a ruler. Or, if you can, do it by eye—when you find the corners of the block under the paper, press with your fingers. Since Jim was arranging roundish shapes (to express his feelings about seeing Stonehenge when he was in the Army) by isolating them in space, he had no edge to his picture, so he inked the edges of the block and printed. That gave him the boundary he needed and at the same time saved the original paper edges.

COLOR PRINTING—MULTIPLE BLOCKS

What I'm most interested in is the one-block watercolor method of woodcutting, but I will explain first how color is printed in the traditional way—the Chinese and Japanese method. It is time-consuming and limits the color you use, but after a lot of work cutting several blocks, you do have the advantage of being able to print, say, 100 prints relatively quickly.

Each color must be printed from an individual block: five colors, five blocks. This is such a drag. A two- or three-color print is a fair challenge, but using ten or more colors gets tedious. (Naturally, there is no limit, except the limit to your patience.) This process takes so long that in the traditional Japanese printing process, there was a three-man team involved—the artist who drew the design, the woodblock cutter, and finally the printer.

For this technique, you need a registration board so each printing will go exactly where it should. If two colors overlap (where they shouldn't), the registration is off. It isn't a big deal to make a registration board. Three-quarter-inch plywood or shelving (unwarped), larger than your paper size, will be the base. Consider the largest size you might be working on in the future so you won't have to make another one. Next nail a strip of wood (1 to 2 inches wide) and almost as thick as the woodblock along both the top edge of the board and the left side. This forms a right angle that your woodblocks can be put up against.

From under the top strip, run two long finishing nails through both base and strip so that the points will protrude a few inches at the top. Printing paper will be registered correctly when the same sheet of paper is placed at different times for different colors through the same nail holes.

Registration board

Now cut a key block (the complete picture). It is placed on the registration board snug up against the right angle. A piece of waxed paper, folded at top for strength, is placed over the block and pressed through the nails; it will be used to transfer the complete inked drawing to all the other blocks. Ink the key block with black and print on the waxed paper. Now

key block

Inked waxed paper is pressed down on an uncut block

lift the waxed paper up while the key block is taken out and an uncut block the same size is placed in registered position under the inked waxed paper. Press the paper onto the surface of the block. Remove. Again, place the cut key block into place and ink, print again on the waxed paper, pull out key block and insert another fresh block the same size and lay under the inked waxed paper. Print again. You will need a different block for each color unless, for instance, you print a red over a yellow, to get the extra color, orange, as a bonus.

When you have transferred the total design to the number of blocks of wood you need, you are ready to cut those blocks. Cut away all the space on each block except the part that will hold the particular color for that block.

The key block is the line drawing part of the print.

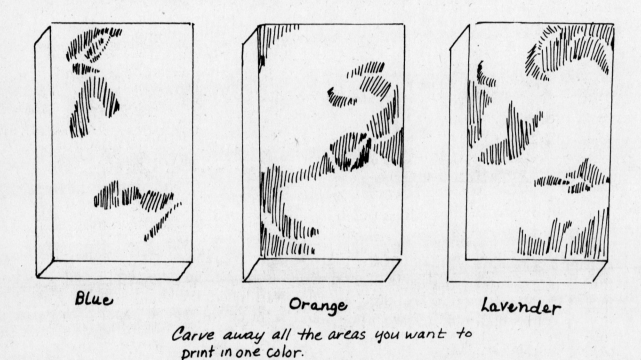

Blue   Orange   Lavender

Carve away all the areas you want to
print in one color.

When printing, do a run of one color on each print, let them dry, and start another color. Paper is placed through the nails and taken off and on again until each color is printed on all the prints.

Try out a few print-runs first to see how you like the color. If you don't, you can always experiment with different tones or different colors before printing up a complete run. The back of a tablespoon is used to rub in the ink.

Note: Try not to allow the nail holes in the printing paper to become larger or the registration may get off. Poor registration is seen in every comic book where the color goes outside of the lines that were meant to contain it. If all this messing around and the prospect of cutting all those other blocks bring you down because more than half the creative work is already done, take a break and don't work in long stretches.

Sometimes when work wasn't going as well as I'd like it to, I'd ask someone around the house to go to the store for me and buy a Fifth Avenue Bar, or whatever kind I was hooked on at the time. But the real thing that happened here was that the idea of somebody doing something exclusively for me, to help me work, was all I needed to get over a creative block or encourage me to continue a stage of work that wasn't all that exciting.

THE ONE-BLOCK METHOD OF WATERCOLOR WOODCUT PRINTING

Most multiple-block woodblock printing is done with oil- or water-base inks. As you've read, the inks are limited in color. In watercolor woodblock, you use one block with watercolor, designer colors, or gouache (the latter two are more opaque than watercolor). This way you have the greatest color choice. I have never used oil paint on the single block, but I can't think of any reason why it couldn't be used. After all, the block can be wiped clean after printing with turpentine. Acrylics would be difficult; they dry fast, and it might be hard to clean the block even with acrylic remover.

I think this watercolor method produces the most sensitive kind of color printing there is. Each print is controlled by the artist's hand—designed, cut, and printed. It does not allow you to print up hundreds quickly, however. After the wood is cut and ready for printing, each print might take you as little as half an hour to as much as three hours (for a very large and/or very complex block) to print, depending on size and how fast you make color decisions.

This method was invented around 1915 in Provincetown, Massachusetts. It seems that quite a few women from France were in Provincetown, all doing woodblocks in the traditional multiblock manner. One woman, Ethel Mars, first developed a shortcut by cutting a line with a penknife within one area of a color block and applying different colors directly to both sections. Nordfeldt, who came to Provincetown at the same time (only from England), picked up on Ethel Mars and developed the one-block method. The prints these people made have the most beautiful color tonality and show the best modern color serse I've seen. The traces of white on the print, caused by the grain in the wood, make a sort of consistency. All the colors have a certain amount of tonality guaranteed them because of the regular amounts of white or off-white coming from the paper through the colors. I started picking up these old prints, and a friend gave us some. I have no idea if enough prints could be dug up to form an exhibit, but I do know both the prints and the method are almost lost. Save it from the grave!

My head has been into this kind of woodblock since I saw some of these single-block prints done by an artist living in Monterey, who had learned the method from one of the few Provincetown people still practicing the technique. She told me I didn't have the patience to do them, and, because most everything she said at the time had the ring of truth, I didn't further my interest in any active way. I was curious, though, as to whether I did or did not have the needed patience, or any patience at all (it was like a teachy fly in my head that bugged me every time I ran into those prints). So for many moons, though this kind of printing is the most obvious and simplest thing to grasp, I had only one eye open to all methods of printmaking. Then a woman on the Cape, who is still doing this kind of color printing, opened my other eye by showing me, in five minutes, how it is done.

<u>DOING IT</u>: A carved woodblock is ready to print. The same piece of paper is going to be brought down on the block each time a different color is brushed on the block.

This is where I used to dash to the freezer for another Heath Bar. Now I try only to drink caffeine-free coffee at this point in the process. It occurs to me that all the names for candy bars must have been chosen by male chauvinists—Mars Bar, Sugar Daddies, O'Henry, Babe Ruth, Three Musketeers, Peter Paul's Mounds, Mr. Goodbar, and M & M is probably for Mister and Master. The rest are neuters, like Old Crows, Twisters (licorice), Hershey Bars, Milky Ways, etc., and there is only one Lady Finger, and it's a kookie cookie. I should start chewing gum.

There are a couple of ways to attach the paper. You'll probably invent ways for yourself after you get into it. If the block you're using is totally carved, with the image filling the entire surface, then an extra strip of wood, 2 inches wide and almost as thick as the block you are using, is nailed

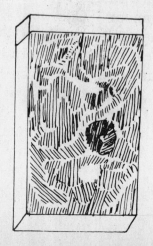

Completely carved block with an extra strip of wood nailed on for attaching your paper.

304

to the top of the block (almost level with its surface). Nails can be angled in from the underside. The reason I say "almost level" is that you might want to rub the top edge of the block to make an edge impression, and, if you do, it will be easier this way. Place a strip of paper on the top edge of the printing paper for added holding power and thumbtack it to the side of the strip. Press the paper into the right angle as it folds over the top of the board so it will come down flat. A good idea, but optional, is to fold another piece of paper over the edge of the paper on the opposite side of the

thumbtacked edge. A few paperclips will hold it on. It will protect the printing paper from getting messed over by paint on hands while working,

etc.   Another way to attach the paper is to use a block larger at the top than your finished carving will be (larger at the top because that's where the paper is attached).   Paper can be thumbtacked right on the top surface of the block above the woodcut.

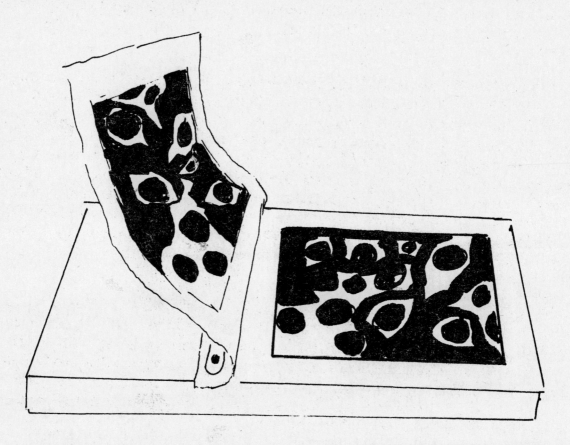

COLOR AND BRUSHES: If you are going to use watercolors, try to use those that say "artist's colors," meaning in most cases that they are the best of the two or three lines every company manufactures. The best usually comes in small tubes, and one of these is Winsor & Newton Artist's Quality, which ranges in cost from 65¢ a tube to $1.65. The difference is in the color. Cadmium colors are always best because the pigment is permanent, will not fade, and is more condensed; therefore, you use less of it. You will only find them in greens, reds, and yellows. Look at the color on the chart, pick out the colors you want—like, need, flip you out, and turn you on the most. Select colors that will somehow give you the full range. If you're short of cash, a red, yellow, and blue, those good old primaries you remember from school, can be mixed to give you a full range. Get a medium (true) red, the lightest yellow (the yellow with least orange in it), and the bluest blue (this is ultramarine). What these basic colors can't give you when mixed together to get other colors is the intensity and purity you can get direct from tubes. A white and a black are also necessary to darken, lighten, or gray any color.

Because watercolor dries quickly, one color at a time is applied to the block and printed, using the back of the spoon. There is no rule. If there isn't enough color transferred to the paper, you can do it over—colors can be reprinted and the color can be made darker, generally by adding a touch of black, or lighter, by adding Chinese white. You can even print another color hue entirely over the first one.

This kind of color printing lends itself best to realizing color. Each print can have totally different color. You can experiment with placement of color until all the colors work together, without having to cope further with the problem of changing shapes, their sizes and placement (though, granted, being able to change a shape might help get what you want with color). A fine painter told me she would set up a color structure and put each color in a different size square—some very large and some small. Then she'd use these colors again and again, moving them around in the squares. The effect is individual in each case, and she learned all there was to learn about what those particular colors could do.

Any color, by itself on a white surface, looks good. It has room to expand its identity. Each additional color you add will alter the first color's appearance. The aim is to alter it so you are still satisfied with the first color. It is hard to put down many different colors without the colors destroying each other. Remember this each time you add a color so you won't settle for less. They have to be chosen carefully so they amplify (add another dimension) and sustain one another.

Each watercolor is placed on <u>part</u> of the block directly with a watercolor brush. Red sable brushes will last a lifetime and hold together well. Also, and most important, they continue to have good spring-back. They are the most expensive brushes you can buy, just like a sable coat is the most expensive fur (fifty to a hundred <u>thousand</u> capitalist pig dollars!). When I went to high school, they used to pass out a new red sable brush every year. You were allowed to keep your old one. I am still using those brushes from a pre-Aquarian age. Well, if taken care of, they do last a long time. Other kinds of brushes I've bought have come and gone, and never could be relied on to do what I wanted them to do. Red sables run from $1 to $8 for small to medium sizes. You probably won't need more than a No. 2 and a No. 5—but that will depend on how fine the areas on your woodblock will be—and how large. If you need larger brushes, you can use either oxhair or sabeline, which are less expensive wash brushes. A large No. 24 pure red sable brush costs about as much as the coat, and only Salvador Dali can afford to Dilly-Dali with those . . .

RAISED WHITE LINE OPTION: After a section of the block has been transferred to paper, apply water with your brush directly on the cut-out lines. Bring the paper down on the block and rub the lines with the back of your spoon. This will raise the paper at the line because the paper has been pressed into the line.

WET PAPER BEFORE PRINTING OPTION: Something that might suit your purpose could be using wet printing paper to get softer and blurred edges on your print. These prints sometimes look slightly like watercolor painting. Heavier paper can be used for this one. After the printing paper is wet, press it between newspaper and use as usual.

MUSIC AND COLOR

Everyone recognizes the analogy music has with color: you can think of a flute evoking yellow, a bass evoking blue, or even an oboe evoking dark orange. You can even go so far as to say F-sharp evokes purple. It is also common knowledge that certain color schemes can reflect different moods and emotions just like certain music. Musicians talk about how Impressionist paintings remind them of Debussy. Painters have painted pictures expressing how they feel about jazz, and musicians have written compositions expressing how they feel about paintings (Mussorgsky's "Pictures at an Exhibition," etc., etc.). Besides relating color to music, there has been much talk about rhythm relationships and symbolic psychological relationships between the two forms of expression. The idea that light and sound frequencies stimulate visual and auditory perception was studied long ago.

When he plays his music, Taj Mahal thinks of his sound as a shape. He especially likes the pure forms of Brancusi and Arp because he feels an analogy to the way a note can swell and mold itself into shape and volume. That must be what is meant by pregnant sound, or when your music teacher told you to play a full note.

Going a little farther than the above in the comparison of music to color is not so common... but it is possible to think of a particular color sequence as being just like a particular musical sequence. Being able to do just that is not my purpose, but being able to think of color in some kind of organized way, as musicians do with musical notes, will stimulate a sensibility to the full range.

Using the ordinary colors you see in nature exclusively, like skin color, grass-green, barn-red, is analogous to musicians' using only thunder sounds, bird calls, or the sounds of a truck coming up the road. The fact is, music has been so much ahead of color that it was put into a man-made scheme (88 notes on the keyboard) centuries ago. It is easy to distinguish one of these notes from the others when you hear them. The intervals between notes in Eastern music is so close that, as Tim Hardin says, Chinese children can't sing their own national anthem until they are twenty-five but they can sing "Silent Night" right off. This is the reason Tim thinks the Western system of music is the perfect system. Everyone can sing it. Thinking of color without intervals is thinking of an unharnessed force, just as sound was before musical scales were invented. Imagine what experimenting must have been like for the Pre-Columbian with his three-hole clay whistle—and that's just about how primitive learning color is in the beginning.

There is the Color Harmony Manual with its 900 separate color intervals in chip form adapted from the Ostwald theory, but it has been discontinued by the Container Corporation; however, you can still get <u>Basic Color</u>, by Jacobson, based on the Ostwald theory. Anyone can start thinking of color in terms of the distances between colors and the amount of black and white that can go into each color. For instance, it is obvious that blue is a long way from yellow, and white is a long way from black, but closer measurements of color can be a tool in your mind much as Do-Re-Mi-Fa-Sol-La-Ti-Do is in sound.

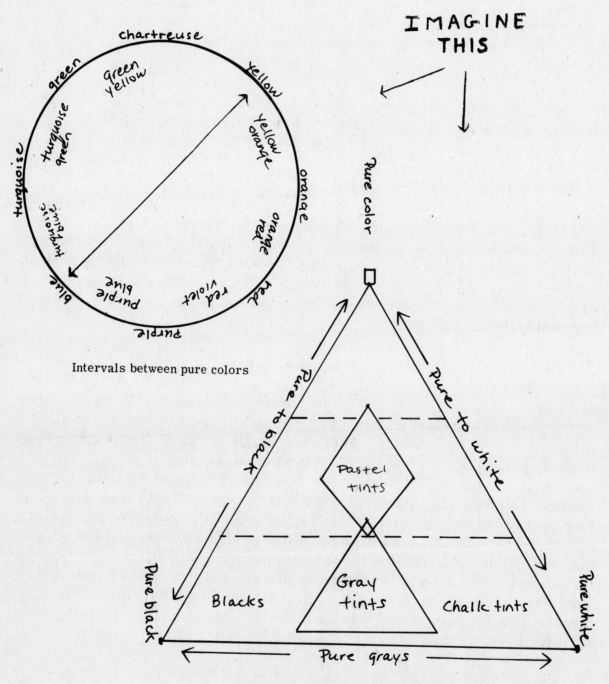

Intervals between pure colors

Mixing a color with white, black, or gray

Single color choices are made from a potential of more colors than there are tones in a music scale. It can be done with less sweat than you'd think. For instance, you can choose color hues out of a certain range of lightness or darkness (tone), which will give your picture a certain all-around tone. You can choose colors that hang around each other, like different hues of blues and blue-greens, which will give the picture a cool feeling. Being aware of color possibilities will make you conscious of when and where you want to limit color.

What is exciting to me is to see a color combined with others so that it appears to be another color than what it really is. A very tuned-in color that does this becomes unique and powerful. These colors have an effect beyond their separate individuality. For example, if only the warmer colors are used in a picture, such as yellow-green, yellow, orange, and orange-red, solid black or black-gray will appear bluish in the same picture (if it doesn't occupy too much space). The same applies to a green mixed with a touch of black (it will appear bluish, as will a red-orange— it will look for all the world like a purple-blue!). Also, a deviation from any group of close colors (such as bright or dark yellow, yellow-green, yellow-orange, orange) will suggest to the imagination a color more brilliant than it actually is. If you use a light pink with the above colors it will appear the dominant color, even if it is a very small area of the picture. You will see when you do it.

Older painters harmonized one local color with another until Rubens' innovation in the seventeenth century. Roger Fry, the good friend of Virginia Woolf, said, "In the golden key of some of Rubens' compositions, a touch of gray made by mixing black and white will count as a definite blue, or the dullest earth-reds will shout like vermilion."

Color can be dissonant in the smoothest, least obvious way, much as in modern classical music or in Coltrane and jazz, when you choose colors that jar, that are close together. It is also interesting to think of using color in places like feedback in music. Feedback can't be notated because there are no notes for it, and a color that is augmented so slightly (slurred into another shade or intensity or into another color entirely) will act much the same as feedback.

Something along this kind of thinking will give your one-block color prints a head start in showing an awareness of color. Since you can actually experiment more with color than with forms (you can't recarve blocks as

easily as you can simply print them with different color) you will discover
a new excitement in color.

The most interesting kind of inspiration happens when you find some
unique quality in your work. It can happen that your whole plan worked out
right or that you're surprised at what you did that was accidental. I hope
woodblock will be a medium where you will be inspired by your own work.

good

energy,

Jean

Bronzeworking

Checko Miller

ILLUSTRATIONS AND ASSISTANCE BY SANDEE SHAW

Why bronze? First of all, it is a strong metal, yet easily worked with the aid of an oxygen-acetylene torch. It can be polished to shine and look like gold; it can be left to dull into an earthy hue, or, with the aid of chemicals, appear as copper and very dark. Also, this alloy is relatively easy to obtain and is inexpensive—around $2 a pound. Bronze can last for thousands of years.

With developed skills and proper tools, you can create, from rigid hard metal, fluid shapes with which your imagination tells a story. Designs are created by joining rods of bronze together or combining the fluid, melted form with the rigid rod: concrete realizations of forms from your mind.

What really inspired me to work in bronze was not so much the final product, but watching Sandee, a craftswoman working in bronze. My initial involvement with Sandee was not directly related to her bronze. However, I soon found myself fascinated with her work. The closer I felt to her, the closer I felt to the bronze... the closer I felt to the bronze, the closer I felt to her, and, within this magnetic energy, all were brought closer to one another. When you see the torch being handled right you sense that the assurance and skilled movement are directly related to your own eyes. If you think because you see it you can do it, you're right. You can! Bronzeworking: the art so graceful you feel you are actually <u>seeing</u> what it takes to make it happen. Actually you <u>are</u> feeling it! You are hooked! If the opportunity arises for you, don't pass it up.

1. Gentlemen prefer bronze

I had to try it myself. But after I first wielded the torch, a new insight presented itself: it is not so easy to translate your ideas and feeling into a piece of work. I had always considered metal simply something machines were made of, something merely functional. Now I've come to know it can be a very creative medium to work in. Bronzeworking is not the simplest of crafts, but the rewards from it more than balance out the effort. The concentration put forth creates a new world for you, and it is not one of escape, but one of birth, a real sphere of your own. As your ability increases, the inner satisfaction and confidence increase. Soon you can be making belt buckles, chains, rings, bracelets, hair pieces, pendants, and pins. You don't have to limit your efforts to male-female jewelry either. I know this welder in Laguna, California, who made a bronze chair; another in Provincetown, Massachusetts, made a fantastic toy tricycle about eighteen inches tall. Both people are really involved, but there are all kinds of other projects like soap dishes, animal sculpture, faces, just designs like God's Eyes that aren't hard to do. If you have an inclination to make something different, try it. Do what makes you happy.

ABOUT EQUIPMENT

Getting the equipment means spending some money, but once you have acquired some skill in bronzeworking it's possible to sell your work and then regain the initial investment.

Most of the materials and tools are relatively easy to acquire. Some money is involved, though there are always ways of cutting down on costs. Certain materials are not immediately necessary and some you may already have. The basics cost under $200. A really nice shop costs under $500. You can cut down on the equipment cost by exploring old barns, attics, cellars, the dump, and junk yards; or try purchasing secondhand tools, tables, benches, etc., from friends. Also, keep your eye out for any garage sales and auctions. Try and get to use equipment in industrial arts shops, in schools, in auto-body repair places—or maybe the person next door has an idle torch in the garage. Enough money for rapid acquisition of tools will get you started quicker, but searching for good deals is always an adventure; in fact, the whole bronzeworking trip is an adventure.

A BRONZEWORKER

A bronzeworker can be lost from the rest of the world for hours, with a torch in one hand and uniform bronze rods in the other. The metal melts this way and that way—flux (don't let this new word put you off, I'll elaborate shortly) is sprinkled with a sizzle on the hot metal. Bronze is added, removed, hammered, and cooled according to touch and feel. There is a steady concentration, with hands guiding the tool—be it the torch, pliers, hammer, saw, or polishing equipment. Behind the dark goggles the bronze-worker may appear strange—invisible eyes guiding the hands. How does it all come about? Once you try it the strangeness evaporates through your own self-discovery. You can no longer observe the strangeness, you _are_ the strangeness. If you get off on that, well then get it on.

THE SHOP

Your working area should include certain basic things arranged in a handy way. First, build or obtain a large and flat workbench. It is pref-

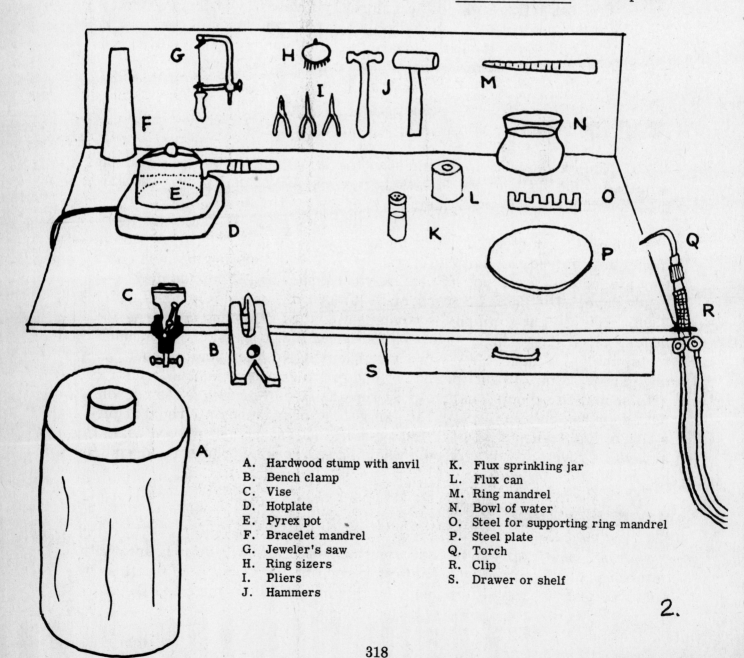

A. Hardwood stump with anvil
B. Bench clamp
C. Vise
D. Hotplate
E. Pyrex pot
F. Bracelet mandrel
G. Jeweler's saw
H. Ring sizers
I. Pliers
J. Hammers

K. Flux sprinkling jar
L. Flux can
M. Ring mandrel
N. Bowl of water
O. Steel for supporting ring mandrel
P. Steel plate
Q. Torch
R. Clip
S. Drawer or shelf

2.

erable to cover the bench with asbestos sheeting, obtainable at a lumber yard, to avoid burning the wooden bench with the torch flame.

Next, get a steel or iron plate large enough to work on; a 9- by 12-inch piece will do. A junk yard or dump will usually supply this item. I use the top plates from an old wood stove, found in a barn. This is one item you shouldn't have to dig into your pocket for.

The <u>lighting</u> where you work is important. It should not cast shadows on the area or cause any glare. A good position for the light source is above and just a little in front of you.

Good <u>ventilation</u> is also important. <u>Make sure that it is adequate</u>. When using a fan in the shop, place it far enough away so as not to affect the torch flame.

You should have a <u>spring clip</u> like those used for brooms attached to your bench so that you can put the lit torch somewhere and leave both hands free. Attach it so that the flame will be aiming in a direction away from you and everything else but air. A burn from a torch is not something you'd soon forget. The clip is also used to hold the torch, freeing both hands for shaping the bronze.

3. The set-up: torch attached to the bench by a clip, bronze rods, and hammers. To get the photo in focus, we had to show the torch pointing more or less toward Sandee. This should never happen in your shop.

A piece of peg board is good for keeping tools in order and out of the way when not in use. A lumber yard will be able to supply you with this. You might enjoy making the hooks for the peg board yourself out of bronze. If you ever need a hook with screwable threads, you can easily make one by attaching a hook-shaped piece of bronze to a common screw by joining them with your torch.

A pan of water handy on your bench is good for cooling hot bronze in a matter of seconds, when you need to handle it right away. If you can cool it naturally, though, do, for the above method tends to make bronze brittle.

I should mention that a small vise attached to the bench can also be a valuable addition to your working area. Besides holding materials firmly it can be used to straighten irregularly shaped rings, etc. Place a thick piece of cloth in the vise and the bronze in the middle and then tighten. The cloth keeps the vise from scratching the metal and holds the piece more securely.

MATERIALS AND TOOLS

If you can't find a welding-supply store in the Yellow Pages, information on where to find materials can be obtained through several sources. Inquire first at a plumber's or at a gas station or auto-body repair shop.

The bronze you'll use is brazing bronze, and it comes in rods of varied thickness. Flux-coated rods are better for sculpture, where a lot of heat is used. Uncoated rods work best in jewelry-making. For best selection and economy, go to welding-supply stores.

The flux can be purchased where you buy the bronze and gas. Flux is like powdered glass. It gives the metal an easier and more even flow when you are joining two pieces together. Flux also helps prevent the metal from burning. If the metal spits, blackens, or wrinkles, you are burning it. Sprinkle flux on the area with your fingers or an empty spice jar with small holes. Garlic-salt jars are about right because the holes match the flux particles. Flux is also useful to help clean the piece you are working on. Slightly heat an area, sprinkle flux on, and let it melt into the metal. This process can clean, smooth, and correct burned areas all at once. It is also good when you wish to blend connections more smoothly once a design has been executed.

You have to be quick in removing the flame once the flux melts into the bronze or you will change the shape. When joining or connecting a piece of rod, heat the end of the rod slightly and dip it into a small pile of flux on the asbestos.   Flux will not adhere unless the surface is heated first.

The following tools can also all be obtained at a welding-supply store:

The <u>oxygen-acetylene torch</u> used to melt the bronze comes in several sizes and styles.

I suggest one that is light in weight, so it can easily be held steady. Torches are sometimes sold in kits.   These include a <u>cutting tip</u>. You won't need this unless you plan on cutting steel or iron bars or plates. If you have ever thought you'd like to change your car into a camper, like I have, you'll want that cutting tip.   Also included are <u>torch tips</u> in several sizes. Larger tips give you a hotter flame. The kind of work and rod size you use will determine the tip you'll need. If you're going to do jewelry work, you'll want small tips: 00, 0, and 1. A finer flame allows the beginner more time to develop control. Check what sizes come with the kit. If they are not the right size, ask to exchange them.

The <u>hoses and gauges</u> that come with the kit are essential. Make sure that the hose is long enough. Before you buy the torch set-up, figure out where you want your tanks placed in your shop area. Make sure the hoses will reach.

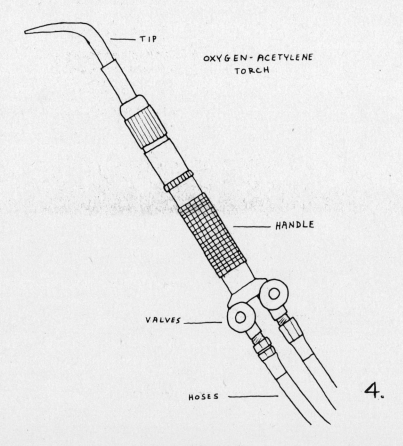

TIP

OXYGEN-ACETYLENE
TORCH

HANDLE

VALVES

HOSES

4.

Before leaving the welding-supply store with your tanks, hoses, and gauges, ask them to show you how to set up the gauges on the tanks. Don't leave until you are sure you understand exactly how they are operated. Don't plan on figuring it out yourself or on asking your friendly neighbor who knows how to fix his lawnmower or truck with baling wire.

You'll need a crescent or adjustable wrench to attach the gauges and hoses to the tanks. From time to time the torch tip will get clogged. So make certain to have tip cleaners about. When cleaning the tip, select a file tip cleaner that fits into the hole where the flame exits. The fit should be snug. Move the cleaner in and out several times and then light the torch to see if you get the proper flame. It should come straight out, not aiming off at an angle or split into several flames.

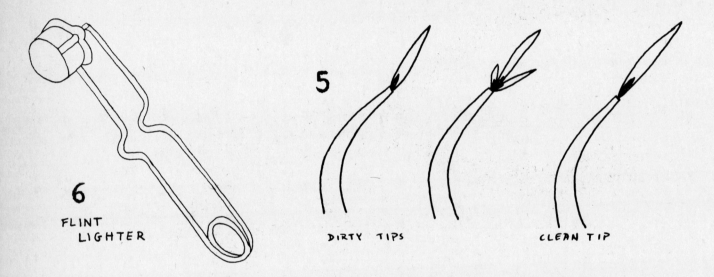

5

6
FLINT
LIGHTER

DIRTY TIPS   CLEAN TIP

To light the torch, use a flint lighter made especially for this purpose. They are also handy for lighting old gas stoves when the pilot light doesn't work. Get an extra supply of flints when you get the lighter. When lighting the torch, hold the lighter within an inch of the tip; rubbing the flint against the steel grater will make sparks to ignite the gas.

The welding-supply store carries the dark protective goggles. You'll need them any time you work on the torch. The bright light from the flame and the hot metal that might spit at you necessitate their use. A pair of clear protective goggles will be handy in other operations, like grinding and polishing. The nose needs protection. Constant exposure to bobbing compound, ammonia, liver of sulphur, and other potential irritants I will tell you about calls for the use of a nose mask. For complete protection you can use a welder's mask, but I find them burdensome, and the shades are too dark.

You'll also need two pairs of <u>pliers</u> with insulated handles.

One pair should be needle-nose and the other flat-nose. Both are good for bending warm metal (cold metal is stiff) and for holding short pieces of rod being melted. Heat gradually moves up the rod to your fingers as you work, so pliers solve the problem of burnt fingers. And they should be small enough to be easily operated with one hand. You can't always find good ones at hardware stores, so also check the craft, hobby, or art stores in the area. Oil the pliers occasionally so that they continue to move easily and to prevent rust. Remember, too, that damage to the pliers will occur if the torch flame comes too close to them. If this happens, a grinding wheel or file can sometimes repair them.

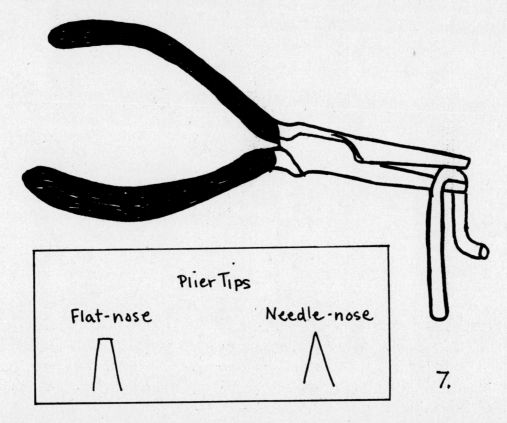

Plier Tips

Flat-nose   Needle-nose

7.

A ball-peen <u>hammer</u> is used to flatten the metal. Both the flat head and rounded end should be smooth to avoid marking the heat-softened metal. A grinding wheel, file, or sandpaper are good to have to keep the hammer in good condition. Avoid hammering on any steel surface directly because this will scar your hammer. A suitable size <u>steel anvil</u>, depending on how large the work is, is the other half of a hammering operation. Always keep any bronze you are flattening between these two steel surfaces. For some purposes, as will be seen later, a hardwood stump or log is better than an anvil. Metal should be warm-to-hot when you hit it. Never hammer molten or cold bronze. Molten will splatter, cold might crack in weak

8. using the ball-peen hammer for cup-making

areas. It may take a while before you can hammer efficiently and accurately. (It's in the wrist.)

There are different ways of hitting the metal. It's not just a matter of striking it. In delicate situations it's better to hit it several times lightly than once hard. It is best to approach metal thinking that you're going to hit it several times rather than to try to get right with just one shot. If you are flattening a small area, you can strike it coming straight down on the piece; when flattening a large area, though, you might try coming in at an angle so that when you strike you can move the metal toward the outside edge.

The round head of the hammer can be used to make curved pieces or cups of metal. Keep hammering the center and it will curve up—heating it, hammering it, heating it, and so on. Interesting effects on flat surfaces are achieved by striking the metal all over lightly, making slight indentations.

Remember, any time you flatten metal you are also making it thinner, and more sensitive to heat. Thin metal reaches a molten state quicker; therefore, you must be more careful whenever you heat flattened metal.

Never hammer bronze until the flux is removed, which you do by heating the metal in a <u>sulfuric acid solution</u>. The acid can be obtained at some automotive-supply places. Mix the solution in a Pyrex container: 10 parts water to 1 part acid. Add the acid slowly to the water—<u>never the reverse</u>, or it will explode. This operation should be done with plenty of ventilation, for the fumes are dangerous to inhale in any quantity. Use a small electric hotplate or electric stove (gas stoves can crack some glass). Or you can put the Pyrex pot in another (ordinary) pot full of water and heat the acid indirectly that way. Slowly heat a solution of acid until boiling in the Pyrex pot and drop your piece in for a few seconds. Remove it from the acid with pliers and drop it into a pan of water that has an adequate amount of baking soda—2 cups of water to 2 heaping tablespoons of soda. This neutralizes the acid. Be very careful handling the undiluted acid, as it burns. If you spill it, pour on a lot of water or milk quickly. Be sure to store it in a labeled container.

A rawhide hammer is useful in reshaping a piece once it is polished. Rawhide will not mark the metal. This inexpensive hammer is good to have, but not essential. Never use it on hot metal.

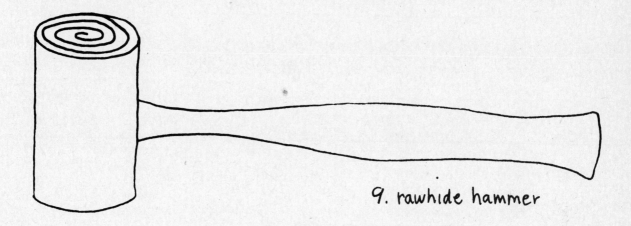

9. rawhide hammer

Files, as previously mentioned, are good tools, too, both for repairing other tools and shaping the bronze. Files are good for smoothing sharp or rough areas, and, in a pinch, they can function in the place of a grinding wheel. When working on a piece with the torch, don't fuss over an area you can fix later on with a small file and grinding wheel. If you don't have a grinding wheel, you must have both large and small files. You'll need both round and flat files, all of finer grades, for if files are too coarse they'll grab the metal. Six-inch hand files are suitable for jewelry-making.

Sometimes you'll use a clamp or vise to hold a piece while filing. Files are designed to work away from you on the forward stroke only. Start at the tip of the file and work toward the handle (see Fig. 18), exerting firm pressure in that direction. In order to make edges of a piece parallel, rub them across the file placed on a work bench (this is especially good for rings).

Grinding wheels are obtainable from most craft suppliers. You might also check with a jeweler, who might just have a good second-hand one for sale. Hand-cranked models are available, but a motor-driven wheel is vastly superior. The latter leaves both hands free, and this makes for much greater control.

Grinding wheels are also good to have around for sharpening kitchen knives or garden tools. Discs of different coarseness come with the wheel. For jewelry, use a finer grindstone. Usually the edge, or primary grinding area, is coarser than the sides. The sides are good for smoothing tools, such as the head of a hammer.

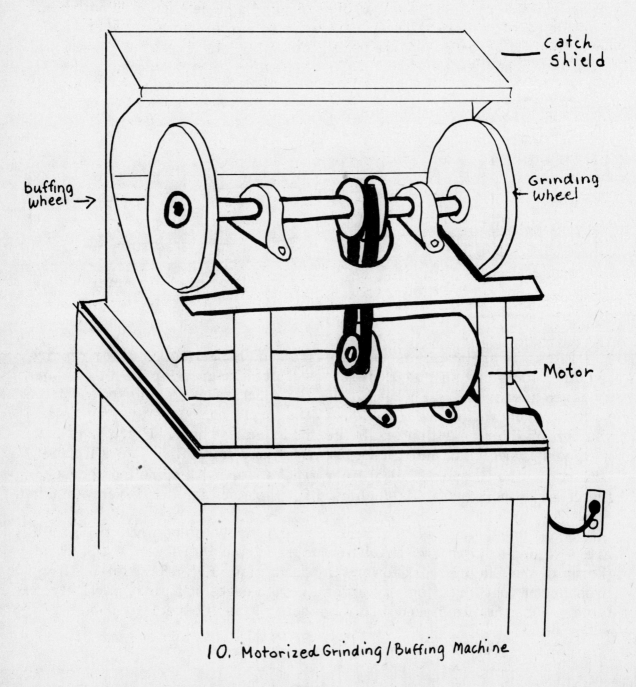

10. Motorized Grinding / Buffing Machine

A buffing wheel attached to the shaft of your grinding wheel makes polishing and smoothing faster and easier. If you are going to purchase a grinding wheel, get one that has a long shaft so that you can connect a buffing wheel. Polishing a piece by hand is more involved—but, I find, better for one's head—than wheel-buffing.

A jeweler's saw is another useful tool, for removing sections of bronze, or for resizing rings when, for example, you want to make a ring band smaller. I find medium grade blades work fine for most cutting purposes. To put a blade in a jeweler's saw, tighten one end of the blade into the compressing thumbscrew farthest from the handle. The teeth of the blade should be facing toward the handle and outward. Press the curved metal arm of the saw against something solid so as to shorten the distance bebetween the two compressing thumbscrews. Tighten the blade into the screw by the handle and relax the tension so that the blade becomes taut in the saw. It will take a little practice to get this operation down. When the blade is at the proper tension, it will make a pinging sound when plucked.

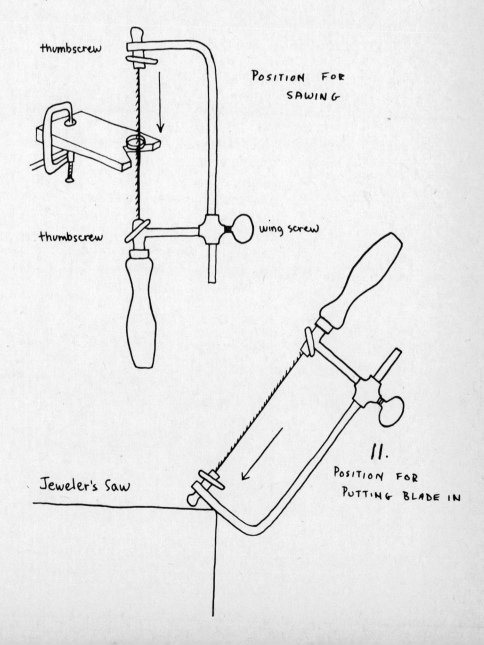

thumbscrew

POSITION FOR SAWING

thumbscrew

wing screw

Jeweler's Saw

11.

POSITION FOR PUTTING BLADE IN

You may find it easier to start a cut with a few upward strokes, but the actual sawing is done with downward strokes. When sawing, hold the saw frame in a vertical position. This helps to control the sawing and minimizes blade breakage. Let the blade make its own cut; do not force the blade or exert strong forward pressure. Too much pressure and the blade will break.

There are two ways to remove the blade from a cut after sawing partially through a piece. Either move the saw blade up and down while backing out along the cut, or loosen the wing screw, release the saw blade from one end of the frame, and pull the blade through.

When a shape is to be cut from the center of a piece of bronze, the first step is to make a dent with a center punch or nail. Drill a small hole through the dent with a hand drill or flexible-shaft machine (see below). The dent will prevent the drill from slipping over the surface of the metal. Release the saw blade from the end of the frame, insert it through the hole, and tighten it back into position. Proceed with sawing in the usual manner and, when it is completed, release the saw blade once more and remove the cut-out metal.

A flexible-shaft grinding machine is the best all-around jeweler's tool and is a necessity in your shop if you plan on large production (one good model by Foredom costs about $100). It's similar to a dentist's drill. Many attachments come with this machine, such as: grinding wheels, sanding wheels, wire wheels, rubber wheels, drills, buffing wheels, sanding discs, brushes. These are all good for doing fine work or getting into small areas. The flexible nature of the tool enables you to do much more than can be done with hand files.

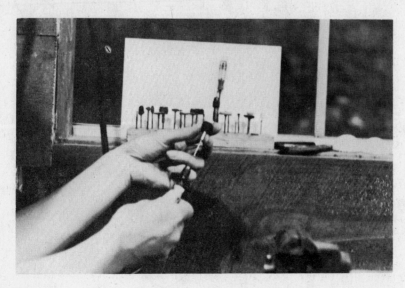

12. Flexible-shaft grinding
    machine with attachments

While using a flexible-shaft, you should be careful not to get the shaft too hot and, whenever it does, to let it cool for a while. It comes with a foot pedal that enables you to vary the speed. The harder you press, the faster it spins. Important: wheels come in both left- and right-hand models. Get the correct one, otherwise the wheel will spin toward you, throwing off particles in your face. Wearing a nose mask will prevent you from breathing in particles and fine dust.

THE TORCH

The flame of the torch consists of two ignited gases mixed together, oxygen and acetylene. By combining them you can produce a flame of 6,000 degrees F.—well above the melting points of all metals.

Getting the proper flame is vital to working in bronze. First you must have the proper pressure settings on your tank gauges. This pressure setting varies with the size tip you use and the style.

Tank Gauge Settings

Types of Tip	Tip Size	Oxygen	Acetylene
Style 112	0	15-20	3-5
	1	35-40	5-7
Style 145	00	15-20	3-5
	0	15-20	3-5
	1	30-40	3-5
Style (General) except 112 & 145	00	25-35	2-4
	0	25-35	2-4
	1	30-40	2-4
	2	40-50	2-4

To light the torch, open the valves by the torch just slightly, after you have set your tank gauges correctly. With the valves open, strike the flint lighter in front of tip. It might be difficult at first to get the gas lit. This is usually due to an excess of oxygen or not enough acetylene, so lower the former or increase the latter. An orange, yellow, or white flame signifies an excess of acetylene. This flame is wasteful and will not be hot enough for efficient work. Too much oxygen will sound windy or will extinguish the flame altogether. This flame will burn the metal instead of allowing it to flow.   (Oxygen is in the mixture to increase the heat.)

While you are trying to get the flame lit, the gas may pop loudly. Don't get nervous, just readjust your valves. The proper flame is light blue with a slight touch of orange. Never get oil or other flammables near the torch. They might explode.

Once the flame is lit, you will notice that within the larger flame there is a small bright blue flame. The hottest area is at the tip of this flame. Hold the torch so that this point is near the metal. The flame and the bronze create a bright white light. As the metal heats, it turns red to reddish-orange, when it becomes liquid. At this molten point it usually has areas of a silvery color. In order to join two pieces securely, both surfaces to be joined must be in a liquid state. Control at this point, as you will find, is essential. Too much heat will cause the two pieces of bronze to separate on either side of the flame. Too little heat and they will not form a secure joint. The smaller the rod you use, the trickier it gets. Larger rods take longer to heat and require a steady hand. I suggest using the second or third smallest size to start. You can control the amount of heat by adjusting the size of the flame and/or the size of the tip. The smaller the number, the finer the flame. Naturally, before you attempt to do anything specific, experiment and get the feel of the bronze.

I am right-handed, so generally I hold the torch in my right hand and the rod in my left. If you haven't used your left hand much, you'll find that the necessary coordination takes some time to develop. But mostly you must develop patience with yourself, which is one of the benefits of this craft. You are establishing a sense of control, coordination, and rhythm between your hands, eyes, and mind.

Gravity is another force at play here. When bronze is in a liquid state, it flows not only with the heat but with gravity also. You might feel that's obvious, but it's important to be conscious of all you have working for you. Each force in the operation is like a part of a symphony.

If you want to remove an area you can't reach with the grinding wheel, hold the piece with pliers, and heat the area until it approaches a liquid state; then shake the piece so the area will fall out.

The heat and flame are something to be very aware of at all times. The plate you work on, the piece, and whatever the torch comes near enough to will be hot! Be cautious, things may not always appear to be hot. If you're unsure about a piece, use pliers and place it in a pan of water first before touching it. The importance of all this caution will be clearer

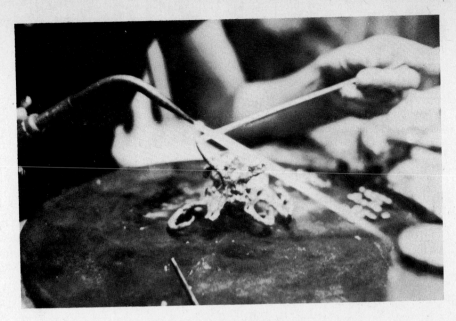

13. Cutting a rod with the torch

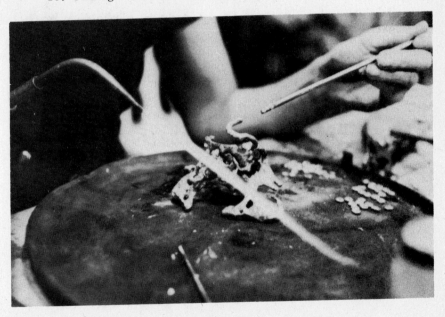

to you after the first time you forget. For some reason I've found that—
with a minor burn—if I immediately place my fingers to my cheek, it helps.
I guess it absorbs and distributes the heat, I'm not sure, but it works. If
the burn warrants it, use ice and cold water. For bad burns, try squeezing a capsule of vitamin E on the area for fast healing and so there won't
be any scar tissue. Also (for sometimes the metal will spit) I suggest you
wear clothing that covers you well. You will be using sulfuric acid, and
so wearing a full-length apron is a good idea.

You'll find out that once you learn how to use the torch the word will spread and you'll soon be asked to do all kinds of crazy favors, like fixing hooks for a gate, cutting kerosene drums in half—they make calypso drums and great indoor fireplaces—and of course everyone will want something done to his or her car. Your new skill will be much in demand and you will be having fun.

FORMING THE BRONZE

Here are some basic methods for forming bronze. For the lack of a better word, blobs or balls will probably be the first method you will encounter. Always use flux when forming a blob or else you will burn metal. You might try dipping the heated rod into the flux and then rubbing it onto the blob you are forming when you don't want the flux all over. Warm the bronze rod end (using flux), heat the area at the end of the rod until it melts off. If it hasn't formed into a ball, heat it some more while it's on the plate. As mentioned previously, this liquid will gravitate toward itself— thus, the blob. When you want to add a blob or ball to a piece, attach the rod to the piece first. Then using your torch separate the two, leaving the amount of metal desired. Sprinkle flux on the area and then heat. The rod will shorten, forming a blob as it does. Placing several blobs near each other requires some doing so that you don't melt previous work. It is important to aim the flame so that it doesn't affect delicate areas. Using a small fine flame will also help your control.

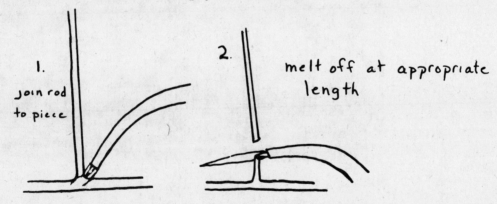

1. join rod to piece

2. melt off at appropriate length

SPRINKLE FLUX THEN HEAT
ALL SIDES SO BLOB FORMS EVENLY

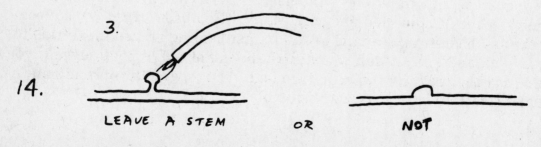

3.

14.

LEAVE A STEM   OR   NOT

Holding the flame so that it warms the metal rod enables you to bend the rod easily. However, there is a method of stretching bronze to make lines with more texture than the plain cylindrical rod. This is called drawing the bronze out, and requires good coordination between your two hands. Your torch flame moves up the rod, just slightly melting the bronze, while the hand holding the rod directs where you want it to go. You'll find that to make a continuous line without a break takes some practice. Drawing metallic lines can follow you into your dreams at night. You may find it helps to sprinkle flux on the heated rod from time to time as you draw it out. Remember, it's also good for smoothing the bronze, but too much flux will tend to make the bronze blob (sometimes you might want to add blobs to break up definite lines, though).

As you are learning these techniques, it will help if you try and visualize the movement and coordination you are trying to achieve with your hands. Don't let frustrations send you away. Believe in the power of the guide inside you.

There will be times when you will attempt to construct some definite form. At other times you'll want to be loose and casual. In both instances, know that the bronze is partially dictating your next move. And you should be as open to the same flexibility as is the bronze. The outcome may be possibly something that (only) you will recognize the significance of, leaving others to use their imagination. In time you discover yourself connected to the bronze rod; when you change it, you change yourself.

Flattening a rod or a partially worked piece involves warming the metal on the anvil and hitting it with your hammer. (Remember to wash off any unfused flux with acid first.) The method is described earlier in the section on tools under "ball-peen hammer." You can flatten out the design or create raised designs on the top of flat surfaces. To make flat areas, melt off a blob large enough to be flattened to the right size and work it flat on the anvil. This requires some hammering. (To repeat: never hammer metal until the flux is removed or it will mark the bronze.)

Sometimes it is handy to attach a rod temporarily to the piece to be flattened to help hold it steady.

Annealing bronze is another method to form the metal. This is done by heating the rod and then letting it cool slowly. This process leaves the cooled metal less brittle. In this way, maybe with the aid of gloves, you can form the bronze rod with your hands. This is also a good approach when you are hammering the bronze repeatedly.

Bronze can also be brazed to copper, steel, or brass. This is an area where you can strike out on your own, after becoming acquainted with bronze.

DOING JEWELRY

MAKING BEADS: To be able to form beads is useful in jewelry-making. Bronze beads look like miniature doughnuts. To make beads for a necklace or bracelet, it is first necessary to heat the rod enough to enable you to bend it. Place one end of the rod against your steel plate at an angle, say 60 degrees. Apply a balanced amount of pressure and heat so that the end curls up and around into a circle. When it just about overlaps, apply flux where the circle will join, at both ends. Aim the flame back and forth between the beginning of the circle and the point where you will connect, until the joint forms by itself. You might find that at first it is easier to hold the two ends of the circle together with pliers. You may not always get the beads even all the way around, but an irregularly shaped bead has a beauty all its own. In every case, make sure there are no sharp areas that might be uncomfortable next to the skin.

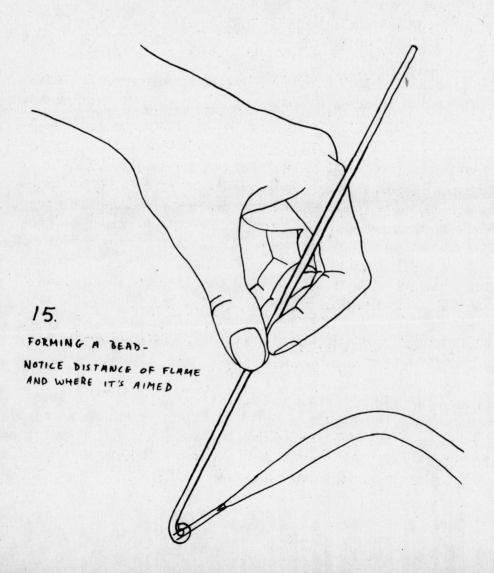

15.

FORMING A BEAD -

NOTICE DISTANCE OF FLAME
AND WHERE IT'S AIMED

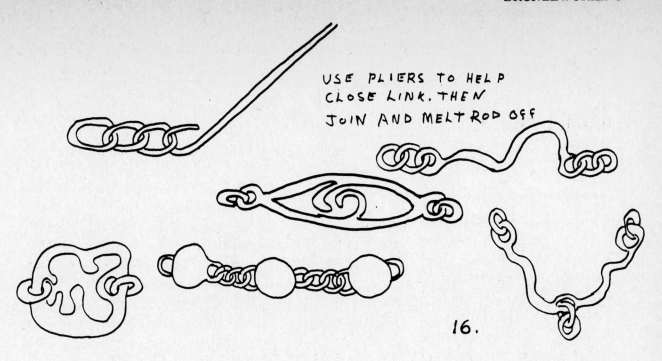

USE PLIERS TO HELP
CLOSE LINK. THEN
JOIN AND MELT ROD OFF

16.

To make chains for a necklace or bracelet requires more dexterity.
You'll need to pass each link hook through a closed link before joining the
ends of the new link. Continue hooking open links into each link you have
closed until the desired length is obtained. Keep the flame aiming (only)
in the area necessary to join links so you avoid affecting finished areas.
You can also insert a solid design in between links.

The ball-and-bead combination is another way of joining movable parts.
This arrangement involves a bead or some design that has a hole in it at
the end you wish to attach to another piece. To this other piece join a rod
that will stick out. Slip the rod through the hole and then melt the rod so
that a ball (head) larger than the hole it is inserted through is formed on
the end. Sometimes a bead can be hidden underneath a design. You have
to be careful not to join the rod-ball to the bead or else the piece won't
move freely.

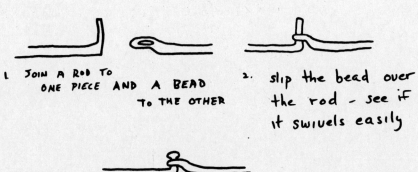

1 JOIN A ROD TO
ONE PIECE AND A BEAD
TO THE OTHER

2. slip the bead over
the rod - see if
it swivels easily

3 blob the end of the rod, large enough so that
it is larger than the hole of the bead   17.

RINGS: One type of ring is a flat band with designs in it that goes all around the finger. Another kind has a design rising above the finger with one or two flattened rods circled underneath.

Study the shape of your finger and how it joins your hand. Each finger is a little different. Study the finger and design the ring to pleasingly fit its form.

In order to make rings, you will need a steel-graduated ring mandrel. This is a tapered cylindrical piece of steel that has the different ring sizes marked on it. You can get one at a craft-supply store. If you want to make a ring to fit someone in particular, you should also get ring sizers. These are bands of steel that are also marked with the different sizes. (A number with a dash after it signifies that it is one half-size larger than the number.) A ring clamp is another handy tool to have. It holds the ring while you're polishing, sawing, or filing. It really isn't essential unless you plan on making a lot of rings.

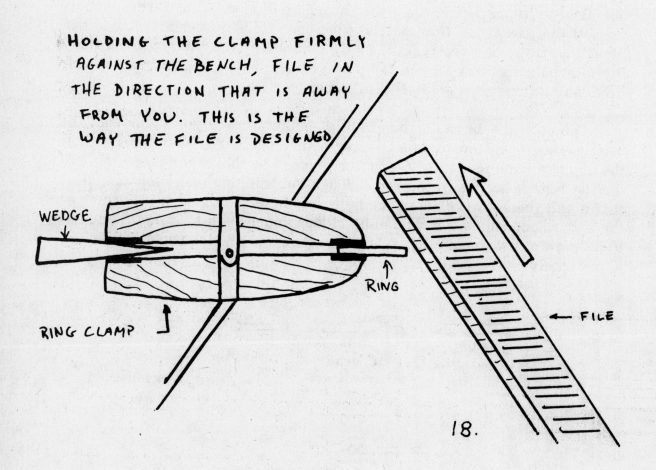

HOLDING THE CLAMP FIRMLY AGAINST THE BENCH, FILE IN THE DIRECTION THAT IS AWAY FROM YOU. THIS IS THE WAY THE FILE IS DESIGNED

WEDGE

RING CLAMP

RING

FILE

18.

Technique:

Using enough heat to allow the rod to bend, move the flame away from the end as you smoothly and evenly apply pressure to the rod, forming a circle. It is much like forming a bead, only the result is larger. Once you have joined the ends, wash off any flux with acid. Use your pliers and slip the piece onto the mandrel. Get the ring to fit tight on the mandrel by forcing it down with your hammer. This is where a hardwood stump would come in handy, because if you use an anvil the two steel surfaces will damage each other. Set the mandrel on the edge of the stump or log in such a way that the bottom of the band is up against the wood.

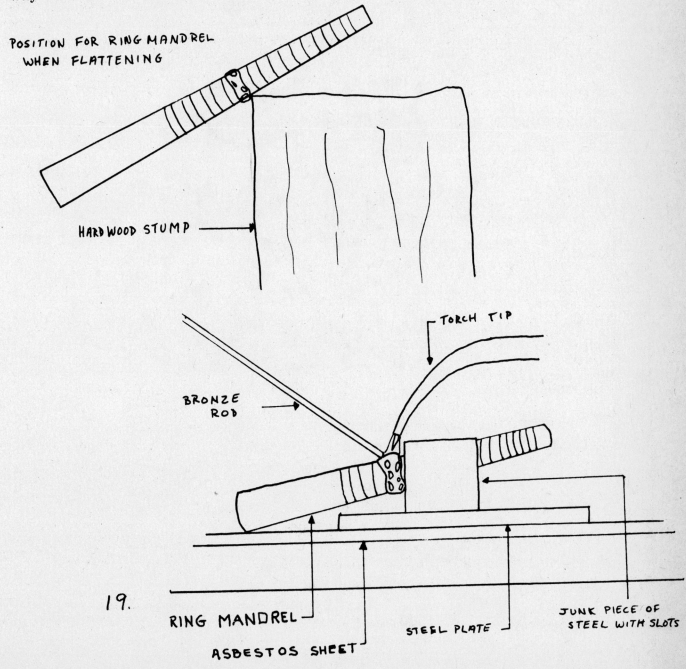

POSITION FOR RING MANDREL WHEN FLATTENING

HARDWOOD STUMP →

TORCH TIP

BRONZE ROD →

19.

RING MANDREL

ASBESTOS SHEET

STEEL PLATE

JUNK PIECE OF STEEL WITH SLOTS

This keeps the band on tight while you flatten it and maintains the ring's round shape.

Hold back on hammering the first side of the band completely flat, for when hammering the other side, some additional flattening will occur in your band. Also, as you flatten the metal, it gets somewhat thinner and the band size increases.

At this point, it is good to have some junk piece of steel that will steadily support the mandrel while keeping the band above the plate. Obtain this by the adventuring-forth method: junk shops, etc. The band of bronze should also fit tight up against this piece of steel to keep it from moving forward.

20. Adding bronze to a
    ring on a mandrel
    braced against a piece
    of junk steel

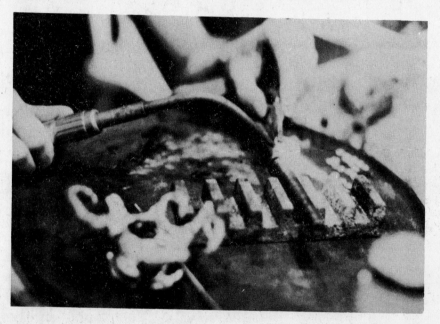

Begin to add bronze to the band in a design that suits you. You might like to use rods of different widths. Experiment. Variety adds to the beauty. The initial band should be made from one of the smaller sizes. Work first on the larger side of the mandrel, turning the mandrel so that the area you are working on is facing up. As you work, keep in mind that you are creating both a ring and a design.

You will quickly discover that a pot holder, preferably wet, is handy in maneuvering the mandrel. You might have a pan of water large enough to put the mandrel in to cool it occasionally. In the winter it's great to throw the hot mandrel into the snow.

Once you've gotten a fairly satisfactory design on one side, use your hammer to flatten it. You still shouldn't flatten it completely, not until you're finished. This hammering gives you a better idea of how the design will look after the final hammering. Now turn the ring around on the mandrel so that you can complete the design. You may have to tap it off with your hammer. When you've finished the basic design, check all the connections to see if they are good and smooth. To clean and/or blend the design into one flowing piece, add flux to the heated metal and slowly move the heat over the piece, melting the flux in. Remember flux prevents burning the bronze.

If you would like to remove part of the original band to break up any definite line you don't want, do it now. Holding the ring with pliers, heat the area you want removed until it reaches a molten point and shake so that it falls out. You will find that an ability to direct the flame on one area without affecting others is, once again, essential.

Before a final cleaning and polishing, but <u>after</u> removing unfused flux, hammer the ring gently once again to make sure that it is round and smooth. When it's cool, try the ring on. An important aspect is how comfortable the ring feels on the finger. Aside from the smoothing that comes from polishing, you might want to make some changes now.

Another method of making band rings is to work the design out first on a flat surface and, if you like, decorate the outside edge of the design with a piece of rod. This sometimes helps hold the design as you curve it into a ring. Of course, care must be taken if you add a rod for trim, not to affect other parts of the ring.

If you don't have access to a ring sizer, cut a piece of string to the circumference you want. Work out a design and flatten a rod on the anvil to the length of the piece of string. Curve the design as you did the band in the first style. You may want to use your pliers to assist you. Join the two ends together and put it on the mandrel. Make sure that it is securely joined or else it will crack when you flatten and round it out on the mandrel. If you like, finish off by melting the surface into a blending pattern.

To make a ring where the design rises off the finger, you start off by forming a simple narrow band again. The larger the design, the wider the band will have to be. When you're just using a narrow band, it is sometimes a good idea to make the bottom of the ring wider or heavier than the sides in order to balance the top design properly. Once you have the band, add your design using the techniques described in "Forming the Bronze."

Cleaning and polishing your bronze ring is described later; note here though that your files or flexible shaft grinder are used to smooth the finger side of the ring.

For bracelets, you will probably need a bracelet mandrel obtained from craft suppliers. You can make chain or ball-and-bead bracelets that are completely movable, adding whatever slight curve you need with the round end of your ball-peen hammer. However, if you wish to make a bracelet that is one solid piece, you'll need the mandrel. This mandrel is also made of steel (hollowed out) and is tapered; they come oblong or round. It is easiest to construct an open bracelet by starting on a flat surface. Work up your design keeping in mind all the basic procedures. One way is to make a flat design and then a slightly raised design on top of it. Whatever you like. Once this is done, add a piece of temporary rod to one end and curve the bracelet around to join the rod to the other end. Place the bracelet on the mandrel and shape it into the correct curve. The temporary rod you attached can be removed when you get the curve right. The two ends of the bracelet should be either wide or thick so there will not be any uncomfortable edges that will cut into your wrist when you put it on.

To make a hair piece requires no additional equipment. A hair piece can keep the hair back off the face or also hold a section of the hair in place. It has two parts. One is the main part of the design, constructed in such a way that a flat curved bar, the second part, can pass through and out and still be able to turn. The curved bar goes through the design behind the hair and back through the design. Then it's turned around so that it's tight and follows the curve of the head.

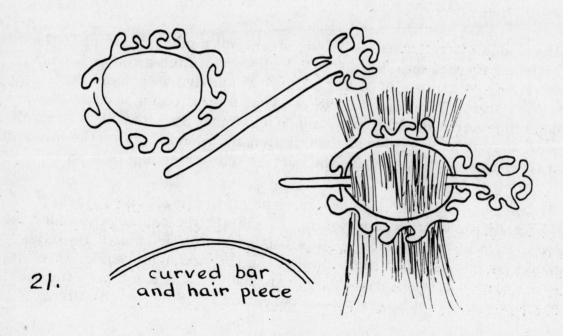

21. curved bar
and hair piece

The opening in the center of the design should be from 2 to 3 inches across and 1 to 2 inches from top to bottom so that the bar will be able to bend and turn. Both the design and the bar have to be slightly curved to fit right.

The bar should be around 5 inches in length, not including any design you might add to it. If you have short hair, find someone with long hair for testing the fit. Keep in mind while working that the bar has to be flat on the design piece in order to lie correctly.

Pendants that hang from around your neck are fairly simple to make. Remember, though, that the hole in the bead the chain goes through should be attached at a right angle to the design so that the whole thing will hang right. Also make sure that the bead is large enough to accommodate what will be passed through it: a leather strip, etc.

Pins are a good way of displaying bronze designs. One very simple method of making them is to curl one end of a suitable length of rod on which you have (maybe) made a design and taper it to a point by pulling the rod as you heat it. Then make a hook on the underside of the rod, at the end, to hold the pin in place. Another method is to make a hinge for the pin by connecting two small beads, standing up side by side, to the back-side. Then insert a rod through them and blob the ends so that the rod won't fall out. In the center of this, connect another longer rod perpendicular to it, and taper it to a point that will go through cloth and fit into a hook on the other side. Make sure to place the pin bar in the top third of the back of the pin.

22.

Place bar in rear upper third. Make sure blobs are large enough.

Barrettes can be made in a similar way. Connect two small beads on the back of your design again and run a long rod through them. Bend the two ends of the rod around to the opposite end of the piece and melt off with a blob on the end of each one. Make two small hooks with blobs on the other side, side by side so that they will hold the two transverse rods in place. The barrette itself should have a slight curve to it.

Barrette

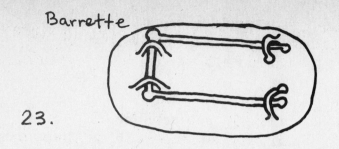

23.

the hooks should be connected on the outside and curve toward the inside

Belt buckles are relatively simple to make also. There are a few important features. The construction of a T shape on one outside edge will be what you connect the belt to. On the other end and underneath, attach a short blobbed rod that will go through the holes in the belt to fasten it tight around the waist. Take note not to have any sharp protruding edges around the outside. The wearer bends over now and then and that buckle could jab.

connect belt to → this T

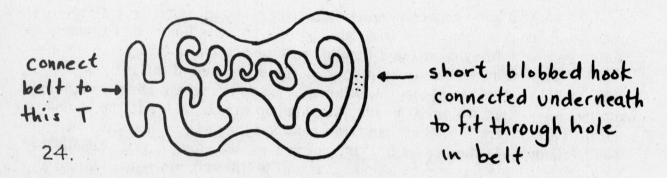

← short blobbed hook connected underneath to fit through hole in belt

24.

Necklaces can be made using any or several chain styles. Chains move and follow the lines of the neck. On the same principle, solid designs can be connected with links. The ball-and-bead combination also is a good way to join movable parts.

Stringing beads on the thinnest bronze wire or good strong cord can also be attractive. Wooden beads are best made out of hard wood. You can use your grinding wheel to help shape them. You might consider making some ceramic beads with a low-fire clay that can be done in the oven, or you may come across some attractive ready-made beads that you can use in a bronze necklace.

It will take some doing to get a nicely balanced necklace that lies evenly. The more complicated and intricate the design, the more difficult it is, but that didn't crimp Michelangelo.

25. a simple clasp for a necklace

connect to string or link

Clasps at the back of the neck should be easy for the wearer to connect and comfortable.

FINISHING AND POLISHING

To finish a completed piece, it's good to treat it with a sulfuric acid solution (see the description of this process earlier in the chapter). This treatment gives the bronze a coppery color as it cleans. Dry the piece and polish.

To polish bronze, you will need bobbing compound found at craft stores, but if you use emery cloth you won't need the compound. Rub the compound on your buffing wheel by holding it next to the spinning wheel for a second or two. Keep adding the compound as you need it, but don't put a whole lot at once on the wheel. The buffing process not only polishes and smooths the surface, but it also can be used to change the shape slightly if desired. For more major changes, use the grinding wheel or file. The grinding wheel can add to the form by making indentations into thick areas.

If you have a piece that isn't flat and you would like to give it more dimension or more color contrast, use liver of sulfur. This can be purchased at a craft-tool store. The liver of sulfur reacts with the coppery coloration that the acid makes. To use liver of sulfur, first treat the piece in sulfuric acid. After cleaning the piece in sulfuric acid, put the bronze into the water with the baking-soda solution, then put a small piece of liver of sulfur into warm (not boiling) water. (This should be done in an enamel pan.) Continue to reuse the same liver of sulfur solution until it gets cloudy; at this point the solution has lost its effectiveness. The smell of the liver of sulfur is hardly pleasant, but it quickly disperses. Leave the piece in the solution until the bronze is as dark as you want it. Then rinse with water. Polish the areas you want shiny and leave the rest alone. A solution of diluted household ammonia and soap will clean off any bobbing compound residue on the bronze and your hands. Unlike gold, bronze rapidly oxidizes to a dull finish. This gives it a more earthy and ancient appearance. When you're choosing your design, make sure it will still be attractive when dull. Sometimes not making the bronze completely smooth will leave texture that goes well with a dull finish. To return the shine, use silver polish or even rub the piece on a rug.

Sandee likes to think her bronze work will be discovered a thousand years from now because bronze lasts a long time, but it is enough to fulfill the personal need to create at the moment ... I know you will have the same satisfaction working with it as I do.

Bronze, metal, metal of the Earth,
  ancient, ancient in the hands of Man—
 Valued as tool, weapon, wealth, and decoration.
 Stronger than praised gold and silver
  and oxidizing in varied colors,
 Bronze, ancient metal of the Earth
  remains a fascination in my eyes
   for its beauty of strength, color, and form.
Flame, fire heat, burning gas of the Earth
  timeless is the mystification it creates—
 Valued as tool and weapon, as life and death.
  Flame is the music that makes Bronze dance,
   though the melody is formed from the properties
    of each.

In the end Bronze remains Bronze, Flame remains Flame.
The Craftsman uses the power of love heat
  to soften the rigid strength,
 as they, too, use the Craftsman.
  There is a balance of power, a balance of beauty.
 Each direct and bend with the nature of each.
For the Craftsman seeing the metal soften into fluid forms,
  it is as if some rigid tension was soothed
   in his own mind,
  as if disjointed thoughts blend together
   in a conception.

There is a romance formed between the
 Bronze Flame Craftsman

Tipi-Making

Steve Raleigh and Paul Alexander

"Everything the power of the world does is done in a circle. The sky is round, and I have heard that the earth is round like a ball, and so are all the stars. The wind, in its greatest power, whirls. Birds make their nests in circles, for theirs is the same religion as ours. The sun comes forth and goes down again in a circle. The moon does the same, and both are round. Even the seasons form a great circle in their changing, and always come back again to where they were. The life of a man is a circle from childhood to childhood, and so it is in everything where power moves. Our tipis were round like the nests of birds, and these were always set in a circle, the nation's hoop, a nest of many nests, where the great spirit meant for us to hatch our children. But the Wasichus have put us in these square boxes. Our power is gone and we are dying, for the power is not in us any more." — Black Elk

We got into tipi-making not out of any strong (at the time) interest in Indian lore, but because we'd both had it with camping in tents. We'd been camping together for a long time, and one day we started looking for an alternative. The tipi was an answer.

At first it looked a little difficult, but after we got into it (with the exception of a few minor hitches along the way) it turned out to be pretty easy. The Laubins' book on tipis is the one most people consider the best. When it comes to the history, symbolism, etc., of the tipi as home for various Indian tribes, that book is the best we know of. As for how to make a tipi,

345

we want to offer here detailed step-by-step directions.

So as you won't be put off by what only <u>looks</u> complicated, we'll give you a sort of brief description of a tipi so that you can visualize what you'll be doing before you start yours.

A tipi is basically a cover of material wrapped around a bunch of poles positioned in a tilted frame of three more poles. The cover is made of strips of canvas (or skin, in the old days) sewn together and then cut to form a semicircle. The smoke- and door-holes are cut out of the canvas beforehand. Then the radius point (center of the straight edge) of the semi-circle is fastened to the top of a pole, which is then dropped into place on the tilted cone of poles. The canvas is then pulled around the poles until the ends meet, and then laced together.

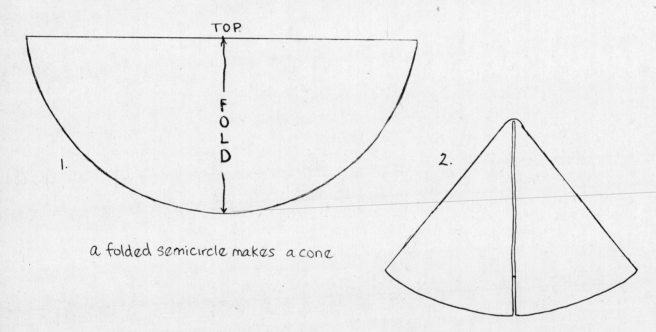

a folded semicircle makes a cone

When the hole at the top is open, you can build a heating and cooking fire inside the tipi. If the tipi is constructed right, it will be watertight when the hole is closed. We guess we did ours right because, during the first stormy night we spent in our tipi, only a little water got in, and now, over a year later, we're still dry inside when outside it's pouring buckets and the lightning is flashing all around. (We've come to really love the sound rain makes as it hits the tipi!)

That smoke-hole should be just above the center of the circle where the fire is. Somebody once said that living in a tipi is like living in a giant chimney, but this is not really true if you build good fires, and have a good lining around the bottom part of the tipi. Linings also help to keep bugs out. A few of the friends who stayed overnight in our tipi have complained of a spider or two, but they don't know how lucky they were not to have been there while the ants were still around. For the first couple of weeks, we were plagued by ants, but then they just packed up and went away as the earth inside the tipi got drier because of our fires. At least this is probably why they left. But maybe they just didn't like our company.

The lining is like a second cover, but it runs only 6 or so feet up from the bottom of the tipi. It is attached to the inside of the poles with ropes and, in addition to its other functions, it serves as good insulation. We've never stayed in our tipi in the middle of winter (although we will this year), but we know a family of five nearby who've lived in theirs year-round for three years. They have all the conveniences, including a plywood floor, and they say they're warm as toast even in the roughest part of the winter. One of the reasons for this is the lining. People who haven't been around tipis very long think the cover is a complete tipi. It isn't.

The tipi is still used by Indians on reservations, but now mostly for religious ceremonies. Tipis are used by a lot of young people who want to go back to the land. And it's not really roughing it, because with a few books, perhaps a chessboard (we play chess, sometimes all day), and sufficient food, say some brown rice, potatoes, canned and fresh fruit, powdered milk, pancake mix, instant soup, etc., you really soon forget the outside world. We've stayed in our tipi for over a week without having to go out for more provisions. We also had a harmonica, a guitar, and a jew's harp (which no one could ever figure out how to play).

Besides being one of the most beautiful shelters, the tipi also has many advantages over the modern, commercially made tent. The average tipi has more room than the average tent. It is probably the cheapest shelter you can live in permanently, and the biggest advantage is the indoor fire for heat, light, cooking, and beauty.

You should pitch your tipi in a place somewhere near your house and spend weekends, holidays, or whatever out there—or maybe use it as a tent for parties, but we disapprove of this because it is not what a tipi is meant for.

Your campsite should be in a field, near a source of clean water (remember to boil any drinking or cooking water you're not sure of 10 to 15 minutes). The reason for being in a field is so that you get lots of sun; the tipi won't mildew, and sun is great anyway. Falling branches from close trees won't puncture your tipi, and there will be less bugs. Also, if you are under a tree it will keep on dripping on the tipi after a rain (or heavy dew) which causes a very loud and annoying noise.

Tipis can be made in many sizes, starting from about 12 feet in diameter all the way up to 25 feet or larger. We've seen some 30-foot tipis. A 12-foot tipi is not large enough for both fire and people and should be used as a play tent for children, and a tipi much larger than 22 feet is hard to heat and hard to put up, hard to find poles for and hard to move. We feel that an 18-footer is an ideal size, that's why we'll show plans for an 18-foot tipi, although if you want to live permanently in a tipi with a family, you should try for a larger one.

MATERIAL, SIZES, AND AMOUNTS FOR AN EIGHTEEN-FOOT TIPI

CANVAS: We paid for our 18-foot tipi by doing odd jobs—gardening, babysitting, etc., with no financial help from our parents. We split the cost right down the middle as well as the work. Altogether it cost us about $75 for canvas (this was first-rate canvas) and another $25 for odds and ends.

The cover and door-flap will take 39 1/3 yards of 72-inch duck. The canvas can be purchased at various weights, the lightest being about 8-ounce duck, and the heaviest up to 16-ounce. The lightest is naturally the cheapest, and if you plan to move your tipi a lot, use a 8-to-10-ounce, lightweight canvas. If your tipi is going to be set up in a place where there are a lot of storms and as a semipermanent placement, then use a heavy-weight canvas, 12-to-14-ounce. We recommend 10- and 12-ounce, which is the weight usually used, as it works for almost any weather and is not that heavy.

Be sure and get canvas that is already waterproofed. Although it costs a bit more, it is really more effective against wetness and lasts longer. Also you don't have to allow for shrinkage, as you will if you waterproof your own. Should you want to do your own waterproofing, you can buy about 6 gallons, 3 for cover and 3 for lining, of waterproofing at camping-supply stores or hardware stores. Follow directions on the can. Shop around until you find the best canvas for the least amount of money. 72-inch wide will not entail the work and labor that 36-inch material demands, and is more effective. (This is the size our instructions are geared to.)

The lining takes about 17 yards of 72-inch duck. It can be made of lighter-weight canvas and also should be waterproofed (by the manufacturers or by you).

THREAD: The supplier of the canvas should also have thread. Any strong rot-resistant thread will do. I bought mine wholesale in $10 spools. You will need a good 5,000 yards.

TIE-TAPES: These can be made by folding a 3-inch-wide strip of canvas over twice and sewing it down. You can also purchase tapes by the roll from the dealer you buy canvas from. You will need 10 to 15 feet of tie-tape. They will be attached to the top and bottom of the smoke-flaps and tied together, as described later.

PEGS AND PINS: We started collecting pegs while we were sewing the cover and lining. You will need 20 to 25 wooden pegs 18 inches long and 1 inch thick for pegging the cover to the ground. Any hardwood you can find will be good enough. If you know trees, you can look for cedar, maple, ash, oak, or chokecherry.

The pegs are sharpened to a point at one end, and you should leave about 6 inches of bark at the other to catch the rope you will be tying to it. Another way to catch the rope is to carve a ring around the top of the peg.

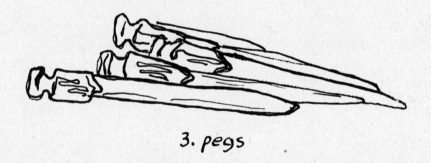

3. pegs

You need 10 lacing pins (used in buttoning up the cover around the poles). These sticks should be pointed, too, and about 12 inches long and 3/8-inch thick. Lumber yards have dowels you can buy and cut to size, but of course that is very un-Indian.

Get together about thirty 2-to-5-inch sticks, 1/4- to 1/2-inch thick. These will be used after your lining is up, and inserted between the rope that ties the lining to the poles and the poles themselves, so that water running down the poles will not get sidetracked and run down the rope.

ROPE: Hardware stores should have manila rope. You need about 45 feet of 1/2-inch manila rope to tie the poles together at the top. To tie the pegs to the bottom of the cover, you will need about 100 feet of 1/4-inch nylon cord. And lastly, at least 200 feet of 1/2-inch cotton rope for tying

the lining onto the poles, for the smoke-flaps and a few odds and ends. Don't worry about buying too much, it's impossible. You can always find use for rope later.

MAKING THE COVER

We first tried sewing on one of our mothers' very small portable Singer machine. But it didn't work; the needles kept breaking. We finally gained access to a Sears heavy-duty machine. This worked for us. Probably any good, heavy floor-model number would work for you, though. Some people run long extension cords to their machine so they can work outside. We sewed ours in the winter so we missed this.

A semicircle when folded in half makes a cone. A tipi looks like a tilted ice cream cone upside down (see Fig. 2). The way to make the half-circle is to sew strips together and then, when they are laid out on the ground, cut a half-circle shape out of the big piece as we will explain later.

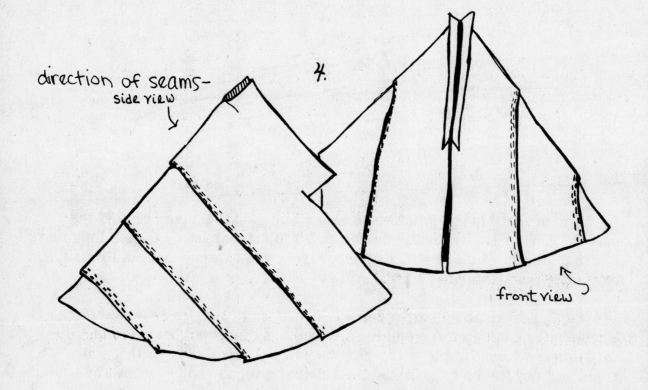

direction of seams- side view

4.

front view

First cut 3 strips from the 72-inch canvas. Strip One is 38 feet, 6 inches long. Strip Two is 36 feet, 7 inches long, and strip Three is 30 feet, 10 inches long. It's a good idea to cut them all a few inches longer than you

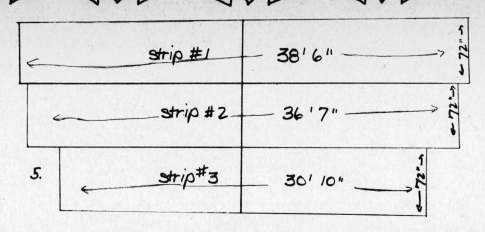

5.

actually need, just to be safe. Next fold each strip exactly in half and, with a marking pen or heavy pencil, mark the center where it folds, both on the top and bottom of the fold and on both sides of the canvas where it folds.

6.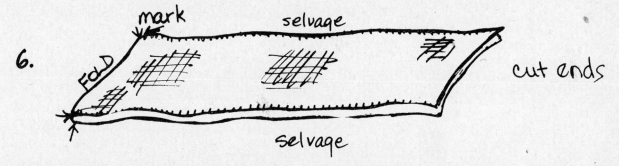

This makes 4 marks altogether. Roll up Strips Two and Three with a string around them and attach a tag telling which one is Two and which one is Three. Put these away for later on.

7.

STRIP ONE IS THE HEAVY TRIP

Strip One is the strip that you are going to be doing most of the sewing and cutting on. It is the strip that will have both the smoke-flaps and the door in it.

Cut a piece 11 by 2 feet out of each end of Strip One and sew them together so that the piece is then 21 feet, 10 inches long (see Fig. 8). This will be Strip Four to complete the semicircle shape. Roll Strip Four up and label.

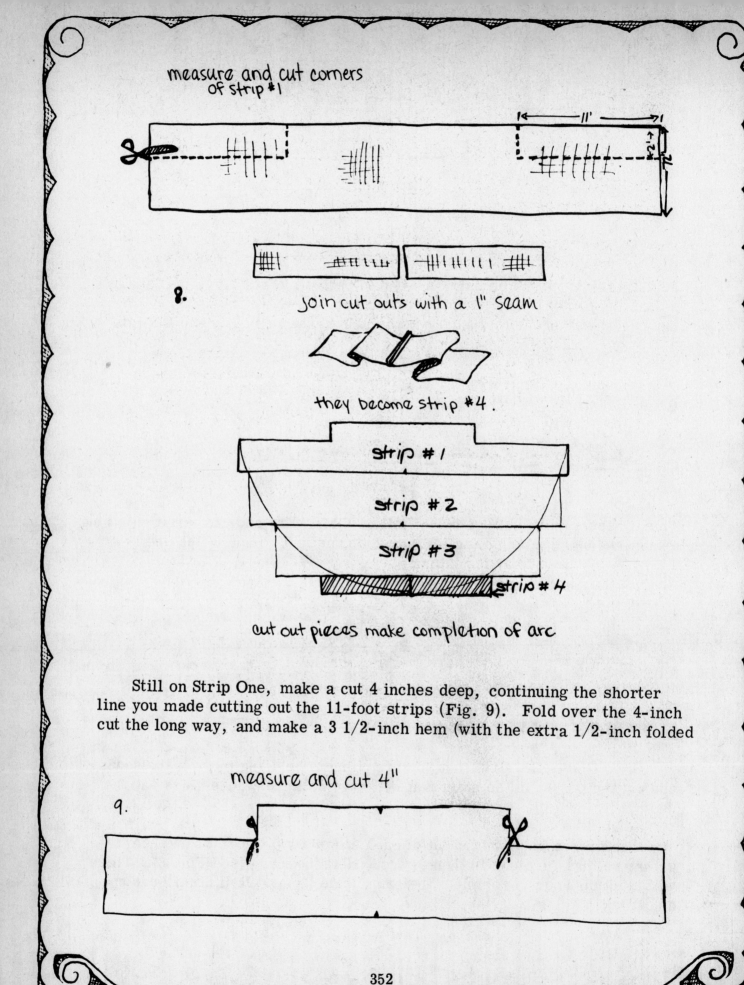

measure and cut corners
of strip #1

11'

8. join cut outs with a 1" seam

they become strip #4.

strip #1

strip #2

strip #3

strip #4

cut out pieces make completion of arc

Still on Strip One, make a cut 4 inches deep, continuing the shorter line you made cutting out the 11-foot strips (Fig. 9). Fold over the 4-inch cut the long way, and make a 3 1/2-inch hem (with the extra 1/2-inch folded

measure and cut 4"

9.

under again at the cut edge). With the machine sew the hem down two or three times in parallel lines (double stitching) 1/4-inch away from each other to secure it well (Fig. 10). These 3 1/2-inch folded sections will be where you will make buttonholes in both sides; they will later be attached by lacing pins to hold the cover together.

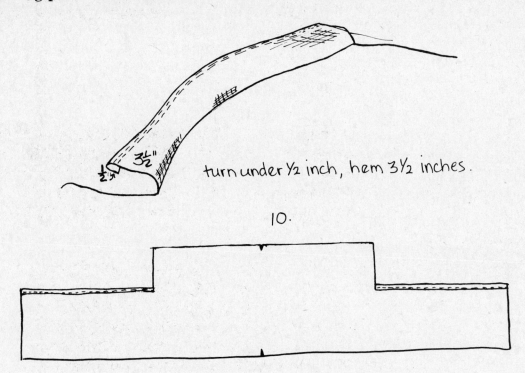

turn under ½ inch, hem 3½ inches.

10.

After you have sewn the lacing-pin reinforcement down, cut out the two halves of the door. Starting 1 foot from each end of Strip One, on the side where the 3 1/2-inch hems are folded over, cut a semicircle 46 inches long and 10 inches deep at both ends. Sew over a 1/2-inch hem on the same side as you sewed over the 3 1/2-inch hem all around this door-opening area (Fig. 11). The pieces you have cut out can be used later to back the top of the cover for reinforcing.

11.

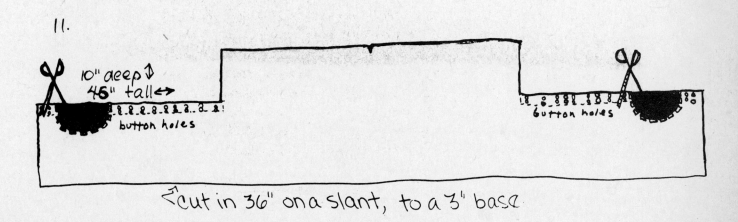

10" deep ↕
46" tall ↔
button holes

button holes

⟵ cut in 36" on a slant, to a 3" base

The large center piece in Strip One is going to be the smoke-flaps. Starting at the middle of that piece, cut two lines straight but on a slant, ending 1 1/2 inches to either side of the center, 36 inches from the top (Fig. 12). This will form a narrow triangle when you cut it out, but make sure you leave a 3-inch-wide tab of canvas at the base of the triangle. This tab is what supports practically the whole tipi, and this area should be backed with three or four layers of canvas reinforcement.

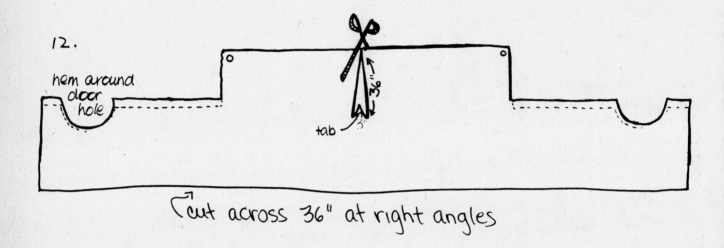

Cut across 36" at right angles

At the base of the tab, and to either side of it, cut a line at a right angle to the center line, 36 inches long (Fig. 13). When these cuts are opened up, they form a triangle, on either side. What happens now is that separate pieces of material in a triangle shape (called gores) are fitted into these two triangles and sewn in place with a 1-inch seam again on the wrong side (seam and hem side). Cut the gores 40" x 40" x 9"; this allows for

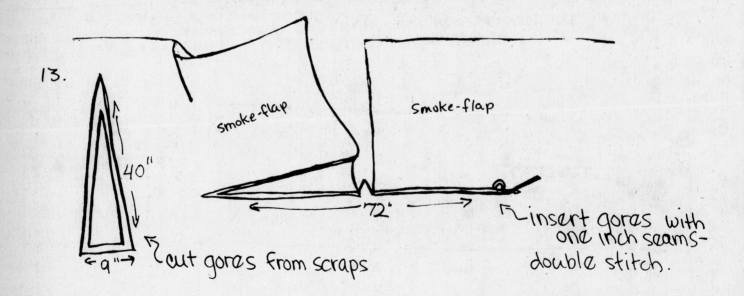

the 1-inch seam, and, when sewn in place, the areas will measure 36" x 36" x 7". Now hem 1/2-inch on all three sides of the smoke-flaps. (All sewing should be in double or triple lines of stitches except for the smaller 1/2-inch hems.)

The tab in between the smoke-flaps is the tie-flap area, and, to repeat, it needs reinforcing. Reinforcement pieces look better if kept on the inside of the tipi because the poles at the top will cover the pieces from the inside. (Remember which is the outside and inside of your cover.) Place two pieces on the inside of the tipi reinforcing the tab area. Sew all over the place with your machine. Some people like to do this by hand.

Attach two 3-foot tie-tapes to the center where the tab is (Fig. 14). Slap another piece of canvas on top of the tapes and sew firmly (Fig. 15). These tie-tapes will tie the cover to your lifting pole (the pole that lifts the whole cover up and onto the rest of the poles). Two more tie-tapes, 1-foot long, are to be sewn at the base of the smoke-flaps in the inside corner (Figs. 14, 15). The tie-tape on the right side of the smoke-flap is placed on the hem side and the tie-tape for the left side is placed on the outside (or right side). When lapped over, they will tie best in this position. These tie-tapes will act as the top lacing pin. Reinforce these too, but not as much as the tie-flaps at the top of the tipi.

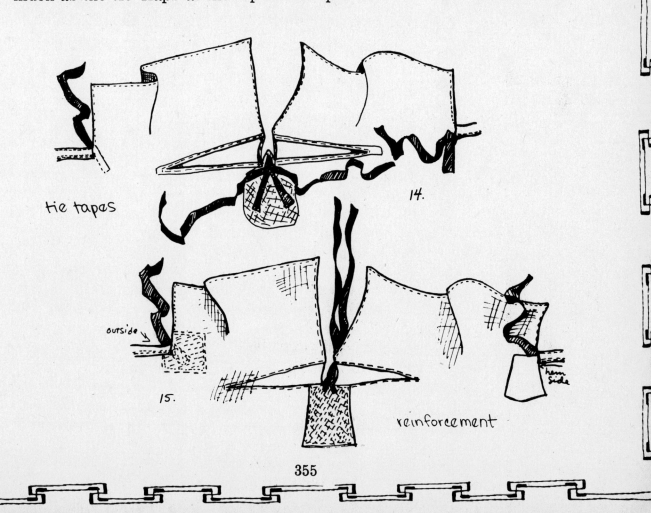

tie tapes

14.

outside

15.

reinforcement

hem side

Next are the smoke-pole pockets. They must be on the outside. Cut four pieces, as shown in Figure 16. Each pocket will be made double-thick by using two pieces of material together. Hem under the 2-inch edge 1/2-inch and then fold and sew three times so this pocket will hold well (Fig. 17).

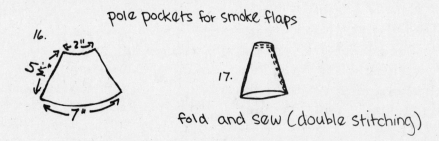

pole pockets for smoke flaps

16.

17.

fold and sew (double stitching)

Before you attach the pockets to the upper corner of the smoke-flaps, reinforce the smoke-flaps from the outside (poles will hide this later), slapping on a triangle of extra canvas. Then attach the back of the pockets to the corners using many rows of stitching (Fig. 18).

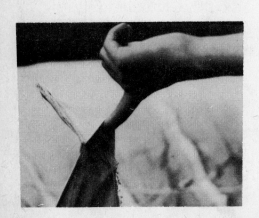
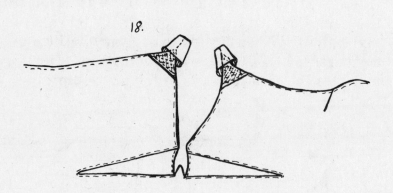

18.

sew pockets so they're on the outside of flaps

Now you are ready to do the last part of this complicated fooling around with the first strip, sewing on the buttonholes! You will need to make altogether 59 holes for the entire tipi so get comfortable: 13 in the lining, 44 to lace together the cover, and 1 on the bottom tip of each smoke-flap (2 in all).

The cover should have 2 rows of 9 buttonholes on each side of the 3 1/2-inch hem area (36 in all), starting near the tie-tape at the base of the smoke-flaps, to the top of the door opening. Add 2 rows of 2 buttonholes (4 in all) on both sides (8 in all) under the door. All should be really round and about 1/2-inch in diameter. Try and space them out evenly. The outside holes should be about 3/4-inch in from the edge. The rows on the left flap should be 2 inches apart, and the rows on the right flap 1 1/2 inches apart. When the left side laps over the right, this variance in distance will make the insertion of the pins easier. The top holes under the door will be for a lacing pin and the bottom holes are there to attach to the ground pegs with rope.

Sewing the holes is difficult because you have to really pull the thread hard. Linen twine (thread) used for sewing braided rugs together is good and strong. You have to go out of your way to get this; large needlecraft-supply houses, boating-supply houses, and sometimes people who deal in leather have heavy threads that will be great for the buttonholes. Actually any tough cotton thread will do. Coat the thread with beeswax, purchased at hardware or sewing stores, thread it on a strong needle with a thin head, and fold double. Twist and coat it again with beeswax. You now have the strongest and most effective thread going for you. There are several ways to make a buttonhole, and we have illustrated the easiest (see Fig. 19). The buttonhole will become almost like a wooden ring. Hammer it to flatten it out on a piece of wood.

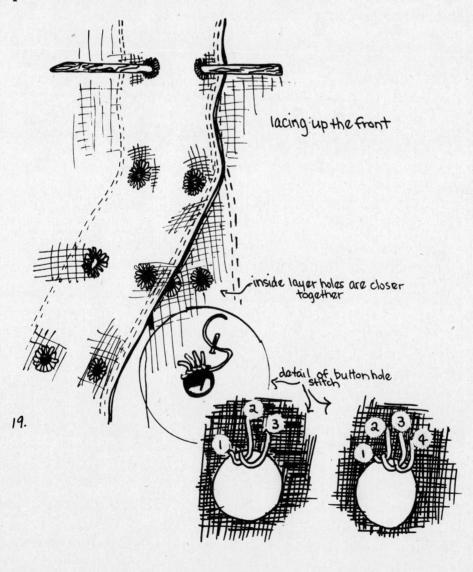

lacing up the front

inside layer holes are closer together

detail of button hole stitch

19.

There are two more buttonholes to make on the cover: one on each smoke-flap—bottom outside tip (see below). Strings will be tied there to pull the flaps out.

20.

ON TO STRIPS TWO, THREE, AND FOUR

Now you are ready to really move. Get out the second, third, and fourth strips. Here's where that center mark comes in handy. Line the strips up so that the center marks join (see Fig. 8). Start with Strip Four, which shows the center with its seam. Pin Strip Three on top of Strip Four so that center marks meet and so Three overlaps Four about 3/4-inch. Sew them together using two rows of stitches 1/4-inch-apart. After that is sewn down, you can join the center marks of Strip Two and Strip Three, making sure that Two overlaps Three, and sew down. Next is the final piece to sew on: Strip One should be placed overlapping Strip Two with the centers joined up. The reason for the overlapping is so water will run off well and will not get caught up in the seams. It is like shingles on the roof (see Fig. 4).

CUTTING OUT A HALF-CIRCLE FROM THE SEWN STRIPS

Find a flat dirt or grass surface to pin down the pieces you have just sewn together. We used a dirt surface, and the canvas ended up with a lot of footprints all over it, as well as some from the dog and cat. Grass is best if you have it around. Stretch it out tight. Drive a stake in the lower corner of both sides of each strip (Strip Four is the bottom strip). Don't worry about tearing it because this is the waste part that gets cut away any-way. Drive a stake in the ground 25 inches above the tie-tapes. Attach a 19-foot, 2-inch rope. Swing the rope in a semicircle across your material and mark the end of the rope swing with a piece of colored chalk or a cray-on. Cut out on this line and <u>do not</u> hem. You don't have to worry about the material unraveling along this line because the material is cut across the bias. The cover is finished, except for minor details you can attend to while pitching the tipi.

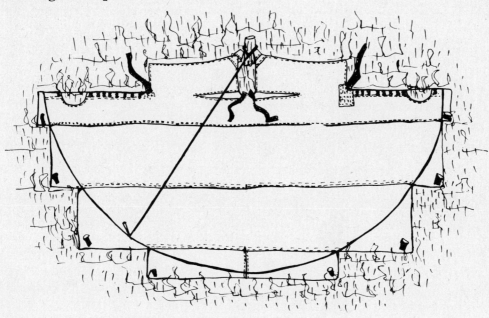

21. marking the lower edge

LINING

Some people consider a lining unnecessary. Wrong. It keeps out most of the bugs, adds an unbelievable amount of beauty, keeps you much drier, keeps you warm in winter and cool in summer, and, because it acts with the cover to create a draft, it helps ventilate the fire, and aids in clearing smoke out of the tipi. We would not consider living in or making a tipi with-out a liner.

The lining is hung on a rope stretched around the poles and measures a little under 6 feet tall. We drew some plans for a lining that is the one we use (Fig. 22). It is not perfect. If you are striving for perfection, we refer you to the Laubins' plan for your liner. Their lining is made so every seam meets at a pole and fits perfectly. Ours does not fit so per-fectly and the seams don't correspond with the poles, but it is a lot simpler to make. We are satisfied with it. The directions we give apply <u>only</u> to our plan. If you use another plan, follow their directions for an 18-foot tipi.

If you are using 36-inch material for that lining, cut the entire length in half and sew the strips horizontally together to produce a 72-inch width (it will be a little under 72 inches because of the seam). If you are using 72-inch material, you're set. Lay out the strip and cut 10 panels, 5 feet, 7 inches on the bottom, 3 feet, 8 inches on the top as the diagram shows.

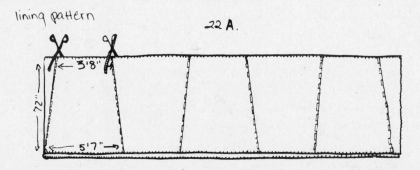

lining pattern

22 A.

3'8"

72"

5'7"

If you use 36-inch canvas, you are going to have to make sure that, when you sew the panels together, the center seam overlaps in the same direction on all the panels in that section. If you use 72-inch canvas, obviously it doesn't matter since there is no center seam.

Most linings are made in three sections, which makes putting it up easier. In each section you sew together subdivisions called "panels." On our lining, two sections (#1 and #3) have three panels, and the back section (#2) has four panels. (The Laubins' has 15 panels in all, which gives you an idea of how complex theirs is.) There are buttonholes across the top, which are there so you can attach the lining to a rope that is tied around each pole and strung from pole to pole. The bottom of the lining of our tipi can be secured by pulling it outside of the tipi and placing heavy rocks on it; or you can sew tie-tapes to the bottom and tie those to the poles, but this usually will not work because you cannot be sure if the poles will line up with the tapes.

22 B.

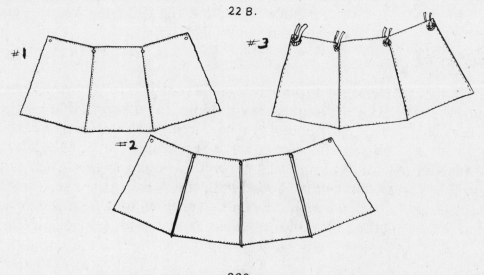

#1   #3

#2

Sew the lining panels with the same thread as the cover. The sections are not to be sewn together. By leaving them open, it is easier to pitch the tipi.

After you sew the panels together, sew buttonholes at the top of each end of a section and one at each seam (all about 1 inch from the top). You will end up with 13 buttonholes. Cut thirteen 6-inch lengths of thin rope or soft leather (leather looks far better than rope). This is to tie the lining to the lining rope when pitching the tipi.

We previously said that the cover looks better unpainted. That is not true of the lining. Almost any tipi expert and all Indians will agree that it is <u>necessary</u> to paint the inside of a lining. But imagine the inside of the tipi at night, fire flickering, black sky with a few bright silver pinholes through the smoke opening, the poles against the light brown, smoke-colored canvas, and, lastly, beautiful Indian designs around the lining. The Laubins' book and almost every Indian craft book has Indian lining designs. Spread the three sections out on a flat surface (if you're outside, place rocks on it so the wind will not blow it around). Draw lightly (with charcoal or pencil) the outline of your pattern, and then paint. Leave the lining exactly where it is until the paint is completely dry.

If you want, you can sew 5 or 6 buttonholes up the sides of section #2 and up one side of sections #1 and #3 so that you can close the gaps up after the tipi is pitched. Sections #1 and #3 are not connected on the side that is near the door.

In the winter, we suggest the use of an <u>ozan</u> to trap the heat at the base of the tipi. An ozan is a semicircular sheet made of canvas. It is attached to the poles and/or lining in such a way that it acts as a roof for the rear half of the tipi.

THE DOOR-FLAP

The door-flap can be made a number of ways, and the only advantage of one over the other is the way it looks to you. Doorflaps can be cut in many shapes as long as they cover the door hole. Cut a shape about 54 inches long and 26 inches wide (where it covers the door area), fanning out to 40 inches wide at the bottom, and narrowing into a triangle shape near the top (see Fig. 23). It should be hemmed 1/2-inch all the way around. The bottom is folded over a dowel or stick and sewn down on the inside, or you can attach the stick to the outside. This will help keep the flap from curling. Nylon rope or any scraps of leather you have lying around can be

used to tie to each end of the stick;
these can be fastened to stakes in the
ground on both sides of the door when
you want to tie the door-flap down.
You can also handle it as in the photo.
Another stick further up can be tied
on to the canvas with a strip of leather.
Sewing two buttonholes 2 inches apart
in the triangle at the top of the door
flap will add a third layer of buttonholes
to the two sets of buttonholes just above
the door hole in the cover. These are
joined up by a lacing pin. If you make
these holes last, you can line them up
and make sure the door comes to the
base of the tipi. When the bottom stick
is not tied down, the lacing pin
allows the door to swing to the side so
you can enter. And of course you can
take the door all the way off if you like.

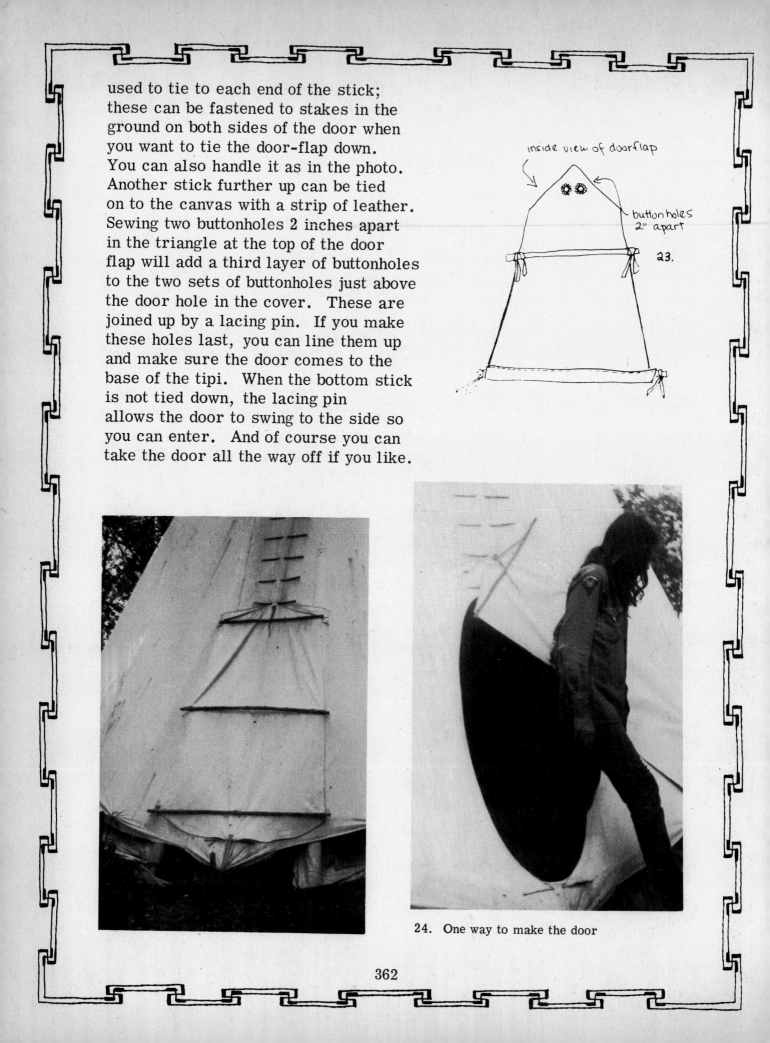

inside view of doorflap

button holes
2" apart

23.

24. One way to make the door

362

A STORM DOOR

A good thing to have around is a storm door made from a piece of 4-x-6-foot canvas. When it rains, tie the storm door to the poles on the inside of the tipi, and pull the edges outside at the bottom and tie to pegs. It sheds the water very well.

Whether you paint the cover or the lining, the paint should be waterproof after it is on. The only paints that will be waterproof and durable are oils and acrylics. We suggest acrylics because they will not tend to rot the canvas as oil paint will. The best acrylics can be bought in art-supply shops in tubes or jars by the color. Different colors are different prices so it would be difficult to lay any costs down here for you. Also, we would have to know how much of the surface you wanted to cover. Acrylics are water-based, but after they dry they are permanently proof against weather and water—and have a tough surface. The Laubins' book recommends using casein colors, but casein available on the market is water-based and is not waterproof. If you use it you will have to spray it with a clear plastic.

POLES

Our cover was made in the winter. In the spring we had to start getting our poles together. Getting the poles for your tipi will probably be the most difficult part. One of us still had his leg in a cast when spring came, so the other was alone in getting the poles. It was the hardest part, because from where he lived mountains had to be climbed and each pole dragged back. The poles had to be zigzagged all the way to get them through the heavy forest, and an axe used. It took at least fifteen trips up and back to do it.

The poles should be as straight and as free of knots as possible. When it rains, whatever water gets in through the top will run down the sides of the pole and drain off and away from the tipi. If there are bumps or knots, the water will drip from these and down to the tipi floor.

The larger the tipi, the more poles you need. The tipi we are giving you plans for is a Sioux tipi. It needs 15 poles for the structure, 2 poles for the smoke-flaps. Its diameter is the same as its height: a Sioux tipi 18 feet in diameter is also 18 feet high. The poles should stick up over the top of the finished tipi about 5 or 6 feet. This means that for an 18-foot tipi the poles should be about 24 or 25 feet long; they don't all have to be exactly the same length. While the lengths can vary, try not to get them shorter than 24 feet. It does not really matter what type of tree you use, although some wood is heavier than others and some is straighter. Cedar and pine were probably our best bet, for they grow very straight, are light, and there are a lot around. You can do what one of us did and just hike around in the woods until you come across trees that look good. When he found a good tree, he just cut it down. The poles you choose, when finished smooth, should be about 3 or 4 inches in diameter at the bottom and about 2 inches wide at the top where they cross. The two smoke-flap poles should be much thinner, for they don't really support the main structure. Be sure to choose the trees slightly thicker than the needed diameter to allow for shrinkage and for the loss of the bark, which has to be peeled off.

The best time to look for tree poles is in the spring when the juices are running through the inner bark. This makes the job of removing the bark much easier than at other times of the year. You should pick only young live trees, for dead trees usually have worm holes and other imperfections in them.

As you find right-on-looking trees, look at them from all angles to be sure that they are really straight. It may take a while to learn to estimate the height of trees and if they are straight or not, but every tree we thought was the right height just happened to be the right size. Maybe that was because we had seen Darry Wood's poles for his tipis lying around, leaning against trees. Trees that are about the right thickness you need are also about the right height. We used an axe at first, but it broke so the rest of the time we used a saw. After felling a tree, the first thing to do is to remove all the branches from it to make it easier to carry to where you are going to strip it. Also sharpen the butt end of the tree with an axe so that you can force the poles into the ground when the tipi is set up. If your cover seems too short you can adjust by pushing your butt points further into the ground after the tipi is up. (It should clear the ground by an inch or two everywhere except just in front.) You can also cut it off. Because your poles are long, it is a good idea to look for trees close to where your tipi will be, if possible, because it is hard to transport 25-foot poles any distance through the woods or even along a road, as one of us had to.

You should strip the poles as soon after felling them as possible. Strip them in a fairly open place so that it is easier to maneuver them. Lay a pole on two sawhorses (or something similar), hammer two large nails in each sawhorse, about 3 inches apart in one and 5 inches apart in the other, and have them stick up about 4 inches. This makes it easier to keep the poles in place while you strip them.

To strip the bark off the tree, use either a draw knife (a two-handled

25.

carpenter's tool) or a meat cleaver. We
were never able to get our hands on a draw
knife. One of our mothers suggested using
the meat cleaver and when we tried it, it
worked real well. Whatever you use, it
should be very sharp, and you will probably
have to sharpen it after every tree or two.
Strip the bark off with the knife or cleaver,
being careful, and using strokes that go
from bottom of tree to top with the grain
of the wood. Be sure to get all the bark
and inner bark off, so you get all the way
down to the real wood. If you leave any
inner bark, it tends to grow mold on it,
which doesn't look good. It's pretty
startling after a rain to go out and find that
some of your poles have turned completely
green. If your poles mildew in wet weather,
rub them with Clorox, full strength.

26.

After you have stripped all the bark
off, you must remove all the knots by level-
ing them down to the rest of the wood.
For this, use either a very sharp axe or
your meat cleaver. Sand knots down so that
the entire pole is smooth and straight. Lean
the poles up against a tree or other support,

and let them season in the sun for about three weeks. It is a good idea to paint the finished poles with canvas waterproofing paint (sold at camping or hardware stores) to keep them from rotting. Do this after you have finished all of your poles. One gallon is enough to give one set of poles one heavy coat and one light coat, and there should be enough left over to waterproof your pegs, too. Use any cloth rag and slop it on the poles. Don't use creosote on the poles, because it rots the canvas.

If you can't find trees for poles, some tipi manufacturers make them. But these are usually quite expensive and will drip all over when it rains, because they come in sections that must be assembled like a typical tent pole, and when it rains water will drip at the joints rather than run the length of the pole and into the ground. If you can, make the poles yourself; if you can't, buy the best two-by-fours with almost no knots. But this, of course, is not very Indian-like.

PITCHING THE TIPI

Before building your tipi, you should consider where you are going to put it when it is finished. Ideally, as we said before, the tipi should be in a field far away from any trees. If it is situated under a tree, and rainwater drips on it after the rain has stopped, mildew will form on the cover, causing dampness inside the shaded tipi, and the sun cannot dry it out. (Should this happen, use Canvak—rub it on with a rag.) Also, falling branches can puncture the cover. Because we had to use someone else's land, we got permission to use a little corner of a field. There were a few trees around so we got permission to chop off overhanging branches of the nearest trees.

Plains Indians have traditionally faced their tipis east, partly because of their religion and also because of wind directions. Because of the way a tipi is built, a wind blowing toward the door forces the smoke from the fire back down into the tipi, causing problems. The winds in inland America seldom blow from east to west, so an east-facing tipi is often best. Consider the direction your tipi will face when choosing your spot. The tipi should if possible be close to some clean water source, most likely a stream or lake. It shouldn't be too close, though—say, not closer than 100 feet, because water is home for bugs and mosquitoes. Also your tipi could be washed away in a flash flood. There was a stream about three minutes away from our site, and five gallons of water lasted the two of us for about three days.

To clear the space where your tipi will go, first get a piece of string a foot or two longer than the radius of your tipi. Drive a stake into the ground at the center of your spot. Tie the string to it and mark a circle as far as the string will reach. This is the area you will have to clear. First, get rid of all the shrubs and then rake. Clear out all the rocks and roots, so that it is pretty level. You can leave the grass for a cushion. Try and find a space relatively flat with no bumps or holes. If you don't, you'll see why after you have spent your first night there.

Now, of course, you will probably want to make a fireplace. It should go slightly toward the front of the tipi's center. This allows more room for living in the back, where you will be most of the time. The fireplace should be dug into the ground a few inches and shouldn't be too big—about 2 feet across. A good trick we learned from a friend of ours is to run a gutter pipe a few inches under the ground from the inside of the fireplace to a few feet outside the circle you have cleared. Here, on the outside end, put on a curved attachment so that it sticks up out of the ground. Put another curve on this, so that when it rains water will not get into the pipe (Fig. 27). This creates a draft and the fireplace burns better, which is very helpful, especially in the winter when your tipi will be closed up most of the time and not much extra oxygen will be able to flow into it from the outside.

27.

drainpipe for fire draft

Pitching the tipi will only require about two people, but the more the better. No tools will be necessary except maybe a measuring tape and a pencil. The first thing to do is mark off a circle around your original center point, the same diameter as that of your tipi. This will guide you in putting down the poles. For the main tripod of poles, pick out your three heaviest and strongest poles. Measuring from the bottom up (beginning above the butt points), mark off the distance from the edge of your tipi cover to the corner where the tie-flaps are on one of your poles (Fig. 28). Again from the bottom up, mark off the distance from the middle of the arc to the center where the tie-flaps are on your second and third poles (Fig. 28). (The distance measured on these poles should be shorter than the distance measured on the door pole.) Mark off these lengths with notches. Lay the poles on the ground as in Figure 29, having them cross on the notches you have drawn. Bind them in a clove hitch with your 1/2-inch ma-

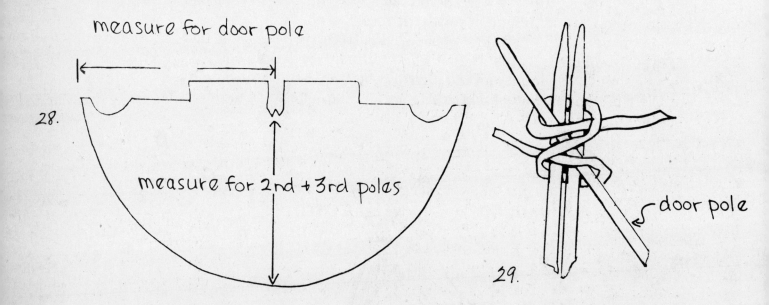

measure for door pole

28.

measure for 2nd + 3rd poles

door pole

29.

nila rope. A clove hitch is the easiest and most practical way to tie them together (see Fig. 29). Don't cut it! Wrap the rope around the poles a few more times tightly and tie that with a square knot. The door pole has to be on the east side of the circle (or, anyway, the front—if your front door doesn't face east). So to set up the tripod, put the butt of the door pole at the east side of the circle and pull the butts of the other two down to a position where they more or less balance, on the south side. By having someone pull on the rope and someone lift the poles, it should not be too hard to get the poles upright. After this, pull out the inside pole of the two that are next to each other, and bring it over to the north side of the circle, toward the person who is holding the rope. This will form your tripod. Now space the poles evenly apart, making sure not to move the door pole. Your tripod should look like the one in Figure 30.

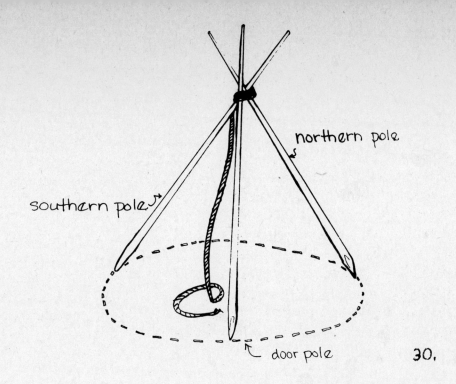

southern pole

northern pole

door pole

30.

Now lay the rest of the poles on the tripod consecutively according to the plan in Figure 31. Lay the first four "A" poles (A1, A2, A3, A4) in the FRONT CROTCH of the tripod. Lay the next four "B" poles (B5, B6, B7, B8) consecutively ON TOP OF the first set of "A" poles, also in the front crotch. Now place poles 9, 10, and 11 in the places indicated in Figure 31 and lay them in the rear crotch. Do not put up the lifting pole yet (this is the pole that will lift your cover). Wrap the rope around the poles starting at pole "S". Walk to the left pulling the rope tight. Wrap it around tight four or five times and then bring the rope down over pole "N". Let the rope hang straight down. Now drive your anchor peg in. It should be placed right next to the fireplace toward the back. Drive it in at a 45-degree angle. You can also use two pegs if you like. Drive them both in at 45-degree angles so that they cross each other. Tie the rope tightly around the pegs. You are now ready to start on the cover.

Pole Sequence

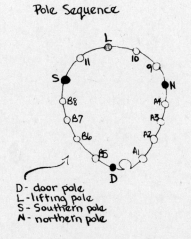

D - door pole
L - lifting pole
S - Southern pole
N - northern pole

31.

32. Looking up through poles

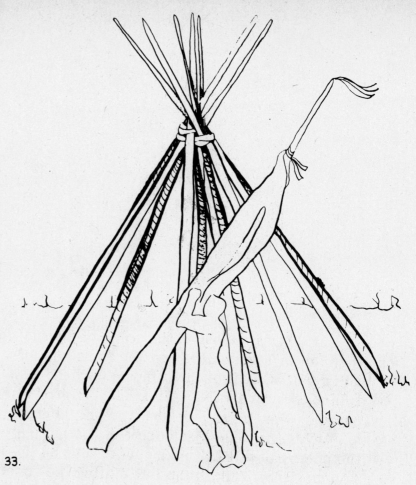

33.

PUTTING UP THE COVER

Lay the cover down on the ground with the outside showing, slip the last pole you have left under it so that it is aligned with the center mark down the middle of the cover. Tie the tie-tapes around the pole very tightly so that they won't slip. Fold the corner of one side over to the center where pole is. Do the same with the opposite corner. Continue this pattern until the cover is folded up into two rolls. Pick up the pole and the cover and lift it into position. It will be obvious where it has to be laid, with the cover on the outside. Now it is a simple matter to unroll each roll around the frame. Find a sturdy stick about 4 feet long and tie tightly horizontally across the two front poles, one being the door-pole, about 5 feet from the ground. By standing on this stick, it should not be difficult to tie the smoke-flap tapes and insert the top lacing pins. While you are up there, get someone to help you fit the smoke-flap poles into the pockets of the smoke flaps. It will be quite difficult to do if you don't do it now. If you don't expect cold

370

34.

weather or rain, you'll sometimes want to pull the lower corners of the smoke-flaps back against the tipi or attach them to poles a short distance from the door, depending on the ventilation you want to get (Fig. 35). So tie ropes through each buttonhole now. Take down the stick and finish lac-

35. Smoke-flaps and
the door open for
maximum ventilation

ing the cover down. The cover will probably fit loosely around the frame so go inside and push out all the poles an equal amount to make the cover fit tightly. Now you have to peg down the cover.

PEGGING DOWN THE COVER

The idea is to space pegs attached by ropes to the canvas evenly all around the tipi. Have two pegs by the door. To attach the 20-25 pegs to the cover of our 18-foot tipi, you will need as many 3/4-inch marbles or round rocks as you have pegs. You will also need the same number of 2 1/2-to- 3-foot lengths of 1/4-inch nylon cord. Hold each marble on the inside of the cover a few inches from the bottom. Tie a length of cord around the marble from the outside with a square knot. Make sure to have an equal amount of cord left on both sides of the knot. Tie the two ends around the top of a peg. Twist the peg until the cord is tight. Then drive the peg into the ground, tilting it away from the tipi. Do this with all the pegs all around the cover. Watch out for rocks in the ground. A really good idea is to drive an iron stake first in the place where you will drive your peg, so that you won't ruin the peg.

36. Cover peg in position

HANGING THE LINING

Now that you have finished with the cover, you can start on the lining. For this you will need a long length of cotton cord or clothesline. Tie one end to the lifting pole about 6 feet from the ground. You start from the lifting pole so that if for some reason you have to take down the cover, you won't also have to take down the lining. Bring the cord across the pole next to the lifting pole and around it. Bring the cord across the next pole. You have a loop around the first pole. Continue to do this all around the tipi, making sure to keep the rope 6 feet above the ground. When you have gone all the way around, go around the whole thing again. Go around to each pole and pull the rope as tight as you can. Now tie the end of the rope to the last pole next to the lifting pole. Go around to each pole and shove two 2-to-5-inch-long sticks in each loop around the poles. Space the sticks about 2 inches apart on the side of the pole facing toward the center of the tipi. This will keep water running down the poles from running off down the rope for the pegs provide a channel for water to go. Now take the four-paneled piece of lining and the 6-inch tie-tapes you cut and tie the middle buttonholes to the rope right next to the lifting pole. Take the next tie-tape and tie that to the cord, and so on until the whole piece is up. Now take a three-paneled piece and tie one end to the cord next to the door. Tie the next tie-tape to where it reaches, working your way to the back of the tipi. Do the same with the other three-paneled piece. The pieces should overlap each other some. From the outside, pull the bottom of the lining so that there's no sagging and pull it back in the direction of the cover. Put a rock on top of the lining where it touches the ground. Do this all around, and use plenty of rocks. Every now and then you will have to go around and pull the lining back a little. The rocks sometimes tend to slip.

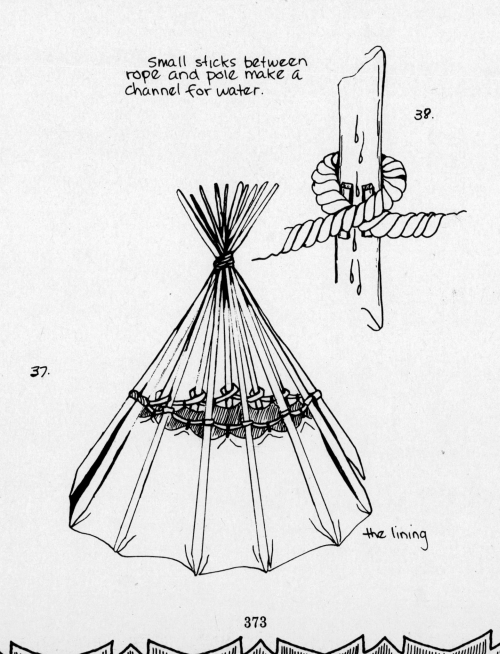

Small sticks between rope and pole make a channel for water.

38.

37.

the lining

FINISHING UP

There is one more thing you have to do. Dig a trench all around the outside of the tipi a few inches out from the base of the poles. Also, dig a run-off channel at the lowest point of the trench. The trench should be 3 or 4 inches wide and 3 or 4 inches deep. After a few rains, you will have to redig the trench because it tends to shallow out. This trench is quite necessary, especially if you are situated near a hill. It keeps water from running through and swamping the middle of your tipi when it's raining.

Depending on the type of lining you make for your tipi, there are many different kinds of floor you can use. The Plains Indians used a layer or two of animal hides for rugs and, as the bottom ones wasted away from dampness or use, just replaced them with no trouble. Today, animal hides are not as easy to come by. In our tipi we have burlap around the fire-place so that any rain that might happen to find its way into our tipi will run through the burlap into the ground. A couple of feet away from the center we have a waterproof tarp all around and then rugs on top of that, except in front of the door. We find this is a realistic floor layout. Paul's mother gave us a rug she wasn't using and Steve's mother gave us a few she didn't want. A friend just found a perfectly good rug at the town dump for his tent. Don't take good rugs into your tent until the ground gets really dry, or you will have moldy rugs. The first time we put up our tipi we had a plastic tarp covering the whole floor with a hole in it for the fireplace. The plastic tarp reached out to the edge of the tipi and was tucked under the lining. Water that came off the outside of the tipi lining dripped on the plastic. That night it rained and we found out why this is not a good thing to do—we were soaked! Water came in from all over. If you plan on living in your tipi permanently, you might want to build it on a wooden floor. You can use plywood, although a friend of ours says that plywood warps. He recommends using floor boards. If you build a wooden floor, build it above

39. Darry Wood and
    Barbara Wood
    making a tipi floor

the ground a few inches to avoid unnecessary dampness, and for insulation. You can even use linoleum; that reminds us too much of kitchens, but okay if you don't have anything else! If you are traveling light with your tipi, don't use anything.

A sleeping bag and maybe a small foam mat under it is all you really need to sleep in. Anything else just winds up getting dirty. If you are living in your tipi, you will probably sleep under blankets instead of a sleeping bag, so have anyone who comes in remove their shoes. Tipis can get dirty in just one day. Always have a small broom around. It comes in handy.

BUILDING A FIRE

It will probably take you a while to learn how to build a decent fire unless you are really an experienced camper. I guess we're not. I believe we smoked ourselves out three times our first night. First rule of the tipi fire: don't build big fires. Second rule: never let the fire smolder or go out, or at least not until you know what you're doing. If you get the fire going right, there is nothing like sitting around the fire at night. When you're building fires in a tipi, you have to watch out what kind of wood you use. Don't use any kind of pine, as it throws live sparks that burn large holes in whatever they happen to land on. Try not to burn too much green wood either. It makes a lot of smoke. Probably oak or maple are the best woods to use. They're good hard wood, burn slowly, and don't throw sparks. Dried-out pine twigs are great for kindling, but not for firewood.

TIPS

If you take proper care of your tipi, it should last eight or ten years. If your tipi will be exposed to the weather all year around, there are some basic maintenance rules to remember. In the winter after a snow, check your cover and clear away any snow banked up around the outside. Be sure to clear all the way down to the base of the tipi. You must do this because air might get in under the cover to create an unwanted draft on the fire. It is a good idea to get all the snow off the entire cover to insure long life for the canvas. Your fire will melt any snow above the level of the lining, so don't worry about the top half. Most people find that it helps to build some sort of wind-breaker around the tipi to keep cold drafts from blowing under the cover. It shouldn't be too hard to make one out of hay. If you are planning on living in your tipi during the winter months, be sure to have a lot of wood stored up, for you will be having your fire going all day long. A friend of ours made a wooden walk leading over the field to his tipi. It was easy to shovel in the winter, also when it is muddy it's good to walk on.

40.

For cooking, you can use a small Colman stove, but you don't need it. We have found that you can cook anything over the fire just as well as over a stove. You can bake, fry, broil, grill, or just heat up things. You can even toast bread by putting a slice on a stick and holding it over the fire. Any camping book will tell you how to do this. At first we had a small stove, but we haven't used it for months. Cooking over the fire is almost easier, and much cheaper too.

The Indians had their special ways of cooking. To boil water they heated rocks red-hot over fire and then dropped them in water, and instantly the water was boiling. To cook things, they dug a pit and lined it with rocks. Then they built a fire in it. After the rocks had heated sufficiently, they cleaned out the coals and put a buffalo skin over the rocks. Then the food was put in and covered. They also cooked things over the fire. Many Indians made jerky, which is strips of dried-out meat. The strips could be stored almost indefinitely if they were not subjected to dampness. The jerky could be eaten straight or boiled in water to regain its tenderness.

If you are going to leave your camp overnight or longer, make your food inaccessible to animals. Put it in a sack and hang it 4 or 5 feet from the ground on the rope hanging from the top of your tipi. If you don't do this, when you come back bring more food and something to clean up with. Raccoons have a habit of making an awful mess out of any food they can get their hands on. This has happened to us many times. Sometimes they will just take one thing and eat it outside, but most of the time they will eat it inside. One time we came back to our tipi and found oats, powdered milk, and flour all over the floor. We also found little raisin skins scattered about.

We have always worried about someone stumbling on our tipi and slashing the canvas, but no one ever has. Once when we went to take the tipi down from Steve's house to Paul's we found some beer cans, broken bottles, plastic spoons, and .22 cartridges lying around. Obviously some hunters had used the tipi. That is one reason to have the tipi near your house if you're not going to be actively living in it.

A survival book that helped us a lot was The Golden Book of Camping, published around 1940. It was corny-looking, but the contents turned out to be helpful.

Did it ever occur to you how the Indians and other people living in the elements dealt with the elementary problem of building a john? Along with Fire, Water, and Air, you need to dig out a latrine at least a hundred yards away. Keep a shovel handy. Cover up and dig another one every couple of weeks. We made a seat out of a split log with each half resting on rocks. Latrines should be far away because of bugs.

Well, that's about all we can tell you. We hope that you have as much fun in your tipi as we have had in ours. Good luck, and keep a stiff upper lip.

Stephen Haleyh   Paul Alexander

Video

Making Media

True Light Beavers / Tobe Carey

When's the last time you turned on your TV set and liked what you saw? When's the last time you thought the show you were watching had any relationship to reality? When's the last time you were really happy watching TV?

Today there are people working with inexpensive video equipment who are committed to making strong personal statements on television. You can join their underground ranks easily.

The new video movement has spread rapidly across the North American continent, and has turned on numbers of people who had never thought they could influence TV programming, never mind create their own shows. These video groups, widespread in both urban and rural areas, are the vanguard of the electronic revolution. With their own or borrowed equipment they are producing significant programming for both regional and national audiences.

Many video groups live collectively and share their equipment and editing facilities. They strive to involve their local community and to turn on individuals to the potential in video tape. They regularly demonstrate the equipment to the community, and give people the opportunity to try their hands at producing TV. It's truly giving media-power to the people.

And the fact is that there is nothing mysterious about television. There is no shrouded secret about techniques behind the shows that reach you through your television set. All you need to know about basic television production can be absorbed in a few hours of using video-tape equipment. After a demonstration, people are much more aware of what they are watching on TV, and can better discriminate between shows. Visual literacy is an important attribute for anyone living in twentieth-century America.

Since the inception of half-inch video format there has been a problem in getting completed tapes viewed by audiences. One major hang-up is the unwillingness of the high-powered broadcasting industry to consider using half-inch tapes for its productions. They claim half-inch standards aren't rigid enough and the on-the-air quality leaves much to be desired. But it seems as though what they are really concerned about is keeping the doors to broadcast facilities effectively closed to those without broadcast-approved union cards. In effect, they are maintaining a monopoly on the television system, keeping it in the hands of the big money people. It simply costs too much to equip a two-inch or even a one-inch television production facility that can produce what THEY have determined to be the standards of the industry. To further complicate matters, they cloak their reluctance to use half-inch video in Federal Communications Commission regulations, insisting on engineering standards that don't apply and serve to effectively bar the new video from being broadcast.

In the disastrous 1972 floods in the Wilkes-Barre area of Pennsylvania, one local-broadcast TV station lost all its cameras and "professional" studio equipment. They did, however, salvage their transmitter and antenna system. All they needed was cameras and video-tape recorders to get back on the air. Then local high-school students came by with half-inch equipment and offered it to provide emergency coverage of flood conditions and relief efforts. The station, having no alternative, took the half-inch equipment and went back on the air. The signals went out over their regular broadcast channel with excellent results. The point is, once the effort is made, the engineers can successfully broadcast half-inch video over existing transmitting facilities.

Fortunately, while this has been happening, the burgeoning cable systems have begun to play more and more half-inch tape. They are able to connect half-inch equipment directly into their local-origination cables, and to push the signal out with at least as good quality as signals captured either off the air from broadcast stations or from their own one-inch production facilities. This has opened new opportunities for half-inch productions to be seen by relatively wide audiences.

I have produced shows on half-inch video for Cablevision, Kingston, N.Y., and, with few exceptions, the quality has held up extremely well. There seems to be no excuse for excluding half-inch from a share of the video market (no reason other than the rigidity of the broadcast industry).

Other distribution outlets have begun to open in the last few years. One alternative has been the video-access banks managed by alternative video groups such as Raindance (New York), Johnny Video Tape (California), Intermedia (Canada), Media Access (California), Videfreex (New York), and Community Video Center (Washington, D.C.). These groups collect and swap or sell software (tapes) for individuals and groups. Check them for details.

Other outlets are growing on the college and high-school campuses. Many schools already have their own half-inch equipment and are using it to show prepackaged materials. Much of this programming is coming from lecture bureaus—commercial agencies that make money by packaging a whole documentary-type show. They are trying to promote and tap the commercial potential of the half-inch video field. The bureaus are developing programming that is sometimes interesting, since it takes advantage of video's ability to present uncensored material.

There are also a number of video theaters springing up. Located mostly in urban areas, they provide yet another source for software distribution. Often they are linked with the prepackaging people, but sometimes they can be persuaded to show what you have produced. Already such theaters are in operation in New York, Boston, San Francisco, Chicago, etc. Check local entertainment sheets for specifics on this changing scene.

Along with the collective video groups that are spreading the word and producing low-cost television, there are individual artists working personally within the medium. Many of them have been turned on to video tape by seeing their work immediately after recording it. Many former filmmakers have switched to the video medium because of this important capability of video tape.

My own background in media stems from film, and now embraces both film and video. And it was the instant-replay quality of video, the considerably shortened time between shooting and editing, that first attracted me. No longer do I have to wait for film to be sent to a lab, to be processed, to be sent back, before I can start editing. No longer do I have to work with silent footage while composing a film. (The sound's already there.) Now I can have the video tape completely shot and ready for viewing in the literal flick of a switch.

The video process is exciting and immediate. In McLuhanesque terms, it is involving and personal. It is, as any TV freak can tell you, a totally absorbing medium, one that sucks you into its grip almost without your knowing it.

This makes it all the more important that people become aware of its power and equally aware of how they can add their vision to it. Personal and collective statements belong on television, and individuals and groups beholden to no broadcast power-system must be encouraged to produce television shows that will reveal the true character of America.

BASIC EQUIPMENT

Video tape is the thing that television is made of. And, due to recent innovations in the field of camera and recorder/playback design, television can now be made in the home.

The minimal equipment needed for recording and playing back your own television shows is a camera with a video-tape recorder capable of recording and playing back through an ordinary TV set. There are a growing number of available video outfits on the market, such as Sony, Ampex, Panasonic, Craig, Toshiba, and AKAI. All the above make video units that use half-inch tape format, with the exception of AKAI, which uses a smaller, quarter-inch tape size. (It's really unclear yet whether there is an advantage in half-inch over quarter-inch, or vice versa. Time and experience will tell.) All of these units are considerably cheaper and less sophisticated than the "professional" one-inch and two-inch video-tape machines used by TV stations. They offer greater portability and savings in tape costs, while providing a picture and sound whose quality rivals some of the larger units.

As the video movement has developed, and as the hardware (equipment) has improved, individuals and groups have chosen their units on the basis of versatility. In this chapter I emphasize the Sony AV 3400 VideoRover II (Portapak) as the standard recording equipment, since it is the most popular recorder in use, and still seems to offer the best in portable recording AND playback capabilities.

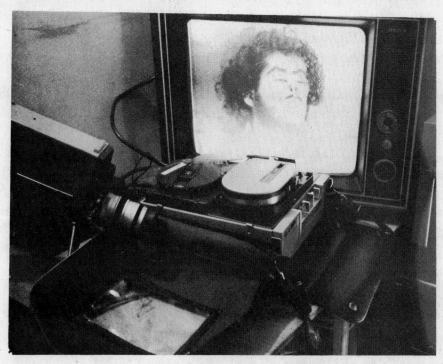

Portapak and monitor set-up

When you get access to a portable video-tape recorder (VTR) and camera, you will be able to record on a roll of tape up to a half-hour of synchronous-sound (meaning, when the lips move, the words come out) black-and-white video tape. Also, you can usually play back the tape on the same machine, viewing through the camera viewfinder (actually a miniature TV set), and listening through a small earphone.

The units will function either on AC-110 house current or on an enclosed rechargeable battery. The battery may provide as much as 45 minutes of running time on a 6-10 hour recharging time. However, some batteries have been known to give out in as little as twenty minutes, so be sure to know what your system is capable of doing.

Part of making video is getting the chance to show it off. To do this, using the portable units, you have to get an RF adaptor that plugs into the bottom of the unit. This converts the video output of the VTR to a broadcast frequency that can be picked up by a television set tuned to the channel corresponding to the RF unit used. The RF unit is connected from the VTR to the TV set by two leads which attach to the antenna terminals. Nothing could be simpler to hook up.

With this equipment, you are set to record and play back video tapes.

A word about technical information: The instruction manuals that come with the equipment are fairly clear and straightforward. All the basic stuff about handling the equipment is in the manual. Be sure to read it through before you go off shooting.

A final equipment note: as far as I know, all half-inch gear now being manufactured meets standard industry specifications. Most brands are now compatible with one another. The system used is called the EIAJ-1 standard. All Sony equipment with an AV prefix meets this standard. Any equipment you run across with a CV designation does NOT meet this standard. Sometimes the older CV equipment is offered on sale—don't get it, because it won't fit standard equipment. Whenever you buy used equipment, make sure you get some kind of guarantee, as a lot of equipment is on the market because it's broken down. (There is an adaptor called an octopus cable that can be used to convert CV signal to AV equipment.)

HOW IT WORKS

In the video-tape system the image received by the camera is converted into a series of electrical impulses that are fed to the video-tape recorder.

The record head receives the impulses and, as the half-inch magnetic tape (similar to quarter-inch sound recording tape) passes over it, the impulses alter the polarity of the iron oxide coating on the tape. When the tape is played back, the VTR receives a weak electrical current from the altered polarity pattern on the recorded tape. This current re-creates the pattern received originally by the VTR from the camera, and makes the images you see on the TV screen.

LENSES

The fine thing about video-taping is not having to wait for the developer— you can see what you are recording right as you record it. You really don't have to be hip to all the technical details of lenses. If things look weird on the monitor screen while you're recording, all you have to do is find the controls and do a little experimenting. Or take another look at your instruction book.

The 12.5-50 mm. zoom lens provided with the portable camera is sufficient to use outdoors under daylight conditions, and indoors with adequate light. The lens has an adjustable focal length (the longer the focal length, the smaller the area of the subject that will be seen, but the more it will be magnified). When the lens is at the wide-angle position (12.5 mm.) the field of view will be larger than normal (25 mm.). This lens position tends to distort the image some. In close-up, telephoto position (35-50 mm.) the perspective will appear flattened in the scene.

With portable VTR cameras you can change lenses. The camera accepts all lenses with a screw-type C-mount. Most 16-mm. film cameras accept this same type of lens. They can be used from an extremely wide angle (8 mm.) to a very long one (1000 mm.). When using long lenses (or when the zoom lens is in the 50 mm. position) you must be careful not to jar the camera. If you do, the image will jump much more noticeably than if you were using a lens of a shorter focal length. Tripods and monopods are very helpful to steady the camera.

Since the video system requires adequate light to record a decent image, you must be sure that your lens allows enough light to pass through it. This means being sure that your lens iris (the adjustable opening in the lens that lets the light through) is opened to the correct place. This means checking the F-stop (the numbers on the lens barrel nearest the camera).

The F-stops range from 1.8 (wide open) to 22 (closed down). Each time you turn to a higher number, the light passing through the iris is cut in half. You can visually check whether or not you have enough light to shoot by placing the VTR in record mode, removing the lens cap from the camera, and looking into the small viewfinder/monitor. If the image looks sharp and the blacks and whites look clear, then the signal being received by the camera is good. If things look gray and dim, check to see that your lens is opened to the correct F-stop. Chances are that most of your taping will be done at F-1.8. Experience has shown that this opening generally gives "correct" pictures.

FOCUSING

A note on focusing: when using a zoom lens, always focus on your object with the lens at its longest focal length (50 mm.). Once in focus at this point, it will remain in focus throughout the zoom range (as long as you don't shift the camera to another position). By watching your image in the camera viewfinder, you can see if you have a correct focus. This will be very clear in a close-up (telephoto position) but much less clear in a wide-angle shot. So, be sure you are in correct focus before you zoom back to a wide-angle shot.

THE CABLE

The camera is connected to the portable VTR by a length of gray cable. For some obscure reason, they've made the cable just long enough to trip on, and just short enough to make you nearly immobile. Wherever you go, the VTR must follow. This is O.K. when you feel like carrying it, but there are other occasions when an extra length of cable would be helpful. Fortunately, there are extensions available from all the manufacturers (at an extra charge).

LIGHTS

If you aren't prepared beforehand, lights for indoor taping can be a problem. Should friends call and say to hurry over with the Portapak and catch the baby as she plays on the rug, first ask about the lighting. If they're not sure, bring along your own.

There are many high-powered quartz lights available for video and film work that are excellent. Usually they come rated at 600 watts or 1000 watts, and one light is often adequate to flood smallish rooms in homes. To tape in larger spaces, you will want to add still more lights, and then I recommend following the standard three-light set-up preferred by most professionals (see diagram below). Light stands and clamps are available from manufacturers (Colotran-G.B.C. and Lowell-Lite).

If quartz lights are not available or outside your budget, think about spots and floods that can be bought from the closest hardware store. Most hardware outlets will also carry hand clamps and reflectors that can house the 150-watt or 200-watt bulbs. Photography stores are another good source for these lights and clamps. Don't forget to get enough extension cords.

If you can't get any of these lights, try ordinary lamps and put aluminum foil inside the shades to reflect the light. Or you can put aluminum foil in flat sheets on cardboard or make a cone shape to direct the light a bit. Experiment around.

ONE CAUTION ABOUT LIGHTS: Never point the video camera directly into any bright light source (lamp or sun). The light will mar the delicate vidicon tube with sometimes a permanent "burn," which will appear as a dark line on the video image. Cost to replace: $85.

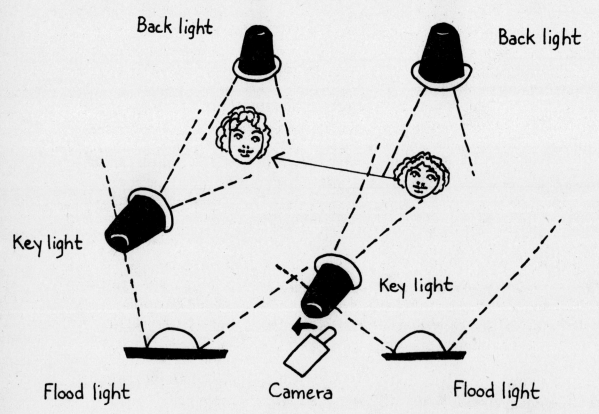

Lighting set-up for action. The subject is moving from right to left, with the camera following in a panning movement. Each half of the lighting set-up can be considered a standard three-light set-up.

When a subject will be moving, you must cover the area into which it will move. In the diagram above, use is made of strong key lights (spotlights) for casting shadows, floodlights to illuminate the general area of the scene, and back lights, which aid in clarifying the subject from the background. All the lights are aimed down on the subject from a 45-degree angle in order to closely approximate natural lighting. For a scene in which there is no movement, the basic three-light set-up (see above) provides ample lighting. In cases where you have to rely on less than three lights, be sure that enough illumination is on the section of the scene where you expect most of the action to occur.

MIKES AND SOUND

Most half-inch systems have a built-in omnidirectional mike (I'll explain this in a minute) just above the lens. This allows you to work the entire unit by yourself, and makes for nice personal video. But the quality of the sound you will get leaves something to be desired. In a small room with just a few folks it'll be OK. But outdoors, or in a large gathering, the VTR's Automatic Gain Control (AGC) will seek the loudest sound and adjust the recording level to receive that sound (and oftentimes that particular sound is not the one you want to emphasize on your tape). This sound problem came home to me very acutely when I was doing a tape of a childbirth in Mexico. The house in which the birth was taking place was situated on the Yucatan Peninsula, right on the Caribbean Sea. The night of the delivery, a storm was blowing up, and the waves were loud and clear in the room. The VTR picked up this sound of wind and waves as the loudest general sound and, throughout much of the beginning portion of the tape, these relatively unimportant sounds were muffling the conversation between the people involved in helping with the birth.

So you may want to supplement the built-in mike (which also picks up mechanical clicks from the zooming of the lens) with an external mike that can get close to your subject. Fortunately, most systems provide an exterior mike input, or jack. What you will need is an auxiliary mike with a mini-plug. Or, if you want, you can deploy several mikes and run them through a sound mixer to combine the sound of one or more mikes before they get to the VTR. The mixer in use, however, must provide a mike output, or the audio signal will overload the circuit of the VTR.

There are several kinds of mike to choose from and, without getting into a course on sound, a few differences bear mentioning.

Omnidirectional: these mikes accept sound from all directions. They are useful for getting the feeling of a crowd scene, a rock or folk group, or in other situations where a number of people are involved.

Unidirectional: these tend to emphasize sounds coming from the front of the microphone and are useful to control (decrease) sounds that might otherwise impinge on the recording. Shotgun mikes are an extension of this idea, and some sophisticated ones (Sennheiser's, for example) are particularly good in candid work. They allow the sound-man to remain quite far from the subject while still picking up and getting a good recording.

All mikes should have about 15 to 20 feet of cord attached for greatest mobility. The more independent the sound and camera, the more versatile the taping situation can become. Of course using an external mike means using a sound-man or -woman.

The sound-person should be supplied with a good set of earphones that can also be jacked into the VTR. Using the small plastic earpiece that comes with the set is really not adequate for determining how good the sound is.

Most half-inch systems allow for the addition of a separate voice track. You can dub (add a sound track without erasing the visual track) while playing back the prerecorded tape. It is a form of editing.

EDITING

Many people like to record things they see and leave them unchanged. They are not interested in altering the dynamics of a situation through editing. For recordings like that, the portable video systems serve well.

But for those interested in building on, adding to, and/or dramatizing their original recorded material, editing is a must. In addition to all the currently designed portable video equipment, you need an editing deck to edit. That also means cables and wires connecting it to the VTR deck and monitors on which to view the editing. A monitor is a TV receiver that can take a signal (picture and audio) directly from the video-tape recorder by way of a connecting cable. Most monitors can be used like an ordinary TV set.

The original recording (also called "original," "master," and "first generation") is never physically cut when you use this electronic editing system. This is a major difference between film and video tape. In video there is much less handling of the basic material, the tape. Although the images may be compared to frames, unlike film they cannot be looked at with the human eye alone for visual information.

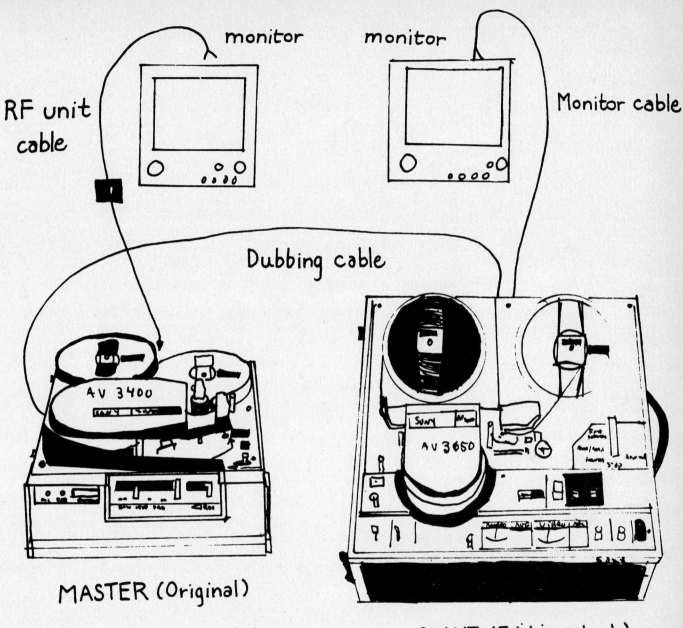

monitor   monitor

RF unit cable

Monitor cable

Dubbing cable

MASTER (Original)

SLAVE (Editing deck)

In a simple editing set-up, the original taped footage is copied by the slave unit in an edited sequence. You may build on this system, adding new sounds and more visuals to already collected materials. A key to the operation is timing and you may want to invest in a stopwatch.

The copy ("second generation," "slave") when completed will be an edited tape, ready for viewing by an audience. The editing process allows you to add sound and to change the sequence of material. It also allows you to shorten sequences for dramatic or other effects. And it allows you to add material from more than one reel of tape to the composite (edited) copy.

Most editing of half-inch video tape is done by matching master-slave tapes on two VTR systems, either Portapak to editing deck or editing deck to editing deck, and watching both tapes on TV monitors attached to the video sources. When you see the picture you want on monitor #1, you hit the edit button on the editing deck, which duplicates the signal on the slave tape and monitor #2.

There are a number of home-grown systems for editing being developed as people get more familiar with the available equipment. The Sony and Panasonic editing decks have a built-in editing function that can give rock-solid edits when things work just right. The problem is to get the correct edit points in synchronous line-up on the two machines. If the counter on the portable unit turned at the same speed as the counter on the editing deck, it would solve some problems. As it is, you'll probably want to develop your own system for achieving effective synchronization after some experimentation.

Some systems already in use involve marking X's with felt-tip pens on the tape itself, and lining up these spots with the skew bar (first post after the supply reel on the VTR). This is one system that sounds complicated on paper, but when shown by someone using the method is quite simple. Others incorporate counters that have been added to the machines, which allow the editor to get both edit points in line and then back off a given amount of numerals, to begin the warm-up or the "roll-in." Once you have the exact beginning of the section to be added ready for playing, and the exact end of the previously edited section ready to be added to, you must back up enough to allow the two machines to lock up in sync (synchronization: signals that lock the horizontal and vertical scanning in step; if sync is off the picture will roll or flutter). This means that both machines need ample run-in time before the actual edit is made. If they don't have adequate lead-in, the edit will be unstable, and the jump from sequence to sequence will be noticeable on the edited tape.

The key is to move both supply reels of tape back far enough to allow for proper roll-in, while ensuring that the original tape reaches the playback head of its VTR at the same time that the second-generation tape reaches the record head of the editing deck. When you know your machines well, you may be able to do this simply by counting the number of turns you have to make on both supply reels. Or you can use a measuring device that fits on the reels. This tells you how many revolutions you need to have the scenes in sync.

As I said, one key to editing is accessibility to two monitors: one for the output of the master tape and the other for the output of the edited version. This will allow you to see and hear the editing points on the two tapes as they reach the critical places. If the edit looks like it'll be all right, punch up the edit button at the proper moment, and you should have a suitable edit.

Playing back an edited tape should be done on an editing deck. If you try to play back an edited tape on the portable unit you will again see the edit points as they roll by. This is simply because the playback mechanism in the portable VTR is not up to handling the impulses from the edit points. There are several proven techniques that may be of use in editing collected material. When contrasting and opposing views are placed against one another, in succession, the viewer gets a synthesis of the material that is stronger than if each scene were presented alone.

Cross-cutting can be effective to make a point, or to dramatically build towards a moment of crisis. Remember the dramatic film scenes where the heroine is tied to the railroad tracks, and the train is seen rushing towards her? The effect is heightened by showing a shot of the helpless girl, and than a separate shot of the train coming closer to the camera. The girl is then seen struggling again, and then the train looms larger. This is a classic example of cross-cutting.

Keep edited scenes to their essentials, paring back until the compiled version is sparse and taut. But you may also want to add complementary or contrasting visuals to a scene without disturbing the audio portion. Often these are cut-aways, shots of things other than the main action, that add to the viewer's interest, information, or mood.

DIRECTING

Everyone must develop her or his own way of handling video situations, but it may help you to jot down a few thoughts before beginning. The better prepared you are for any situation, the better will be your tape. But if it's not necessary to have anything like a script, you can also simply trip out on the event as it occurs.

Be aware of a few things. When taping with the portable half-inch unit, always leave ten seconds from the time you begin recording until the time

when you want your information to begin on the tape. This will allow enough time for the VTR to get up proper speed and sync. If you fail to do this, you'll have trouble making solid edits with material at the beginning of your shot.

Keep in mind that TV can give a lot of information in a short period of time, and that constant changes of the image may keep viewer interest high. On the other hand, don't keep zooming in and out or panning around without having a purpose. Every shot you make should have a reason for being on the tape; otherwise it is wasted effort.

Don't get so hung up on the synchronous sound capability that all your tapes become interview or talk shows. Use the portable nature of the camera and recorder to get into action situations.

Be aware of framing and composition. Leave anything out that is not essential to what you want to show. Be aware that camera angles can affect the way your material looks. A high angle (looking down on the subject) can make the figures less imposing, while a low angle (looking up from the floor) can make a small person look more menacing. Generally a head-on approach is comfortable for viewers, although a dramatic effect can be achieved by using other carefully chosen camera angles.

The relatively small TV screen does not show long shots well.

Long shot (L.S.)

Medium shot (M.S.)

Close up (C.U)

These are the typical TV images:
    Long shot (l.s.)—the figure and surroundings
    Medium shot (m.s.)—head and shoulders of a person
    Close-up (c.u.)—head of a person

If you know your scene doesn't call for much action, you might want to use a tripod. It helps steady the image, and keeps viewers from feeling seasick as they watch. It's especially vital to steady large and heavy telephoto lenses—and it will give your weary hand a rest.

Don't be afraid to direct a scene to get what you want. Every piece of art has a point of view—there is no objectivity in TV—just don't claim to be objective, and your statement can stand by itself. Every video tape is automatically "exclusionary," automatically places a frame around certain objects and not others. If you want to present two sides of a story, go ahead, but remember that most stories have more than two sides—many shades of gray.

Pacing and rhythm are vital parts of any video production, be it documentary or dramatic in nature. They determine the length of each shot and the way in which shots are placed in order. Shots that last more than six or seven seconds each are relatively long, and may call for shortening in the editing process.

Keep in mind certain edits you may want as you work, and look for material that might help fill in whatever scheme comes to mind. If you have an idea beforehand of how much material you want the final tape to have, you'll know about how much you want to shoot. Video tapes can be erased and reused, so don't be afraid to shoot more than you end up using.

A good way to fantasize what you want the tape to look and sound like is to close your eyes and imagine the scenes on a TV set. That will be your visuals. Then hear the sounds in your head. That will be your audio. The next step is to try to recreate the scenes as you imagined them.

Once the material has been gathered, you will want to review it several times, jotting down notes (it's a good idea to carry a little notebook) about the tapes. The half-inch units have a counter that can be used to help locate material when the editing time comes. Simply line up your first scene and get the counter to 000. Then you're ready to log the tape, jotting down a short description of the scene and the counter number where it appears on the tape.

If you want to go beyond a simple one-camera system, you will need a few more pieces of hardware. To run more than one camera into a recording deck, you need a camera switcher (also called camera selector) and a sync generator (to keep the camera signals in line with each other) or a special effects generator (SEG), which can accept up to four cameras at once, and which will allow you to change from one signal to another while taping. This will give you the capability of covering a scene from three or four different angles at one time, and creating an edited tape by choosing your shots while the initial taping is going on.

SEG's can supply interesting visual effects.

Cut: one shot immediately replaced by another.

Fade-in: starting with a black screen, the shot is gradually brought up to full brilliance.

Fade-out: starting from a fully brilliant picture, the shot is gradually brought to black.

Split screen: two shots share the screen at the same time.

Mix (dissolve): one shot is gradually faded out while a second shot is faded in to replace it. The signals cross to make a superimposition at one point.

Superimpose: placing one shot over the other—good for titles, cut lines, etc.

Wipe: one shot pushes the other off the screen. There are several ways the wipe may enter the screen.

Note: To make fade-ins and fade-outs without using a special effects generator, you can use the F-stop ring on the lens. Simply close down the lens all the way (turn to highest F-stop number) when you begin shooting, and gradually open to the correct F-stop. That will give you a fade-in. Do the reverse (from wide-open lens to closed-down) for a fade-out.

EQUIPMENT CARE

Here are some tips:

Watch out for extremely hot or cold situations. In very bright sun or intense heat you might drape a piece of white muslin over the VTR to save the battery from being drained. I did that in Mexico, and regularly preserved the battery charge.

Keep the heads clean. The portable units come with a cleaning kit, but if the fluid runs out, pure alcohol on chamois leather will work as well. If the heads get clogged, the VTR may not record at all. (Use a demagnetizer periodically on the heads.)

The covers on the portable units have a tendency to loosen. This is especially likely to happen if you leave a unit on its side. Then, while you're taping, the cover may rub against the take-up reel and cause the tape to wind itself around nearby rollers and capstans. When this happens, the tape is like useless spaghetti and has to be cut off.

Lens tissue: be sure never to touch the lens glass with your fingers. If the lens does get dirty, use lens tissue only (not eyeglass papers—they scratch). Carry some with you and, before each taping session, check the lens for dirt. A few circular wipes with the soft tissue will prevent dirty spots from appearing on the tape.

VIDEO TO FILM

Since the number of video playback units is far less than the number of 16-mm. film projectors, you might want to think about transferring a completed video tape to film. There are outfits that will do this for you at a fairly reasonable rate, and there are also ways to do it yourself.

To have a commercially done transfer made will cost between $9 and $12 per minute of film for one composite (sound and picture) print. Some places to check for prices and quality are: Rombex Productions Corp., 245 West 55 St., New York, N.Y.; and Windsor Electronic Systems Corporation, 230-08 South Conduit Avenue, Laurelton, N.Y. 11413.

If you want to try your hand at transferring video to film, simply set up your playback deck corrected to a monitor, and begin the tape. Put your movie camera in front of the monitor, set the correct F-stop, and film away. Film speed should be comparable to the number of frames per second of video playback—about 30 frames per second. The sharpness you usually expect from a film image will, of course, be lacking in a video-film transfer. But you'll have a copy that can be shown on a projector. Needless to say, unless you have very sophisticated film equipment, you will just get the visuals without the audio. So you'll need a sound-tape-recorder running at the same time, to pick up the voice and music track. Then, when playing back the film, you'll have to use the sound tape as well.

A FEW PROJECTS

There's plenty you can do—here are some projects I've found to be good. The use to the community of half-inch video is limitless. Say you wanted to show local groups how certain industries were polluting the environment, you could really do it with video: waste going down the streams, smoke in the air, etc. Not everyone can show up at the town meetings but you could tape them for replay to community groups, schools, and cable television, which is looking and will sometimes pay for such programming.

In fact, the political uses of video tape are fantastic. Candidates can record their opinions. Talk a shopkeeper into using his shopwindow for replay, and people will stop by to listen and watch. Also you can record political rallies, speeches, and all the rest. This way both issues and candidates will get broader coverage, particularly local ones.

Every area has its special events and there isn't always a commercial operation around to record them. Last summer in nearby Phoenicia, N.Y., a group of architects got together from all over the East Coast and formed what was called "quick city": simple shelters that could be both erected and inhabited in a day. Tipis, domes, tents, plastic structures were all put up in a grassy meadow, high in the mountains. And it was great to have all this on tape. I've used it and shown it many times.

Making a permanent record of other kinds of craft is important. Somebody makes something special and then either sells or gives it away. If you have video equipment you can make a record of it, and if possible how it was made, for the use of craftspeople as well as the general public. Public libraries are showing active interest in forming a collection of video tapes and, from my experience, their initial interest has been in the crafts. The Mid-Hudson library system (Market St., Poughkeepsie, New York) has started a collection, which is available on a loan basis to schools.

The video recording is a natural for musical events. Folk concerts very often happen sort of spontaneously or at least without enough time to get a complicated recording system ready. The portability of the video system makes it easy to record these visually exciting popular music concerts.

Locally, the women's lib groups are using video in their consciousness-raising sessions. They want to document and view themselves at these sessions. It has answered questions like who is overly dominant, how does one physically react to a particular subject matter, what mannerisms are evident, and why are they there in the first place. It would be a good idea if they could watch men interact in similar situations.

Group-encounter sessions are particularly helpful if experienced for

the second time through video. I heard that followers of Janov use video for both group and individual psychotherapy. One person who teaches autistic children has gotten his first real response from certain students through video.

What you can do with video in teaching is wide open. In the first place,

398

because of the simplicity of the equipment, students can use it inside and outside the schools. They can produce their own current-events, dramatic, and historical productions. And on and on.

How-to-do-it instruction will probably introduce the first widespread use of video equipment. Almost anything can be taught through sight and sound. And hopefully the informal approach, which is the right approach, of video will liberate people into happy and productive creativity.

ACCESS TO TOOLS

Looming above all the questions of how to do it, and what programming best serves your needs, is the problem of access to equipment. Although, when comparing film to video and portable video to "professional" TV equipment, the half-inch gear is cheap, that doesn't mean most people can afford to put up the dollars needed to get equipped for the video frontier. So details follow as to where and how you can get hold of video equipment cheap.

Let's start by looking at the typical community and surrounding area. These days there are cable TV systems just about everywhere, and they are a logical first place to look for equipment. Maybe they invested at one time in half-inch gear but couldn't find a way to make it profitable for local origination. Chances are they have keyed their programming to local commercial ventures. Perhaps you can help liberate these locked-up gear-goodies by offering a solid program that will interest the community. Prove that you can sell the show (commercially) or get a sponsor, or maybe you can afford to agree to underwrite the minimal production costs in exchange for access to the equipment. Little by little, the cable people can be nudged into giving you and your group more and more control over the equipment if you play your cards right.

Another vital source is the local school. Most of them have some video equipment now, usually locked up where even the teachers can't get at it. Often there are departments called Instructional Media, or some such, that control all the stuff. Since it was all purchased in the public's name for use in the school system, perhaps you can get access to this equipment by running a workshop for students and teachers. Turn the kids on to video and they'll demand that the equipment be made available to them, instead of being held in some dark corner encrusted with cobwebs.

Local community colleges are a good source of equipment, but it seems harder to open them up. Chances are they have a full TV studio which is empty most of the time. Try to stick your finger in that pie, and offer to organize a course in video for students and faculty. The trick is always to get the gear out of the clutches of the administrators, who are overly worried about breakage and concerned about guarding their unused toys. Problem is, they never want the toys played with at all—unless they can directly control the process. Work through the art department or the humanities people to free up the gear, if you have no luck with a head-on confrontation with the Instructional Media folks.

Other local groups with video possibilities are social service organizations (government and private), such as community action offices, OEO programs, VISTA, United Way, etc. They may have used them in encounter groups, and perhaps they can be loosened up to allow other community groups access.

A real possibility is to band with friends and operate as an organized media group, get community status, and buy or lease your own equipment. Then you can hold public showings on your own monitors, and not have to worry about when and how you can use the equipment. As I said earlier, there already are many video groups around the country, and with a bit of searching you can find one willing to help you get going.

FUNDING YOUR PROJECT

One way to get funding is to set up a community access group and look for government or private foundation monies to support your work. To pull this off, you have to be able to demonstrate that you are already doing something worthwhile, that the thing you want to do cannot be done without their help, and that you are responsive to the community's needs. Also, you will need to show some kind of community monetary or equipment support. Most of these groups are not into funding entire programs, but will help fund part of a project. It's still up to you to show that it can work. Check the local library for The Foundations Directory, which lists foundations that aid the arts and other areas.

Speaking of libraries, check them out to see if they would like to have video demonstrations and projects carried on under their sponsorship. If so, maybe they'd even be willing to front some money to help pay expenses of hardware and tapes.

At the present there isn't any big money to be made in doing half-inch video—as a matter of fact, most outfits in a position to show your work will try to rip it off, saying how pleased they are to let you show your tapes on their system ... nice of them. eh? Remember that if they are a commercial concern, and any tapes you do for them support their organization, it must be worth something to them ...

The more people there are who can swing the financing and be active participants in the relatively low-cost portable half-inch video process, the sooner there will be a major communications breakthrough and the less power over us private television will have.

SOME COSTS

Portable video-tape recorder/playback unit with camera and omnidirectional mike	$1700
Editing deck	$1400
Monitor (9-inch screen)	$ 225
Unidirectional mike	$ 50
RF unit for portable VTR	$ 55
12-volt standard battery (45 minutes operating time)	$ 35
Long-life battery pack (3 hours operating time)	$ 120
Audio/video extension cables for camera	$30-65
Special effects generator	$ 600
Camera selector (up to 3 cameras)	$ 50
Sync generator	$ 175
Mike mixer	$60-250
Tripod	$ 50
Lights (quartz)	3 for $150

For the most current information on the rapidly changing field, check: (1) Radical Software Magazine, Box 135, Ruby, N.Y. 12475; (2) Video Exchange Directory, c/o Vancouver Art Gallery, 1145 West Georgia, Vancouver, B.C., Canada.

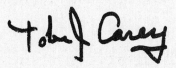

Needlepoint

Carol W. Abrams

It was the day of the unveiling. The invitation said "formal"—whatever that is. I brushed my teeth and sat on the windowsill to watch a skinny sparrow pick at a clump of dried mud. There had been many secret meetings, with Frank Sinatra crooning through the closed door. The invitation said "formal"? I pulled on my new jeans and tagged a ride. She'd been hiding herself in her tiny studio for months. It had to be something special.

The room buzzed with controlled conversation. Everyone was hungry. Luscious smells floated from the kitchen. There she stood, bright as a poppy in her Lord & Taylor hostess robe, flushed with excitement. It's time. The unveiling. I sat eagerly on the edge of the coffee table. The room hushed as she moved to the double doors and, amid much murmuring and expectant whispers, flung them open. Candlelight and silver warmed the room. And there they stood, eight of them, all matching, carefully arranged to face the crowd, their wood polished to a deep lustre ... What was she doing with Aunt Lydia's chair covers? Or were they Maybelle's sister-in-law's neighbor's chair covers? Then again, I thought they might be Cousin Bertram's Cincinnati client's chair covers, or maybe they were the milkman's mother's chair covers ... There were gasps. Ahs. "How lovely. She's so talented." "You did it all by yourself? I could never ..." Oh wow, there's no room for doubt, I saw those chair covers before—last spring. Ooooh (choke) ... that's it! That spring needlework catalogue. Kit # 65297J ... and the flowers were already worked in! She was saying, "They were a delight to do." Imagine having to say to her grandchildren some day, "Yes, my dears, I colored in the backgrounds all by myself."

I excused myself as tactfully as I could and pressed my way through the crowd. No, I wouldn't be staying. I stepped out of the light and into the dampness of the evening. I was saddened. She had missed so much. The exhilaration of planning and executing her own patterns, the sensuality of choosing her own materials, the excitement of discovery with each new stitch learned. She had missed so very much. Needlepoint, my needle-point ... how I love it. It's a crazy, tension-reducing, soothing, rhythmic, downright addictive new/old craft. It's a way to be alone in a supersociety, giving you a chance to clear your head and concentrate on only the stitch-ing, only the rhythm, only the color, only the terrain to be covered. Best of all, it's not complicated.

With very little equipment, some vision, and very little time you can master and enjoy needlepoint. And, unlike most other needlework crafts, learning the initial techniques doesn't eat up hours. With only one or two basic stitches you can explore new regions of visual space, or you can hit the canvas in coloring-book style. It's so flexible that it covers the whole range in between.

Needlepoint starts with a canvas that looks more like three-dimensional graph paper than canvas and ends up with a solidly filled-in, heavy fabric. Sometimes it's called needlepoint tapestry, because at first glance it looks as if it were woven like a tapestry. Unlike embroidery, where the fabric is as much a part of the pattern as the stitches, needlepoint stitches com-pletely cover the fabric, actually becoming one with it.

Go to a well-supplied needlecraft shop and browse. Really browse; check out canvases, for one thing, but really concentrate on the yarn. Sort of get an idea of what you are letting yourself into. See what you will have available for your projects. Touch the wools and cords, put them next to each other, let their colors sink in, look at all the yarns and stuff—don't restrict yourself to "needlepoint yarn." Anything you can thread through a needle might do. Super-raw beginners may want to stick to the classic wools, while the more adventurous may move into the exotic macrame cords and such. Just remember—you're browsing right now.

When starting needlepoint, designing a project should be first and foremost on your list of priorities. A pleasant sojourn in a needlecraft shop will arm you with ideas. After that, you will probably know pretty much what colors and yarns and possibly the size canvas you'd like to work with, and you can then approach designing with more ease. A sampler is fun and a useful vocabulary-builder—it can be played with, and gives a place to explore textural possibilities, color combinations, and exotic yarns, strings, and cords. It's the perfect place to record stitches learned, measure yarn lengths, and generally doodle around. I am always working on a sampler of some sort right along with my projects.

For design ideas, go for a nice long, slow walk or sit by a window for a while. Soak in all you see. Really look. Piles of cement blocks; marigolds blinking in a neighbor's garden; empty-lot collages of bottles, cans, papers, weeds, a butterfly, and rocks; rows and rows of store windows; purply mountains stacked one behind the other; tremendous glass-skinned buildings; fences covered with roses and grapevines; cows on a very green field; a river; a gutter; a couple of dumb pigeons—there are possibilities everywhere. Look. See. Remember and note carefully. What are your favorite things? What are "your" colors? Do you like geometrics? Are you into art deco, do you really, really get into Jean Arp? How about a dog, a kid, cooking, music, cybernetics? What about the bottoms of your shoes? Get it?

Take out your box of crayons and some paper and express yourself—work with what you like, move into colors and lots of spaces. Don't get hung up with "My, that doesn't look like Uncle George," and don't give me that garbage about not being "artistic," whatever that means. You dig being, don't you? You know what colors please you (so they're not Harriet's favorites, and who cares if she'd never have them?). You know what turns you on, right? As I said, don't give me that junk about not being artistic. Freedom is the word. Loosen your head and move out. Get it out on paper. It's best if you do your drawing about the size you'd like to stitch.

Now you've got it—how to get it on canvas is next. But first you've got to have the canvas. The number of warp and weft threads per linear inch (warp threads run the length of the material, weft threads the width of the material) determines the mesh of the canvas. The range runs all the way from very large mesh, with only 5 threads to the inch, to teeny-tiny, eye-

Two sizes of
penelope canvas

popping 40 threads to the inch. The mesh is not the only factor in deciding what canvas to use. Needlepoint canvas comes in either of two varieties: mono canvas with single warp and weft threads, and penelope canvas, whose threads run in pairs. I prefer penelope canvas to mono because I can move from a large stitch to a smaller one on one canvas—it's like using canvases of different meshes together. If you can't make a decision as to the mesh canvas to buy, pick a middle range of penelope with 10 threads to the inch. This will let you see the stitches fairly well. It also covers relatively quickly, and you'll get to know what needlepoint is all about. The smaller mesh canvases permit more detail. So choose whatever you need to suit your pattern. If it's your first piece, think about it. Be logical—unless you want to spend years on one piece. The reverse holds true also; it's silly to pick 5-mesh penelope canvas for a tiny piece—you'll just get started and—zap!—it's done. The little demon in my head, though, asks if that's all bad. Just think, it'll be done quick. Okay—I'll concede—it's not so bad and could be rather fun, though limiting in detail. Rug canvas (5 to 3 1/2-mesh canvas) needlepoint has become very popular in this instant-result-craving society, and it's certainly a legitimate form, so move where your head takes you.

Buy as much canvas as you'll need for the size piece you've decided to work on. Add 3 inches more all around the area to be covered for a blocking, mounting, and working edge—and 6 or 8 inches more in length for messing around on (a sampler).

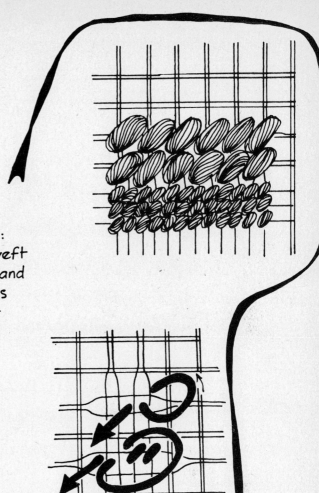

Stitching small on a penelope canvas :
spread the closely spaced warp and weft
thread pairs apart with a blunt needle and
proceed to stitch as usual. The stitches
will be about half the size of the surrounding stitches.

The problem of moving the pattern off the paper and onto the canvas has now presented itself. There are two basic methods I find most useful; one is painting or coloring it on, the other is "following the coded square." For a pattern that has bold areas and well-defined colors and is already the size you want to work up, the painting or coloring routine is fun. You need a sheet of thin, clear plastic. You can find the stuff in hardware stores on wide rolls sold by the yard. Get a good-size piece, a yard by a yard at least, so you can use it over and over again on canvases of almost any dimension. With this you also need crayons, an iron and ironing board, masking tape and/or adhesive tape, and a sewing machine or needle and thread. Set the iron at a very low heat. Tape the pattern down to a table and lay the plastic over it. Tape the corners of the plastic so it doesn't shift. Trim the canvas to size, leaving an excess of 3 inches all around the pattern. Be sure you trim along one single warp or one single weft thread on all the sides so the canvas remains square at the corners. Posi-

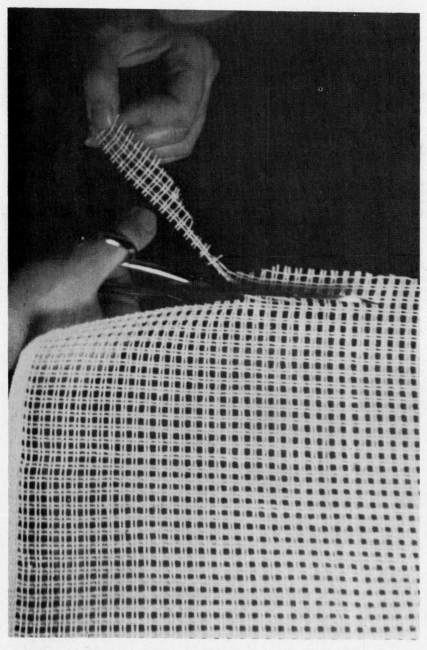

Cut along one single warp or weft thread of canvas to get right-angle corners.

tion the canvas over the plastic and pattern so that the centers of the canvas and pattern coincide. Tape the corners of the canvas. You should be able to see the pattern through the holes in the canvas. With your crayons retrace and color the pattern on the canvas. Remove the canvas from the plastic and place it, face down, on the ironing board. Slip a sheet of paper or an old cloth between the canvas and your ironing board to save the cover from possible staining. Gently press the canvas, using circular motions. (The heat of the iron melts the crayon wax into the canvas fibers, making your pattern permanent and waterproof.) Don't use a steaming iron—it'll stretch your canvas out of shape.

If you'd rather use paint to transfer your pattern you'll need—in addition to your pattern—trimmed canvas, plastic brushes, a palette (an old china plate or ashtray will do), acrylic paints in the colors you need, and water for cleaning your brushes. Acrylics are easier to handle than oils, as they dry in half an hour or so and can be cleaned with water while wet. Tape down your pattern and plastic, lay your trimmed canvas over them, and paint the pattern as described for the crayon method. Mix your paints with a little water if they are very thick, until the consistency is like heavy cream, using your palette as the mixing surface. When your canvas is complete, carefully remove it, and retape it to a flat surface so it stays flat while drying. Clean the plastic and brushes with water before paint dries. Whether you use crayons or paint, save your pattern for future reference.

After the canvas is pressed or dry, whichever the case may be, the edges must be bound to prevent raveling. With my sewing machine I run a long basting stitch all around the perimeter of the canvas about 1/2-inch away from the edge. Then I fold surgical adhesive tape or masking-tape over the edge. Bias tape or grosgrain ribbon can be sewn down over the edge also. This protects hands from being stabbed by the rough, prickly canvas threads bristling out from the edges. It also adds strength to the edges for later blocking. Always follow straight single warp and weft threads while binding the edges, to keep the corners square.

If your pattern has subtle colorations and shadings the "following the coded square" transfer technique is best. This way you get to see pretty much how your pattern will look in needlepoint. The curves you may have in your pattern are broken down into squares on a graph, exactly the way they will be with stitches on the canvas. The advantages of this technique are many: you can enlarge or reduce your pattern on any size canvas without elaborate techniques, and you can very easily change colors consistently throughout your pattern using simple substitution.

You'll need drawing paper, graph paper (found in most good stationery stores), a lead pencil, fine-pointed felt-tipped markers, crayons or colored pencils, and your prepared (edges bound, corners square) canvas. Freely draw your pattern on the drawing paper with colored pencil or crayon. With a dark crayon or marker, outline your pattern's major shapes. Lay the graph paper over the drawing with centers matching. With the lead pencil, lightly trace the pattern on the graph paper disregarding the paper's squares. A draftsman's lightbox or taping the pattern and graph paper to a sunny window would ease the tracing. With felt-tip markers or colored pencils carefully color in each square as it would appear on the canvas. You are

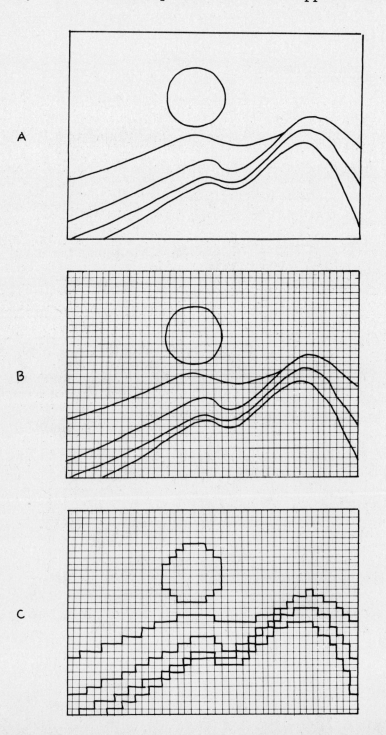

breaking your pattern down into squares, completely square squares; as you can't stitch half a square, don't divide them. If your pattern has very subtle shadings or if you don't like to color, you can code each color with a symbol: orange is ":", red is "/", green is "0", brown is "-", etc. Fill each square that is to be colored with a symbol of that color. This approach is really fine if you happen to change your mind about what colors you are going to use. All you do is substitute the new color for the original and use the same code in working from a chart. Mark the center of the canvas and the center of the chart. This mark will provide a reference point for counting. As you stitch, count the mesh of the canvas, as the holes correspond to the chart's squares, starting from the center and matching yarn color to the code.

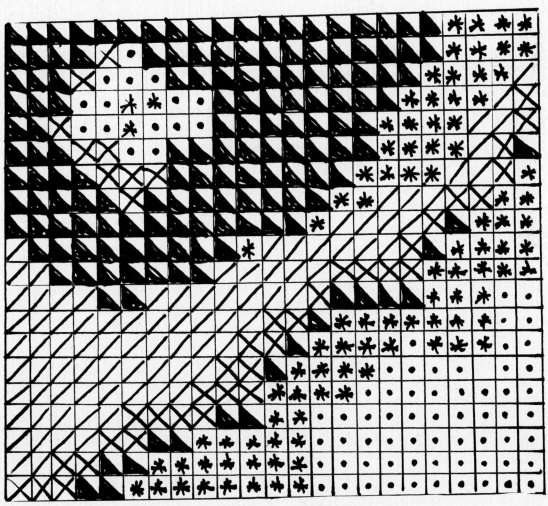

⊠ One color   ⊡ A light color
⊛ Another color   ⊠ A dark color
       ◪ Any color

Needles are basic, and most needlework departments carry a range of needlepoint or tapestry needles. If you are working on large-mesh rug canvas the heftier yarn needles are needed. In all cases the needles are large-eyed and blunt-ended. For the life of me, I can't remember needle numbers, so I have a wide assortment always on hand—something I urge you to acquire. That way you'll be prepared for anything. I can't figure how you can keep the needle numbers straight anyway, they're not printed on the actual needle and I don't know of anyone who can use them without taking them out of the package. If it fits too tight in the canvas it's too big, and if it falls right through it's too small. Easy enough?

The real far-out trip is the yarns. A supreme exhilaration. The colors are lush and the textures deep. Shiny bright silks and pearl cottons and soft, compact English crewel wools for those mini-needlepoint projects; smooth, elegant Persian and French tapestry wools in absolutely stupendous colors and rugged, nubbly rug wools for larger canvases and whatever comes in between. The tapestry wools are the standard wools associated with needlepoint. The color ranges are fantastic. They are strong and easy to work with and give an even, warm, touchable surface to the piece. Persian yarn is the most versatile; it comes three-ply (three strands per length) and can be split to fit a range of the middle-size mesh canvases, the colors are good, and it's available at most places that sell "art" needlework supplies in bulk. The French tapestry wool is a twisted, tough yarn that is fantastically durable and works beautifully for projects that will undergo lots of physical wear. It is difficult to split successfully so it's best to use with the middle-range canvases. Recently a domestic yarn manufacturer has produced a terrific Persian-type three-ply yarn in great colors.

If you are working on a larger mesh size, check out other materials—some macrame cords are beautifully adaptable to needlepoint. Satin-covered rattail and tight, pliable nylon cord, sisal, jute, and seine cordings are interesting. Good old packing or butcher's twine can also be tried. An eclectic approach is most exciting. I say if you can get it through a needle and into a needlepoint stitch, then use it. I use knitting worsteds also. They offer textures and colors I can't find elsewhere and they make an interesting surface next to some other wools and cords. Knitting wools do stretch and shred easily—so don't use long lengths. Some cords are not as flexible as you might like—try using a crochet hook along with your needle. Learning to compensate for whatever problems the "alien" materials may have will make the experience worth much, much more in the long run. Use your imagination. If something doesn't work, you've learned why at least. Biblical-type commandments—thou shalt nots—are not to be obeyed unless you've discovered their practical value. Hell is not in store for a needlepointer who's tried and failed.

The thing that makes needlepoint needlepoint is that the yarn used covers the canvas <u>completely</u>, so fitting the yarn or cord size to the canvas mesh size is a good idea. You can't fit a thick yarn into a small hole, the old saying goes, without just a little trouble—fraying, shredding, and pinched stitches, for instance. Pick up bits and pieces of the kinds of material you'd like to experiment with, along with the classic reliable tapestry wools, and you can mess around a bit on the leftover canvas trimmed off the piece for your project. You'll then know what's good to work up and what you can abandon for the time being.

Bind the edges of the "messing-around" piece and have fun. Try each stitch. Put different yarns against one another. Discover the idiosyncrasies of each yarn. Figure out what yarn you want to use where and get a general picture of what you will use for your project. Work out your problems here.

Determine how much yarn you'll need for your piece by figuring it out on your messing-around hunk. Measure off one square inch on your M. A. (messing-around) canvas and fill it, in the desired stitch, with a <u>measured</u> length of yarn. See how much yarn it uses. Note it down for future reference. Each yarn covers differently, so a notebook listing the type of yarn, the stitch, and the mesh canvas will be of great assistance later. (It's also nice to have for noting design ideas, supply resources, and stitch diagrams.) Measure the length and breadth of the area you want to cover with that stitch and that yarn. It doesn't matter if it's an odd shape—you want a general figure. Take the measurements of the area and convert to square inches. Multiply that number by the length of the yarn used to cover one square inch. Convert this number to yardage and—blare of trumpets— you've got the amount of yarn you'll need for that area. Repeat this process for each area to be filled with different stitches and yarns. Now you don't have to over- or underestimate the stuff you'll need to finish your canvas. Your friendly neighbor hoop & yarn shop is always willing to help. Remember, though, better more than less material, for after all everyone makes mistakes and that loses yarn. Matching dye-lots is a pain. (Make sure <u>everything</u> is <u>colorfast</u>.)

I don't care to use a frame when I needlepoint. I like the feel of the canvas and I find stitching easier without one. Others feel more confident with a frame and say they can see progress better and understand what relationships are developing on their canvases with one. For very large

pieces a frame is necessary, as the weight of canvas and yarn can be difficult to manipulate. In either case, a square frame is perfectly adequate.
These are available in needlework-supply houses and can be very simple,
screw-together wooden slats or very beautiful, floor-standing jobs. You
can make one from four 2 1/2-to-3-foot-long trellis strips from a lumber
yard and four long screws with butterfly nuts. Drill six or eight holes
along either end of each slat about an inch or so apart. The drill bit should
be as big as the screws you'll be using. Staple the unfolded edges of a
folded piece of canvas duck along the edge of two slats (see below).

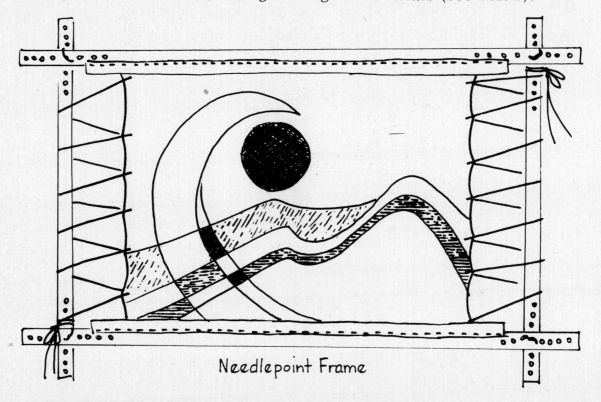

Needlepoint Frame

To mount the needlepoint canvas in the frame you'll need heavy thread
like that used for braided rugs, and a needle. With the edge of the needlepoint canvas slightly over the edge of the canvas stripping, centers matching, baste the two together with short running stitches. Place the screws
in the holes and tighten with the butterfly nuts. The number of holes in
each slat makes the frame adjustable for different size pieces. If the needlepoint canvas is much longer than the frame, then roll one end over one
of the slats and unroll later when you come to it. (The canvas can be longer
than the frame in only one direction so you can secure the piece in the
frame.)

Now you can stitch. There are many many stitches that have been developed for needlepoint. Because of the restrictions of needlepoint (i.e.,
the canvas must be completely covered, the warp and weft must be wrapped

with yarn, and the canvas mesh itself is angular) most of the "stitches" are simply classic patterns made up of very few actual stitches. Here I have included my favorites, which, as you can see, are very few. What is lacking in number is made up in versatility. I have added a few of the classic pattern stitches to show you that, if you examine them closely, they are just derivations of the few basics. So use your imagination and play with them. You may come up with a new "classic" needlepoint stitch or two of your own.

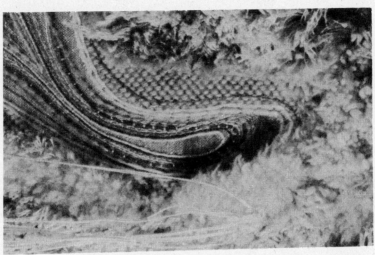

THE STITCHES

KNOTTING OFF/FINISHING OFF:

A.   From the front insert the needle into the canvas four or five mesh squares away from the point at which you will start stitching. Leave a tail hanging from the surface. Bring the needle to the front of the canvas. On the back of the canvas there should be a long "stitch" spanning the four or five meshes from the point of insertion to the point of the stitching (the broken line in the illustration, next page).

B.   As you stitch, cover over the long "stitch" on the back as you pass the needle through the canvas.

C.   When you reach the tail, clip it off very close to the canvas and continue stitching. This process should be done with each new length of yarn, and, though the Continental stitch is used as an example, the procedure is the same for all the stitches described here.

D.   To finish off, turn the canvas over and push the needle through four or five stitches on the back. Clip the yarn close to the stitches.

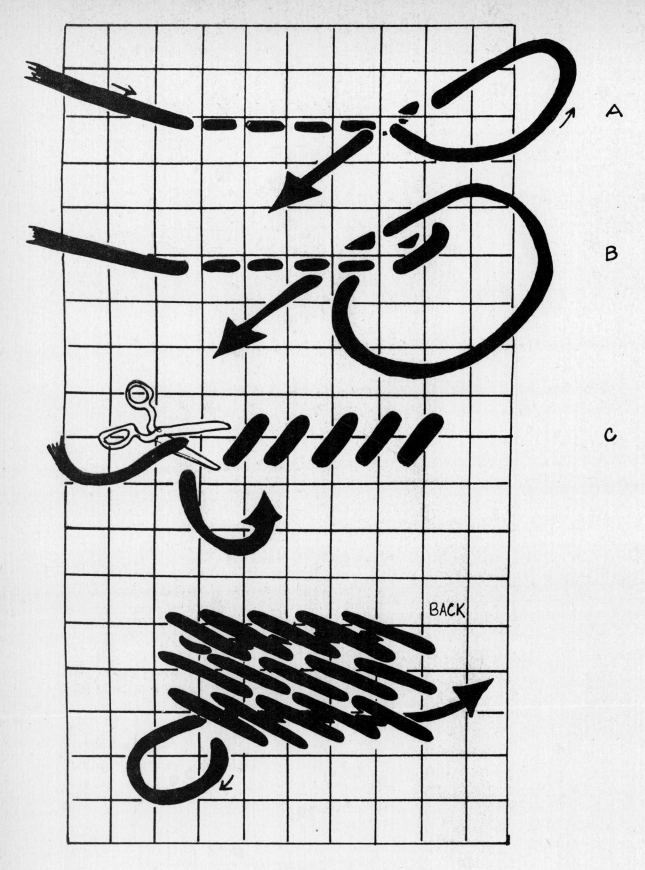

A

B

C

BACK

Knotting off/Finishing off

HALF CROSS: Turn the canvas around to work each new row (B). The raw end in (D) is finished off as in the previous illustration.

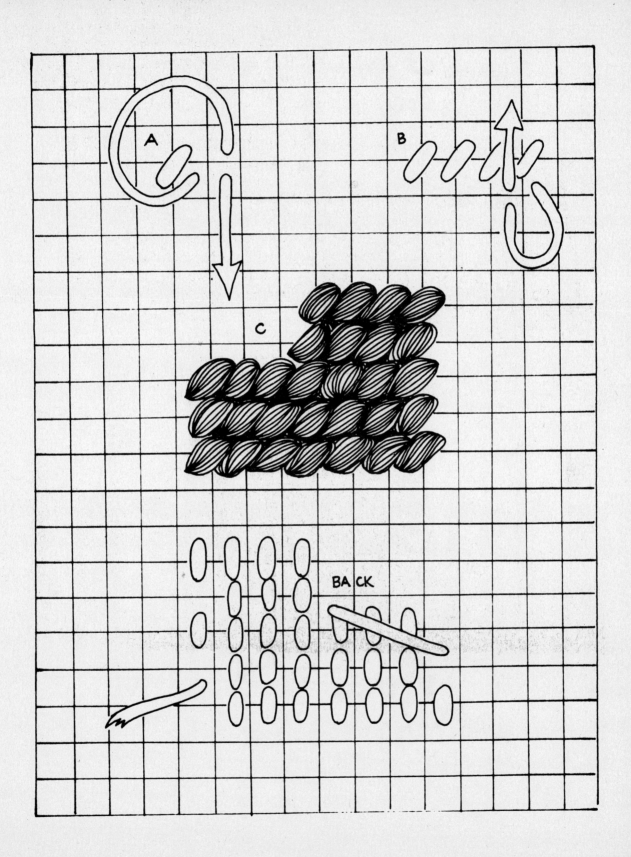

CONTINENTAL: This is the stitch usually associated with needlepoint. Again, turn the canvas around to work each new row, and finish off as shown on page 416.

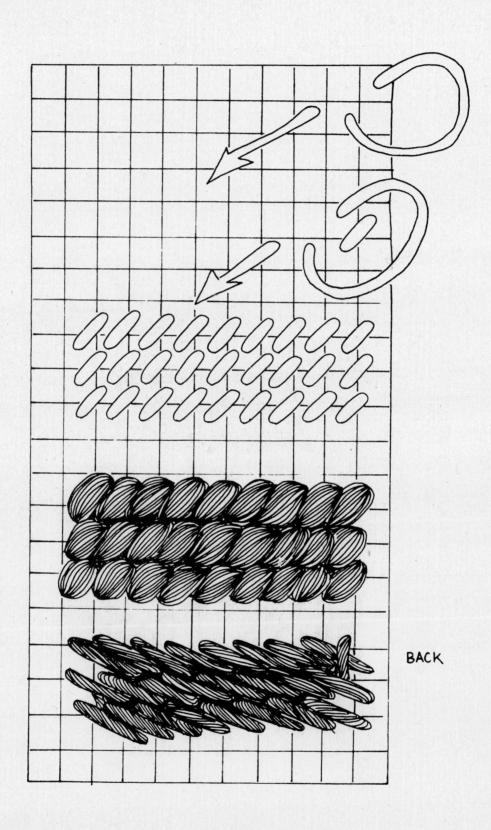

BACK

THE GOBELINS:

Basic Gobelin:

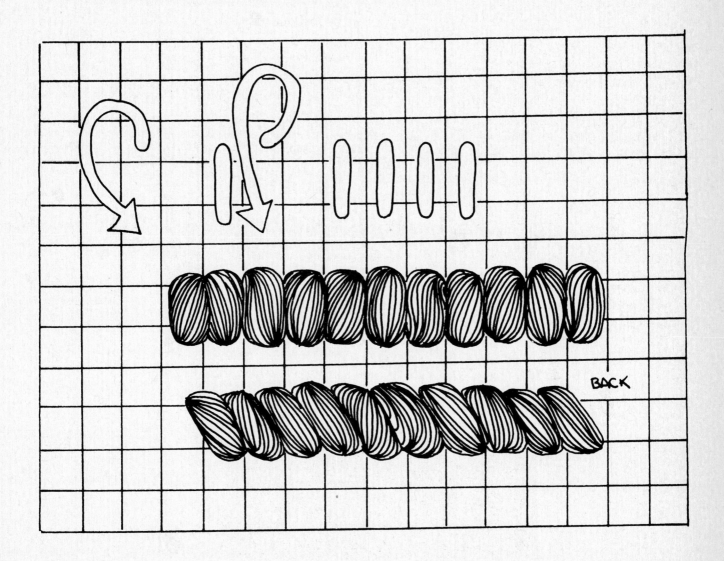

A Few Variations on Gobelin:

(A) is a stitch in its own right, and if you use it this way, work it as (C) and (D), but it's also the basis for (E). (B) is worked like basic Gobelin, only you skip every other mesh square. In (E) the rows cross over each other. As Gobelin is worked left to right, there is no need to turn the canvas over to start a new row in a different color. If you choose to use the same color throughout, you can turn the canvas over and reverse the direction of the stitch. Any empty spaces left at the edges are filled in with a smaller stitch running in the same direction as the stitches in the filled area.

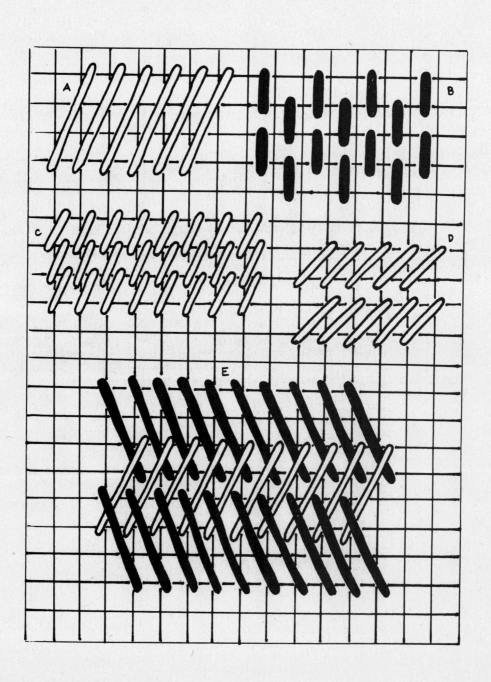

CROSS:

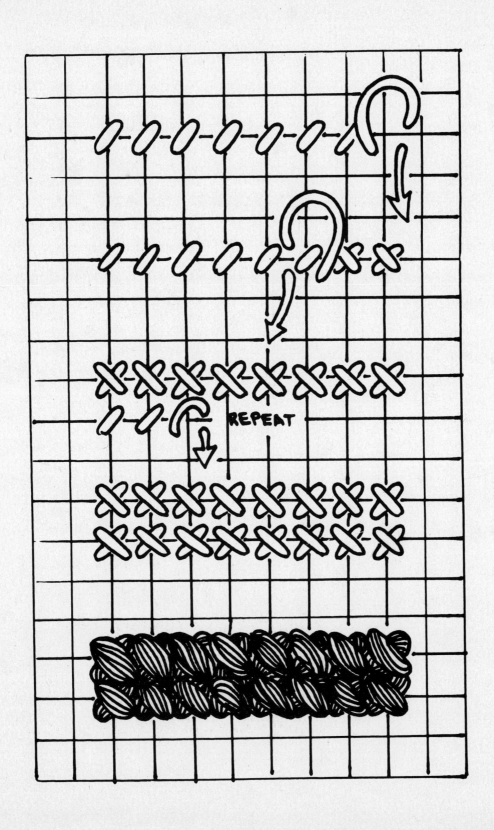

REPEAT

EYE: A really fine large filling stitch as a border or as an isolated stitch.

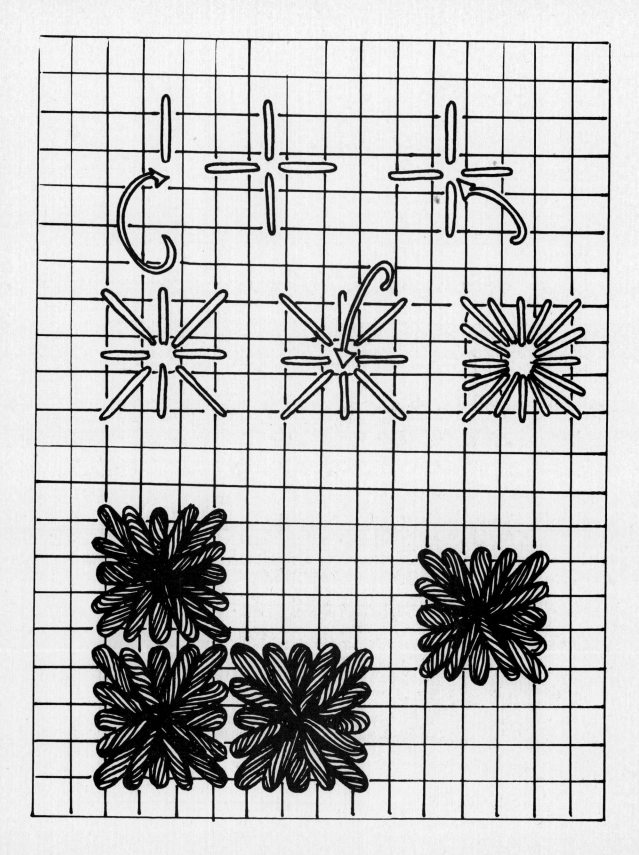

HERRINGBONE: The Herringbone stitch is one of my favorites for background and large-area filling. Each row must be done from left to right, and you should not turn the canvas around to do any of the rows.

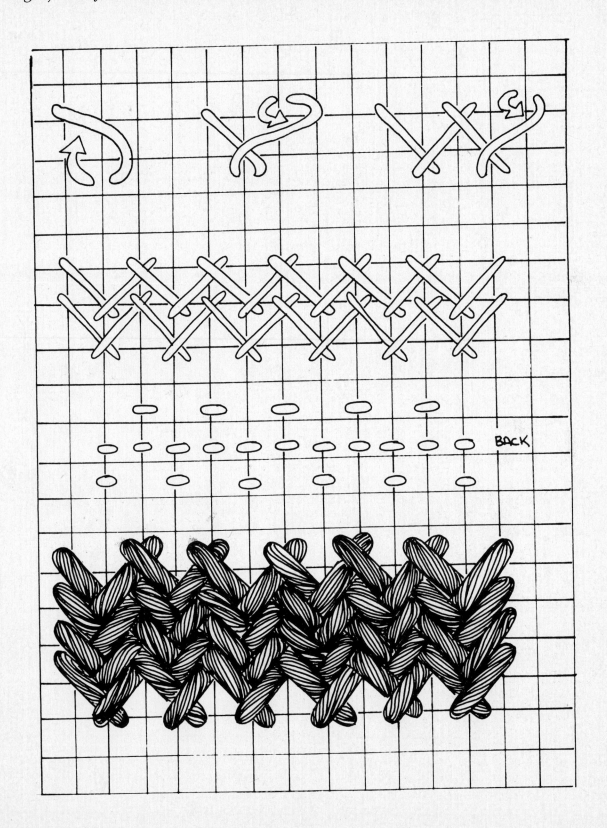

BACK

MOSAIC: Work this one diagonally. It's interesting done in strips—
every other row a new color.

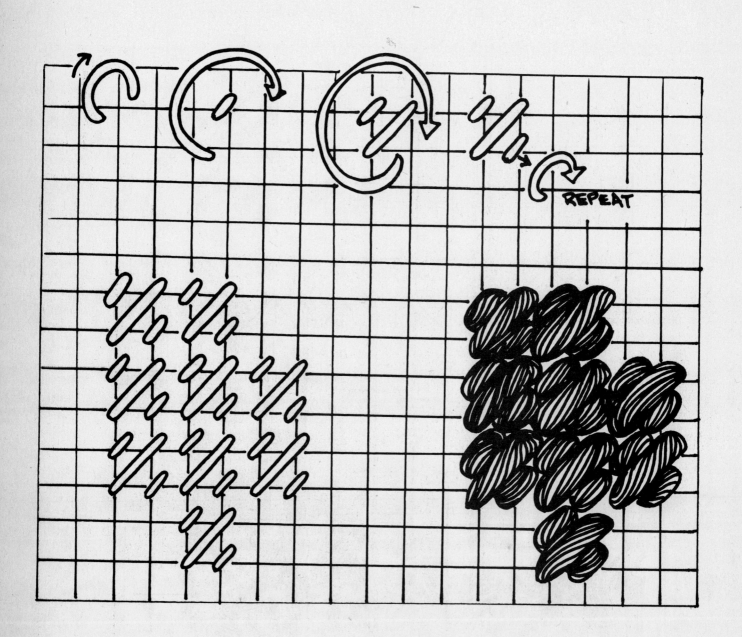

SHAG: To create a thick, ruglike pile, use a crochet hook and short lengths of yarn. Trim to the height desired.

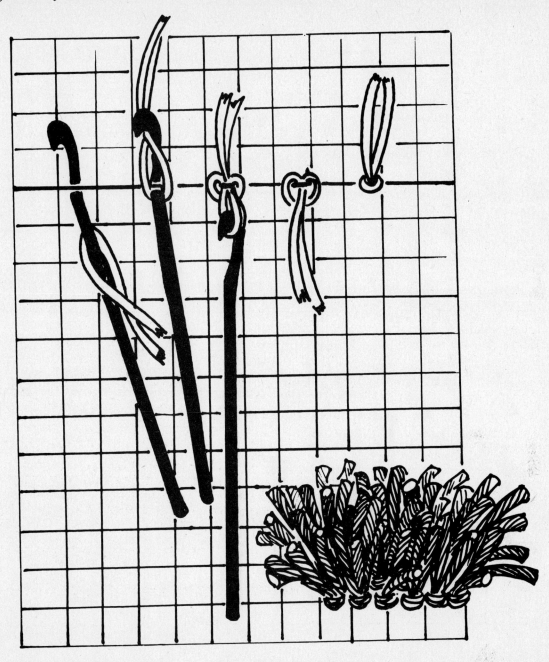

BARGELLO: If you are put down with the whole idea of making a pattern and all that, Bargello stitching is where it's at for you. Sometimes it's called Flame or Florentine stitching, and it works up into designs reminiscent of television interference patterns or an electroencephalogram (remember Dr. Casey?). The first set of stitches establishes the pattern, and you're off into a vibrating growth session: shades of one color growing from light to dark and the reverse, subtle tones of one color with a fantastic slash of shiny cord. Rainbows on jagged mountains. To get an idea of what it's about, play around with felt-tip markers on graph paper and you'll see what I mean.

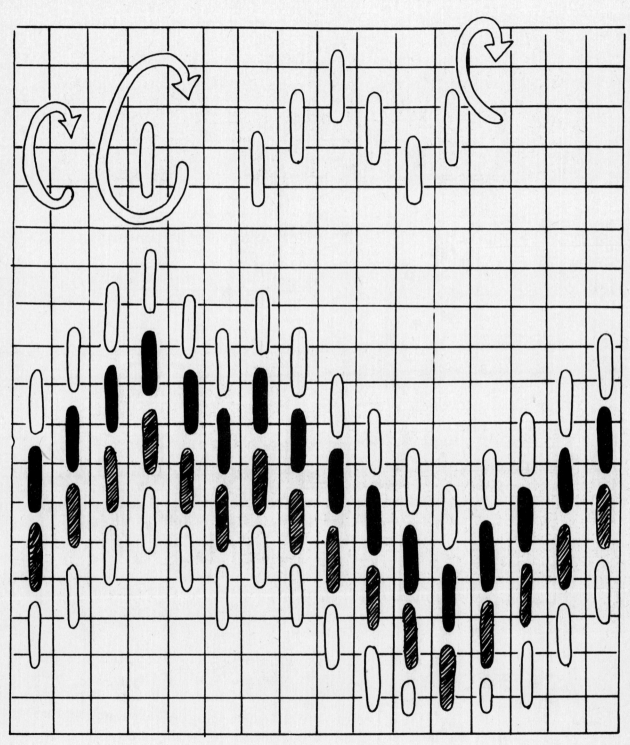

Bargello (stitches must be vertical)

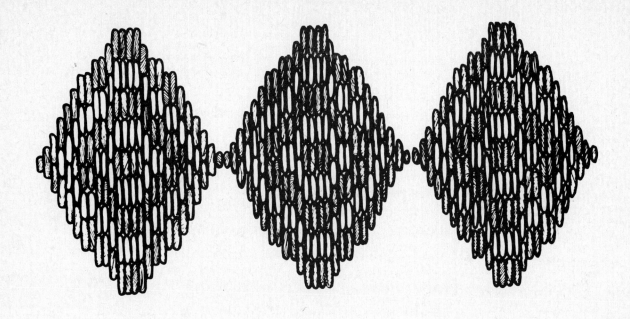

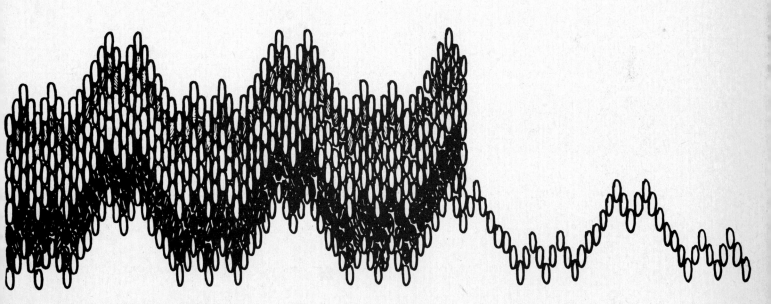

When you've stitched as far as you care to go, it's time to stop. Stop. Now you've got to finish it off. Zounds! You mean there's more? Blocking is the name of the game, and block we must. Your canvas is probably all lopsided and looking more rhomboid than square. This is the cure.

You'll need a sheet of plywood larger than your canvas, a few old sheets or smooth cloths to cover the board, some rustproof tacks, a pencil, a small light hammer, a pair of household pliers or canvas pliers, Woolite or Ivory soap flakes, a sheet of paper (butcher's paper or brown-wrapping), a right-angle, and a bucket or sink of cold water.

On the brown paper, mark the dimensions that your canvas should be with sides parallel and corners square. Fill your sink or bucket with cold water and swish up some thick suds with the Woolite or soap flakes. Sink your canvas into the bucket and slosh it up and down a couple of times. Rinse well in cold water—soap left on the surface will just attract dirt. Spread the sheets over the board and lay the marked paper over them. Place your canvas, face up, on the paper. It's wet. Match the edges to the penciled outline. With tacks and hammer, tack down one edge, following the penciled outline and stretching the canvas to fit if necessary. Move to the opposite side and, starting from the center of the canvas edge and the center of the pencil line, stretch and tack. You may need a friend to help pull the canvas with the pliers while you tack. Do this on all the sides. Make sure your corners are at right angles. Let the piece dry in place.

The easiest and most universal mounting technique is using canvas-stretcher strips. The strips (get them from an art-supply house) should be slightly smaller than the dimensions of the needlepointed surface. A row or two of stitching should be wrapped over the edges of the strips when you mount, so plan on this when you buy the strips. Once your piece is dry

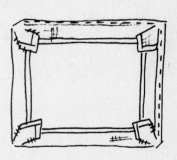

Mounting

(which may take a few days) remove it carefully from the plywood surface. With tacks, once again, tack one edge of the excess canvas down on the back of the stretcher strips. Then tack the opposite edge, starting from the center out. Do this again for the other two sides. Slip the mounted canvas into a frame and tape or glue brown paper on the back and hang it.

Fantasmagoric visions of tremendous needlepointed ceiling covers, door covers, slipcovers, toaster covers, dog covers, feet covers, book covers, box covers, wall covers, bag covers, birdcage covers, typewriter covers, window covers, body covers, belts, bands, boots, and banners pass through the mind in dizzying succession. Soft, plushy piles interspersed with tight textures. Maybe some beads or mirrors could be fun. Throw in a little embroidery, stitch on leather patches, or a dash of weaving here, a little knitting there. How about cutting some holes in the canvas and mounting another needlepoint, a painting, a mirror, some velvet (can you dig it), or just empty behind? String cords off the edge of the canvas of a needlepointed piece and macrame, or string some beads off them. Picture it done in natural shades. Do up a screen or wall hanging with open spaces to hang pieces of glass, pottery, metal, or bamboo that sound with the slightest breeze.

Need a new knapsack? Make a cover for it in rug wools and tapestry yarns and you'll have one that will last forever. Feels better than canvas to lay your head on and is a pleasure to lug. What about that old bicycle seat-cover? Museums and old historic residences are full of old needlepointed objects. Take a look at them if you can.

Really look at what you see. Do you like it? Interpret it as it strikes you. Get into it, enjoy it, rejoice in being able to see the colors, to feel the textures, to do the stitches. It's a gas to be here.

Got all that?

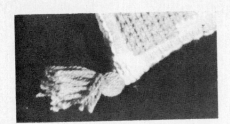

Fragments

Stained Glass

Howard Raab

Most people agree that stained glass is beautiful but inaccessible. The art itself has always been surrounded by an air of mystery, and many think it is about to die with the last of the "old master" stained-glass makers. The fact is that stained glass is very much alive, and a revival is taking place in the homes of individual craftsmen.

There are only three or four studios in New York City now that do church windows. Churches seldom commission work any more, and only occasionally is there a church that wants traditional stained-glass technique used for windows. The studios in the city are down to half their labor force and are half empty. When I go into one of these studios to buy glass for my work, the workers are always questioning me—"Are you busy?" or "Are you working?"—because they are anxious about their jobs. They know that stained glass is practically a dying industry. Today, the interest in this traditional form comes mostly from the individual, and this chapter shows how a person without previous experience and with little investment and a small space allotment can make stained-glass objects as beautiful as the imagination can envision.

I got into stained glass by being in the right place at the right time... A friend of mine loaned out his shop to someone who knew how to do stained glass in exchange for teaching him the craft. I happened to be there and I picked up on it. I only learned the basics then, and it took a good two years of meeting a lot of people who do stained glass to pick up more about it. A little bit here and there—and I eventually learned. I had only a few skills, like carpentry and making scale models for architects. I also took baby pictures for a year. That was fun, shooting 300 kids a week for department store promotions, but I was always living in hotels and traveling around. It was mass production, but fun.

433

After spending two and a half years on Madison Ave. in advertising design, I wanted to do something on my own. I thought that stained glass was the field with the least competition in it, and I thought I might make a living at it. At that time there was no one who did stained glass. Later I found out that not too many people buy it because the expense is high, due to the amount of time it takes in making a piece. I can't tell you that you'll make a living selling it. But it is a great thing for people to do for themselves in terms of personal reward. I teach stained glass, sell some pieces, and trade things I make to other craftsmen in exchange for their work. (Recently, I traded some stained glass for some dental work I had to have done.) And I give it away for presents.

I joined the Craftsman's Marketplace in the city and met a lot of good people there when I got into it. I was working with a girl at the time, and we did well selling to stores and doing craft fairs, but you have to do production work to make any real money from it. We wanted to leave the city and eventually move to Rochester to join a craft commune. I made up my mind to do the stained glass that I liked and not do production work. This girl is still doing production work, making money at it, but I think she has ended up not liking it.

The technique I want to discuss is that of copper and solder, or what some people call the "Tiffany" method. It is most suitable for today's artist/craftsman because of its extreme flexibility and tolerance for error. This method is easy to master and allows for more delicacy than the cumbersome and difficult lead techniques used in most church windows. With copper and solder, you can make beautiful and delicate objects such as small windows, lampshades, jewel boxes, jewelry, and anything else you can think of once you have learned of the possibilities and limitations of stained glass.

Occasionally I'm asked if it wouldn't be simpler to work in plastic. I think that plastic can be very beautiful and useful, but a good deal of it has been used to imitate other materials such as glass. As a result, people have become disconnected from glass and many times can't even tell the difference between it and plastic. The difference is, however, very great. The rich color and qualities of light of stained glass can never be matched by any synthetic, and even a little time spent with it will make this apparent. There are also more practical reasons for using glass that result from its extreme durability. It does not dull or scratch easily, is not affected by the heat of soldering, and has textures and surface qualities that are beautiful even when it isn't colored.

GLASS

Here are the two most popular and easily available kinds of glass to work with. (Look in your Yellow Pages under Glass Suppliers, and in the index at the end of the chapter for addresses.)

Commercial Sheet Glass: This glass is mass-produced in the U.S. and is distinguished by its regular surface texture and even color. Some types have been made that show some color variation, texture, and even bubbles, and these are quite nice. Commercial sheet is useful because it is inexpensive, and its unobtrusive qualities do not interfere with overall designs as more elaborate glass does.

Antique Glass: The beautiful color and handmade qualities of Antique make it very desirable, even though it is much more expensive than mass-produced glasses. The name Antique is used because the manufacturing method is very old, though the glass itself is still made at the present time. The process is very interesting. First the glass is blown into the shape of a large bottle (Fig. 1a). The ends are cut off leaving a cylinder, which is cut down the side (Fig. 1b). Then the cylinder is heated until it unrolls into a flat sheet (Fig. 1c). A certain type of Antique is called "flashed

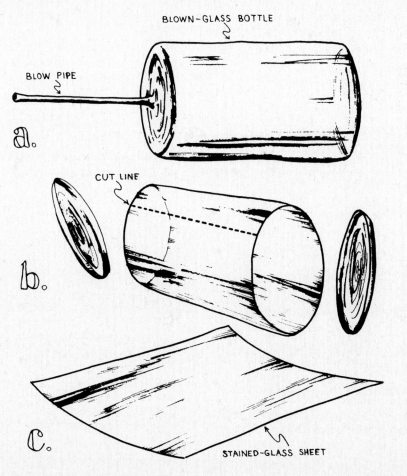

BLOWN-GLASS BOTTLE

BLOW PIPE

a.

CUT LINE

b.

c.

STAINED-GLASS SHEET

Fig. 1

glass." This is a light-colored or clear-base glass onto which a thin layer or "flash" of another color is added. It is used mostly for reds and oranges, which are very expensive, and some blues. To tell when glass is flashed, take a small piece and hold it up to the light. Looking into the edge, you can see the two layers of glass (Fig. 2). Antique is made mostly in Europe and by only one American company, but still all these kinds of glass are available.

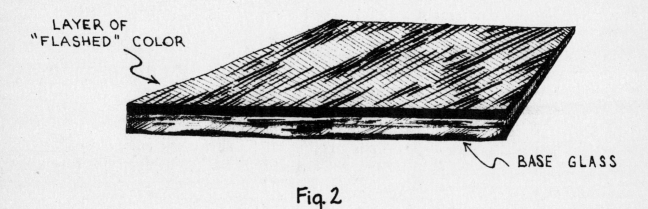

LAYER OF "FLASHED" COLOR

BASE GLASS

Fig. 2

For practice, you will want window glass. You can go to junk yards and get a whole lot of storm windows, or you can go to people who always save big pieces of glass that break in their house. It's better to practice cutting on old glass because it's brittle and harder to cut. New glass is so easy to cut you get fantastically overconfident, but if you want to use it you can go to the hardware store and get pieces that have been cut to order.

There is a lot of glass available, once you start to look for it. But it is difficult to find a variety, specifically of the opalescent glass. The increasing demand for it cannot be met unless the few small factories now producing it get new, expensive machinery. I run into places that are going out of business and get remnants of glass jewels and chandelier parts. Optical companies (listed in Yellow Pages) often have seconds on lenses.

TOOLS AND MATERIALS

Now that you know about glass, you should know about the things you use to cut and shape it. Again, see the index at the end, or try your local hardware store when you set out to buy.

Glass Cutters: There are all kinds of glass cutter on the market. I prefer the common, inexpensive, household glass cutter available at almost all hardware stores for under $1. It is thin, light, easy to use, and cheap to replace (Fig. 3). Diamond cutters are for plate glass and difficult to use on the irregular surfaces of stained glass. There is a tungsten carbide cutter, which is too hard for stained glass, and a cutter with a bunch of wheels that can be rotated, which I think is too big and clumsy but which you may like (Fig. 4). Another cutter, which I use for more delicate work, has a thick wooden handle and a smaller wheel than the common type (Fig. 5).

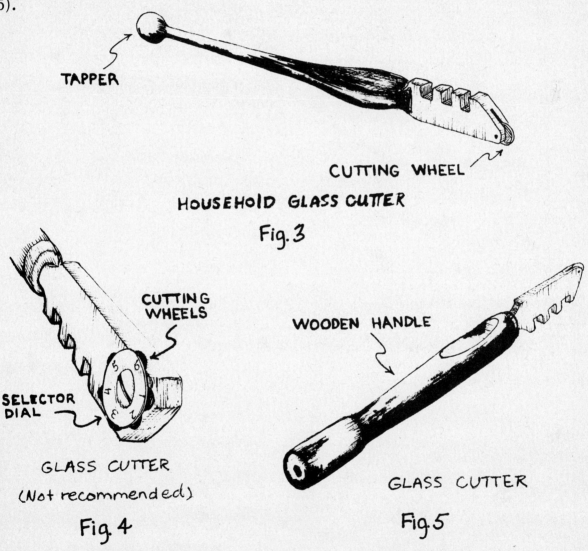

TAPPER

CUTTING WHEEL

HOUSEHOLD GLASS CUTTER

Fig. 3

CUTTING WHEELS

SELECTOR DIAL

GLASS CUTTER

(Not recommended)

Fig. 4

WOODEN HANDLE

GLASS CUTTER

Fig. 5

Glass cutters should be kept lubricated with light oil or kerosene and should be replaced when dull. I keep a little glass jar filled with oil mixed with kerosene. You can dip your cutter in while you're using it and also store your cutter in the jar.

Buy the cheapest cutters at the hardware store. They are the best. It takes experience to know when the cutter wears out, but this is something you will learn in time. So change cutters often.

<u>Glass Pliers or Plate Pliers</u>: These come in different sizes and shapes, but all work the same way. They are used to break pieces of glass that are too small to grip with the hands (Fig. 6).

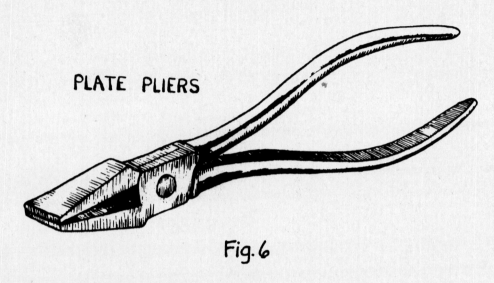

PLATE PLIERS

Fig. 6

<u>Grozing Pliers</u>: The grozer is another plier and is used to trim the edge of glass. It has flat insides and is made of soft, untempered steel (Fig. 7). (You can save money buying a regular pair of pliers instead, which some people find more versatile.)

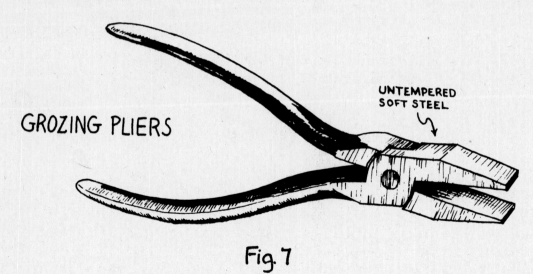

GROZING PLIERS

UNTEMPERED SOFT STEEL

Fig. 7

Hand Grindstone or File: Either of these can be used to clean up rough edges, which make the glass hard to handle. If you use a glass grinding machine, you should wear a dust mask. The glass will be almost powdered and you want to protect your lungs. Hand methods of grinding will not cause a powder and you won't have to worry.

Soldering Iron: This is a very important tool and here quality makes an especially big difference. It should be 80 watts or more, but not over 150 watts, with a fairly large tip. Tiny electrical irons are too slow for the large amount of soldering to be done on stained glass.

Copper Foil: The basis of the structure that will hold your finished piece together is copper foil. It is available as an adhesive tape in a few widths, the most common being 1/4-inch (Fig. 8). However, if you're buying in quantity, you can get a 6-inch-wide roll (not adhesive-backed); you pay for it by the pound, and save a lot.

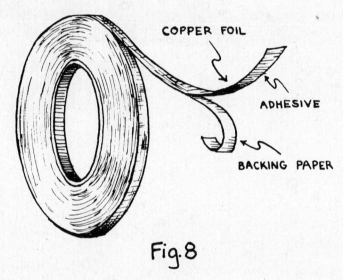

COPPER FOIL

ADHESIVE

BACKING PAPER

Fig. 8

Solder: A 60/40 grade, 1/8-inch solid-core solder seems to work best for stained glass. The grade means that 60 percent of the solder is tin and 40 percent is lead. Most household solder is 50/50 and does not flow as well as the 60/40.

Good ventilation is very important because of lead content when you're working with solder.

Solder Flux: In order to ensure a clean surface for the solder to adhere to, a flux must be used on the copper. Any plumber's flux will do; however, they are usually difficult to clean off and toxic. There is a soft solder flux available that washes off easily and is not as harmful to breathe. You can get it at Rainbow Studios in N.Y.C. Other places have it, too.

Patina: This chemical, when applied to solder, causes it to turn to a dark brownish color, as in old stained-glass shades. It is certainly not necessary, but I've found it to improve the look of most pieces.

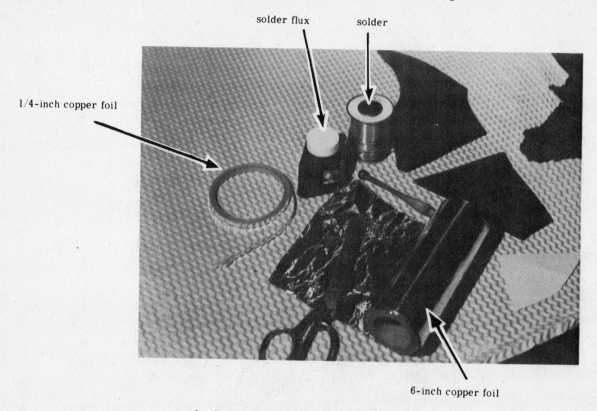

solder flux   solder

1/4-inch copper foil

6-inch copper foil

9. Some of the things you'll need

DESIGN AND TRANSFER

Some people who teach stained glass tell people to use ordinary children's coloring books for ideas of simple designing. This is all well and good as a last resort, and to absorb the idea of black lines breaking up areas. Then go home, start making line drawings of anything you like. Nature is full of material, and what you have to do is zero in on an aspect of it and develop it in pattern form. Tiffany was fond of using trees for his inspiration, and the Art Nouveau period is full of leaf patterns, vines, butterflies, and flowers over and over again. The human figure is also a good source to draw from. Arranging different shapes and putting them together in a stained-glass piece is always going to be easy, pleasing, and fun to do.

There are many ways to transfer your design to the glass for cutting. You can lay the glass over the design and trace on the glass with a grease pencil. This is pretty easy when you can see through the glass, but this is hardly ever the case.

Another method is to cut out the pattern pieces from a carbon copy of your original drawing and lay them on the glass. Then you trace around the pattern piece with the grease pencil or use the glass cutter directly, as is done in many professional studios, if you feel confident. The method I use most often involves a light-box. This is easy enough to make and is very useful in stained-glass work (Fig. 10). You lay the drawing on the light-box and the stained glass over the drawing. The light enables you to see the drawing and to trace it on your glass.

If you make a light-box, the glass top should be made out of 1/4-inch clear plate glass. Frosted glass is not really necessary because it cuts off a lot of light and the stained glass itself diffuses light. You want as much light as possible.

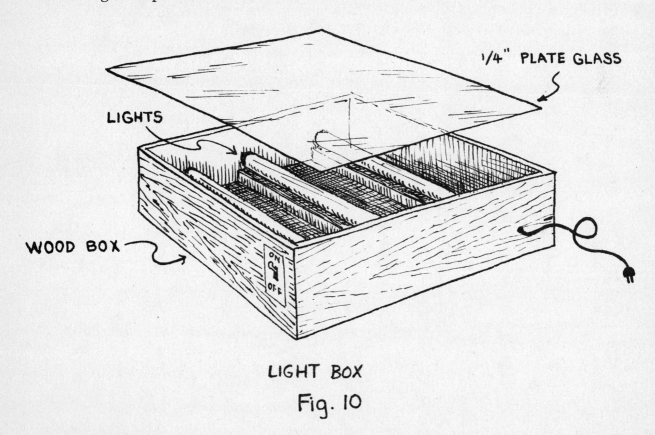

LIGHT BOX
Fig. 10

GLASS CUTTING

For a lot of people, cutting glass seems to be the most difficult part of the stained-glass operation to learn. With practice, however, cutting can become almost as easy as drawing.

I don't usually get cut working with glass. You get used to handling glass and learn to keep your fingers away from the edges. However, when

I go out to buy big pieces that I am not used to handling I invariably get some cuts. You <u>can</u> wear gloves, but I don't recommend this when you're actually working with glass, as they mask the sensitivity of your fingers.

When cutting, you should follow the inside of your pencil lines. This will make the piece slightly smaller than the design and automatically compensate for the space later taken up by the copper foil, which you will use after all the pieces are cut and trimmed to the proper size and shape.

Hold the cutter with the flat part between the thumb and index finger and the narrow part resting in the crotch between the index and middle fingers. Try to consider the tip of the cutter as an extension of the index finger. The cutting wheel should always be perpendicular to the glass and the handle tilted back toward you (Fig. 11). You can cut in any direction but it is easier to see what you are doing if you start away <u>from</u> and cut <u>towards</u> yourself.

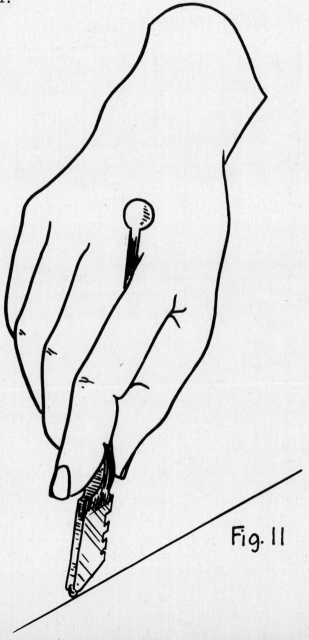

Fig. 11

Earlier I mentioned a glass cutter with a thick wooden handle and smaller wheel. This cutter is very difficult to hold in the manner just described and so I use a method that is a little unorthodox. I simply hold the cutter in my fist as one would hold a dagger (Fig. 12). This may seem a bit awkward and even childlike at first, but I've found that for small, delicate curves this method gives me more control. The small wheel makes turns easier, and the thick handle fits nicely in the fist.

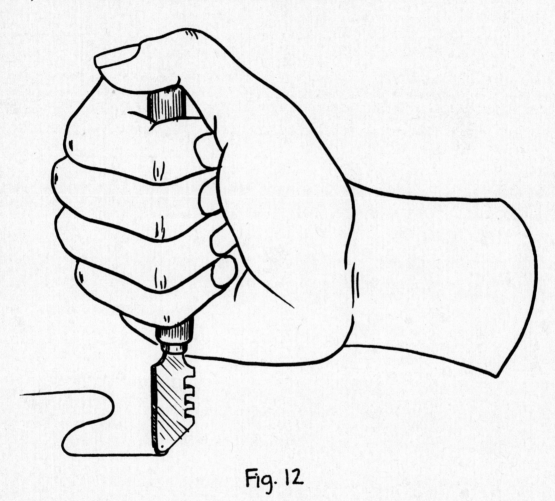

Fig. 12

Most stained glass is textured on one side and smooth and polished on the other. It is important to cut on the smooth side only. If both sides are smooth, it doesn't make much difference unless the glass is "flashed." Check carefully for flashed glass (see Fig. 2) and always cut the base glass. Glass cutting should always be done smoothly and continuously and never jerkily or unevenly. Pressure on the glass should be firm and constant from the beginning to the end of the cut. Some people tend to press with all their strength, which is not only unnecessary but results in a rough cutline and lots of broken glass. The scratch should be a thin, almost invisible line, and the moving cutter should sound like a soft whine, not like a

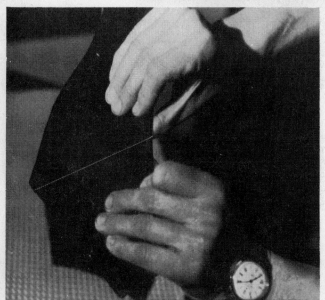

13. Scoring and breaking glass by hand

railroad train. NEVER GO OVER A CUT. That is the surest method of ruining a glass cutter and almost never improves the cut. If you feel the cut is not satisfactory, then make another one elsewhere or turn the glass over and try it on the other side directly under the first cut.

Now, get yourself a big pile of scrap window glass and cut like the devil. Try to control the cuts by following specific lines and patterns.

After making a cut, the object is to break the glass along the cut line. This, for many people, is accompanied by a good deal of nervousness.

After all, we have been taught the dangers of breaking glass since we were children. The best way to do it, in most cases, is to grip the glass on either side of the cut line and snap down and apart quickly and with confidence (Fig. 13). To overcome your fear of cutting and breaking glass, you simply have to do it over and over again.

Glass acts like a crystal. When you make a scratch in it you are causing a fault. When you put pressure against this fault, it cracks all the way through and the glass is cut through. If you wait too long to break the glass, the scratch will "heal" and the piece will not break right.

If one side of the cut is too small to get a good grip on, then you must use the plate pliers. Place the pliers on the small side of the glass with the front edge against the cut line and, holding the other side in your hand, snap down and away with the pliers (Fig. 14).

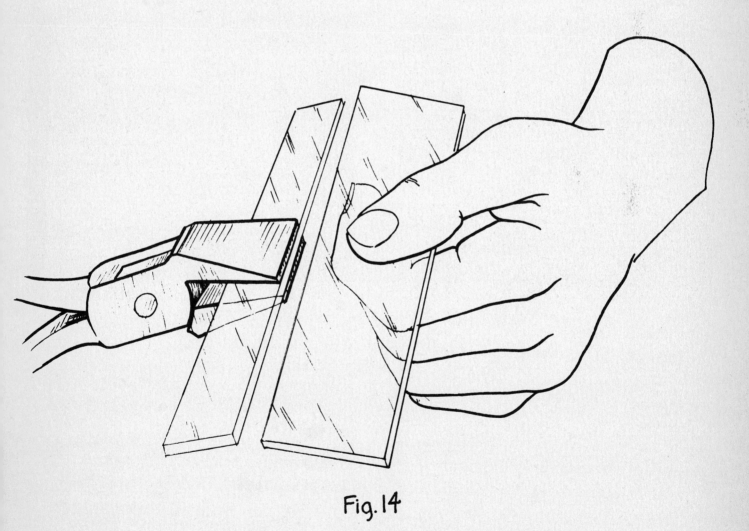

Fig. 14

When you are cutting curves, snapping the glass usually does not work very well. The cut line in these cases must be "tapped" in order to break the glass. This is done by using the top end of the cutter, which, in the case of the metal ones, is usually a ball shape. Never use the cutting wheel for this. By tapping the cut line accurately from <u>underneath</u> you will cause the crack to go all the way through the glass and the pieces to separate easily (Fig. 15). Whenever you are cutting a deep, inside curve, it is best to do it in stages. First, make a shallow-curve cut and tap it out. Then keep deepening the cut until it is where you want it (Fig. 16). For outside curves and circles you should also use multiple cuts (Fig. 17).

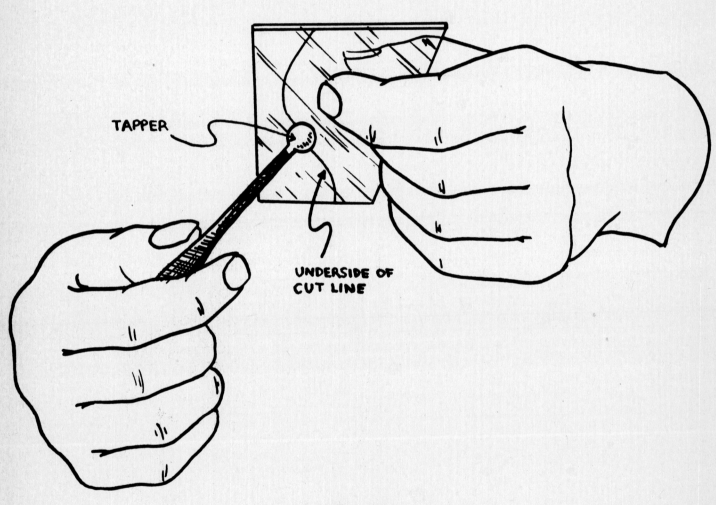

TAPPER

UNDERSIDE OF CUT LINE

Fig. 15

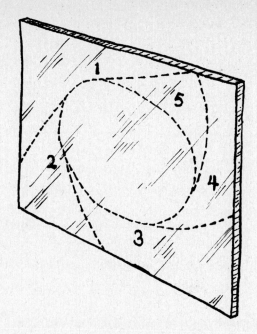

Fig.16

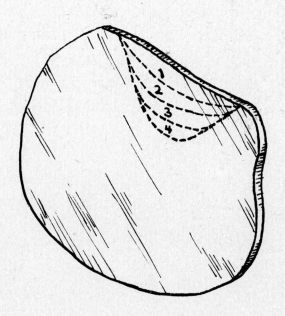

Fig.17

After you have cut a shape, you may find that it needs some adjustment or trimming to suit your design. For doing this, you will need the grozing pliers which are used to chip away the glass edge. With the tips of the pliers just pinch the very edge of the glass and it will chip off. Do this until the edge is adjusted. Then finish it with the grindstone or file. When you must trim a long straight edge, it is better to use the sides of the pliers as you would use a pair of scissors. With practice, you can alter the shape of a piece of glass very quickly and easily with this tool (Fig. 18).

Now that you have a large pile of broken glass pieces at your feet and it feels comfortable, you are ready to try cutting stained glass.

JOINING THE PIECES

Copper Foil: Using copper foil can be tricky, but dexterity will come with practice. First, peel off some of the foil from the backing paper and start it along one edge of a glass piece, holding it in place with the index finger. The foil should be centered on the edge of the glass. Then continue

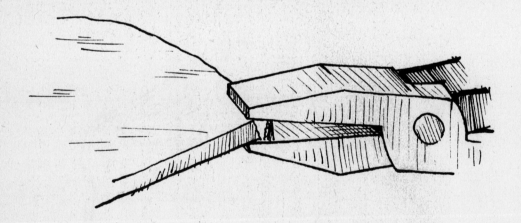

Fig 18

to wrap the foil around the entire piece, folding the overlap down over the sides of the glass as you go. When you reach where you've begun, overlap the foil about 1/4-inch (Fig. 19). You will eventually evolve your own way of doing this, but the result should be neat and uniform. Do this to all the pieces in your design and place them on the original design as you do them. This will keep you from losing track of where they belong. Remove the design before you begin soldering.

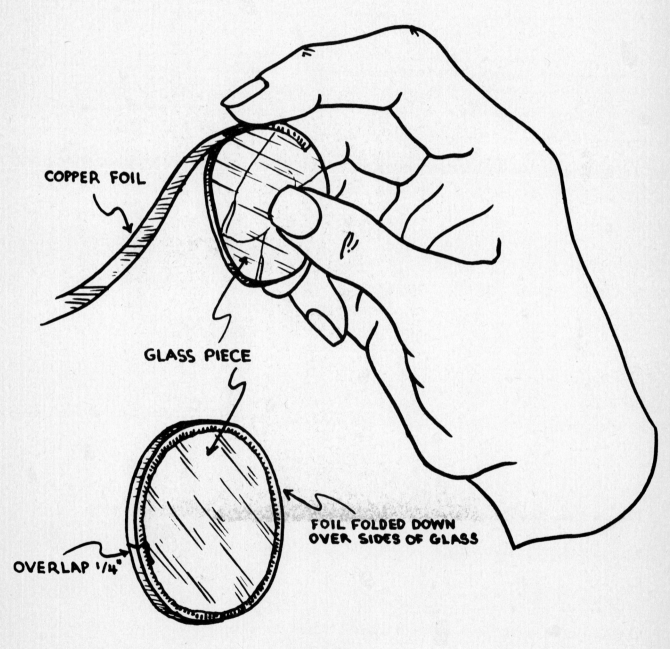

COPPER FOIL

GLASS PIECE

FOIL FOLDED DOWN OVER SIDES OF GLASS

OVERLAP 1/4"

Fig. 19

Soldering: Once the pieces are all wrapped and in place (lay them on any expendable surface—board or even paper), the next step is soldering. You get your soldering tool at a hardware store, and it comes with instructions—basically all you do is plug it in, wait for it to get hot, and then touch the solder with it. With an acid brush apply the flux to all the copper foil showing on the face of the design. Then tack the pieces together at one point where each piece touches another (Fig. 21). "Tacking" is soldering one drop at the joints to hold the pieces in place. Be careful not to move the work while it is being soldered. If this is difficult, then you can keep the pieces in place by putting pins or nails into the work surface around

20. Soldering

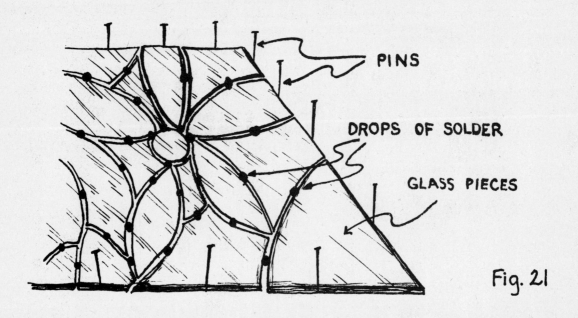

PINS

DROPS OF SOLDER

GLASS PIECES

Fig. 21

the glass (see drawing). Once the work has been tacked with solder, it may be moved around to make the final soldering easier.

Using a good deal of solder as you go, try to run a "bead" along all the copper joints until they are completely soldered together. A bead is a raised puddle of solder that covers the whole joint (Fig. 22). If there are any open spaces between the pieces of glass, they can be filled with solder if the gap is not too great. Once the first side is finished, carefully turn the work over and solder the other side. After the entire piece is soldered, it must be washed with soap, hot water, and a scrub brush. If the flux irritates your skin, try and find a thin, tight pair of rubber gloves. The flux will corrode the solder if left on.

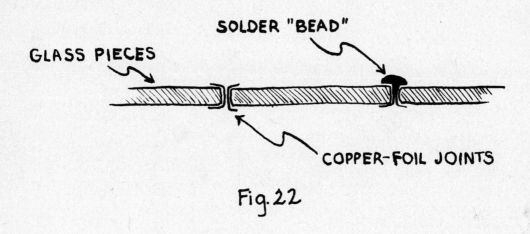

Fig. 22

You may now use the patina if you prefer. Using a stiff brush, such as an old toothbrush, apply the patina to all of the solder, rubbing it in well. Then, with a rag dipped in the patina, rub the solder until the color is satisfactory. You will find that the color is not very consistent but the over-all effect will usually be good. Let this sit for a while and then wash the piece again, because the patina will form a powder and look bad unless washed off. This time, use a soft sponge or your hands for washing. Steel wool or any abrasive cleaner will scratch or even remove the patina. Your piece is now finished and can be framed or simply hung from a wire loop soldered to a joint at the top.

THREE-DIMENSIONAL SHAPES

The process is similar for 3D-shaped objects, such as lampshades, boxes, sculptures, etc. A mold is very helpful, and many fire- and heat-proof things you find around the house can be used to form interesting shapes. For example, a Chinese wok would be just fine to form a lamp-shade. The pieces in the design must be small so that they can follow the curve of the mold easily. Otherwise, you must bend the glass, and that requires much different equipment and skills. Just build up the forms on the inside or outside of an object and solder the pieces together (Fig. 23). Be sure that you will be able to remove the piece from the object after it has been soldered on one side (don't use a basket with a handle, etc.). You will be amazed at how much strength the glass form has after it is completely soldered on both sides.

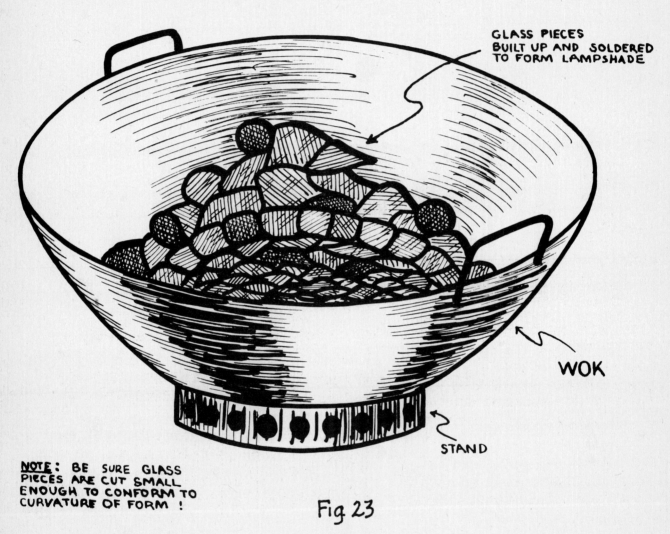

GLASS PIECES BUILT UP AND SOLDERED TO FORM LAMPSHADE

WOK

STAND

NOTE: BE SURE GLASS PIECES ARE CUT SMALL ENOUGH TO CONFORM TO CURVATURE OF FORM !

Fig 23

Glass boxes are simply six flat pieces joined into a box shape with one side hinged if it is to be opened. The hinge can be anything from a store-bought device to simple interlocking wire loops soldered in place (Fig. 24). The top of the box and edges of the lid are edged with copper foil and then soldered.

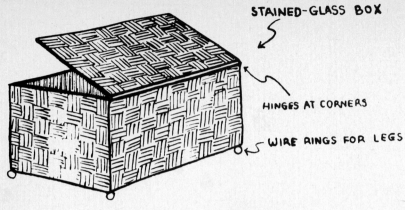

STAINED-GLASS BOX

HINGES AT CORNERS

WIRE RINGS FOR LEGS

HINGES

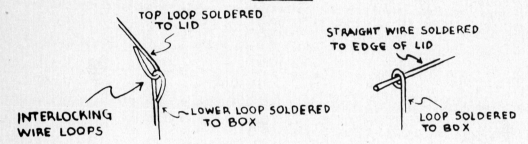

TOP LOOP SOLDERED TO LID

STRAIGHT WIRE SOLDERED TO EDGE OF LID

NOTE: BE CAREFUL NOT TO SOLDER THE WIRES TO EACH OTHER!

INTERLOCKING WIRE LOOPS

LOWER LOOP SOLDERED TO BOX

LOOP SOLDERED TO BOX

Fig. 24

Stained-glass objects can also be done in a freehand manner without using forms. By holding the pieces in place while soldering, you can build up amazing shapes, which can also be combined with other interesting materials. I have used marbles, wire, lenses, and many other things to add interest and texture to things I make.

Once you have mastered the cutting of stained glass and the use of copper foil and solder, the possibilities are endless. Sunlight is probably the best way to illuminate stained glass, but electric lights can also be very exciting.

I would like to do structures that you can sit in or picnic in ... environments where stained glass produces light against a background—town, country field or trees, or whatever. Even the biggest churches are stifling to a degree, because you are still between walls. I think that an outside structure lit by stained glass—where you wouldn't even look at the glass itself but at the light being shaped and colored by the glass—would be a very beautiful environment. That's my fantasy right now.

There are qualities glass has that are visual, and tactile, and maybe even spiritual. It responds like no other material and, once mastered, yields great freedom. I've written this chapter hoping that other people can learn to appreciate and make stained glass in order to further its revival and beautify our environment.

SUPPLIERS

Rainbow Studios, Inc.
97 South Broadway
Nyack, N.Y. 10960
- copper foil
- tools
- patina
- flux
Catalogue on request

S. A. Bendheim Co., Inc.
122 Hudson Street
New York, N.Y.
- glass

Glaziers Hardware Products
1689 First Ave.
New York, N.Y.
- tools

Westphal, Henry & Co., Inc.
4 East 32nd St.
New York, N.Y.
- tools

Whitemore-Durgin Glass Co.
Box 2065
Hanover, Mass. 02339
- everything by mail (ask for their catalogue)

Getting It in Print

PREPARING COPY AND ARTWORK FOR OFFSET PRINTING

Rick and Glory Brightfield

It's easy to sit around rapping about the kind of book or magazine you would like to do. The real thing is to <u>do it</u>. One night Glory and I got the idea for the <u>Woodstock Guide</u> and three weeks later it was printed and we were giving it out to friends. Some stores gave it away, some sold it at 20¢ apiece. We ran out of copies quickly. Glory was half way through her pregnancy, but she still did most of the frantic running around that was necessary to get all the information. While she was doing this, I pitched into the paste-up, and with the help of a couple of friends, one doing the typing (Annie) and the other checking on details (David), we moved fast. We, of course, already knew how to do it, but everything we needed to know is in this chapter.

Just don't get uptight with the relatively few hassles you have to go through. You want to know what you are doing, but learning to prepare artwork, photos, and mechanicals is an easy craft to master.

People have individual reasons for wanting to get their poetry, protests, stories, philosophies, politics, messages, drawings, and other raps out to the public and to friends. The printed page is a good way to spread the word about your individual or collective consciousness.

The form of the material when you give it to the printer determines the way it will look when it is printed. What you should give him is a set of "mechanicals." There are a number of things you can do while you're getting it in shape that will save time, money, headaches, and even battles. All of this we will try to lay on you in the hope that getting your thing printed will be an easy ride. There are, however, a lot of technical chores you will have to do. This is because the printers are pretty straight and not into improvisations, so you want everything as clear as a clenched fist.

Mechanicals are ruled-up pieces of illustration board on which the artwork (drawings, photographs, etc.) and type have been assembled in the position you want them to be in. This artwork and type are pasted (or stuck) onto the board with rubber cement, wax, or Scotch tape. For this reason they are sometimes known as "paste-ups and mechanicals," even though a paste-up and a mechanical are the same thing.

The first thing that should be done is to "rule up" the boards. This is done by drawing parallel and perpendicular lines describing the dimensions of the final printed product, be it a book, handbill, newsletter, or anything else. To do this, a drawing board or drafting table is needed.

An inexpensive pinewood drawing board can be purchased at almost any art store. The smallest practical size is 18 inches by 24 inches (and 3/4-

inch thick). This fits on almost any table or desk top and can be conveniently stored away when you are not using it. Since a slightly tilted surface is the easiest to work on when you are ruling up a board, it is a good idea to get a pair of doorstops (the rubber-tipped metal fastenings that keep doors from slamming against the wall) and screw them into two corners of the drawing board. The doorstops can be positioned so you can use the board horizontally or vertically, and they can easily be switched from time to time, depending on the shape of the mechanical you are ruling up.

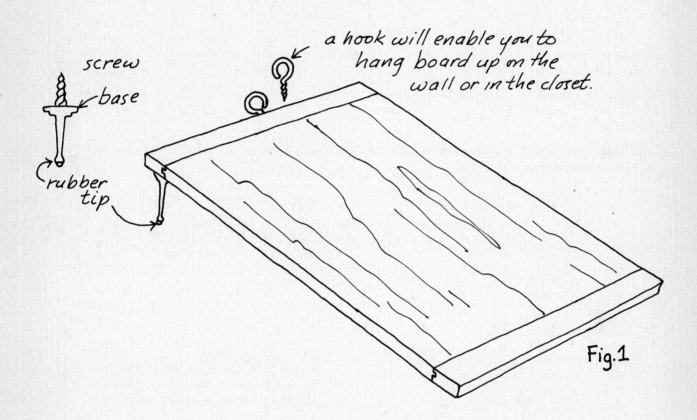

screw

base

rubber tip

a hook will enable you to hang board up on the wall or in the closet.

Fig. 1

Wooden drawing boards usually have a fairly straight edge on one of the sides of the board. Pick this side for the working side. You can test this (in the store) when you buy the board by sighting down the edge. Hold the board up to your eye as shown in my diagram. If the board has warped at the factory or the store, you will see a slight rise or depression in the surface of the edge.

More expensive drawing boards have a permanent metal edge built into a side of the board. This is usually very straight (but test it anyway).

If you already have a board and the edge is not straight, you can buy a "straight-edge." This is a metal strip with clamps that fasten it to the board.

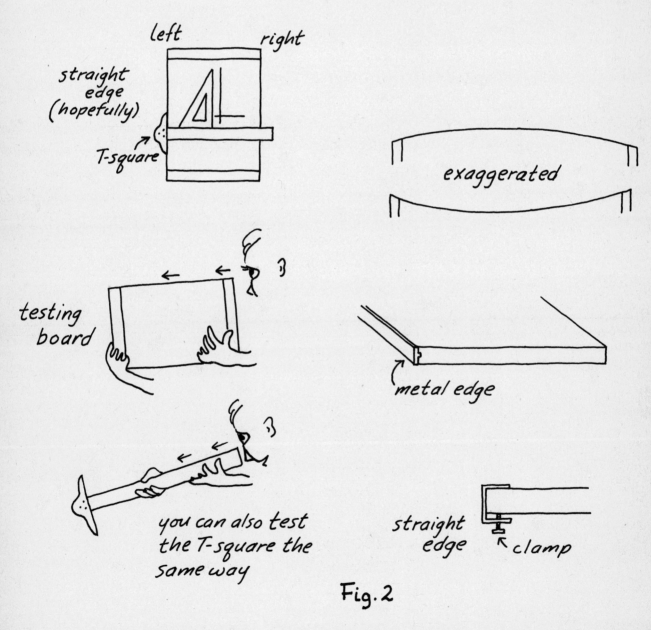

Fig. 2

When you set up your board at home, you should test it again to make doubly sure that a line drawn with the T-square at the top will be parallel with a line drawn at the bottom. If the distance A is different from the distance B by less than 1/16-inch, you're all right (unless you're an absolute perfectionist).

Other basic materials you will need are one 30°/60°/90° right-angle triangle (preferably one measuring 12" x 6-7/8" x 13-3/4") and a T-square (one having a working edge of at least 18 inches). The T-square and the triangle work together to give you parallel and perpendicular lines (and, of course, right-angle corners).

testing board edge II

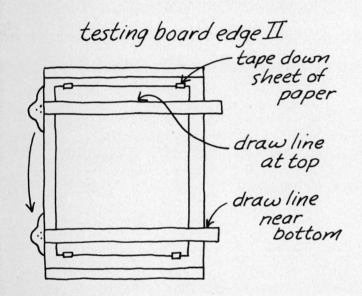

tape down sheet of paper

draw line at top

draw line near bottom

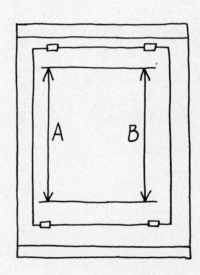

distance A should equal distance B

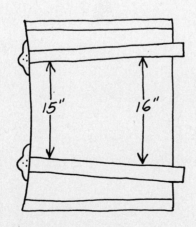

Fig. 3

if this happens get a straight edge. If you are using a straight edge— get a new one

There are inexpensive T-squares of wood or plastic that are completely satisfactory. There are also stainless-steel T-squares, which are (over a period of time) worth the extra investment. The latter usually have a minimum working edge of 24 inches, which is a convenient size for working on an 18- by-24-inch raised drawing board.

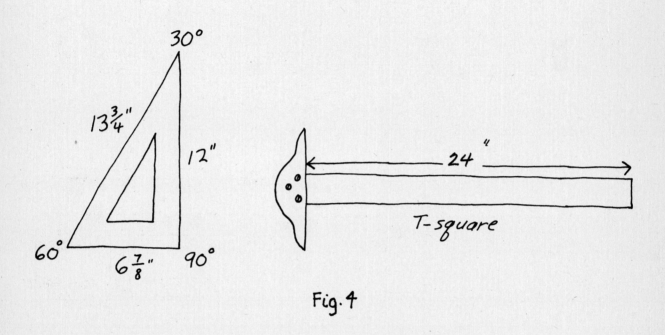

Fig. 4

You will need a bottle (or can) of rubber cement. The smaller sizes usually come with a brush already attached to the top. Also, get a rubber-cement pick-up. This is a small square of rubber that cleans up (like an eraser) excess rubber cement as it dries. There are a few other small things that you will need, like single-edge razor blades, pencils, etc., and these are listed below.

Last, but not least, you will need a supply of illustration board. Start out with a dozen or so 15- by 20-inch sheets of lightweight, "one-sided" (gray back) illustration board. Illustration board comes either "cold-press" or "hot-press." If you are going to do just paste-up, the cold-press is better because it has a tougher surface. It is also slightly rough in texture. If you are going to do a lot of drawing or illustration directly on the board, get the hot-press, as it has a smooth surface and therefore takes ink and other media more smoothly.

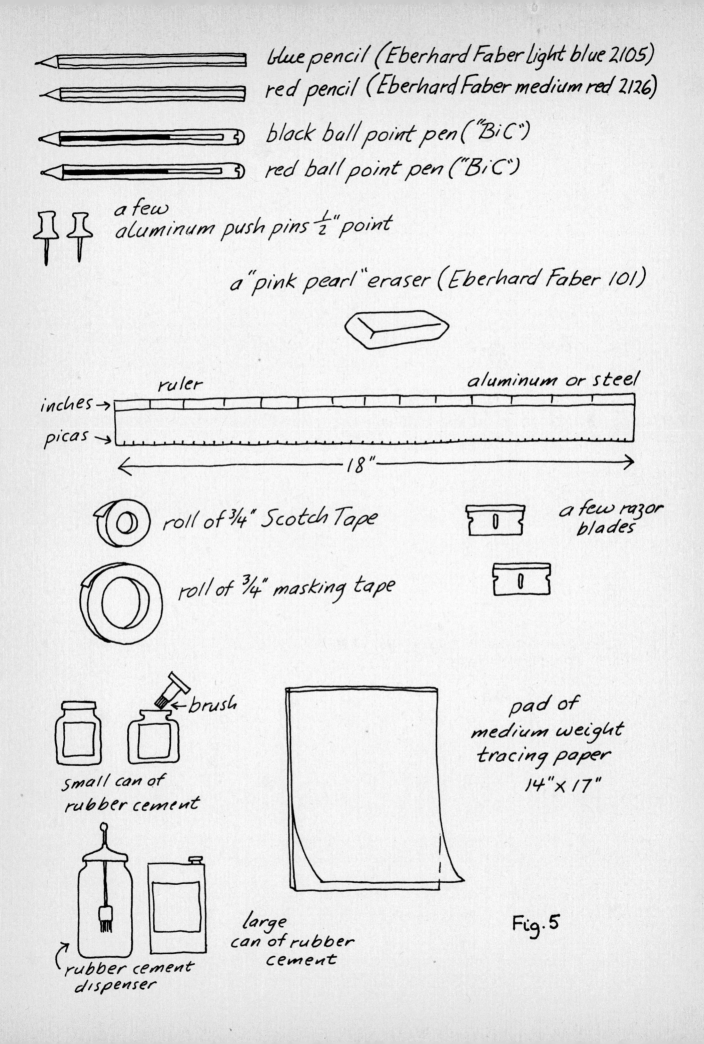

blue pencil (Eberhard Faber light blue 2105)

red pencil (Eberhard Faber medium red 2126)

black ball point pen ("BiC")

red ball point pen ("BiC")

a few
aluminum push pins $\frac{1}{2}$" point

a "pink pearl" eraser (Eberhard Faber 101)

ruler   aluminum or steel

inches →

picas →

←————————— 18" —————————→

roll of ¾" Scotch Tape

a few razor blades

roll of ¾" masking tape

brush

small can of
rubber cement

pad of
medium weight
tracing paper
14" x 17"

large
can of rubber
cement

rubber cement
dispenser

Fig. 5

So far we have:

drawing board	$ 6.00	
doorstops	$ 1.00	
triangle	$ 1.50	
T-square	$ 3.00	
pencils	$ .60	
ballpoint pens	$ 1.00	
ruler (18-inch, aluminum or steel)	$ 2.00	
Scotch tape (3/4-inch-wide, small roll)	$ 1.00	
masking tape (3/4-inch-wide, small roll)	$ 1.00	
tracing paper (lightweight, 14-by-17-inch pad)	$ 2.50	
illustration board	$ 5.00	(dozen or so sheets 15 by 20 inches)
razor blades	$ .15	(5 at 3¢ each)
rubber cement (medium can)	$ .80	
rubber-cement pick-up	$ .25	
and a frisket knife (more about this later)	$ .50	

Total: .... $26.30 (approx.)

This is all the basic equipment you will need. With this you can prepare almost any mechanicals.

If you want to do paste-up on a professional basis, then there are a few more things that you may need, and you may want professional quality in a few items (like the T-square, which can cost up to $15). A hand waxer (which will be described later) is also a good thing to have, but it is somewhat expensive (around $25). Don't worry about these other things now, as you will not need them to start out.

Every job that you do will probably involve some small individual expenses. You may need to buy Artype (which will be discussed) to do the headings. Special pens or brushes may be needed to do an illustration. However, over a period of time you will build up a collection of these things so that, as each new job comes up, you will probably have enough of a lot of things left over from a previous job to make do.

A PERSONAL TOUCH [STATIONERY]

Granted your own stationery isn't the most revolutionary graphic project, but it's an easy one, and since it's personal, you're at liberty to do anything. The printer doesn't care what you do, as long as you square up your board.

1. Cut one of your illustration boards in half (to 10 by 15 inches), using a razor blade and the aluminum ruler as a cutting edge.

2. Tape the illustration board down to the drawing board with a piece of masking tape on opposite sides of the board, or (if you can find a couple) tack it down with two push-pins at the top.

3. Determine the center point and draw a <u>very</u> light, vertical blue line with the triangle (and the T-square).

4. Measure 4 1/4 inches on both sides of the center line and draw two more vertical lines through them.

5. Draw a base (horizontal) line near the bottom of the board (using the T-square).

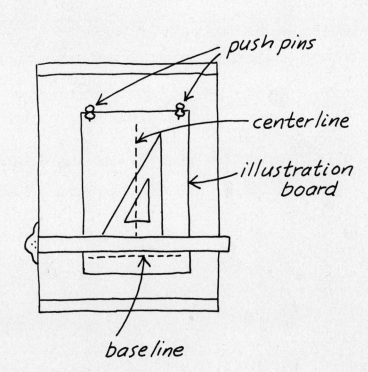

Fig. 6

6. Measure 11 inches up from the base line and draw another horizontal line.

7. Now draw a slightly heavier blue line along the rectangle you have created.

8. All we have to do now is to put "crop marks" at the corners. These should be in black about 1/2-inch long and 1/8-inch from the rectangle. These indicate to the printer that the final job should be trimmed to exactly this size (8 1/2 by 11 inches).

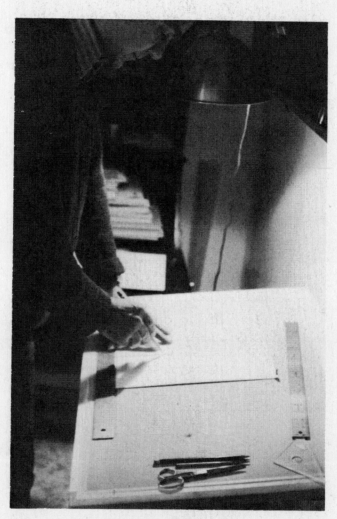

Fig. 7 Marking the center line

The reason for the blue lines is that blue does not show up when the artwork is copied photographically in the process of making printing plates. If, for some far-out reason, your artwork is in blue, the printer can put special filters on his plate camera to pick it up, but under ordinary conditions no blue lines will print. This is why the black crop marks are so important. Otherwise, all the dimensions marked on the mechanical would be lost when it is photographed. Red will also photograph like black. But this color is usually reserved for making "holding lines" (which we will go

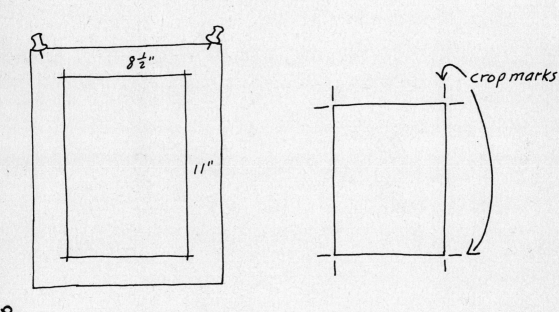

Fig.8

into later). Usually, any black lines within the "live" area of the delineated rectangle will be printed.

Now, since you are doing your own stationery, find some lettering and paste it down. Let's say you have one copy of your old stationery left and you want to get some more printed: you then cut out the type (if it is in red or black) and paste it down in the same position as the original on the new mechanical.

Cut the old lettering out of the stationery. Smear a layer of rubber cement on the board where you want to paste the lettering. Lay the lettering down on top of the glue and line it up (horizontally) with the T-square. When the glue has dried, clean up the excess around the lettering with your pick-up.

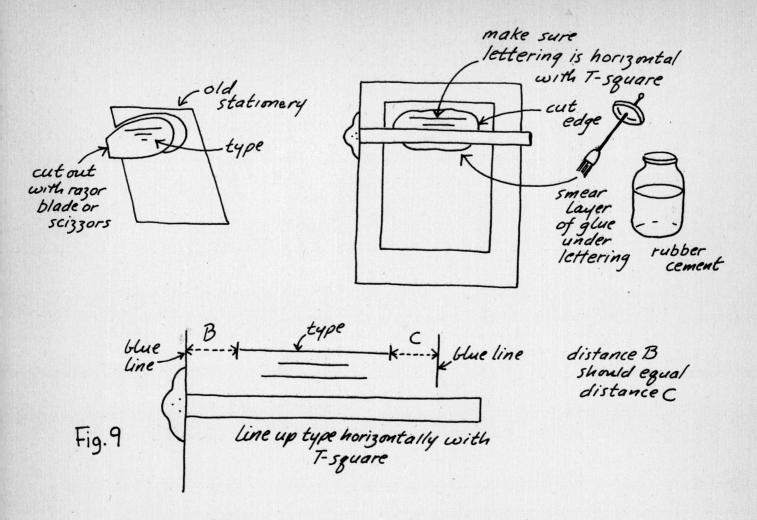

Fig. 9

distance B should equal distance C

Line up type horizontally with T-square

Use a strip of masking tape to attach a sheet of tracing paper over the lettering to protect it. The finished mechanical should look like this:

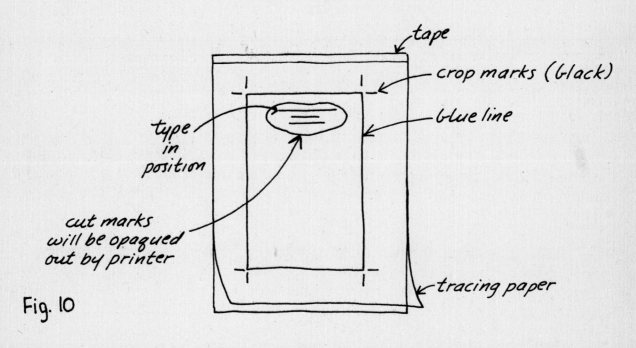

Fig. 10

This is about all there is to it. This is called a "ready-for-camera" mechanical. It is the kind that printers want to get and it is also the cheapest to get printed.

If you can do <u>this</u> mechanical, you can do <u>any</u> mechanical. Is it really that easy? Well, almost. As someone has said, "You can learn to do a mechanical in an hour, but it takes longer to master the finer points of paste-up." But don't worry about that. If you are going to make your living doing paste-ups, then you can worry about it.

The art of ruling up the mechanical boards and positioning the type and illustrations is the basic craft of preparing copy and artwork for printing. Type, illustrations, etc., will only be printed as well as they are assembled on your boards.

HEADINGS, COPY, AND ILLUSTRATIONS

Most books, brochures, handbills, or posters, etc., contain these three elements. Each element poses its own problems, and then there is the problem of putting them together in a layout so that they will relate properly to each other.

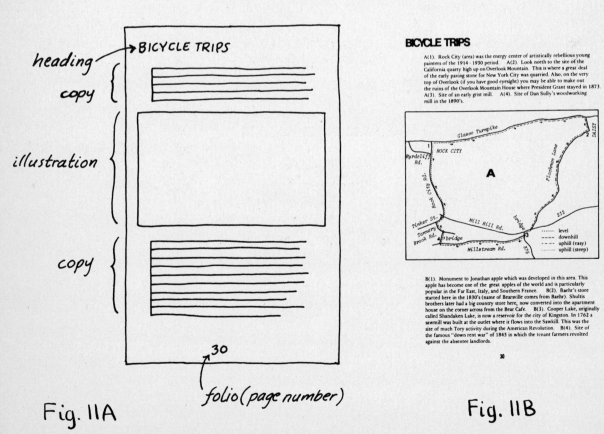

sample from "WOODSTOCK GUIDE"

Fig. 11A   Fig. 11B

The simplest method of producing headings is by hand lettering. This can range all the way from calligraphy, which is done with a flat lettering pen and takes considerable skill and love, to block lettering, which can be done casually with a great deal of freedom and spontaneity.

Block lettering should be done with a good solid black pencil. L.&C. Hardmuth Black 350 No. 2 is a very good and very black pencil; also, a

Fig. 12 Calligraphy

black Pentel marker can be used effectively. Be careful not to smear hand lettering with your fingers. For added protection it can be sprayed with a fixative like Krylon.

I am assuming that you are limited as to the amount of money you can spend on any one project. Therefore, you do not want to have "foundry" type set by a commercial typographer. You should, however, know what it is. Foundry typesetting is the traditional process of setting movable type and running a proof of the type on a proof press. This process produces excellent "repros" (short for reproduction proofs of type) that can be easily pasted up. Unfortunately, this kind of heading is very expensive to have set.

You don't have to use foundry type headings because there are several methods of producing headings using sheets of letters that can be cut out and then stuck down, or made to transfer onto a sheet of paper or other surface to produce headings. This takes patience but it can be easily learned.

Woodstock Crafts ← *calligraphy*

WOODSTOCK

WOODSTOCK

Woodstock

} hand lettering

← surface of type
inked and pressed into
paper to produce a print of
the letter

frisket knife (approx. exact size)

mailing labels
(especially "AVERY"
self adhesive unprinted
labels, 200 labels 2"x 4"
$2.¹⁵ no. 5-6432)

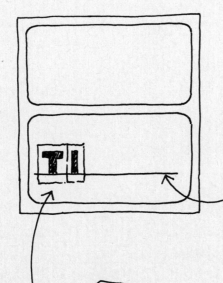

score a line with
the point of frisket
knife

Fig. 13

The two main types are Artype (a brand itself) and transfer type. Letra-set and Instantype are two popular brand names of transfer type that are readily available in most big art stores.

One of the best tools to use for both Artype and transfer type is a small "frisket knife." These are usually used for cutting stencils and are very cheap. Frisket knives are razor-sharp when you buy them. For the purposes of moving Artype around or transferring transfer type, these frisket knives should be dulled down by rubbing the sharp edge against a piece of sandpaper until the edge can be rubbed against the palm in safety (don't use your palm to test the blade as you are dulling it).

A good trick is to stick the Artype letters down on a self-stick mailing label. These can be purchased at stationery stores and are used for ad-dressing packages on a typewriter. They are stuck onto the packages after peeling off a paper backing. Cut out each letter from the Artype sheet with a razor blade and carry it with the frisket knife to the label. Be careful not to cut through the backing of the Artype sheet as this will make holes in the sheet, making it difficult to handle.

Score a line on the surface of the label against your ruler with the back of the point of the frisket knife. Use this to line up the letters. Ignore the guide line below the letters put on by the manufacturer as it is not accurate enough. Also, tape the label down to your drawing board and check the horizontal and vertical lineup of each letter.

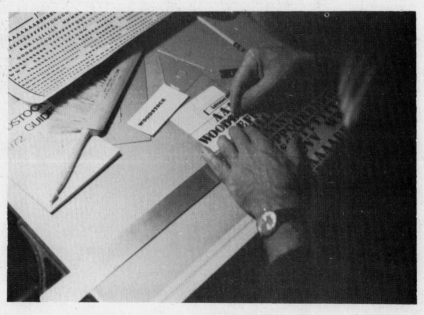

Fig. 14 Working with transfer type

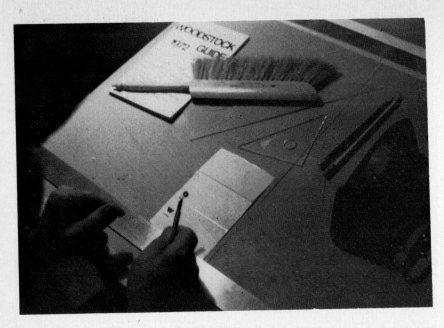

Fig. 15 Cutting out Artype and sticking it on a mailing label

When doing both Artype lettering and transfer lettering be careful about letter spacing. You should always be conscious of the equivalent spaces between each letter. Take the word THE; here the T and the H have to be close to each other while the E is placed a bit away from the H to preserve the equivalent spaces between the letters.

The hardest letters to cope with are A, T, and L. The combination of L and A is very tricky, since it is hard to make up the equivalent space in the rest of the word unless you exaggerate the space between the other letters.

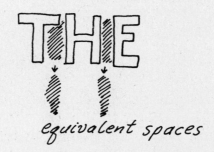

equivalent spaces

good→ LAKE

bad→ LAKE

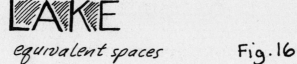

equivalent spaces   Fig. 16

This will take some practice, but if you keep yourself (at first) constantly conscious of letter spacing, you will eventually do good letter spacing unconsciously.

For word spacing, use about two-thirds the space of a full character (letter).

NOTE: The advantage of having your Artype lettering on self-stick labels will become apparent when you come to do your layout on the mechanical board. If you try to paste down Artype on paper with rubber cement, the solvent in the cement will come through the paper and dissolve the sticky backing of the Artype, and all the Artype letters will move or, sometimes, just fall off. With the self-stick label you can just stick the type down where you want it without the hassles engendered by trying to glue it.

Transfer type does not seem to transfer to mailing labels too well. Transfer type is very fickle about what kind of surface it wants to transfer to. You may have to try a few different kinds of white paper before you find a good surface to use.

To line up transfer type, draw a <u>thin</u> blue line on your paper. Put the letter directly over the blue line (and lined up carefully on the bottom). Then rub down <u>gently</u> with the <u>flat</u> side of the frisket knife blade until the undersurface of the transparent sheet adheres to the surface you're transferring to. Then press firmly down with the <u>flat</u> part of the blade. With practice you can tell by the slight change in tone when the letter has transferred. Then carefully pull off the sheet. Don't press with any kind of pointed or rounded tool, as it will cause the letter to crack or even go to pieces when you pull off the sheet. Besides being a lot of fun once you get the hang of it, transfer type is probably the quickest and most efficient way of producing type headings.

edge of transparent sheet

Line up letter to be transferred

using flat part of knife, rub down over whole area

rub letter until it transfers

pull up sheet carefully

Fig. 17

After being transferred, the surface of the letter is very delicate and can be easily damaged even by gently touching it with your hand. To protect the lettering after you have set the whole word or the whole heading, you can cover it carefully with a strip of transparent Scotch tape.

After you put the tape on the lettering, burnish it down with the flat side of your frisket knife. This makes the lettering fairly permanent. The only caution is that in very cold weather you cannot let the lettering covered with Scotch tape go below freezing as the tape will shrink and crack the letters.

In Figure 11B, the headings were done with transfer type and then covered with Scotch tape. This particular type was "packed," that is, put down so that each (or almost every) letter touches the letter before it. This is one of the many tricky techniques that can be done with both Artype and transfer type, though transfer type is really better for this sort of thing. The A in the middle of the map was put on with Artype.

COPY

The main block of information, that which is introduced by the headings, is called the "copy" (or sometimes "text").

Up until the invention of the linotype machine, most copy was produced by setting hand type in the same way that foundry type is set. Each letter was an individual piece of separate, movable type. The letters were lined up in a handstick (a sort of tray) to form words and sentences and then "locked up" in a frame and used to print directly onto paper. In 1886, Ottmar Mergenthaler first demonstrated his linotype machine (to drag in a bit of history). This machine casts a whole line of type from a row of matrices (or small molds) lined up by typing on a keyboard similar to a typewriter. Molten type-metal (mostly lead with a bit of tin and antimony) is poured into the molds, giving a rectangular piece of metal with the line of type in one piece. A few copies (reproduction proofs) are printed from this type. This kind of type is referred to as "hot-metal" type. As with foundry type, it is too expensive for our (and your) purposes.

The kind of type you will be able to afford is called "cold type," to distinguish it from the hot-metal type described above. There are basically two methods of producing commercial cold type. These are by phototype-setting devices and by the IBM Composer typewriter. At the moment, with a few exceptions, the phototype is not cheap enough to make it feasible for low-budget underground printing. On the other hand, the IBM Composer system is being phased out by IBM (IBM officially denies this but admits that they are no longer manufacturing them). The rumor is that IBM intends to come out with some dynamite system of phototype in the near future that will make all other typesetting systems obsolete. Be that as it may, quite a few small shops, like the Woodstock Times Type Service, have IBM

Composers and produce copy of a very good quality at a price not much greater than typists charge for straight typing.

Cold type is either "justified" (that is, with the lines flush left and right) or "unjustified" (flush left and ragged right). The linotype and phototype systems usually justify the type automatically. One model (a very expensive one) of the IBM Composer also justifies the type automatically: after storing the information from a preliminary unjustified typing, it then automatically retypes the copy, justified. To justify the type on the cheaper model of the IBM Composer, which is still rather expensive, the copy has to be typed twice by hand. This is tedious and not too practical since it doesn't always work the way it is supposed to. So resign yourself to unjustified type. In our opinion it looks better anyway. Most lines of type are justified at the expense of the internal spacing of the words so that, particularly on short lines, you often get exaggerated word spacing.

The IBM Selectric typewriter, though not cold type in the strict usage of the term, produces a very satisfactory type. The Selectric is the machine that has changeable balls, each ball for a different "font," or style, of type. The Selectric, like the Composer, produces a much sharper letter than the ordinary typewriter, since it uses a tape instead of a ribbon, which gives a fabric texture to the letter. Selectric type is particularly effective when it can be reduced (photostatically or in printing) by 15 to 20 percent. The Selectric is now standard in most executive offices and so is often available on an after-hours basis.

The copy in Figure 11B was produced by an IBM Composer typewriter (flush left, ragged right) set in 11-point type but reduced 20 percent. The type on the map was typed on an IBM Selectric typewriter (light italic ball). It was typed onto a mailing label which was cut by word and stuck to the map on the mechanical.

ILLUSTRATIONS

There are two main kinds of illustration that can be used fairly inexpensively in printing. These are "line drawings" and "halftones." Four-color-process illustration, which actually produces all colors using the primaries red, yellow, and blue plus black, is, alas, not for you, unless you win the state lottery. It is very expensive.

LINE DRAWINGS: These are illustrations or drawings that are reproduced from lines and masses of solid black. The final printing is not necessarily in black—this depends on the color of the ink on the press when it is printed. However, the artwork is usually prepared in black. The map in

Figure 11 is a typical line drawing.

The important thing to remember here is that line drawings do not have intermediate gray tones, which must be reproduced either by halftones or Bendays, which will be discussed in a moment. Zip-a-tones, also described soon, are sort of on the borderline, since their gray tones are produced by larger dots than the halftones; however, they can be photographed like line drawings (in technical jargon, "shot as line") if the dots are large enough.

Any medium or technique may be used to create line drawings as long as the areas produced are solid black and white. These include india ink (but not "wash"), black crayon or pencil, or black Pentel marker. The map in Figure 11B was done with a Rapidograph pen.

HALFTONES: These include wash drawings, drawings with Benday tones, and photographs. Halftone is a method of screening artwork or photographs for the printing press during the plate-making process, in which the drawing or photograph is broken up into little dots. If you look at any halftone photograph (that is, virtually any photograph you will see in a newspaper, book, or magazine) under a magnifying glass or small hand microscope, you will see that it is composed of a collection of dots of various sizes. However, they are so small that the eye blends them into a continuous picture of various grays and blacks.

NOTE: You cannot take a photograph that is already screened and use it as a halftone illustration unless the dot is large enough to be shot as line. If you try to rescreen a halftone what you often get is a moiré effect where the superimposition of one screen over another causes an interference pattern, which sometimes obliterates the original.

There is a photographic process called "velox" where the dot itself is large enough to be shot as line by the plate camera. Veloxes are "pre-screened" photos or drawings that are done at commercial photo houses and pasted into position on the mechanical, ready for camera. This may save you a great deal of money if you have photos, since the veloxes are much cheaper than halftones. However, the velox screen is heavier (cruder) and will not look quite as good as ones screened by the printer.

BENDAYS: These are areas of solid tone that can be stripped into the plate by the printer if indicated by the artist. For example, if we had wanted to further highlight the map in Figure 11B we could have asked the printer to put a 20 or 30 percent tone of light gray behind the map.

ZIP-A-TONE: These are sheets of cellophane that you can buy in most larger art stores. They have a pattern of dots (grays) printed on one side and a waxy coating on the other side, like Artype, so that it will stick to your mechanical. A line drawing can be made to have areas of tone by rubbing down Zip-a-tone, then cutting around the exact area with a razor blade and lifting off the excess. These areas of Zip-a-tone can be photographed as line.

Zip-a-tones come in all types of dots and textural effects.

SCALING ARTWORK

The ideal thing is to make all artwork the same size as it should be when printed, and to paste or draw it in exact position on the mechanical. However, this is not always practical or possible. Most photographs (except in the case of prescreened veloxes) have to be scaled and then "stripped in" to the mechanical by the printer.

The exact area and position of each piece of artwork and photograph must be indicated exactly on the mechanical with a red "holding line." It is a convention that red is used for holding lines, which indicate the position of artwork only, and that black lines are rules and are to be printed. Again, any black line that you put in the live area of the mechanical will most likely get printed.

In order to scale a piece of artwork or a photograph to the size you want it, you must understand how a diagonal line is used to figure out proportion. In Figure 18, all of the rectangles in the top drawing are exactly proportional.

If you have a photograph or any piece of artwork that has to be stripped in, first determine the amount of the photo you want to include by putting a piece of tracing paper over it and very lightly with a very soft pencil carefully sketching out the rough cropping you want on the final printed photo. It is important not to draw a heavy line with a hard pencil on top of the photo as this will leave a line on the photo, which may show up when the photo is printed.

Then place a heavy piece of cardboard between the photo and the tracing paper, and with your triangle draw in a heavy rectangle over the light preliminary sketch. Remove the cardboard for a moment to check the cropping of the photo. Now, with the cardboard back in place, draw a heavy line from the lower left-hand corner of the rectangle to the upper right-hand corner.

SCALING ARTWORK

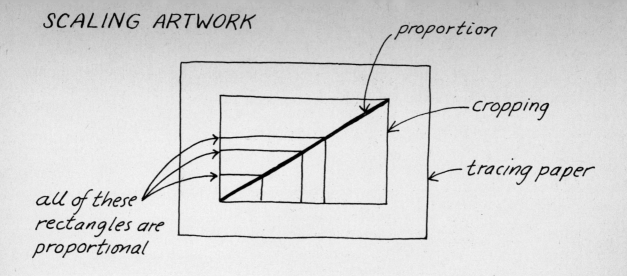

proportion

cropping

tracing paper

all of these rectangles are proportional

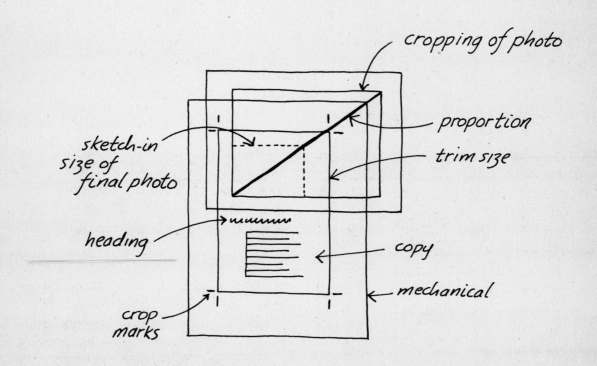

cropping of photo

sketch-in size of final photo

proportion

trim size

heading

copy

mechanical

crop marks

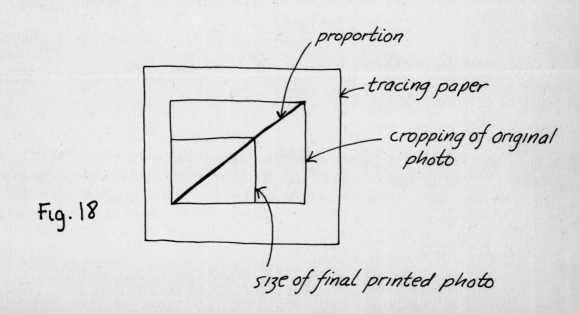

proportion

tracing paper

cropping of original photo

Fig. 18

size of final printed photo

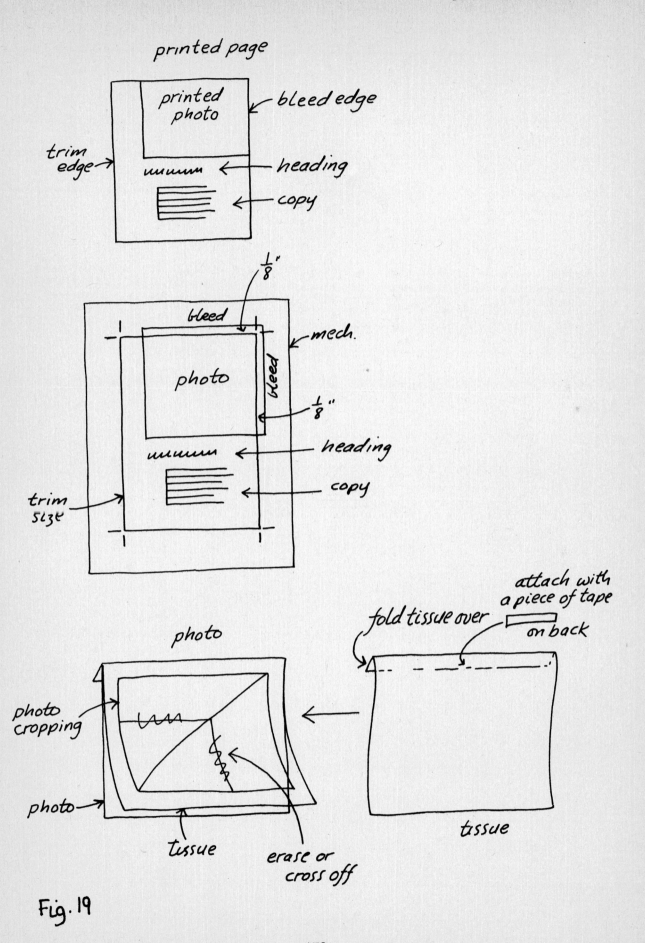

Fig. 19

This is your proportion.

Now, drop the tissue flap on your photo, but do not detach it, and place it over the area on the mechanical where you want to place the photo. Draw in a new rectangle the size of the final printed photo, using the diagonal to keep the same proportion.

Once you have the final photo rectangle, you can move it around over the mechanical to get the exact position. Use a push-pin (or any pin) to make little holes at each of the four corners, through the tracing paper into the mechanical. Use these as a guide to rule in the holding line for the photo on the mechanical. Draw this in with a <u>red</u> ballpoint pen.

Working through tracing paper and using pin holes is a very efficient method of getting exact positionings of all sorts. Pin holes do not show up when the plates are made from the mechanical, and, in any event, will be opaqued out by the plate maker if they do happen to show a bit.

In ruling in holding lines, etc., make sure you always use your T-square and your triangle. All lines should be either horizontal or vertical.

When you have your holding rectangle ruled in, write "strip-in photo" in blue inside the rectangle. All directions such as this should be printed legibly and neatly. Always put yourself in the place of the worker in the printing plant who is going to have to read and interpret your instructions.

BLEEDS

When a photograph or illustration "runs off" the edge of the printed page, this is called "bleed." This is indicated on the mechanical by running the holding rectangle 1/8-inch outside the trim size of the page on the mechanical. This 1/8-inch is later trimmed off by the binder so that the photo runs up to the exact trimmed edge in the final printed page.

Write "bleed" in black (it is outside the live area) in the margin of the mechanical on each side that bleeds.

RUBBER CEMENT VERSUS WAX

Rubber cement has always been <u>the</u> way to glue artwork to the mechanical in commercial art. However, if you are using rubber cement all day, especially in not too well ventilated quarters, it can become very toxic. Nobody knows the long-term effects of inhaling the naphtha (hydrocarbon) fumes from the solvent used to make rubber cement liquid. There is a

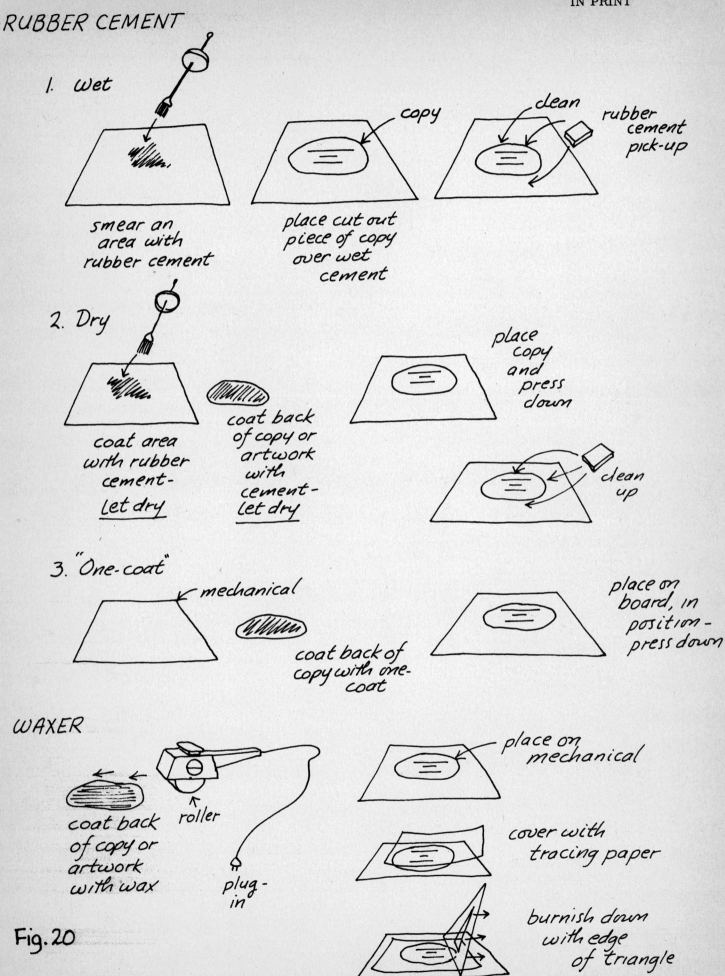

RUBBER CEMENT

1. Wet

smear an area with rubber cement

copy

place cut out piece of copy over wet cement

clean

rubber cement pick-up

2. Dry

coat area with rubber cement— let dry

coat back of copy or artwork with cement— let dry

place copy and press down

clean up

3. "One-coat"

mechanical

coat back of copy with one-coat

place on board, in position— press down

WAXER

coat back of copy or artwork with wax

roller

plug-in

place on mechanical

cover with tracing paper

burnish down with edge of triangle

Fig. 20

growing suspicion that it may have some very bad effects on the body. A limited amount of use probably does not have any particularly bad effect, but if you are going to do a lot of paste-up over a long period of time, using wax is a better method.

Up until recently, the only waxing equipment was very expensive and had the further disadvantage of being unreliable. Sometimes the machines just shredded your copy and other times they did you the favor of waxing both sides, which is a sticky proposition.

This situation has improved with the introduction of small, foolproof hand waxers, which are relatively inexpensive and easy to use. All you have to do is place your copy face down on some scrap paper and roll the waxer over the back. This puts a thin coating of wax on the back and enables you to stick the copy down easily wherever you want it on the mechanical. Keep all your scrap pieces of tracing paper as these are very useful in covering your copy while you burnish it down (use the edge of your triangle).

Waxed repros are much easier to pick up again and move around than rubber-cemented ones. You still have to be careful picking the copy up again as it will sometimes suddenly tear if you are not careful.

OFFSET PRINTING

This method of printing has been around for some time, but in the last few years it has taken over the printing field almost completely. Letterpress (locking up movable type in a frame and printing directly with the type, which is also the way reproduction proofs for offset are made from hot-metal type) when it is still used is used mostly for special printing jobs and special effects such as embossing. It is more expensive than and usually not as good as offset printing.

Offset is the only method of printing that is practical for most underground printing projects. Also, this is the type of printing that we have been showing you how to prepare artwork for.

When the printing plate is developed, the areas that have first been exposed to light through a film negative will now take ink. The other areas now reject the ink. The area that takes ink is not raised as in letterpress printing but is even with the surface of the plate. This printing process is often called "planography," that is, printing from a flat surface. It is also called "lithography," since it was first used in printing from a stone surface drawn on with a grease pencil. The stone was kept wet, so that when an

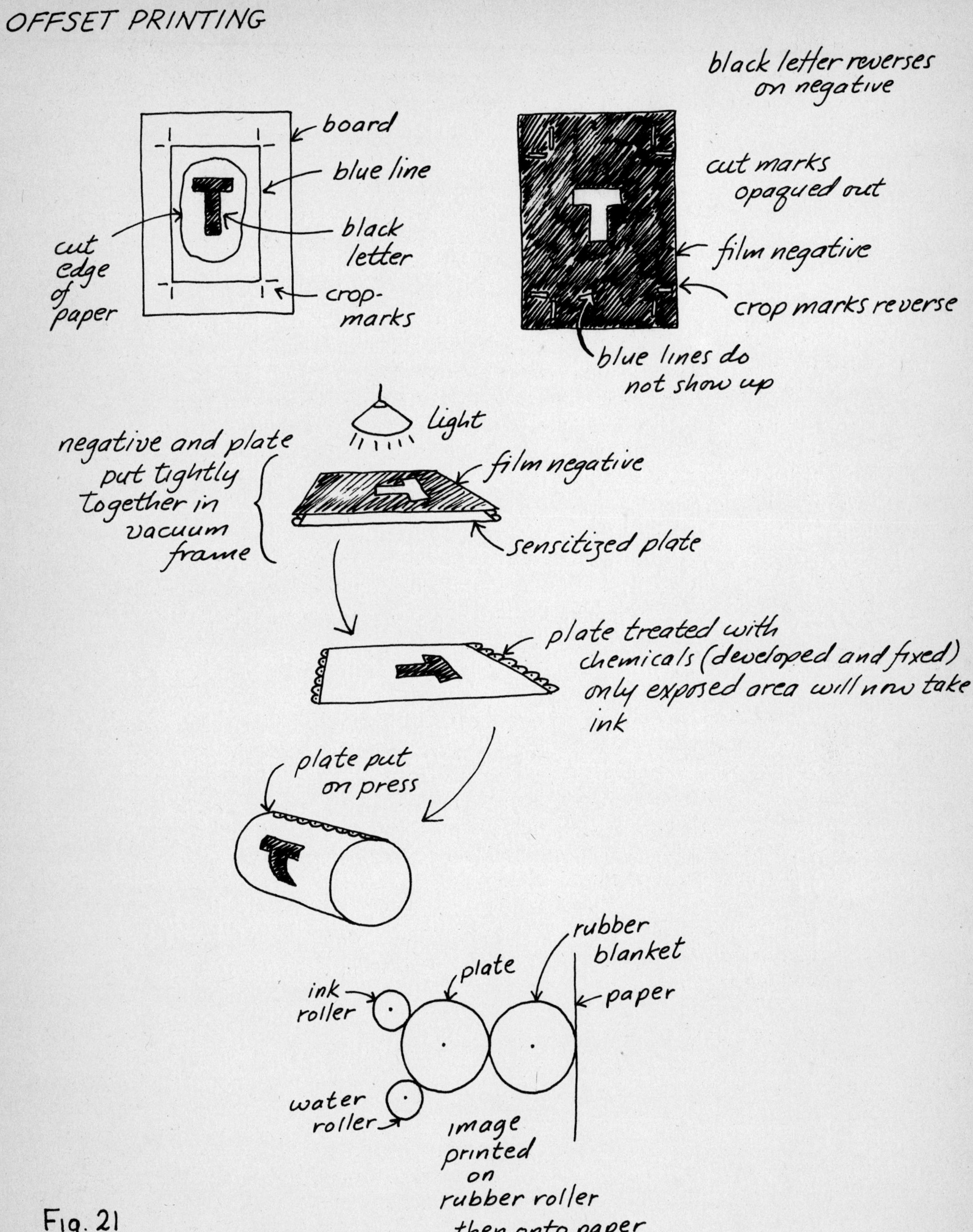

OFFSET PRINTING

board

blue line

black letter

cut edge of paper

crop-marks

black letter reverses on negative

cut marks opaqued out

film negative

crop marks reverse

blue lines do not show up

Light

negative and plate put tightly together in vacuum frame

film negative

sensitized plate

plate treated with chemicals (developed and fixed) only exposed area will now take ink

plate put on press

ink roller

plate

rubber blanket

paper

water roller

image printed on rubber roller then onto paper

Fig. 21

ink brayer was rolled across the stone only the grease-pencil lines took the ink. Offset printing uses the same principle. The plate is kept wet and only the areas that have been sensitized by light will take the ink. The correct name for the whole thing is "offset lithography."

This printing surface is much more delicate than a bed of metal type, so that the image must be printed first (or "offset") onto a soft rubber roller, which <u>then</u> prints on paper.

BINDING

The term "binding" is used by printers to indicate everything from trimming and folding to complicated sewn bindings. Forget about the sewn bindings—they are too expensive.

The three kinds of binding that are practical for you are called "side-stitch," "saddle-stitch," and "perfect-binding."

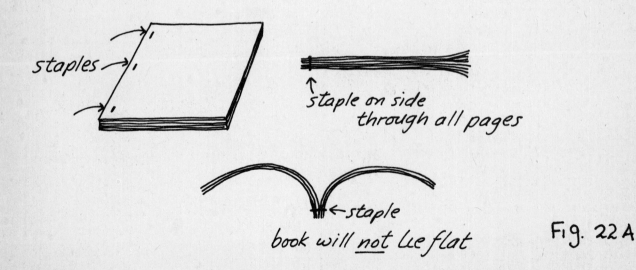

BINDING

8-page booklet, self-cover

all same stock (paper)

cover stock

8-page booklet plus cover (=12 pages)

cover stock *text*

1. Side stitch

staples

staple on side through all pages

staple

book will <u>not</u> lie flat

Fig. 22A

2. Saddle stitch

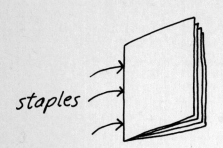

staples

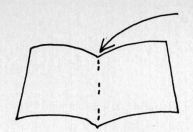

staples through center of book (or "gutter" as it is called)

staple in gutter

book will lie flat when opened

Fig. 22 B

3. Perfect binding

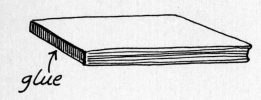

glue

this permits a "square-back" binding which is useful if you want to put information on the edge (spine)

glue →

this binding is always done with a separate cover to cover the glued edge

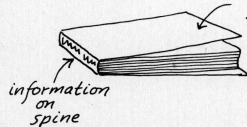

separate cover

information on spine

will lie flat when opened

Fig. 22 C

PAPER

Two main kinds (weights) of paper are used. These are "cover stock" (the heavier paper used for the cover of your pamphlet, or whatever, if you need one) and "text."

The most common and popular text paper is called "70-pound text." This term derives from the fact that a carton of this paper (usually 1,000 large sheets) weighs this much. "60-pound text" is cheaper and is also a good paper, but is lighter and thinner.

Cover stock paper is most often "65-pound cover." This term seems to indicate that cover stock is lighter, but in fact it is heavier than text paper. Reason is, a carton of cover stock is smaller.

Also, the more expensive text papers are termed "opaque." This is because they have more filler and the paper is less likely to have "show-through," which is seeing the printing from the other side of the sheet faintly through the sheet itself.

As far as the actual surface of the sheet goes, it can be "vellum," which is a smooth mat surface; a "fancy-finish" (textured), or a "laid" stock, an artificial imitation of old-fashioned paper in which the crisscross pattern of the paper fiber shows.

There is also "coated" stock that has a shiny finish and is the kind of paper ultra-slick magazines are printed on. This is usually very expensive and is also much harder to print on.

For most purposes try to use vellum stock, or "70-pound vellum off-set," as it is usually called. This comes in all different grades, some expensive and some inexpensive. Try to get your printer to find you a job-lot of paper, which is a batch of paper left over from some other job, or paper that was ordered but for some reason not used.

Paper also, of course, comes in different colors. The best thing is to get a sample book of inexpensive and readily available papers from your printer.

SENDING YOUR MECHANICALS TO THE PRINTER

Ways to save money:

1. Make sure you have crop marks on all your mechanicals.

2. Try to have all your artwork as nearly as possible ready for camera.

3. If you can get the "imposition" plan (the way pages are physically lined up when they are printed—this is not the order the pages fall in eventually) for your job from the printer, you can do your paste-up in imposition order rather than in a sequence of facing pages. The printer can usually give you a lower price for the whole job if you do it this way, as he has less work in setting up his plates. Ask the printer about this ahead of time.

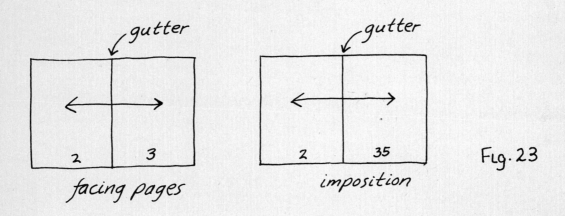

Fig. 23

4. Try to make the size of your job fit the presses of whatever printer you are sending it to. Certain paper sizes fit different presses more economically than others. Your printer will have to give you all this information so that you can plan your job. Make <u>sure</u> you get this information first, before you start ruling up your boards.

Printing costs are, unfortunately, fluid and frustrating, as well as differing greatly from place to place. Most printers want to do a good job for you at reasonable costs. From our experience, this is particularly true of small-town printers, who are very anxious to build business and create confidence and goodwill. In the bigger cities it is advisable to get estimates from several printers in order to compare costs. Many printers will give a "knock-down" price—that is, one with a very small profit, if any—to get your initial business.

Generally, you get a package deal, which includes printing, paper, and binding. The printer will order the paper for you and arrange for binding. You want to establish a good working relationship with your printer, and when you do you can use his advice and guidance.

We hope this will get you working it all out graphically in a new craft... new to you, anyway. A lot of people who probably never thought they would be into printing got into it and made it work. The underground press, comics like Zap and Fritz, political pamphlets, self-help books like the Volkswagen Manual, books of personal statement like Living on the Earth, newspapers and magazines like Rolling Stone and the Free Press, ecocommercial catalogues like The Whole Earth, were all done by people who picked up on printing in order to communicate.

Gloria Brightfield

Rich Brightfield

A PERFECT PATCHWORK PRIMER

Beth Gutcheon

This is the most complete book of patchwork instruction ever published. *The Perfect Patchwork Primer* differs from other quilting manuals by teaching you not only how to reproduce old quilts but also how to create and execute your own quilt designs. (It also outlines more than seventy other patchwork projects—from coasters and mats to tote bags and wall hangings.) Here you will find everything you need to know about choosing and handling materials, making attractive patterns, and using modern technology without loss of quality. Once you learn the techniques, Beth Gutcheon shows you how to earn money by quilting, how to organize quilting parties, where to send for supplies, and much, much more. Among the topics covered in this book are quilting as a communal activity—for parents and children, husbands and wives, friends and lovers; quilting by hand with a frame—or without one; adapting any traditional pattern for machine-sewing; quilt names, stories, history, and superstition; album quilts, memory quilts, freedom quilts, and bride quilts—and the parties at which they were made; and why men make quilts.

THE QUICKEST WAY TO DRAW WELL

Frederic Taubes

This popular book gives a concise course for the student who wants to develop skills in drawing in a short period of time. The author gives detailed but easily understood instruction in basic good draftsmanship and materials as well as a variety of special techniques—for the beginner, the Sunday artist, and even the practicing professional. Frederic Taubes covers figure, landscape, and still-life subjects; perspective; and composition from both classic and contemporary viewpoints. For those who want the shortest path to proficiency, this book provides all the necessary steps for further accomplishment in any medium.

WAYS OF SEEING

John Berger

"Seeing comes before words. The child looks and recognizes before it can speak. But there is also another sense in which seeing comes before words. It is seeing which establishes our place in the surrounding world; we explain that world with words, but words can never undo the fact that we are surrounded by it. The relation between what we see and what we know is never settled." So begins this book, based on the acclaimed television series. *Ways of Seeing* widens the horizons, quickens the perceptions, and enlivens new vistas as we look at art, the world, and ourselves.

EVERYTHING RAW
The No-Cooking Cookbook

Jennie Reekie

Like to eat? Hate to cook? You'll love *Everything Raw*—the last word on preparing food *without* cooking! Here are recipes for more than two hundred sensational no-cooking dishes. A fantastic array of raw foods is quickly combined into hors d'oeuvres, salads, main dishes, desserts, sauces, and soups. The wide variety of ingredients offers something special for every taste: cheeses, milk, yogurt, meats and fish (smoked, dried, and fresh), all kinds of nuts, eggs, fresh and dried fruits, and vegetables. Here are recipes aplenty for dieters and vegetarians as well as for cooks who are looking for delicious and simple new dishes. This is also an ideal book for the college student, for whom cooking facilities are often less than ideal.

FRENCH PROVINCIAL COOKING

Elizabeth David

Elizabeth David always succeeds in inducing a desire to use each recipe as soon as it is read. Whether she is describing the preparation of a plain green salad or the marinading of a haunch of wild boar, she writes with the same imaginative directness. Recipes like pot-au-feu are described in all their delicious simplicity, which, it is made clear, means cooking without elaboration and has nothing to do with the higgledy-piggledy "let's hope it's all right" technique. Some excellent advice is included on the choice of the tools that would always be needed in any kitchen. "It is difficult to think of any home that can do without Elizabeth David's *French Provincial Cooking*.... One could cook for a lifetime on the book alone"—*Observer*.

GYMNASTICS FOR GIRLS

Dr. Frank Ryan

The most exciting event in the past Olympic games, women's gymnastics, has come into its own as one of the great sports of our time. It is also a breathtakingly beautiful sport, in which each competitor must demonstrate her skills in four unique and demanding categories: floor exercise, balance beam, uneven parallel bars, and the vault. In these pages Dr. Frank Ryan tells you all you need to know about the fundamentals of gymnastics, about individual tumbling and dance skills, about control and precision, about the split-second timing of work on the uneven parallel bars, about the techniques of aggressive performance on the vault, and much more. The author also offers invaluable advice on the development of combinations that will enable the gymnast to devise her own routines. Illustrated with dozens of step-by-step photographs, this is the most comprehensive guide available for today's young student—and tomorrow's champion.

SLIMNASTICS

Pamela Nottidge and Diana Lamplugh

"Slimnastics" is a new approach to the problem of weight control. To slim by yourself is difficult, say the authors, but to do so in a group can be a pleasure as well as a permanent success. All you need are a few interested friends, a tape measure, and a scale. This book gives you the rest: weight guides, progress charts, dieting advice for women of all ages and shapes, and six courses of fully illustrated exercises tailor-made to your personal needs.

THE PENGUIN BOOK OF KITES

David Pelham

The kite is now enjoying a world revival that has partly to do with its
functional beauty and partly with its paradoxical quality of providing
exercise *and* relaxation to both mind and body. This book is a comprehensive and thoroughly illustrated introduction to kites and kiting,
covering in detail their history, their construction, and their flying. It
contrasts the highly decorative models of the East with the more functional
and aerodynamically efficient Western types. Over one hundred detailed
and tested kite patterns are included, giving all the information required
to build kites.

TANGRAM
The Ancient Chinese Shapes Game

Joost Elffers

Tangram, the thousand-year-old Chinese puzzle, is an exciting game that
stimulates creativity and fantasy and can be played either by one person
or by a group. The game consists of seven pieces, formed by cutting a
square in a certain way, with which you can copy the examples given in
the book. This may sound easy enough, but as soon as one starts playing,
it becomes obvious that Tangram presents a real and pleasurable challenge
to one's skill and imagination. A set of the seven pieces in durable plastic
is packed with the book. Also included in this edition are an Introduction,
a bibliography, and a mathematical section that examines the number of
possible shapes that can be formed. There are over 1,600 examples, with
solutions.

The Pelican History of Art Series

For scholarship, readability, and the range of its illustrations, The Pelican History of Art Series has become widely recognized as a unique enterprise in the field of art history. More than thirty volumes have been published, covering the art and architecture of all ages. Written by authorities whose international standing is unquestioned, they have maintained the strict standards set by the series editor, noted art historian Sir Nikolaus Pevsner. In each paperback volume a lavish collection of hundreds of photographs and plates is integrated into the text, bringing the finest examples of the subject immediately to the reader for enhanced comprehension, appreciation, and enjoyment. The paperback Pelican History of Art makes available the finest in art publishing at unusually reasonable prices. Some of the paperback titles are:

ARCHITECTURE: NINETEENTH AND TWENTIETH CENTURIES, *Henry-Russell Hitchcock*

ARCHITECTURE IN BRITAIN: 1530-1830, *John Summerson*

ART AND ARCHITECTURE IN FRANCE: 1500-1700, *Anthony Blunt*

ART AND ARCHITECTURE IN ITALY: 1600-1750, *Rudolph Wittkower*

ART AND ARCHITECTURE OF INDIA, *Benjamin Rowland*

ART AND ARCHITECTURE OF THE ANCIENT ORIENT, *Henri Frankfort*

CAROLINGIAN AND ROMANESQUE ARCHITECTURE: 800-1200, *Kenneth John Conant*

DUTCH ART AND ARCHITECTURE: 1600-1800, *Jakob Rosenberg, Seymour Slive, and E. H. ter Kuile*

PAINTING AND SCULPTURE IN EUROPE: 1880-1940, *George Heard Hamilton*

PAINTING IN ITALY: 1500-1600, *S. J. Freedberg*

PENGUIN STEREO RECORD GUIDE
Second Edition

Edward Greenfield, Robert Layton, and Ivan March

Drawing on profound technical knowledge and on vast musical and historical
learning, this newly revised and updated guide to recorded classical music
deals with over four thousand discs, giving details of title, performers, record
number, label, and price range. For record buyers in a hurry, a starring
system (from one to three stars) is provided; for the enlightenment of
browsers, there is a short but informative discussion of each record. Upon a
few records of outstanding quality the authors have conferred a "rosette"—a
special mark of admiration on their part. This edition has been updated with
American selections. "The authors' scope and zeal are stunning, their
standards of judgment and accuracy high . . . what an achievement"—*Sunday
Times* (London). "The answer to a record-collecting browser's prayer"—
High Fidelity.

Also available from Penguin Books:

AFTER THE BALL: POP MUSIC FROM RAG TO ROCK, *Ian Whitcomb*
IN DEFENCE OF OPERA, *Hamish E. G. Swanston*
A NEW DICTIONARY OF MUSIC, *Arthur Jacobs*
A SHORT HISTORY OF WESTERN MUSIC, *Arthur Jacobs*
THE SYMPHONY, VOLUME 1: HAYDN TO DVORAK, *edited by
Robert Simpson*
THE SYMPHONY, VOLUME 2: ELGAR TO THE PRESENT DAY,
edited by Robert Simpson